Pupils during the 1960s.

A History of
St Joseph's Māori Girls' College

St Joseph's Māori Girls' College 1911.

First published in 2022 by Huia Publishers
39 Pipitea Street, PO Box 12280
Wellington, Aotearoa New Zealand
www.huia.co.nz

ISBN 978-1-77550-621-8

Copyright © Malcolm Mulholland 2022
Cover image: SJMGC Archives
Inside cover image: SJMGC Archives

This book is copyright. Apart from fair dealing for the purpose of private study, research, criticism or review, as permitted under the Copyright Act, no part may be reproduced by any process without the prior permission of the publisher.

A catalogue record for this book is available from the National Library of New Zealand.

Published with the assistance of Creative New Zealand

A History of
St Joseph's Māori Girls' College

Malcolm Mulholland

MIHI IX
ACKNOWLEDGEMENTS XII
INTRODUCTION 01

CHAPTER ONE 11
Sisters of Our Lady of the Missions

CHAPTER TWO 41
St Joseph's Providence

CHAPTER THREE 71
Exemplary Education

CHAPTER FOUR 93
The Fight for Survival

CHAPTER FIVE 119
Growing at Greenmeadows

CHAPTER SIX 157
Producing Quality Teachers, Nurses and Typists

CHAPTER SEVEN 197
A New Dawn

CHAPTER EIGHT 217
Te Wero

CHAPTER NINE 243
Being Bicultural

CHAPTER TEN 269
Rangatiratanga

CHAPTER ELEVEN 291
Swimming against the Tide

CHAPTER TWELVE 323
He Tuāhine Pūmau Sisters for Life
'The Sisterhood'

ENDNOTES 326
SELECT BIBLIOGRAPHY 340
IMAGE CREDITS 344

1. St Joseph's Māori Girls' College 1903.
2. Catholic Church Camp, Rata, 1935.
3. St Joseph's Māori Girls' College 1905.
4. Pageant 1919.

vi   I Ō MAHI KATOA, MAHIA

3.

1905

4.

A HISTORY OF ST JOSEPH'S MĀORI GIRLS' COLLEGE

Prefects 1956.
Back row: Kataraina Millen, Putiputi Te Waewae.
Second row: Frances Carrington, Phoebe Sadd, Lovey Roberts.
Front row: H Hotere, Marian Heke, Matirei Mariu.

Mihi

He hōnore, he korōria ki te Atua
Te tīmatanga me te whakaotinga o ngā mea katoa

He maimai aroha ki a rātou kua mene ki tua o Paerau
Ki te mūrau o te tini
Ki te wenerau o te mano
E au ai tā koutou moe te hunga kua whetūrangitia
Moe mai i roto i ngā ringa o te Ariki

Ka hoki mai anō ki a tātou, te hunga ora, Ngāti Kahungunu iwi, ngā iwi o te motu, ki ngā Whāea Tapu, ngā Kuia Mōrehu o Hato Hohepa, ngā tauira, ngā tumuaki ngā Whāea Ātawhai te Whānau whānui me te maha noa atu o rātou e tautoko ana i te kāreti, i ngā tau kua hipa, o tēnei wā hoki, me ngā tau kei mua i ō tātou aroaro.

He mihi ki a koutou i whakanui, e whakatairanga nei i tō tātou kāreti o Hato Hohepa. He ara roa i whāia mō ngā tau kotahi rau e rima tekau. E tū rangātira ana i tēnei rā, te taha Hāhi, me te taha Māori.

'I ō mahi katoa, mahia'.

Suore di Nostra Signora delle Missioni

Dear Miss Kingi, teachers, staff, sisters, members of the Board, students, parents and friends of the College. Tēnā koutou, tēnā koutou, tēnā koutou katoa.

St Joseph's Māori Girls' College – Hato Hohepa – is a very special college. It is the only Māori Catholic girls' school in the world. It holds a special place in the hearts of the Religieuses De Notre Dame des Missions – Sisters of Our Lady of the Missions (RNDM), not only in New Zealand, but in the entire congregation.

I had the joy of personally being a teacher and hostel supervisor from 1979 to 1986. These years touched and shaped my being and missionary spirit in ways that were beyond my imagination. I learnt something about the very rich gifts of Māori culture and traditions and the warmth and hospitality of the Māori people. The young women I taught and helped to nurture in those years enabled me to see something of the wonderful diversity and gift of God we human beings are. It was a real privilege to be part of your lives and to get to know something of your families and cultural life. Many of you have gone on to do wonderful things, and there are many young women who have followed in your footsteps, maintaining the excellent standards of academic, cultural and sporting achievement. You truly live out your motto: I ō mahi katoa, mahia – whatever you do, do it to the best of your ability.

The story of the RNDM sisters in New Zealand begins in 1865 when the first four French sisters travelled by ship to New Zealand following the inspiration of Euphrasie Barbier, Mother Mary of the Heart of Jesus, the foundress of the Sisters of Our Lady of the Missions. These first sisters demonstrated an intrepid spirit, which allowed them to overcome the many obstacles they encountered in a distant and foreign land.

The sisters' faith in God and their missionary zeal enabled them to establish schools in many parishes throughout New Zealand. Very soon, after landing in Napier, the sisters undertook responsibility for staffing a Providence for young Māori girls. Father Euloge Reignier SM was responsible for the Māori mission in Hawke's Bay, and he was aware that the education of Māori children had been neglected. The sisters were involved with the education of settler children and they also generously took responsibility for teaching young Māori women and girls at the Providence, which later, in 1926, became known as St Joseph's Māori Girls' College.

Euphrasie always took a very close interest in the Māori children and was greatly concerned about the development of the mission. When she visited New Zealand, she spent time with the children and always encouraged the sisters to treat the children with kindness and loving care. She instructed the sisters to pay attention to the curriculum, the preparation of classes and the quality of education. Euphrasie was very clear about the kind of discipline that was to be used with the students. No matter how serious the fault, she stressed that a child should never be slapped or sent to bed without supper, nor given passages from the scriptures or the catechism to write out as punishment.

Euphrasie also had great sympathy for the children in their struggles to learn another language. She knew about this firsthand. She was supportive of the children speaking in their own language and encouraged patience in the learning of English. She wrote several times to the sisters encouraging them to learn the Māori language. In a letter written to the Mother Prioress on 15 June 1884, she was very firm:

> As regards the Māori children I should be very sorry if this work were to prove a failure. Do ask the sisters engaged in it to learn the language. For a very long time I have been urging these sisters to teach the catechism, their prayers (Mass prayers as well as others), and the hymns in Māori. It should have been done already!

Euphrasie would go to great lengths to ensure that there was finance for the children's education, even when the government threatened to withdraw its support. In a letter to MM St Raphael dated 17 April 1890 she wrote: 'We must look after our dear Māori people in a special way and take in as many of them as possible, even if the government should withdraw its help!'

There are many sisters and lay people who have continued the mission of St Joseph's Māori Girls' College to this day. Euphrasie would be very proud of what continues to be achieved at St Joseph's and the excellent traditions that are taught and maintained.

You are faithful to the mission of faith formation (virtue) and the educational attainment (knowledge) of young Māori women. The college makes an outstanding contribution to culture and society in Aotearoa New Zealand.

This is only achieved with quality leadership. I take this opportunity to congratulate you Miss Kingi for your outstanding work as teacher at St Joseph's for many decades and for your dedication and commitment as principal since 1987. You have given your life to championing quality education and the teaching of te reo and tikanga Māori at St Joseph's.

To you students of St Joseph's Māori Girls' College, I encourage you to make the most of every opportunity that you have to deepen your understanding of language, heritage and culture and may you stand tall with pride and dignity in being Māori. St Joseph's enables you to be equipped and empowered to take your place in society with dignity, courage and confidence.

I pray that all who have been a part of the college and those associated with the college today will receive abundant blessings.

Ngā manaakitanga
With blessings of peace and joy

Josephine Kane RNDM
Congregation Leader

Sister Josephine Kane.

Acknowledgements

Ngā mihi nui ki a Dame Georgina Kingi / Sister Sarah Greenlees / Anecia Prentice / Fiona Whaanga / Meriama Taufale / Julie Tangaere / Elizabeth Charlton / Noreen Pakinga / Michelle Taiaroa / Kataraina Millen / Te Arani Barrett / Aroha Harris / Rawinia Higgins / Kereana Bird / Audrey Robin / Maia Melbourne-Wilcox / Pio Jacobs / Takawai Jacobs / Hera Jacobs / Tania Jacobs / Mary Kereopa / Sister Margaret Purdie / the late Sister Beverley Grounds / Sister Muriel Kivell / Sister Maureen Richardson / Ramona Belmont / Tammi Wilson-Uluinayau / Linda Mastny / Jill Cotter / Taria Tahana / John Bishara / Shontelle Bishara / Hine Bishara / Maureen Roger / Val Caffery-Tangimetua / Olive Prince / Nikayla Jonas / Ngatoru Wall / Pania Newton / Te Mihinga Komene / Charisma Rangipuna / the late Lady June Mead / Kaapua Smith / Henrietta Walker / Kataraina O'Brien / Phyllis Peni / Varni Carson / Vicky Peni / John Tangaere / Jade Tuhua / Lisa Ropiha / Fonz Ropiha / Pirihira Ropiha / Erana Bricknell / Kylie Tiuka / Api Smith / Patrick Hickey / Winnie Spooner / Lexi Puna / Mere-Kingi Harvey-Brewster / Ngaroma Ngamoki / Bridget Rika / Anamarie Rika / Ngaroma Rika / Alamein Shoulten / Ripeka Wiki / Paraone Wiki / Charlie Mackey / Te Aranga Rolleston / Beth Dixon / Caroline Roberts / Riria McDonald / Joanna Rameka / Nadell Karatea / Christina Karatea / Kayleen Neho / Te Rina Warren / Janice Wall / Kania Worsley / Tuterangi Nepe-Apatu / Angela Nepe-Apatu / Theresa Nepe-Apatu / Kathy Bates / Katrina Bates / Wiki Baker / Moana Maniapoto-Jackson / Hinewehi Mohi / Maisey Rika / Ria Millen / Terry Gardner / Stephanie Gardner / Megan Gardner / Stacey Hape / Kaa Daniels / Monika Barker / Stella Marr / Hiria McAlister / Paul McAlister / Theresa McAlister / Iulia Leilua / Mereana Hond / Stephanie Tibble / Kimiora Kaire-Melbourne / Kristina Karatea / Moana Beveridge / Edith Crawford / Ariana Roe / Rangimarie Taite /

Aroha Peakman-Walker / Puhiwahine Tibble / Miriama Kereama / Amiria Arapere / Debra Williams / Margaret Walsh / Edith Harris / Peggy Warren / Maru Karatea-Goddard / Danny Karatea-Goddard / Tineka Hall / Grace Allen / Rangireremoana Hau / Aleeta Hau / Hariata Rewi / Toia Lucas-Walden / the late Veronica Huriwai-Hawkes / Puti Nuku / Debra Unahi / Meriana Broughton / Heeni Bartlett / John Cribb / Kararaina Cribb / Tawhiwhirangi Skipper / Hikurangi Edwards / Mere Roha-Stewart / Jacinta Paranihi / Tereihine Roberts-Thompson / Hinematererangi Mackey-Pasene / Mereana Broughton / Jacqueline Broughton / Hinehou Broughton / Alana Broughton / Gay Kahu-Sinclair / Keri Neho / Elsa Hug-Nicholl / Kim Wetini / Te Atamarie Wetini / Sharon Lawton / Unaiki Lawton / Roimata Lawton / Courtney Reneti / Marama Studer / Zoe Studer / Frances Te Kani / Marama Cook / Taini Hudson / Tira Ruru / Maria Maui / Erica Herangi / Hana Gulliver / Huia Borrell / Peter Borrell / Eileen Transom / Connie Purvis / June Collins / Julia Pomana / Makareta Paku / Talalelei Taufale / Derek Bartlett / Turuhira Mohi / Amiria Tapa / Georgina Te Huia / Jacqueline Phillips / Sue Osborne / Cecilia Tawhitipou / Hineatatu Dorset-Paewai / the late Edith Sainsbury / Te Kani Kingi / Sister Josephine Kane / Wanda Brljevich / Jill Williams / Judy Rafferty / Sarah Morgan / Ellie Hutchinson / Jude Tewnion / Prue Kapua / Margaret Low / Bossy Hill / Melissa Irving.

Last, but by no means least, to my whānau: my wife Wiki, my 'research assistant' Molly Rose, Ihaia and Patrick.

St Joseph's Māori Girls' College 1925.

Introduction

Nestled in Greenmeadows, Hawke's Bay, is St Joseph's Māori Girls' College. The school is now 152 years old, having grown from humble beginnings on the school's former site at what is now Sacred Heart College, Napier Hill. Since that time, St Joseph's has become the second oldest Māori boarding school in the country and the Māori boarding school with the largest roll in New Zealand (the school roll fluctuates during the year between 200 and 250). The story of St Joseph's is one of triumph over adversity, of overcoming religious, racial and sexual prejudice, of delivering consistently stellar academic results for Māori, and of becoming something of a 'production factory' of Māori women trailblazers in a variety of fields. Yet, until now, the story is not well known.

St Joseph's has encountered significant challenges during its history. During the college's formative years, nationwide anti-Catholic and anti-French sentiments impeded progress towards establishing the school. Another obstacle St Joseph's encountered was the bureaucracy of the Pākehā male-dominated New Zealand education system. Successive native school inspectors continued to impose their limited worldview of the place of Māori women within New Zealand society, which influenced the curricula they promoted for the best part of a century. The Catholic Māori missionary Father Euloge Reignier was a key figure behind the drive to set up what was then known as 'St Joseph's Providence'. Shortly thereafter, the Sisters of Our Lady of the Missions, led by Euphrasie Barbier, the founder of the order, took control of the school and they have continued to have a strong presence at St Joseph's.

There have been two notable periods of time when the very existence of St Joseph's was seriously threatened. The first was following the Napier earthquake. Despite repeated assurances that the Māori Purposes Fund Board would help improve the school's facilities during the 1920s, a prolonged battle with Wellington officials would eventually result in the release of limited financial assistance during the 1940s. The second period of time when the viability of St Joseph's was in question was during the late 1980s and early 1990s. The financial state of affairs of St Joseph's was tenuous and debt was being accumulated, as parents found it difficult to make ends meet. Compounding the problem was the need to pay the teaching and hostel staff, an issue the school had not encountered in its past as the Sisters were not paid for their time.

The situation was so dire that several members of the Board of Trustees offered to mortgage their own homes to ensure the college would continue. The saving grace came in the form of a strong network of members of the Catholic Church who were prepared to support the school. This period of the school's history coincided with the arrival of St Joseph's first lay and Māori principal, Georgina Kingi. Under her watch, the school has grown from strength to strength academically, with some students receiving the best results in the country. St Joseph's, as a whole, is also consistently above the national average for NCEA and University Entrance results, as the following tables demonstrate.

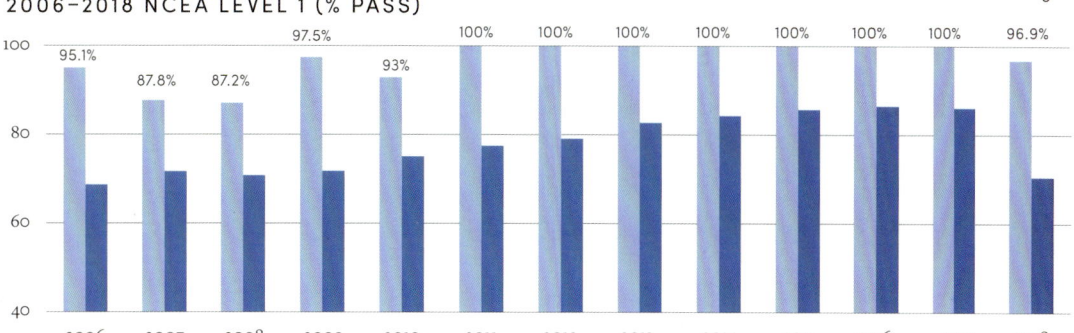

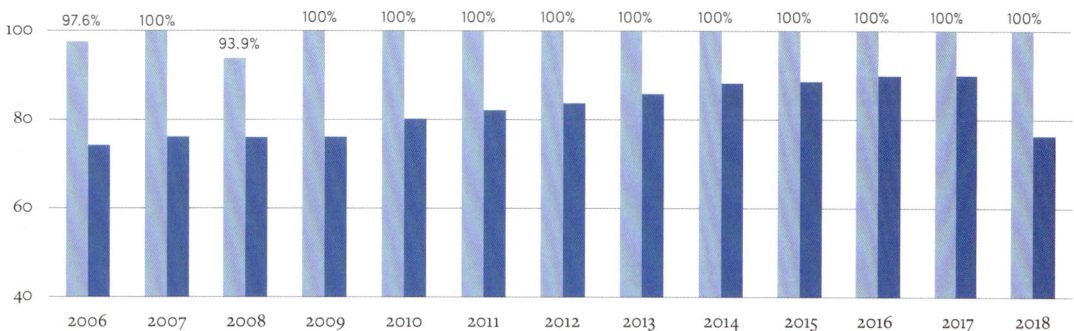

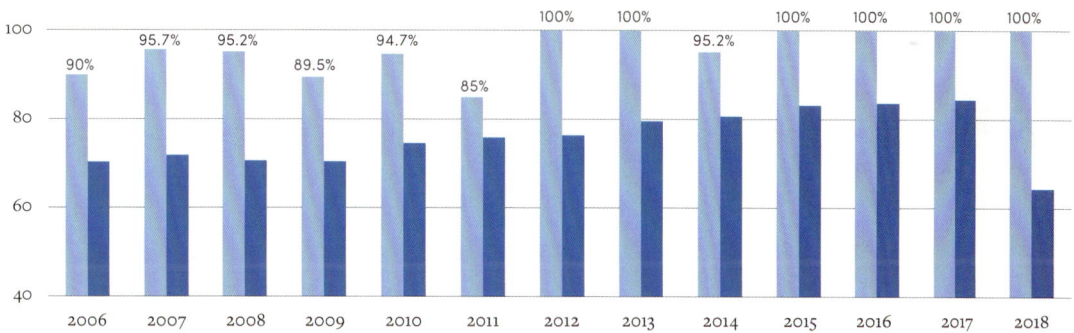

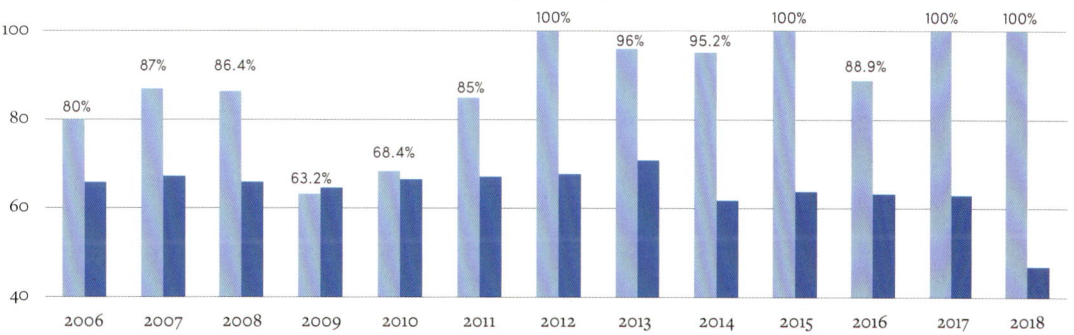

St Joseph's Māori Girls' College 2017.

St Joseph's has a holistic approach to education, promoting students who are well grounded in their identity as Māori, have religious morals as supported by the Catholic Church and have an absolute dedication to achieving academic excellence. St Joseph's has constantly proven to be a national leader in the education of Māori women. Former pupil Rawhia Te Hau conducted her master's thesis on the success factors of the college.[1] Ms Te Hau articulated that the five success factors of St Joseph's are:[2]

1. Whanaungatanga
2. Leadership
3. Māoritanga
4. Religion
5. Academic focus

Underpinning the exceptional academic results produced by St Joseph's is a devotion to seeing Māori women be all they can be through a strong work ethic that is promoted within the school motto: 'I ō mahi katoa, mahia!' (whatever you do, do it to the best of your ability). The culture of excellence within the college is further reinforced by the boards, teachers, hostel staff and the wider family support network (Whānau Whānui).

Throughout the book are recollections from former pupils, staff and whānau (over 160 interviews were conducted) and a number of themes emerge: the significance of religion is one that all interviewees remember, whether or not they are members of the Catholic faith, as are the strong familial connections between new entrants and former pupils; the memories of parents saying goodbye to their daughters or the equally sad time when pupils leave the place that has become their de facto home during their teenage years; the sisters' strict adherence to the rules and their dedication to producing the best academic results possible for Māori girls; performing in the concert party and making the most of the opportunities presented to the girls to travel, both nationally and internationally; and perhaps, above all else, the 'sisterhood' of former pupils. This was the strongest theme expressed by former students of St Joseph's: a bond that each shares with every other girl who has walked through the gates on Osier Road.

This book is their story.

Catholic Church camp, Rata, 1935.

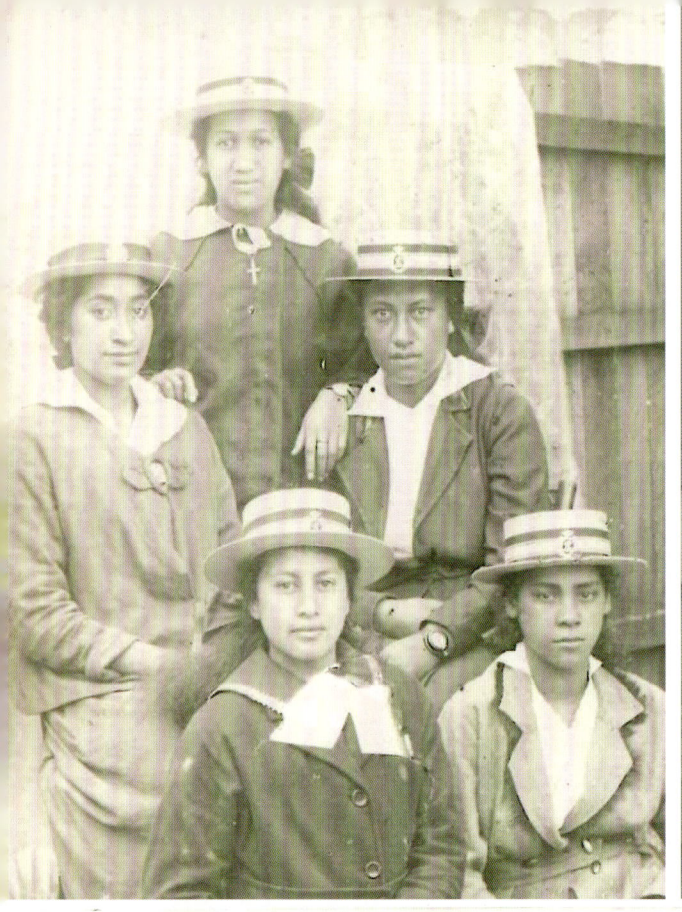

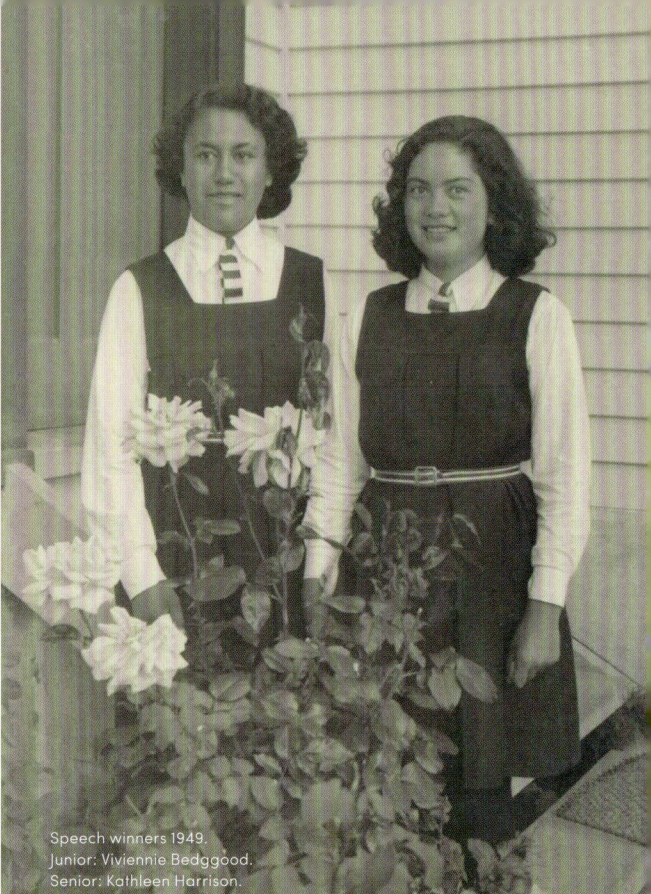

Speech winners 1949.
Junior: Viviennie Bedggood.
Senior: Kathleen Harrison.

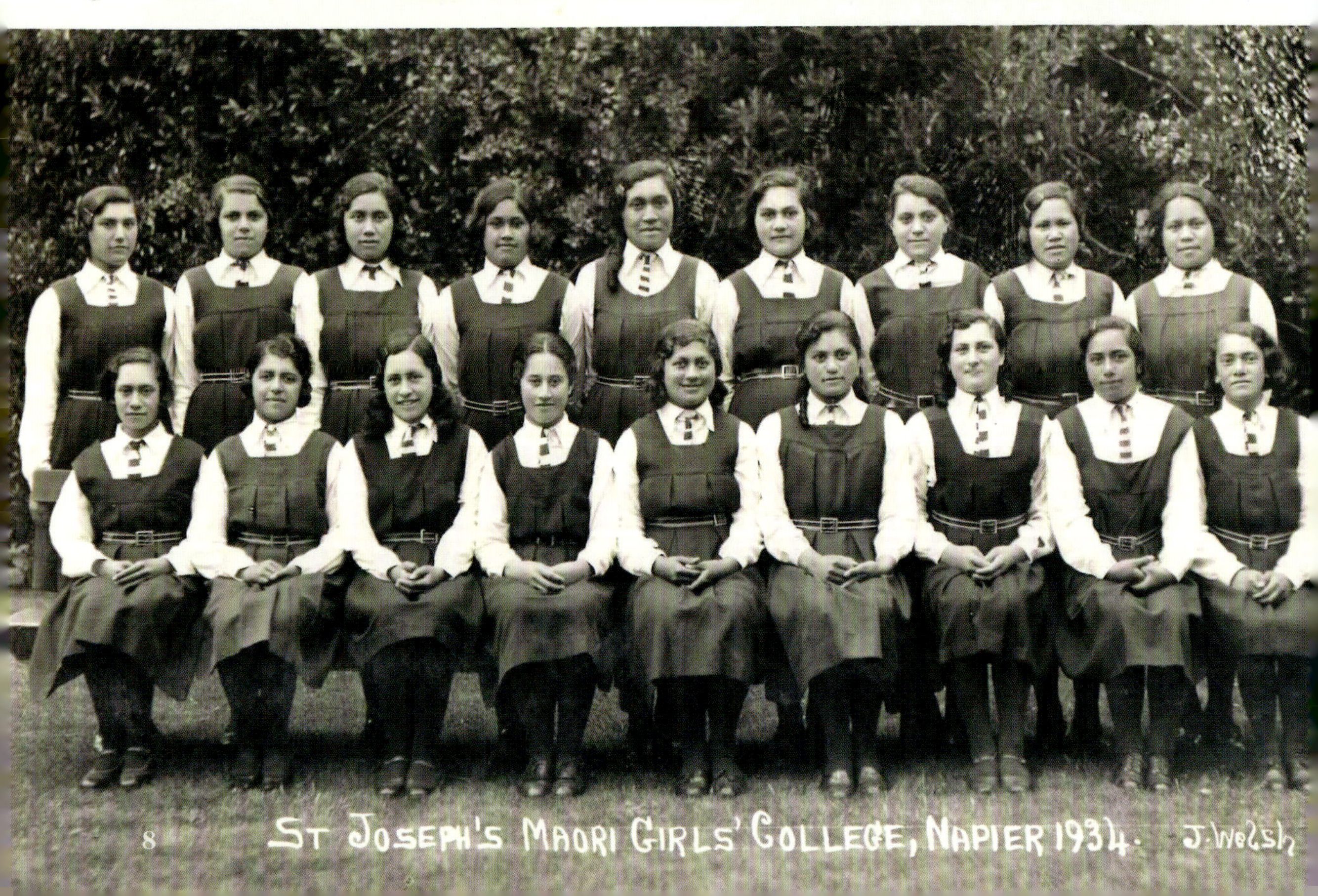

ST JOSEPH'S MAORI GIRLS' COLLEGE, NAPIER 1934.
J. Welsh

'There's a Long Winding Road'

School Drumming Band 1947.

Monika Marr and other old girls recall with clarity a song that was sung by pupils when they were arriving at their school from an outing. Monika states: 'We used to go around the country marching and we would sing all the way. When we got to Osier Road, we would all sing:

*"There's a long winding road to that happy old abode
along the road to SJC.*

*Where the bells are always ringing and hearts are always singing,
beneath the swaying palms.*

*We are proud of our motto, we hold our heads up high,
as we salute our patron, St Joseph up on high.*

*As we march, one, two, three, round the walls of SJC,
we shout hurray, cheerio carry on! Thank you, driver."'

Sisters of Our Lady of the Missions.
Back row: M M St Augustine, M M St Laurentia, M St Gerard.
Middle row: M St Lucine, Rev. M M St Mechtilde, M St Athanasius.
Front row: Sr M St Edward, Sr M St Esther, Sr M St Josephine, M M St Crescentia.

CHAPTER ONE

Sisters of Our Lady of the Missions

Father Jean Forest.

At the time that the Sisters of Our Lady of the Missions was established in 1861, in Lyon, France, by Euphrasie Barbier,[3] Bishop Philippe Viard was desperate to recruit more nuns for his Wellington diocese, receiving constant requests from Father Jean Forest in Napier.[4] He pleaded with the Marist Fathers to send more 'women's religious' to New Zealand. Euphrasie heard the news while working in the slums of London while she was attached to the Sisters of Calvary. Having been based in England for almost a decade, Euphrasie was becoming desperate to fulfil her dream of being an overseas missionary but concluded that her aspirations would not be realised if she remained with the Sisters of Calvary. She approached Father Chaurain at the Marist Church at Spitalfields in London and registered her interest in Viard's call.

In July 1861, Pope Pius IX granted Euphrasie permission to change to another congregation so that she would be able to travel to New Zealand.[5] Accompanying her would be Sister St Wilfrid, an English novice, and Father Favre, who had accepted the offer to be transferred to Wellington, and all three travelled to Lyon with the expectation to set sail for the South Pacific. However, due to Viard having received three new French sisters in Auckland from Bishop Jean-Baptiste Francois Pompallier in June 1861, Euphrasie and Favre received the disappointing news in October that their services were no longer required.

Dismayed but not disheartened, Euphrasie and Favre decided to start a new order to operate schools in the Marist vicariates in New Zealand and the Pacific Islands and so the Sisters of Our Lady of the Missions was established. The Cardinal Archbishop of Lyon approved the new institute and appointed Favre to supervise the development of the new order in his name. The novitiate was opened on Christmas Day 1861. One year and one day after the novitiate commenced, Euphrasie took her vows in 1862. The four sisters who travelled to Napier – Mother Mary St Madeleine (Alexandrine Niel), Sister Mary St Jean (Marie Antoinette Dufour), Sister Mary St Anne (Elise Deat) and Sister des Anges (Marie Moreau) – were professed in August 1864.

Also that year, Father Forest corresponded with Father Yardin, who was also responsible for the development of the congregation, over the matter of supplying teachers for his female pupils in Napier. Yardin wrote: 'I am occupied preparing for you three young Sisters for your Girls' Schools. They will be able to depart only next November …'[6]

In August the same year, Yardin again wrote to Forest:[7]

> The sisters are delighted. They thank you for all your preparations to lodge them so well and to provide for their support … Instead of three Sisters, you will have four of them … The Superioress is Sister M. Madeleine, she is a mature person, with good judgement and a devoted heart. She does not fear sacrifices. Her assistant is Sister St John who was the econome here. The third is Sister Mary of the Angels, who has been a class mistress in England for twelve years and who will be the mainstay of your school. She will certainly succeed; it will be enough to give her head to encourage her from time to time. She is a good religious. The fourth is Sister M. St Ann. She has less schooling than the others but she will make an excellent work-mistress. None of these Sisters is a musician; Sister St John will be able to teach the elements of vocal music. The first two Sisters are in London eight days now to accustom themselves more to the language and to the English teaching methods and school management.

The four sisters from the Sisters of Our Lady of the Missions arrived in Napier on the *Walter Hood* at 8 p.m. on 25 February 1865, having left England in October the previous year.[8] Prior to their arrival in Napier, the sisters heard of the death of Father Peter Chanel at Futuna and had heard that Māori in Napier were like those who murdered Chanel. Fearing for the life of Father Forest, as he did not meet them at the wharf in Napier, the anxiety of the travelling sisters was very high. The harbourmaster escorted them off the wharf, after being assured by Father Poupinel that Forest was indeed alive and safe. They were also greeted with lantern-carrying parishioners before being driven to the church at the bottom of the hill.[9]

Memorial at Pakipaki.

By August 1907, such was the growth of the Sisters of Our Lady of the Missions, that Bishop Grimes announced that the sixteen houses of the congregation in New Zealand would be designated a province, after confirmation had been received from the Vatican.[10] By 1920 there were twenty-four convents and, given the growth of the mission in New Zealand, two provinces were established: the north province was established out of Hamilton and named St Mary's, with the headquarters for the south province being located in Christchurch and named Sacred Heart.[11] Today the Sisters of Our Lady of the Missions operate eighteen provinces in Italy, Australia, Latin America, Canada, New Zealand, United Kingdom, Ireland, France, Vietnam, the Philippines, Myanmar, India, Sudan, Senegal, Kenya and Bangladesh.[12] They continue to deliver programmes in social development, pastoral work, education and health.

1. Pope Pius XI.
2. Jean-Baptiste Francois Pompallier.
3. Father Louis Catherin Servant.
4. Bishop Philippe Viard.

Top row: Sister Mary St Madeline and Sister Marie des Agnes.
Bottom row: Sister Mary St Jean and Sister Marie St Anne.

Founder of St Joseph's Providence
Father Euloge Reignier
1811–1888

Father Euloge Reignier.

Father Reignier was born in Chateaubriand, France, in 1811. Ordained in 1834, he then worked as an assistant priest before joining the Society of Mary and was professed as a Marist in 1841. The following year he sailed with Fathers Jean Forest and John (Jean) Lampila to New Zealand and worked in the Bay of Plenty, stationed in Ōpotiki in 1843. He then shifted to Rotorua and serviced that settlement as well as Taupō. While based at Ōhinemutu in 1849, Reignier was one of the more successful Marist priests, having baptised 1300 Māori in his area.[13] He moved in 1850 to help establish the Pakowhai Mission Station in Hawke's Bay and, after a brief visit to the new Wellington Marist headquarters, Reignier returned to Pakowhai in the following year.[14] Reignier, known affectionately as 'Father Reinie', spent much time with Māori, often walking from settlement to settlement with a Māori catechist before purchasing a horse named Bob in 1857 and becoming a familiar sight on the Hawke's Bay plains with his carved walking stick.

Reverend Dr Mulcahy wrote in 1960:

One writer [Fredrick Sutton] recalls meeting Father Reignier on the Taupō Road north of Rangitāiki in the 1870s. He was riding his horse, Bob, and had one Māori child in front of him and another clinging on to him behind. He had found the parents dead and was bringing the girls to Napier. He had been three days on the road, he told the traveller and expected to be another two. He also used to finance the College [St Joseph's], for the State aid was far from sufficient, and for many years he was its business manager.[15]

Pakowhai Pā 1859.

Mulcahy also notes that sometimes Reignier would take Māori girls to a Napier local, John Mahoney, to 'spruce them up' before dropping them off to the sisters.[16] The sisters were never sure what to expect when Reignier visited, as sometimes when he took off his black cape, up to three Māori girls would 'pop out'.[17] During this time, Reignier established churches at Pakowhai (1851), Napier (1859), Meeanee (1863), Waipawa (1874), Hastings (1881) and Wairoa (1882).[18] Reignier's involvement with St Joseph's extended from arguing for the school to be established during the 1860s, through to resigning as the acting manager in November 1886 due to his 'age and infirmities'.[19]

It is also important to note that Reignier became a 'naturalised' British subject under the Naturalisation Act 1858.[20] This may have been as a result of being frustrated at not being able to purchase land as a Frenchman. After declaring that he had been a resident of New Zealand for eighteen years, Reignier, then aged forty-eight, wrote to the Colonial Secretary petitioning the bureaucrat to be made a 'naturalised' British subject. It was granted and backdated, as per Reignier's wish, to 1 January 1857.[21]

In 1880 Reignier suffered a serious injury when he was thrown from his buggy and his head struck a stone wall. He was not expected to survive, but he did, living life at a slower pace for his remaining eight years. When he died in 1888, aged 77, the *Hawke's Bay Herald* wrote: 'It is men of the stamp of Father Reignier who formed the real strength of the Catholic Church. He was the beau ideal of a French gentleman and a Catholic Priest of the best type. It was due to his influences that, in this district, there was no friction between the holders of different creeds.'[22] Upon his passing, it was said that his cortege was the '... longest procession ever seen in Hawke's Bay – 62 carriages and conveyances and over one hundred horsemen ...'[23] A presentation in 1962 delivered by Rev. Dr M Mulcahy reads: 'His most enduring work – St Joseph's Maori Girls College' (known in 1867 as 'St Joseph's Providence').[24]

Foundress of Sisters of Our Lady of the Missions
Euphrasie Barbier
1829–1893

Euphrasie Barbier.

Euphrasie Barbier was born Adele Euphrasie Barbier on 4 January 1829 and was known as Marie du Coeur de Jesus during her religious life.[25] Euphrasie attended school at the Sisters of Providence in Lisieux, north-western France. She made her first communion aged ten on the Feast of the Holy Trinity, and it was at this point that Euphrasie felt she heard the call of God to work in the church.[26] After encountering a priest who shared his experiences about working overseas in the missions, the seed was sown and Euphrasie decided that her service to God would be to travel overseas and help the poor.[27]

In 1848 Euphrasie entered the newly formed Sisters of Calvary but became despondent over not serving a mission overseas, so she established her own mission titled Religieuses De Notre Dame des Missions (Sisters of Our Lady of the Missions) in 1861. The title of the order reveals that it is Trinitarian (the doctrine of the Trinity).

In the constitution that was presented for approval in 1888, Euphrasie says: 'By placing themselves under the title of our Lady of the Missions, the Sisters wish to honour in a very special way the Divine Missions which were the sole object of Mary's deepest aspirations.'[28] The first set of sisters from the Sisters of Our Lady of the Missions left France in 1864 to teach European and Māori pupils in Napier. Despite her small stature and ill health, 'The Little Mother', as she was affectionately known made regular trips to communities in France, England, the Pacific Islands, New Zealand and Asia.

Euphrasie clearly expressed her thoughts on the kind of education the girls at St Joseph's should receive when she wrote to Father Reignier:

> … first of all to be trained to virtue, an enlightened, simple, solid and practical virtue … Care will also be taken to give the children a knowledge of the sciences, especially those which are essential to their state of life, e.g. reading, writing, grammar and arithmetic, etc. The children will also be trained in the crafts suited to women, e.g. knitting, sewing, etc. They will help in the kitchen and in the different employments of the house so as to be trained in order and cleanliness and all that appertains to the domestic economy.[29]

Euphrasie visited St Joseph's on eight occasions in 1873, 1875 and 1876, and on her first visit the three schools were assembled on the school's veranda and welcomed her with singing. Described as having a 'special affinity' with the Māori girls who attended St Joseph's, 'She was delighted to see that these dear little "native girls" were receiving food, clothing and a complete education appropriate to their strength and capacity. As well as that, she watched over their social advancement, hoping that in turn, they might be capable of educating the young children of their own race.'[30]

On her final visit to the school in 1883 Euphrasie observed that the government now only funded girls who had come directly from their tribes to the Providence and that the roll had grown to about forty pupils:

> Some were still pagans, but nearly all, after having spent a year or two in the establishment, and after having learned the prayers and truths of our holy religion in their own language, begged for baptism, and received Holy Communion and Confirmation. Returning to their people, many became apostles and new Good Samaritans, striving to lead their friends and relations to Jesus Christ.[31]

At the request of the bishops, the Sisters of Our Lady of the Missions established a presence in Christchurch in 1869 and then in Nelson in 1871. In 1870 the sisters founded their first base in England at Deal, Kent.[32] Over the next thirteen years, the sisters expanded their operation to include Sturry in England, Armentieres in France and in Bangladesh.[33] Euphrasie died in 1893, aged sixty, and was interred in the convent chapel in Sturry, England. Her last words to the sisters who surrounded her were: 'Be united, be all united on earth that you may also be in Heaven.'[34]

Sisters of Our Lady of the Missions

Sister Maureen 'Doc' Richardson
TEACHER 1973–1983

Sister Muriel Kivell
HOSTEL MANAGER 1992–1995; TEACHER 2014–PRESENT

Sister Sarah Greenlees
TEACHER 1983–PRESENT

Although the Sisters of Our Lady of the Missions are no longer responsible for running St Joseph's, they remain in residency on the school grounds and have ongoing input into college governance and into the lives of the pupils. Christchurch-raised Sister Maureen Richardson, affectionately known as 'Doc', was a nurse by profession. 'I was going to become a nurse, get married and have twelve children. When at primary school I can remember the teacher saying to me "If you really want to be happy you will follow God's will." I couldn't think of anything worse. Black stockings and no driving! That was a major disappointment because as a little kid I couldn't wait to sit behind the wheel.' Eventually Sister Maureen warmed to the idea of becoming a sister. She worked in geriatrics for a decade, before she became the matron of the hostel at St Joseph's. In that role Sister Maureen 'looked after the girls' health and general well-being'. 'I had more influence with the third formers who needed a bit more mothering.' Past pupils fondly remember 'Doc' who had 'to dish out the medication because the girls wouldn't take them'. 'They all got cough syrup because they all had coughs, even though some of them might have been pretending.'

One humorous aspect to being a sister was the habit (dress) that they wore. 'We had long habits in those days and so the girls would say "Where are their feet?" It was also the time of an American comedy called *The Flying Nun*, and one day walking down the street some children said "Look! There she is, the flying nun."'

Sister Maureen loved the girls, especially the 'rogues'. 'There was this one girl and she had a rough upbringing and was very streetwise but I loved her and she would always remember my birthday. Some years later I was at the funeral of a priest which also happened to be my birthday. She said "Happy Birthday, Doc!"'

Sister Muriel, from a Hāwera family, was attracted to being a sister 'to assist education for children who are disadvantaged' because being both a missionary and a teacher fits her well. 'I returned to St Joseph's in 2014 after six years in Rome and being responsible for the finance and property of our congregation. Georgina [Kingi] knew I was back and asked if I would help teach maths in the college, to which I agreed.'

Sister Maureen Richardson.

Sister Muriel Kivell.

Sister Sarah Greenlees.

Muriel also has memories of people's reactions to her wearing a habit:

All they could see was your face and hands. The religious habits came out of the dress of the poor from the middle ages, and it hadn't changed until the Second Vatican [1965]. [One of the main objectives of the Second Vatican Council was to modernise the Catholic Church.] When it changed, it came up to half calf length, and it had some shape to it rather than being a sack that was tied in the middle. Then we changed into ordinary clothes and a cousin of mine said, "Welcome back to the human race!"

The reward for teaching at St Joseph's for Sister Muriel is the growth she witnesses in the pupils:

One girl had lived on the streets and there was a meeting with welfare and her whānau and no one in her immediate whānau wanted her. One of her more distant relations said to social welfare, "If you would pay for her costs for boarding fees, she could come to St Jo's with my daughter." She said to me, "My father wants me home for the holidays." The girl returned to school and said, "All they wanted me to do was look after the babies while they went down to the pub. I am going to look after myself and do well in my exams." That same pupil passed School Certificate.

Sister Sarah Greenlees is now eighty-seven and was known as Mary St Vincent before reverting to her baptismal name. Born in Christchurch, Sister Sarah was schooled in Christchurch with the Sisters of Our Lady of the Missions:

> When I was only six, I made my first communion with the Sisters. I was chosen to be what they called an angel for the sisters. In their ceremony to enter the novitiate they had little flower girls, and the sisters became a bride of Christ and I was a flower girl for one of these brides. I thought it was the most wonderful thing, and I decided that I wanted to be a bride and I always wanted to be a teacher. I would teach them tables and spelling.

However, having an education with the Sisters of Our Lady of the Missions was a big commitment for her father, a fishmonger, who had to support six children. After finishing her University Entrance, Sister Sarah entered straight into the novitiate in 1950, aged seventeen. 'The sisters were not allowed to go to Teachers' Training College, and you had to do all your qualifications by correspondence because we were not allowed to go there with our religious habit and the rules of the government at the time did not permit it.'

After teaching stints at Catholic schools in Nelson, Christchurch, Leeston and Napier, Sister Sarah was appointed Mother Superior at Mount St Anne's in Christchurch, where she had begun her secondary education in 1946. Being posted to Samoa during the majority of the 1970s and the early 1980s, Greenlees took a year of study in Sydney where she fell ill and required open heart surgery. 'The authorities then said I had to return to New Zealand and I said I wanted to go to St Joseph's because my father worked a lot with the Māori people in Christchurch.'

Sister Sarah teaches music and religious education. On the subject of religious education, Sister Sarah states:

> We teach Catholic Christianity as expressed through the Catholic Church, but in the programme, they study other religions. [Teaching Religious Education] does present its own set of challenges. One of them is why do we have to take the subject when it is not an exam subject. My response is that we teach it because we believe we are teaching the whole person; we teach you for your intellect, your spirituality, your physical side, and your creative side.

The Catholic Communities of Hokianga, Whanganui, Tūrangi and Matatā

After the arrival of the Catholic Church in New Zealand, certain Māori communities became strongly associated with the faith. Four such communities are at Hokianga, Whanganui River, Tūrangi and Matatā. Those communities have, over the years, sent their daughters to St Joseph's Māori Girls' College and their sons to either Hato Paora, just out of Feilding, or the now closed Hato Petera in Auckland. As the following whānau and individuals demonstrate, successive whānau have built a strong connection to St Joseph's that is underpinned by those communities' connections with the Catholic faith.

Puhara Hawaikirangi.

Jacobs whānau: Takawai, Tania, Pio and Hera.

Jacobs Whānau

Takawai Jacobs
TE AUPŌURI

Pio Jacobs
TE RARAWA

Hera Jacobs
1979–1982

Tania Jacobs
1980–1984

The Jacobs whānau hail from Hokianga, and the significance of the far-north harbour to the Catholic Church in New Zealand is not lost on mother Takawai:

> Hokianga was the birthplace of the Catholic religion. That was the cradle of the Catholic faith. In January, every year, they have a pilgrimage to Totara Point. Our tipuna,

Peri Te Huhu, was very much a peacemaker and he brought Christianity into Te Uri o Tai. Our church was built, St Gabriel's, at Pawarenga by the influence of Bishop Pompallier.

When asked what it means to be a Catholic Māori she responds: 'You have a battle between following the Roman religion, but we are not in Rome, we are in Aotearoa, so at times we were battling within ourselves are we Māori first or are we Catholic first? We are Māori first and Catholic second. We are Māori Catholic, not Roman Catholic!'

For daughter Tania, part of her introduction to Catholicism came in the form of a play titled *Christ the Maori* written by Pā Henare Tate:

> It was about what would have happened if Christ had been a Māori. What would the world be like? Our family was involved; Dad played Jesus, Mum played Mary and we were the disciples. Our rōpū was called Te Rangimarie, and we travelled from the top of the north to the bottom of the south. We lived out of suitcases for seven years and the play was performed fifty-two times each year, on weekends.

With six children and the two eldest daughters being sent to St Dominic's in Auckland, Pio and Takawai sent their daughters Hera and Tania to St Joseph's. 'We sent them there [St Joseph's] for them to develop their Māori side in academia,' explains Takawai. Financially it was a struggle to send the two Jacobs sisters to St Joseph's, and they describe the experience as a 'real sacrifice'. Takawai remembers there being 'some very kind people who contributed to their schooling and even today we don't know who they are'.

Younger sister Tania recalls her journey from Auckland to the school in the family car with her older sister, Hera, already being at the college. 'I cried the whole way from Auckland to Napier. I started playing up, and we stopped at Greenmeadows to get changed into my uniform. Mum said: "Do whatever you like, but you are going to that school".' Tania enjoyed having the sisters there:

> Sister Kathleen's nickname was Radar because she knew who you were and where you were. Sister Malia was from the islands and was cool, and we would call her Bob Marley. Doc was everyone's favourite. She knew who was sick and who was just trying to bunk school, and if you were sick, you got this syrup and a jug of hot orange juice that was yum.

Hera once played a trick on the sisters. 'There was one sister who would kiss every girl, every night, but one night we decided we would play a trick on her, so some of the girls turned around in their beds, and she ended up kissing our feet.'

During their schooling, Takawai and Pio were part of the larger Whānau Whānui group that operated in Auckland. Takawai states: 'Our big chief was Tui Swannabeck, and we ended up having three large buses that transported the girls from the North and Auckland to St Joseph's.' Pio also remembers galas: 'They would put us up at the school. All of these people placed their food on a long table, the length of the football field, that was how they were fed that time.' Auckland Whānau Whānui also organised debutante balls for Hato Hohepa alumni in Auckland, with the girls all wearing white. Tania relays: 'Our first ball was at Te Unga Waka and then there was one at Trillos. I know we felt really special. Sister Patricia Huckle and Miss Kingi would present us with a scroll of what we had achieved.' Talk of balls sparks a memory for Hera regarding a graduation dance with Hato Paora: 'Sister Annetta [Sister Beverley Grounds] would be saying that the devil is upon us if we kissed a boy, and she would be praying.'

1. St Joseph's at Totara Point, 1938.
2. Debutante ball 1990.
   Back row: S Peipi, R Rewi, A Thomas, N Tapara, N Transom.
   Front row: D White, D Boyce, M Hotere, M Hoko, G Timu, A Heremaia, V Lewer.

Shontelle Bishara, Debra Whittle and Hine-Matioro Bishara.

Tūrangi

Mary Kereopa
NÉE TAEWA
NGĀTI TŪWHARETOA, NGĀPUHI
1964–1967

Michelle Taiaroa
NÉE HOKO
NGĀTI TŪWHARETOA, WAIKATO
1985–1988

John Bishara
NGĀTI TŪWHARETOA

Shontelle Bishara
NGĀTI TŪWHARETOA, NGĀTI KAHUNGUNU
1992–1996

Maureen Roger
NGĀTI RAUKAWA KI TE TONGA
1993–1996

Mary Kereopa followed in the footsteps of her older sister, Elizabeth, who left midway through Mary's first year at St Joseph's in 1954. Feeling a little bit lost after her sister departed, Mary still had a relation at the school, her aunt, Sister Katarina Mariu. 'It was lovely having her there, and she would remind you that you are representing Ngāti Tūwharetoa. I guess there was a strong relationship between Waihi, Tūrangi and Taumaranui with Sister Katarina.' As a devout Catholic who was raised at Waihi, Mary can vividly recall hearing her kaumātua chant in Māori during Latin mass. 'Aged seven, I remember when Father Nederhoff said, "Kāti! – Stop!" to the kaumātua because the Vatican at the time was going through a change and Latin mass was stopped.'

One of Mary's favourite teachers was Mrs Flashoff. 'She taught us English, like Shakespeare and poetry and literacy. As a literacy teacher, I still use poems to teach phonetics.' Mrs Flashoff stood in stark contrast to Mother Augustine, otherwise known as 'Gussy', whom Mary describes as being 'grumpy'. 'She didn't like it if we danced and would say, "You look like worms in a bucket." She would frown on us for wearing our rompers for PE and would say, "You look like storks! Go and put some clothes on!" because she didn't like us showing our legs.' The attitudes of the principal, says Mary, influenced their ideas on how to be good women. 'From my time at St Joseph's, we were taught to be good mothers, how to act properly, to have a deep sense of pride in ourselves and to remember you have your whānau on your shoulders.'

After St Joseph's, Mary went to Ardmore College, where she trained to be a teacher and met her husband. Currently she is a teacher at Te Kura o Hirangi, a Kura ā-Iwi. 'We teach things to do with our Tūwharetoatanga; our tikanga and our environment.

I am still engaged in teaching in te reo Māori, and I still use what I learnt from my teachers at St Joseph's.' During the 1990s, Mary's daughter, Leila, attended her alma mater. 'My daughter secretly phoned her father to say, "Come and pick me up. I hate it here." He was going and I said, "Don't you dare. You leave her there; she'll get over it." She ended up staying for five years and loved it.'

The whānau of Michelle Taiaroa are 'staunch Catholics'. From the small village of Waihi that is nestled on the southern shores of Lake Taupō, St Werenfred's Church takes centre stage in the community. All of Michelle's family, from her grandparents to her aunties and uncles, had attended schools operated by the Marist Fathers. 'Sister Katarina's parents and my great-grandfather used to go to rosary every day at nine o'clock and every afternoon, and they got an award from the Pope for their service.'

Michelle Taiaroa at St Werenfried's, Waihi.

When asked about why she goes to church, she responds: 'It's our wairua, our tikanga. People ask, "Why do you go to church?" But when something goes wrong, people always want prayers. I say to my children, "When you get upset, go to your chapel, go to a church, go to the lake, or go to the river."'

Michelle Taiaroa was called upon to perform an important reading at the ordination of her uncle, Max Mariu, when he became the first Māori Catholic bishop in 1987. She was encouraged to do the reading by Georgina Kingi, and she practised beforehand at some churches in Napier. 'Uncle Max was awesome. He made you want to go to church. He would have midnight mass. All of his brothers would be drunk, and he would say come in, sit down, get blessed, and then go.'

Joining Michelle Taiaroa at St Joseph's was her younger sister, Nicole, and her cousin, Kahureremoana. Currently both of her daughters, Moengarau (year 13) and Maraea (year 9), attend the college. 'I just wanted them to have Miss [Kingi] in their heads and in their hearts. Miss is the last of the Mohicans. Not many people can say they are teaching third and fourth generation girls. Her whole being is about the girls.' Going to St Joseph's is, for Michelle Taiaroa, about maintaining old-fashioned values. 'Going to St Joseph's widens your horizons. Although it didn't used to be, Tūrangi is a depressed community, and I think my daughter Maraea has learnt more in the last year than she has in the previous five years.'

John Bishara has been involved with St Joseph's for the past twenty-four years, since his daughter, Shontelle, was a student there. He is currently the Deputy Chair of

Top: The daughters of Michelle Taiaroa: Maraea and Moengarau.
Bottom: John Bishara, Nastasia Kopa and Shontelle Bishara.

the St Joseph's Māori Girls' College Trust Board. For John's whānau, their involvement with the school dates back to when his grandmother, Hine-Matioro Tamaira, attended, then his mother, Manaiawharepu ('Mana') Bishara (née Tamaira) and her sister, Ketekiri ('Bunny') Maude Wildermoth (née Tamaira). John's mother, Manaiawharepu, married Edward Bishara, whose two sisters, Charlotte Harvey (née Bishara) and Ngawaiata ('Mei') McDonnell (née Wanikau), also went to St Joseph's and, to cap off the whānau connection, John's brother's daughter, Hine-Matioro ('Hine'), also attended. As John explains: 'In Ngāti Tūwharetoa, the connection with the college is very, very strong, through the Catholic Church. Sister Katarina was Mum's first cousin and they were devoted Catholics.'

During the mid-1970s, John became acquainted with the school when he was a forestry ranger in Mohaka. At the time, Cyril and Waina Gotty, parents of girls attending St Joseph's, were involved with the school, and Cyril would turn up to the forestry camp and tell John they were going to Napier. 'While in Hawke's Bay, Cyril would say, "We are just going to do something at St Joseph's." We would cut the grass and Cyril would do the cooking to give the sisters a rest.' When John became first involved as a Board member in the early 1990s, unemployment was high as various government policies impacted negatively on Māori, and the subsidy many whānau relied on to send their daughters to St Joseph's was coming to an end. John recounts: 'Parents struggled to pay, and we would put things in place to help them. You can put the debt collectors on to them or send the girls home, but at the end of the day, you are only penalising the girl.'

Shontelle Bishara followed her cousin, Hine. It wasn't until after she attended that she realised the significance of going there, following in the footsteps of the women in her whānau. 'It made my great-grandmother and grandmother very proud. My nan used to talk to me about her and her sister going from Taumaranui, about how she was homesick and did not want to be there, crying to her dad until she got to come home. Her sister, Maude Tamaira, stayed and became a teacher there.' After leaving St Joseph's, Shontelle completed a Bachelor of Arts degree majoring in political science at Victoria University and has a graduate Diploma in Economic Development. She now works as a management consultant for GHA, which works with Māori businesses from their Rotorua office.

Maureen Roger, bred in Tūrangi, was born to a Māori mother and a Pākehā father, who was Catholic. 'I was supposed to go to Villa Maria in Christchurch, but I told my father if he sent me there, I would run away. So I ended up at St Jo's.' Cost was an issue for the Roger whānau. 'I can remember Dad pulling over into the gas station after gala. I said to Dad, "Can we afford it because if we can't I'll come home," and he said, "I'll find a bloody way girl."' Sometimes her brothers would contribute money to help her pay for her stationery. Maureen remembers the significant role of the prefects in the school. 'If we played up at night, we had to get out on the courts and do twinkle, twinkle, little star on our tippy toes for an hour or clean the Marian Steps with a toothbrush.'

For Maureen, attending St Joseph's was the first time she had been exposed to her Māori whakapapa:

> Before I went, I hardly had any knowledge of being Māori, and when I left school, I was speaking and writing Māori. I hadn't been exposed to my taha Māori before I arrived. I didn't know my hapū and iwi, and yet all my mates could get up and do their pepeha. I had to ask Mum and she didn't even know.

Olive Prince.

Whanganui

River Rats

Amiria Beamsley
NÉE TAPA
TE ATI HAUNUI-A-PĀPĀRANGI
1962–1965

Olive 'Olly' Prince
TE ATI HAUNUI-A-PĀPĀRANGI
1988–1991

Nikayla Jonas
TE ATI HAUNUI-A-PĀPĀRANGI
2011–2015

Kataraina Millen and Turuhira Mohi
NÉE BAILEY
TE ATI HAUNUI-A-PĀPĀRANGI
1953–1957 AND 1955–1957

Cecilia Tawhitipou
NÉE WHANARERE
WHANGANUI
1959/60–1961

Georgina Hema
NÉE TE HUIA
TE ATI HAUNUI-A-PĀPĀRANGI
1968–1970

Jacqueline Phillips
TE ATI HAUNUI-A-PĀPĀRANGI
1979–1981

Sue Osborne
WHANGANUI, NGĀTI PARERAUKAWA, NGĀTI TAMA
1983–1985

Old girls 1911–1920.

The whānau involvement of Amiria Beamsley (née Tapa) with St Joseph's stems back five generations:

> My grandmother was there from 1914 to 1917, her maiden name being Meri Haami, and she was the godchild to Sister Aubert. Of the five generations who have gone there, two of them have been made dux, Rachael Tinirau and Olive Prince, and two of them, mother and daughter, Olive Prince and Nikayla Jonas, have been appointed head girls. I had a daughter attend, Jacqueline Beamsley (now Delamere), who went from 1982 to 1985.

Amiria remembers well when she first arrived at St Joseph's, having to hand in any pocket money she had received from her parents. Second time round, Amiria, like other girls, hid her money in the seam of her blazer.

When Olive 'Olly' Prince was born, the words spoken by Olly's great-grandmother, Meri Haami, to her daughter, Christine Tapa, were that Olly was to go to St Joseph's. Olly's daughter, Nikayla, also attended the college, and Olly recalls some of the conversations she had with her mother's generation when her daughter was responsible for organising the waiata for the group competitions:

> We sat with these seventy- and eighty-year-olds who went to St Joseph's, listening to their stories about how tough the times were. For my mother's generation, they would bathe once a week, and you could be the tenth person in the water, and they wore long

woollen stockings that were itchy. For my nan's generation, there was a lot of focus on their faith. They were from Rānana and Koroniti, and because our whānau were asset rich and cash poor, not every girl in our whānau went to St Joseph's.

By the end of the first term, Olly observed how attending boarding school strengthened the bond between daughter and father:

Dad is a gruff farmer, and we didn't grow up hugging, and we would show aroha in different ways. The first term was thirteen weeks, and I was sitting outside in the front for gala day and everyone else's parents were coming. He appeared out of the group of parents. I called out "Dad" and screamed towards him and threw my arms out open. I had never hugged my dad like that, not since I was a kid, and when we walked off together, it was the first time I had held his hand, and I can remember how big and gruff his hands were. You missed your parents like you would not believe.

The general appearance of the girls and the school ethos of treating every girl the same operates as a great 'leveller':

Some of the girls look the same as they did twenty-five years ago. Their hair is worn in the same style, regardless of the fashions that come and go, and that is a leveller. Miss Kingi understands that we have girls who come from all walks of life. They have to learn to live and learn together and everyone has the opportunity to do well. It doesn't matter if you come from the most affluent family or if you come by the good graces of CYFS, you are all on the same playing field and you would never ever know. That's a real powerful thing because it allows any wahine who goes there to unlock herself and to choose to do that, not to bring whatever you think it is you can bring because that is what you thought.

Cecilia Tawhitipou (seated) and Kataraina Millen (standing).

Jacqueline Phillips, Turuhira Mohi, Georgina Hema and Amiria Beamsley.

Daughter Nikayla, the fifth generation to attend from their whānau, followed in her mother's footsteps and was also appointed as one of two head prefects (Olly shared the head prefect role with Stephanie Nuku in 1991). 'In the sixth form, I was made house prefect. I was glad it wasn't just me who was made head prefect. It was a shared role with Valerie Houkamau, in 2015, who was strong in Māori and I am strong in English. When it came to public speaking, we would alternate the roles.'

On the subject of personal grooming, Nikayla remembers being growled at when performing kapa haka:

> You were reminded to keep your hair how God gave it to you. You weren't allowed to dye it or use mousse. The only time we were allowed to use product was when we had a photoshoot or a performance. I have quite fuzzy hair, and Miss Kingi would growl me because of the fuzzy bits, so I'd have to use hair gel or wax to smooth out the edges.

Nikayla is now studying at Victoria University and is achieving As due to the 'study ethic that St Jo's has embedded in me'. 'I probably wouldn't have got into university and getting the results I am now without having gone to St Jo's. It made me dream big, and university was definitely a possibility.' The school also contributed greatly towards strengthening Nikayla's Māori identity. 'It [St Joseph's] is a kāinga, a church, a marae. Hato Hohepa taught me all I know about my Māoritanga, my tikanga, my reo and my confidence, and I am forever grateful.'

Another whānau from the river, associated with the college for three generations, is the Takarangi/Bailey whānau. Agnes and May Takarangi (sisters) attended the college, and their cousin, Lucy, also attended and was crowned the Queen Carnival at the Napier Municipal Theatre in 1919. May's daughters, Atawhai, Kataraina, Turuhira, Sheridan and Erana attended, followed by the third generation of the whānau, being Coralee (the daughter of Turuhira) and the two daughters of Kataraina (Trina and Maria). As Kataraina remembers:

> Our grandfather was a convert from the Anglican Church, and he always went to the Catholic Church. St Joseph's was a church college for Māori who went there automatically from the river. Our schools were chosen for us, and we knew where we were going to go. We were from Rānana that had a convent school, and our cousins came from there and all along the river to Kaiwhaiki. We got the government scholarship because we had to leave home to go to high school. We travelled by bus, but our parents' generation commuted by boat.

When speaking of her mother, May, Kataraina remembers:

> She went because our grandfather said you are going and you are going to live in Te Ao Pākehā, so you are going to have to learn those skills even though her first language was Māori and she didn't learn English until she went to school. When Mum went to Greenmeadows, she didn't want to go because of the [1935] earthquake.

The commute from Whanganui to Greenmeadows took two days when Kataraina attended:

It was exciting. We only travelled to Wanganui once a year, and it was our first outing from Wanganui. We caught a steam train from Wanganui to Napier and then by bus. When we got off the train, we saw the sisters, and they were totally different from our sisters [from the river] with their habits. We only saw their face whereas with the Sisters of Compassion, sometimes you might see some of their hair. We used to peek and try and see them without their habits, so we would go under our blankets because they would get up to go to office for their prayers early in the morning, and we would peek through the dormitory windows to see what they would do.

A teacher of te reo Māori, Kataraina reminisces about the language: 'It was all around us as it was Mum's first language, but those from the river never spoke. At school, it was the Coasties and the ones from the north that really spoke te reo Māori.' Following her education at St Joseph's, Kataraina became a secondary school teacher, only to return to St Joseph's as the school's first lay Director of Religious Studies in the 1990s. Kataraina's sister, Turuhira, became a psychology nurse after three years of training 'on the job'. 'I went from the college to a Post Office hostel in Wellington and was placed by Māori Affairs in a trade training-like arrangement.'

Cecilia Tawhitipou (née Whanarere) was raised Katorika in the small settlement of Kaiwhaiki. 'My mother was Catholic and my mum's parents were Ringatū. Even though we had Rātana who lived with us and other denominations, most of them came to our Hāhi because the Catholic Church was there.' As for mixing with other religions, Cecilia remembers that, prior to the Second Vatican in 1965, Catholics weren't allowed to go to other churches:

You would get ex-communicated back in the day if you went to someone else's church! The Church had to change their stance because we wouldn't listen. We would go to tautoko our wānau, no matter what Hāhi they belonged to. If there was a wedding in another church, we weren't allowed to go. You couldn't be a pallbearer at the funeral of another faith. They would say, "Don't go," but we didn't listen.

The former Upokongaro School pupil left her small settlement on the banks of the Whanganui River with her cousin Reti Peina to travel to Greenmeadows. 'There were several girls from our school who went to St Joseph's, including Sheri, Bernadette, Virginia and Miriama Henare. I was the only one from my whānau at the time who went. There were three of my sisters-in-law who attended: Yvonne, Doreen and Helena Whanarere. We all just stuck together, regardless of religion, and we called ourselves River Rats.' Cecilia's mokopuna, Te Oranga Whanarere, attended St Joseph's and was head prefect in 2010.

Memorable sisters during Cecilia's time at St Joseph's included Sister Agnes, who took the girls for cooking, Sister Joseph, who was in charge of the laundry, and Sister Jerome, who was 'my favourite because she would let me sleep in, and if there were any errands, she would let me go to Taradale.' Sister Gabriel took the pupils for French, as it was compulsory for first year students. 'I used to hate it, and I never got to finish learning Hail Mary in French.' For Cecilia: 'I just wanted to learn to speak te reo Māori, and when I went home, Dad would say to me, "Kāore kōrero i te reo," and I would respond, "Well you didn't teach me."' No Māori was spoken in Cecilia's home, although her father was a native speaker and spoke to his cousins in te reo Māori:

> All those ones who came from the East Coast and the Bay of Plenty to St Joseph's used to talk to each other in Māori, flat out. Sister Katarina took us for Māori. At home, we always used to say, "Kei tere," but then Sister Katarina would say, "Ka tere". You couldn't use our mita because she didn't accept it.

Other memories of the sisters include their frugalness and their fundraising:

> The sisters were very economical, and they wouldn't waste a thing, not even the little bits of soap. They would collect them all up in a little mesh bag, hang it on the hot water tap and let the water run. For the Garden Fete, we had to make cakes and lollies. Sister Athanasius would crochet a whole lot of baby clothes and would start at the beginning of the year to get them ready in time. The last old girls' fundraiser that I went to was in Rotorua and organised by Sister Katarina. When we went as Wanganui, we took a bus, and we would always get a koha from Te Ati Haunui-a-Pāpārangi of over £1,000 that we always took back to the college.

Sadly, for Cecilia in her School Certificate year, she changed schools to Sacred Heart in Wanganui so the family could afford to send her brother to Hato Paora:

> I know my koro helped my mum to pay the bills. I think she got a grant, like a family benefit, that used to go to the school rather than to Mum and she also had to pay the balance. I was really sad when I left because I didn't like Sacred Heart. The Sisters were from a different order, the Josephites, and I hated travelling every day to school.

Georgina Hema's mother attended St Joseph's during the 1930s. For Georgina, the name of Sister Katarina Mariu conjures up the memory of a sister who disliked miniskirts. Georgina quips: 'She was in charge of dressmaking, and I wanted to sew a miniskirt to wear to the show. She put an end to that idea.' Georgina's time at St Joseph's coincided with another Georgina returning to the college:

> Georgina Kingi used to visit as a reliever in 1968. Two of her sisters were prefects at the time, and they used to say, "Don't be frightened of her, because she knows nothing." She was very determined to instil mana wahine, and she was a role model for me. I thought, I'm going to be a principal like her, and she was my inspiration.

Eventually Georgina became a travelling principal in the Australian outback, teaching Aboriginal children.

Jacqueline Phillips went to St Joseph's because her mother and her cousins went to the school. 'I went to school to learn te reo Māori and Dad just started to learn it because it was his time to stand on the marae.' However, after she arrived, her late nanny, who had died when she was young, started to visit her in her sleep, causing her to wake and cry. 'It used to scare the girls, and in the end my parents came over. I would go to the chapel and to the holy water because Miss Kingi thought that's what you should do.' Jacqueline also remembers celebrating birthdays at the school. 'When we had a birthday for one of the pupils, we had chips and dip and got sachets of Happy-Ade. You would cut the corner, wet your finger and stick it in. It was like sherbet and we all brought something.'

Having left during the fifth form, Jacqueline enjoys the strong relationship she has with her former school friends. 'After I had left school, one of our good friends died in an accident, and we came together and went to Hāwera. We also got together in Palmerston North because one of the girls from our year is really sick.'

Sue Osborne's whānau lived just out of town and were associated with Hui Aranga. 'I think for our generation there was a big push at the time [to attend St Joseph's] and it has got more to do with being Katorika if anything … our boys went to Hato Paora and then there was a change when some of our boys went to some of the local Catholic schools like St Augustine's.'

Class photo 1952: F4 with Miss Matheson.

Matatā
Marr Whānau

Monika Barker
NÉE MARR
NGĀTI RANGITIHI
1947–1949

Stella Marr
NGĀTI RANGITIHI, NGĀTI TŪWHARETOA,
TE ATI AWA
1969–1974

The Marrs from Matatā have a long and proud association with St Joseph's. Former pupil Monika Barker (née Marr) explains:

> We had a convent in Matatā, and we have just celebrated our 125th anniversary. I was sent to St Joseph's because my sister went ahead of me (four sisters in total attended the college) but my great-grandmother went there also. Kirikau Kaipara was her name and my great-grandfather took her from Kaingaroa. It took two weeks with a horse and buggy to get her there, and when she came home, she came home on a trawler right around the headlands and into the Thornton River. Grandpa sent her there to learn the Pākehā ways. Because my grandmother went there and my older sister, it was a tradition and my brothers went to Hato Petera. I knew from my infant days I would go there. My mother was a fierce Catholic and my father was a Methodist, and when I was seventeen, he became a Catholic because there were so many priests and nuns around our place that he decided, if you can't beat them, join them. He only did it to shut Mum up, to please her.

Monika arrived at St Joseph's aged twelve. With her older sister being an organist before she arrived, Monika stepped into her shoes, as her keyboard skills were often called upon. 'I would play the boogie woogie instead of the Norwegian cradle songs, and I would always get caught.' A friend of Monika's at St Joseph's was Kaa Daniels. 'We used to have dances or concerts, and Monica could play the piano and the organ. She would "jive it up" and we would be dancing away in the chapel. When we could hear the nuns walking, we would quieten it down.'

Teaching Monika music was Sister Chanel:

> If you played the wrong note, God help you. But she used to have the statue of St Joseph on our feast day and if it rained, she turned it or hid it away. I was also Sister Margaret's pet. She was a shorthand typist teacher and she would always send me into town. She gave me nine pence for a sundae and the first thing I would do was hit the music shop because they always had the latest piece of music up on the stand. I would learn the tune and write down the lyrics in shorthand and one of the songs was "If you ever go across the sea to Ireland".

Monika also attended St Joseph's with Te Ao Tamihana 'who could knock Kiri Te Kanawa off'.

With the sisters teaching virtually all the subjects when Monika attended, she remembers having respect for the sisters, bar Sister Petronius who took music. 'She was in the wrong calling, I tell you. I never had a nice word out of that woman.' Sister Athanasius also looms large in Monika's memory. 'She taught us how to sew black bloomers for sport. I hated them. We had to place our gyms under our straw mattresses to press

Monika Barker.

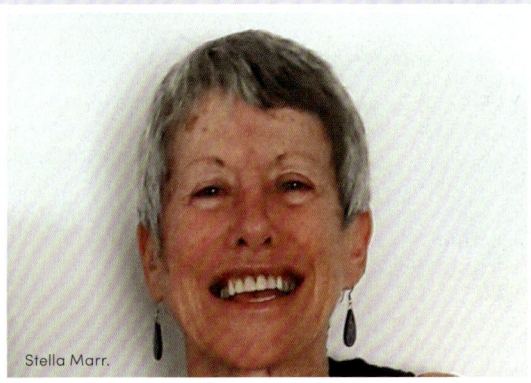
Stella Marr.

them on the wire wove and they would have crinkles all up the back.' Life at St Joseph's was fun for the free-spirited Monika.

> We used to follow Ally the Gardener. He used to pull up in his little truck and the word would go out "Ally is here with the apples", and he would take them around to where the [water] well was. We also used to raid the chicken frames to unwind the chicken wire to make curlers for our hair and we would wrap newspaper around it. We would be winding our hair around these stiff bits of wire in the dark at night.
>
> The only mufti day was Saturday. I had hairy legs and Kereni [Sister Crescentia] would say, "You're not going to look very good with legs like that, working in an office."

Stella Marr is a niece of Monika's and went to St Joseph's with her sister and cousin. With her and her three siblings attending either St Joseph's or Hato Petera, her grandmother became well versed in fundraising. 'I had to sell raffles in Matatā and go to all the local houses.' With eight siblings, Stella was keen to attend St Joseph's. 'Matatā was the second village that Pompallier went to after the Hokianga, and I had already been raised Katorika, although you didn't have to be a Catholic to go there and there were different denominations when I was there.'

On the subject of Kapa Haka, Stella reflects with affection:

> I was the kapa haka leader for two years, and we did amazing things. Miss Kingi was the strictest kapa haka teacher ever, but it worked. We did long hours, and she screamed at us to smile; you may not be liking it but you are going to look like you're liking it. It was the discipline you needed and it was good discipline. We started fundraising for the buildings at the college, and we did things like perform at Rothman's Cafeteria with a hat out, and we used to get the excess filters (the 'tow') for the filling of our poi. Kapa haka was my forte, and we were performing all the time to raise money. I was also the leader of a haka from Ngāti Porou and it was well received. I was also the leader of the record we did that year, and we went to Wellington to a studio like real pop stars.

Other staff Stella can recall include Sister Jerome, who took typewriting, a bright Mr Hannah, Mrs Welsh, who took art, and Raewyn Lawrence. 'Mr Howard who took biology as well as being the school's dentist. You would have him in the morning for biology and then in the afternoon, you would go down the road to Taradale and get your teeth done.'

'The Little Vatican', Napier Hill. St Joseph's Providence is on the highest point of the hill.

CHAPTER TWO

St Joseph's Providence

St Joseph's Māori Girls' College was first named St Joseph's Providence and was officially opened on 10 October 1867. St Joseph's came into being following the establishment of the Catholic Church in New Zealand and, more specifically, Hawke's Bay. Another factor to consider is the role the various religions played in catering, exclusively, for the western-hemisphere educational needs of Māori. This stems back to the early contact period, and it was from this time that the underlying principle of the need to educate Māori in the ways of the English and the Europeans began.

The first western hemisphere school in New Zealand was opened at Oihi, Rangihoua, in the Bay of Islands on 12 August 1816.[35] The small school sat next to the first missionary settlement in New Zealand, which was run by the Church Missionary Society, with Thomas Kendall responsible for the thirty-three pupils ranging in age from seven to twenty. It was during this time the first book on the Māori language, *A Korao no New Zealand* (The New Zealander's First Book), was published in Sydney in 1815.[36] Kendall's school was short-lived through a lack of supplies and trade,[37] yet Māori schooling developed during the 1820s and 1830s as there was a desire among many Māori to understand English.[38]

When the first New Zealand Governor, Captain William Hobson, arrived in New Zealand in January 1840, one of his instructions was to establish schools for the education of the 'Aborigines'.[39] This was reinforced from an 1840 despatch from the future British Prime Minister, Lord John Russell, to Hobson, which read:

> The education of youth among the Aborigines, is, of course, indispensable to the success of any measure for their ultimate advance in social arts and in the scale of political existence. I apprehend however that for the present this is a duty, which cannot be properly undertaken except by the missionaries or at least on some system formed in concurrence with them.[40]

The missionary support spoken of by Russell would materialise in 1844 with the establishment of two Māori church boarding schools in the Auckland region: St Stephen's (Anglican) and Wesley College (Wesleyan). Based in Hawke's Bay, Te Aute (Anglican) would open its doors a decade later, followed by Waerenga-a-Hika College (also Anglican) in Poverty Bay in 1856.

Other Māori boarding schools to open included Hukarere Māori Girls' School in Napier (Anglican, 1875), Queen Victoria School in Auckland (Anglican, 1901), Hikurangi College in Clareville, Wairarapa (Anglican, 1903), Turakina Māori Girls' College in Marton (Presbyterian, 1905), Ōtaki Māori College in Ōtaki (Anglican, 1908), Te Waipounamu Māori Girls' College in Christchurch (Anglican, 1908), Hato Petera College in Auckland (Catholic, 1928) and Hato Paora College, Feilding (Catholic, 1948).[41] Dr Judith Simon writes that the motivation behind the government funding of Māori church boarding schools was to 'create a Europeanized Māori elite ... such an elite by leadership and example was expected to help foster assimilation within the Māori communities and thereby ensure the peaceful maintenance of British rule'.[42]

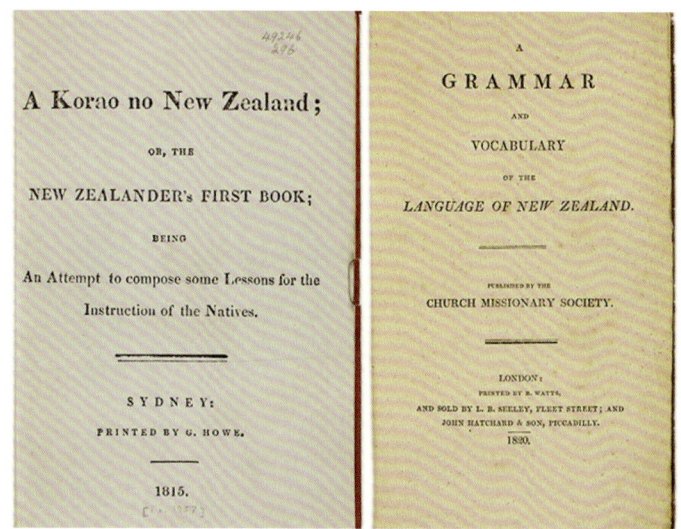

Top: Thomas Kendall.
Bottom: The first book on the Māori language.

A HISTORY OF ST JOSEPH'S MĀORI GIRLS' COLLEGE

Minister of Native Affairs, James Richmond.

Governor George Grey.

Māori Education Legislation
1847 Educational Ordinance, 1858 and 1867 Native Schools Acts and 1871 Native Schools Amendment Act

The Māori education policy of Governor George Grey was enacted with the passing of an Educational Ordinance in 1847. The regulation gave the government the power to:

> ... out of the public funds to establish and maintain schools for the education of youth and to contribute towards the support of schools otherwise established. In every school established or supported by public funds under the provisions of the ordinance, religious education, industrial training, and instruction in the English language shall form a necessary part of the system to be pursued therein ...[43]

The system provided for one twentieth of colonial revenue, one fifteenth of land sales and a fixed sum from British imperial funds to be allotted to the three main denominations providing education in New Zealand:

the Church of England, the Wesleyans and the Roman Catholics.[44] Between 1846 and 1868, the Anglicans had received £29,000, the Wesleyans £18,000 and the Roman Catholics £10,000, with another £20,000 distributed between all three.[45] Governor Grey rejected the petitions submitted for Roman Catholics to be excluded from receiving aid under the ordinance.[46]

New Zealand education historian Arthur Gordon Butchers wrote: 'Among the basic principles, which actuated the policy of both the missionaries and the Government, the Europeanisation of the native race occupied a foremost place. To this end no opportunity was lost to encourage the co-education of the youth of both races.'[47]

The 1858 Native Schools Act provided the sum of £7,000 per annum for seven years for the education of Māori and 'half-caste' children being orphans or the children of 'indigent people'.[48] Every school to be aided under the Act was to be connected to a religious body, and it specified the percentage each religious body was to receive of the total budget: the Anglicans were to receive 49 per cent, the Wesleyans 32 per cent and the Catholics 19 per cent. It was clearly an attempt to partially fund missionary-operated native schools. The focus on teaching Māori the English language was expressed in the 1847 Education Ordinance and repeated in the Native Schools Act 1858. The Inspector appointed under the 1858 Act, Henry Taylor, espoused the following view: '... in carrying out the work of civilization among the aboriginal Native race through the medium of schools ... [t]he Native language itself is another obstacle in the way of civilization. So long as it exists there is a barrier to the free unrestrained intercourse which ought to exist between the races.'[49]

On 10 October 1867, the government passed the Native Schools Act. The Minister of Native Affairs, James Richmond, believed that authorities should be providing education for Māori via a system of secular village primary schools that were to be run by the Department of Native Affairs. New Zealand educationalist John Barrington summarises the debate on the legislation, focusing on two key aspects:

> The first was that schooling in the English language was regarded as essential to "civilise" and assimilate Māori. The second was its "self-help" component, by which the onus was put on Māori who wanted a school not only to request one but also to gift some of their land for the school site and contribute to the cost of the building and the teacher's salary.[50]

The legislation provided the sum of £4,000 to be granted annually for seven years for the education of 'children of the aboriginal race and of half-castes being orphans or being the children of indigent persons'.[51] Despite the Act being passed in 1867, the legislation did not come into effect until 1871 at the end of the New Zealand Wars.[52] Under the final version of the legislation, much of the financial contribution expected from Māori was removed and the responsibilities for such costs were placed with the Governor.

Also appointed at this time was Lieutenant-Colonel Andrew Russell as the Inspector of Native Schools. Russell, although satisfied with the academic progress being made at St Joseph's Providence, constantly wrote of his concerns regarding government expenditure for Māori boarding schools in comparison with the cheaper option of native village schools.

St Mary's Church, Napier, circa early 1870s.

The first Catholic school in Napier was in St Mary's Church on the corner of Shakespeare and France roads in 1860. Named 'St Mary's Boys' School', the pupils were taught by Irishman Denis Hoben[53] and, following Hoben, John Mulhern.[54] In August that year, St Mary's Catholic School for Girls opened on Shakespeare Road near the Catholic convent and was overseen by Mary McGarvey and her sister Sarah,[55] with half of the pupils being Protestant. Mary McGarvey had tried her hand at being a nun at the other St Joseph's Providence in Wellington, as well as being the school's principal, but after a bout of ill-health and having relocated to Auckland, Father Forest approached her to come to Napier.[56] Sarah McGarvey married Denis Hoben, the first teacher of St Mary's Boys' School, and their son Ernest Hoben became the founder of the New Zealand Rugby Union.[57]

In premises that were formerly owned by the Wesleyan Church, which were transported next to the residence of the sisters, St Joseph's Girls' School was opened on 6 March 1865 with twenty-eight students who were predominantly poor children of Irish immigrants.[58] This was the first school the Sisters of Our Lady of the Missions were asked to teach at. Sister Mary des Anges was the main teacher, as she could speak English fluently, with her deputy, Sister Mary St Jean, having a rudimentary command of the language.[59] With the school quickly reaching fifty pupils, Father Forest realised that the current arrangements were inadequate, and he wanted a 'select school' that could admit boarders.[60] In August 1866, Sister Mary Madeleine announced plans to construct a two-storeyed 'Ladies School' for the more affluent girls, with Sister Mary St Anne in charge.[61] 'The parents did not like them to come in contact with poor children, and particularly with some of the native children whom the Sisters were taking care of'.[62] The school, considered to be the first Sacred Heart school of the province and the third oldest existing Catholic college in the country,[63] opened on 1 June 1867.[64]

Father Reignier had, for some time, dreamt of building a Providence where Māori and 'half-castes' could be educated.[65] Reignier was clear about the purpose of the school: it would serve

Donald McLean.

a dual purpose; poor and abandoned Māori girls would be taught alongside the daughters of prominent chiefs. The highest point of Napier Hill was owned by Phillip Dobel, and Reignier considered the site to be suitable for his purposes as it was not far from the Catholic Church and the sisters' convent. He, along with Bishop Viard and Father Forest, purchased the land for £270 in 1866,[66] with Reignier submitting a petition to the government for a grant, proposing a building be built on the land. Provincial records read:

... the education of native and half-caste children of this province which is much neglected and that there are a great many children without means of education. Your petitioner proposes to erect in Napier a school for native and half-caste children of this province and to provide the ground for the building and the teachers for the school but requires assistance in order to erect the building. He would after its erection, require assistance in order to defray, the expense of maintaining and clothing such children.[67]

Father Reignier wrote to Donald McLean, the superintendent of Hawke's Bay, in July 1867 to thank him for the help the Hawke's Bay provincial government had provided to get the materials required to erect a schoolhouse.[68] Reignier also stated that he needed the assistance of central government in the erection of the building, as the last floods had taken a financial toll, and, in order to support the school in the longer term, they had purchased a Māori run. The following month, Reignier again wrote to McLean. In the letter, he relays a previous conversation he had had with Governor George Grey in which '... [Grey] intimated to me and after some officer of the government his desire to have here in the Province of Hawke's Bay such Providence as there is one in Wellington for half-caste and Maori girls ...' and concludes by informing McLean that he now has purchased twenty-five acres of land in Napier from funds canvassed in support of his cause.[69] Reignier in the same month penned a petition to Grey, begging for help to establish a providence.

Governor Grey's interest in Māori education was well known. In February 1851, Grey spoke with Bishop Viard and promised land for a Māori Girls' College in Wellington and a sum for the building. On 8 September 1852, the Providence of St Joseph opened in Wellington, with thirteen Māori girl pupils.[70] Viard was explicit that he wanted '... to form good House-servants' when he wrote his report that was tabled in parliament in 1858.[71]

Grey and his wife continued to take a special interest in the school, with Lady Grey providing all the furnishings. It would be this school, in Wellington, that Grey wanted to see replicated in Napier. Unfortunately for Reignier, the petition he sent to Grey was immediately forwarded to the Minister of Native Affairs, Andrew Russell, whose under-secretary responded that '... it will not be possible to afford you any assistance towards building a Providence'.[72] Expressing his dismay at the

Earliest known photograph of St Joseph's Providence, possibly 1868.

decision, Reignier wrote to McLean that he could not '… do good to so many poor half-caste and native children so much neglected …'.[73]

Continuing in the same vein, Reignier wrote: 'You know better than anyone, how many poor half-caste and native[s] are along the coast and in the country, and grow so ignorant and wicked, the greatest charity and duty of a government settled among them is to do something for the education, and not to throw the burden on the shoulders of ministers, or others.'[74]

The Catholic father also informed McLean that he had sent six 'half-castes' to the providence in Wellington without the consent of parents, who opposed their children being sent away. His final plea to McLean was for him to use his position and influence to secure financial assistance for the building to be erected and for the children to be strongly supported. He concluded: 'Maybe the financial difficulties of the government for the present, yet the civilization and education of the half-caste and native children is a necessity and duty will be the glory of the government settled among them.'[75]

Reignier's pleas for assistance from central government were again put in writing to McLean, who wrote: 'Besides if I were to receive now what the Honourable [James] Richmond promised to contribute for the maintenance of the pupils of the establishment, I could take more children than I have now in our present buildings.'[76] Several days later, Reignier again wrote to McLean regarding the charitable aims of the institution.[77] Reignier again emphasised the need '… to promote the civilisation and improvement of the natives'.[78] He managed to raise £3,000 for the building of St Joseph's Providence[79] through the efforts of '… convent ladies and others busy preparing for a bazaar …' to assist in paying for the buildings.[80] In October 1867, a tender notice was placed in the *Hawke's Bay Herald* for carpenters to build St Joseph's Providence on the hills near Father Forest's residence in Napier.[81]

The official date Reignier provides as the opening of St Joseph's Providence is 10 October 1867, the same date as the passing of the Native Schools Act 1867, with Dr Mulcahy writing that it was

a date Reignier recorded more than once in his memorandum books.[82] The first two pupils were sisters Elizabeth (eight years old) and Maria Lewis (ten years old).[83] Yet St Joseph's Girls' School had already received Māori girls, as evidenced by the wishes of some of the parents who did not want their daughters to mix with the Māori girls, which led to the establishment of the 'Ladies School', and by correspondence written by Reignier himself (one 'half-caste' girl had been boarding since July 1867).[84] As further correspondence will demonstrate, it would appear that the building was not completed until one year after the date the providence officially opened.

In January 1868, it was reported that a large school was being erected for the purposes of a boarding school for half-caste girls near the residency of Father Forest. With another seven months having passed with no assistance forthcoming from the government, Reignier penned another despatch to McLean in July 1868, in which he outlined that he had decided to proceed with opening the St Joseph's Providence building, despite the government not providing £20 for past maintenance of two half-caste girls and with no allowance for two teachers, no grant for starting the school and no yearly sum for the maintenance of the boarders.[85] Reignier again implored McLean to make enquiries to the Minister of Native Affairs, James Richmond, regarding assistance for the providence. The following month, a desperate Reignier pleaded with McLean that he was on 'the eve' of opening the providence and wished to avoid incurring a debt from the lack of government action.[86]

In September, Reignier's prayers were answered with a small contribution of £15 made by the government for the two half-caste pupils, maps and furniture. In correspondence with McLean, Reignier lamented the lack of influence of Richmond within the government as the funds were still sadly lacking, noting the disparity between the funding for the providence and government schools. Despite this, Reignier was determined to push ahead with his plans for the providence.[87] Eventually, through the constant badgering of Reignier, the government released a meagre £100 as a 'Grant

St Joseph's Providence with Father Forest, 1882.

St Joseph's Providence with Marie St Anne,
Marie St Raphael and Father Forest, 1882.

St Joseph's Providence 1886.

in Aid of Buildings' and £10 per head, per annum, for the two teachers.[88] On 29 October 1868, Reignier wrote to Viard stating: 'Our Providence is open. I am starting to gather children.'[89]

McLean remained a staunch supporter of St Joseph's, writing in the capacity of Minister of Native Affairs in 1872 that, although the cost of the school was high, 'the Government are fully aware of the exemplary manner in which the establishment is conducted and of the good effect it produces'.[90] St Joseph's Providence initially provided education for Māori girls aged eight to fifteen (although school records show some were aged between three and five years) and to a Standard IV level.

The first mistress of the providence was Mother Marie St Jean (Marie Antoinette Dufour) who worked for thirty-three years in New Zealand before returning to Lyon in 1893 and then passing away in 1929 at Deal, England.[91]

In April 1869, Reignier reported that, although the providence had provisions for thirty boarders, only six pupils resided at the school (this was a reference to girls who were sponsored by the government, with others being privately funded).[92] He also added that the 'disturbed state of the country and the depression of the times [a reference to the New Zealand Wars]' added to the cost of the building and prevented further progress of the school. The following year, Reignier wrote that pupils at the providence had been given a uniform that was 'pink, white and very bright'.[93]

The cost of running the school was also an issue for the government, with the Inspector of Schools to the Native Minister and the former Minister of Native Affairs, Andrew Russell, reporting in 1872 that 'I feel it my duty, however, to call your attention to the great expense of this small establishment'.[94] Russell calculated that as the providence enjoys a roll of twenty-four students, the school would be able to access £480 per year. This amount was capped due to the lack of accommodation at the providence, rather than Reignier limiting the number of enrolments. Russell stated that:

> ... as a matter of opinion, I thought it unlikely that so large a sum of £600 for a boy's school, in addition to £480 for a girl's school, making together more than £1,000 could be afforded [out of the grant of £4,000 for all New Zealand] for one denomination in Hawke's Bay, particularly as I was already in possession of applications from twenty or thirty parts of the Colony.[95]

Russell continued to argue his case for restrictions being placed upon the funding available for native education. He promoted a formula of distributing the £4,000 among the provinces in accordance with their proportion of the Māori population and expressed a strong desire to favour the funding of village schools over Māori boarding schools, as pupils at the former were housed, fed and clothed by their parents and could educate up to twenty pupils in comparison with one student at a boarding school. This would be a constant issue for Russell, who in 1873 remarked that half-caste children had European fathers who have 'no special claim upon the Colony'.[96] For government-funded students attending Māori boarding schools, Russell proposed a limit of £10 per head, for the number of students to be restricted to twenty per school and for only one child per family to be able to access the scheme. The sisters wrote to Euphrasie about the edict, whereby she told them to use the profits from the farm and on no account to send the pupils home.

Russell continued to reason that:

> ... I doubt whether the Colony derives much advantage in return for the sum of £480 per annum supposed to be expended on it, for I found one if not two of the children belonged to Morena of Pourere, a chief of no great rank or importance, but at the same time well able to pay for the education of his own children.
>
> Most of the others appeared to have come from the Wairoa, being, I imagine, waifs and strays collected by Father Reignier in his missionary tours. It is intended that these children should be brought up for domestic service, an excellent plan in a philanthropic point of view, but scarcely one upon which the Colony would desire to spend £20 a year, for an indefinite number of years, for each child so instructed.[97]

Commenting on the actual operation of the providence, Russell did note that 'everything was in perfect order' and being impressed with the 'cordial tone' struck between the superioress and the pupils.[98] In terms of the physical structure of the school, he stated: '... the general establishment of St Joseph's Providence appears to include a ladies school, a common school for European boys and the Native girls' school ... each of which is fenced off and perfectly distinct from the others'.[99] The following year, Russell focused his attention on the overall operations of the school.[100] The hours of attendance were from 9.30 a.m. to 12 noon and then from 2 p.m. to 3.30 p.m. The other hours were consumed with study and needlework, resulting in the total time attending to school duties being between seven and eight hours.

He also reported that: 'The appearance of the pupils was clean, neat and healthy – their behaviour cheerful, orderly and respectful ... The progress of the pupils in reading, writing, spelling, arithmetic and geography, was good, and their understanding and speaking, as well as their pronunciation of English, better than most in the village schools ...'[101] Another subject taught was cooking, with several girls leaving the school to take positions as domestic servants.[102]

Of bother to Russell were the numerous complaints that were being lodged by the masters of the village schools regarding the loss of their best students to Māori boarding schools. Russell's view was that: 'It will be seen, therefore, that we are in danger of subsidising two different kinds of schools – not one preparatory to, and acting in conjunction with, the other; but both giving the elementary education, and likely to be antagonistic.'[103] As had been the case the previous year, Russell was disappointed with the state of native schooling in Hawke's Bay. Making an example of St Joseph's, he argued that twenty pupils at the providence could educate two hundred attending village schools. Russell complained that the political effect of the schools on Māori was minute and that he did not consider their education to be charitable, as parents were able to pay for their child's education.[104]

St Mary's School for Māori boys.

St Mary's for Māori Boys

The Brother School of St Joseph's Providence

When reviewing the early correspondence involving St Joseph's Providence, one school is constantly mentioned: St Mary's School for Māori boys at Meeanee. This school was established by Father Reignier and clearly, as some correspondence states, was the 'brother school' of St Joseph's Providence. The school was built in 1872 at a cost of £1,200 and was opened on 8 August 1873.[105] The school was able to cater for up to thirty boarders[106] and, with a growing roll, the school built extensions in 1878.[107] But by 1884, only five pupils attended the school and by 1886 it was transformed into a parish day school and a girls' boarding school.[108]

It is clear from the correspondence between Reignier and the Department of Education that Reignier struggled to recruit suitable Māori boys who fitted the 'blood quantum' criteria imposed by the government. In one memorandum written in 1882, the Secretary of the Department of Education, James Hislop, commented that: 'William and George Priestley … are scarcely indistinguishable from Europeans and know hardly a word of Māori … Henry and John Rogers, who are English quarter-castes, and might be regarded as English children'.[109] In response, Reignier wrote that he would do his utmost to uphold the regulations so that St Mary's might enjoy its quota of eighteen government scholars and that some of the boys had now enrolled at Te Aute College.[110]

Control of St Joseph's Providence

In 1873 Euphrasie made her first visit to New Zealand. During this trip, Euphrasie raised the sensitive issue of asking the Marist Fathers to offer some security towards ensuring that St Joseph's Providence had a future and that the Sisters of Our Lady of the Missions would have an ongoing role in the running of the school. Euphrasie's biographer M. Ollivier[111] writes:

> At this particular time, the Congregation of Bishops and Regulars was favourable towards the autonomy of women's congregations. Like many of their contemporaries, the Fathers were convinced that a community of women was not capable of governing by itself.
>
> A letter from Father Yardin to Father Forest is a good illustration of the mindset: "To my way of thinking, it seems preferable that they only have the use of it, and so relieve them of the administration, something that women are not capable of."[112]

The Sisters of Our Lady of the Missions were given the responsibility for the school in 1873 after a discussion between Euphrasie, Bishop Patrick Moran (Bishop of Dunedin and Administrator of the Wellington Diocese after the death of Bishop Viard) and the Marist fathers.[113] The deed signed by Bishop Moran, Father Reignier and Marie du Coer de Jesus (Euphrasie Barbier) allocates eighty acres of land at Greenmeadows for a period of sixty years to the Sisters of Our Lady of the Missions for staffing St Joseph's Providence. Under the contract, Father Reignier also gives the 'whole administration and direction of the Providence', with the use of all the houses and land belonging to the Providence, to the sisters.[114]

Euphrasie was concerned about the long-term viability of the Providence and the role expected of her order in the administration of the school. In September 1873, Bishop Moran made his thoughts on the matter known to Reignier, stating that both the land and buildings must be 'enclosed' and control handed to the sisters, as long as they were in charge of the providence.[115] The following month, Moran implored Reignier to sign the agreement with the Sisters, with the limitation that the order continue to instruct Māori and half-castes, with permission granted to teach a few 'white orphans'.[116] That same day, Reignier wrote to Moran that the providence must remain in the service of 'pure Maori and half-castes'. Wrestling with his 'conscience', Reignier admitted that if this was not the case then he would rather 'withdraw' himself and leave the arrangement to be sorted between his lordship and the sisters.[117] Three days later, Moran again wrote to Reignier, instructing him to sign the agreement.[118] Reignier agreed but strongly suggested the following clause be inserted:

> That this, "Providence", founded for young Maori girls, half-castes and quarter-castes, be always reserved for this purpose and that, should it happen, eventually that these races die out, or for some reason, foreseen or unforeseen, some of these children, or few of them are able or willing to come to this "Providence", then only orphans or other poor children, who would have no other means of receiving a Catholic education, are to be admitted in their place.[119]

At this juncture, a frustrated Euphrasie, perhaps hoping that Reignier's relationship with Donald McLean might help her cause, wrote to the then Member of Parliament for Napier and the Native Minister:

I would be much obliged your Honour, if you could send me by the Porter of this note a word or remark concerning the document [the contract] I forwarded you the other day to tell me either you find therein sufficient security in favour of Maoris in this Providence for perpetuity, that is to say, up to the extinction of the race if it ever occurs and that if you have any clause still in their favour, kindly indicate it to me that we may add it to the document.

Only I pray to remember that the clause concerning orphans or poor children of Polynesian races must remain in sanction the document, but as I have mentioned only in case of extinction of the race so as to solidify and secure the very existence of the Providence, not only during the life of good Father Reignier and ours, but for perpetuity. We can neither accept to remain in this good work without that security, nor to assume the responsibility of it.[120]

After Euphrasie engaged with McLean, a flurry of correspondence took place between Moran and Reignier. The latter argued that, as he had given himself to the service of Māori for the past thirty-two years and that parents had left their children in his care, he feared for the future reputation of the providence and willingness of Māori parents to leave their children with the sisters.[121] Reignier also returned to his earlier argument that there was no guarantee that the sisters would maintain the providence for the 'natives'.

The relationship between Reignier and the sisters continued to deteriorate, with Reignier penning that, when he saw Euphrasie in Napier, she had turned her back on him. By this stage, an infuriated Moran wrote to Reignier: 'If there be failure it will be due to disobedience. There must be obedience or removal'.[122] McLean responded to Euphrasie at the end of October. He wrote that he had viewed the agreement and that, in its current form, it did not appear to uphold the original agreements for which the providence was established: that the school cater for the educational needs of 'Maori and half-castes'. Noting the money that had been contributed by both private and public purses, McLean concluded that Māori sent their children to the providence under the care of Reignier and that '... any change would deprive him of the fullest control, when he is held chiefly responsible might greatly injure the prospects of the Providence'.[123]

On several occasions, Euphrasie explained to Reigner that she did not want ownership of the house and grounds, but rather wanted the sisters to have full direction and administration of the providence.[124] Eventually, Reignier signed the contract in September 1873, but not before adding the following statement:[125]

> By command of his Lordship Dr Moran a formula which is meant to only to ease my conscience with regards to the considerable sums of money I have received from the government and many other persons, which sums I declare to have been used for the building and maintenance of this "Providence", to which I remain wholeheartedly attached and concerned for its welfare, until the end of my life, in so far as it will be in my power.[126]

After the agreement was signed, Reignier wrote to Bishop Moran to say that he obtained legal advice about the insertion of a clause that ensured the providence would remain in service for Māori. After having seen McLean, Reignier was advised that such an undertaking was not in legal form and that the government viewed him as being principally responsible for the providence and objected to him having no involvement in the management of the operation. McLean also '... added that in future he would stop any more money, till he would see more about it ...'¹²⁷ As the Marists were in receipt of £3,000 for the establishment of the providence, Reignier feared that questions would be raised in parliament about the management of the school and that in regard to the capitation of £20 per child: 'I regret very much it is stopped for the present. How can the sisters without it carry on the establishment of which by their signatures appended to the agreement they have taken all the responsibility and full management of the Providence ...'¹²⁸

At the end of the sixty-year lease in 1933 (from the purchase of the eighty acres of land in 1867 from Bowes), Dr Victor Geaney, Rector of the Marist Seminary in Greenmeadows, wrote to the Marist Superior in Rome with a request to renew the lease.¹²⁹ He remarked in correspondence a decade later, that when the lease first lapsed, he wrote to Father General to legally transfer the property to the Sisters of Our Lady of the Missions. Father General concurred but his suggestion about how that should occur was both wrong in principle and harmful to the Society of Mary.¹³⁰ The Apostolic Delegate wrote that he believed certain conditions should be attached to its transfer:

> ... this school is now in a precarious position; instead of forty or fifty there are only eight or ten boarders [due to the Napier Earthquake of 1931]. Though we might have the perfect right to do so it would be an odious thing for us to step in now and take from the school its chief support, giving it perhaps its death-blow.¹³¹

The issue resurfaced a decade later when the Napier City Milk Department, the organisation that took the milk from the farm that was being leased, suggested expensive improvements to the land, expenditure that the sisters were not prepared to support due to the uncertainty of their tenure.¹³²

At this point, the Superioress of St Joseph's asked Geaney for another sixty-year lease, but, with his encouragement, the father said he would approach the authorities with a proposal that the sisters take ownership of the land, with the proviso that if the work at St Joseph's be discontinued, then the land would be returned to the Society of Mary.¹³³

Geaney outlined the reasons behind his position to Archbishop Panico: 'It would be a severe financial loss to a school which, I venture to say, is the strongest influence we have among the Maoris for religion and culture ... Because of their love for children, the future of New Zealand belongs to the Maoris; their birth rate is over forty per thousand.'¹³⁴ He also believed the relationship between the Marist Fathers and the sisters would be embittered as: 'The Sisters, even those in authority, seem to know nothing of the reason why we own the land of which they are in possession ...'¹³⁵ Finally, and in reference to the belief of his predecessor Bishop Moran, Geaney opined that the scholastic already owned a considerable amount of land in the district.¹³⁶ The Archbishop agreed with Geaney's suggestion and a Memorandum of Agreement was signed in February 1944 between the Society of Mary and the Sisters of Mission of Congregation, formally leasing the land to William Halpin, with the revenue being transferred to the sisters.¹³⁷

In 1969, the Ministry of Works, for a second time, approached the sisters to acquire land for the Napier–Hastings motorway. The 'Mission Farm' was purchased by the Crown for $58,050.¹³⁸ A spokesperson for the school stated that profits would be put toward a trust and that the revenue from the trust would be used for the college. The Halpins, who were leasing the farm at the time of the purchase, were to continue using it until the Crown required the land.¹³⁹

1877 Education Act and the 1880 Native Schools Code

Prior to the passing of the 1877 Education Act, the responsibility for education rested with the nine provincial governments. In the case of St Joseph's Providence, although it received state support, it was also championed by the Hawke's Bay provincial government, illustrated by the close relationship between Reignier and the then Superintendent of Hawke's Bay, Donald McLean. The 1877 legislation allowed for free, secular and compulsory primary education throughout New Zealand to Standard VI.

The law established an infrastructure for education in New Zealand, including the establishment of school committees, education boards and a Department of Education. An allowance was made to Roman Catholic schools whereby all seven votes allowed for with a school committee were able to be vested in one candidate or distributed as they saw fit.[140] Of particular interest to St Joseph's were the funding arrangements for government-sponsored scholars (named as capitation grants where children attending primary schools received £3 15s per head) and what was expected to be taught to students: reading, writing, arithmetic, English grammar and composition, geography, history, elementary science, drawing, object lessons, vocal music and, for girls, sewing and needlework.[141] In 1879, control of the fifty-seven native village schools with 1336 pupils was transferred from the Department of Native Affairs to the Department of Education.[142]

The following year, the Native Schools Code was introduced. The code established that if at least ten Māori petitioned the Minister of Education for a native school, if they offered two acres of land and transferred the title to the government and contributed toward the establishment of a school, and that if the site of the school was accepted by the Inspector, and if there was an average of thirty pupils attending, then the government would provide a classroom and a teacher's residence.[143] The schools were to teach Standards I to IV with the subjects covered to include reading, spelling, writing, English, arithmetic, geography, composition (of sentences and stories) and sewing.

Accompanying the code was a memorandum by the Secretary of the Education Department, John Hislop:

> ... teachers will be expected to exercise a beneficial influence on the Natives, old and young; to show by their own conduct that it is possible to live a useful and blameless life, and in smaller matters, by their dress, in their houses, and by their manners and habits at home and abroad, to set the Maoris an example that they may advantageously imitate ...The Department would especially call your attention to the fact that it is extremely advisable that teachers should always keep their houses neat and tidy. In this matter the natives are, as a rule, very careless ...[144]

1. Te Aute, founded 1854.
2. Hukarere Māori Girls', founded 1875.
3. St Stephen's, founded 1844.

4. Waerenga-a-Hika College.
5. Te Waipounamu Māori Girls' College.

1. Queen Victoria School.
2. Hikurangi College.
3. Ōtaki Māori College.
4. Turakina Māori Girls' College.

1.

2.

3.

4.

1. St Joseph's Māori Girls' College.
2. Hato Petera College.
3. Wesley College.
4. Hato Paora College.

The authorities were quick to regulate government admissions to St Joseph's Providence, following the transfer of control from the Native Department to the Education Department in 1879. Restrictions to funding were also implemented, despite constant correspondence from St Joseph's for assistance with expenses, such as water and gas, repairs and alterations to the buildings[145] and stationery.[146] Costs associated with education would be a constant headache for St Joseph's. In 1892, Bishop Francis Redwood wrote to the Inspector General of Schools, Reverend William James Habens, asking for financial assistance in relation to music (piano and violin), vocal music, ornamental drawing and water colours, oil painting, paper flower making and French.[147] To alleviate costs, donations were often called for and bazaars were held as fundraisers.

In 1880, Hislop wrote to Reignier, asking him not to receive any child attending at the expense of the governor unless it was approved by the Minister of Education.[148] This caused some difficulties for Reignier, who expressed that, as some students had been admitted, the government should have the regulation take effect at the end of the current quarter, rather than retrospectively.[149]

In a further blow to St Joseph's, the government capped the number of government-funded students at thirty-three,[150] with an additional eighteen private pupils permitted to attend.[151] As the number was in excess of thirty-three at St Joseph's at the time, the government allowed a three-month period to remove excess students and, once there were vacancies available, the Education Department could consider any new admissions. In response Reignier wrote in January 1881 on behalf of his 'poor dear little children' that they had dismissed two girls aged above sixteen and refused several more children.[152]

That same year, Hislop informed Reignier that the government would not sanction the admission of any Māori child whose parents usually resided within an easy distance of either a native village school or a European public school and cited one particular pupil as an example.[153] Reignier replied that her parents resided within three to four miles of the proposed new native school on the banks of the Wairoa River and that there was no European public school nearby.[154] Also in 1880, the capitation per pupil was raised to £20 per pupil, per annum,[155] and two years later Habens wrote that children from the age of eight could be admitted if no village school serviced the area they lived in.[156]

In 1884, the government established scholarships that would be in place for a two-year period, provided the pupil was able to pass an exam of Standard IV native school standards and that they had made considerable progress in the subjects of singing (theory and practice), drawing, needlework, household duties, speaking and writing in English, and were able to translate a Māori letter or a paragraph from a Māori newspaper or a verse from a Māori hymn into 'good idiomatic English'.[157] Also in 1884, Standards V, VI and VII were added to the St Joseph's curriculum.[158] By the end of the century, the government was willing to support a maximum of thirty-three students for St Joseph's with nearby Hukarere being allowed up to twenty.[159] The discrepancy was on the basis of 'accrued rights' (this is not explained in the correspondence).

The three eldest former pupils from St Joseph's at the centenary celebrations: R Chadwick, M Keefe and T Paratene.

Blood Quantum in Māori Education

Further regulations were placed on St Joseph's in 1880 with the Secretary of the Education Department, John Hislop, writing: 'the Government have resolved that in future no half-castes the children of European fathers will be admitted to any Boarding school at the Public cost unless for very special reasons after very full consideration of the case'.[160] This was further reinforced in September that year when Reignier received a memorandum from Hislop that the government had to adopt a set of principles to reduce expenditure for St Joseph's, St Mary's and other native schools.[161]

At the end of 1880, the government would not fund any European child or 'any child who by descent is more nearly related to the European than to the Maori or of any child of mixed race whose parents are living in European fashion', nor would the government financially support the maintenance of any Māori boy who exceeded the age of fifteen or any Māori girl who exceeded the age of sixteen (the youngest age pupils could be admitted was ten), except in special cases decided by the Minister of Education.[162]

The categorisations of race were as follows:[163]

LETTER	CATEGORY
M	Māori
M.Q.	Between Māori and half-caste
H	Half-caste
E.Q.	Between half-caste and European
E	European

A 'stocktake' of pupils attending St Joseph's according to race was taken in 1880. Twenty-two girls were Māori or between Māori and half-caste, eight were half-caste and the remaining ten were categorised as being between half-caste and European.[164] Criteria were constantly raised in correspondence to Reignier. In 1881, Hislop questioned the suitability of pupils on the grounds that they were either 'more European', if the parents 'live as European' or if the girl was aged sixteen.[165] A total of nine girls were listed as being questionable, with Hislop requesting either an explanation or further information.

Reignier's response touches on the family environment of the pupils: Julia Borrell had a European father who lived in the poorest of circumstances with Māori and lived a 'Māori' life; Mary Hale was brought to the providence when her father was ill and too poor to keep her, with her mother having already died; Elizabeth McCarthy's mother's whereabouts was unknown and her father was married to a European; Amelia Priestley's father lived in a very distressed state with many children and could not afford the clothing the child needed; and Mary White's father was a servant in the bush with many children and he gave her to another man who in turn brought her to the school as she had no home to go to.[166] The government reply was that, as the pupils attended the school before the regulations came into force, they could remain at St Joseph's, with the exception of Mary Hale, whose father resided in Gisborne and was able to educate his daughter.[167]

The issue of how 'Māori' certain pupils were was again raised the following year. In a memorandum from Hislop to Reignier, the secretary classified nine girls as being 'English quarter-castes'.[168] Hislop reminded Reignier that: 'The native school vote is for Maori children only, namely the children of pure Maoris and children one of whose parents was a pure Maori – No half caste is to be deemed a Maori however unless he or she is living as a member of some native tribe or community.'[169] In 1883, due to concerns being raised regarding some of the pupils in 1882 being 'virtually European', only nine students sat examinations, as the roll had 'fallen-off'.[170] In 1885, James Pope, the Inspector of Native Schools, commented that: 'I suppose the "Europeans" are children who are partly of native race, but near to pure European that we decline to pay for them'.[171] Often the inspector would judge how 'Māori' a pupil was by their appearance, such was the case with Ema Nepata in 1888 who came from Wairoa and spoke Māori better than English '… but does not differ from a European as far as appearance is concerned'.[172]

In 1899, the then Secretary of the Department of Education, Edward Gibbes, wrote to Father Grogan informing him that more information was required regarding Mary King, as he had been informed that her father was working as a roadman and living at a house on the Napier–Taupō Road rather than living in a pā with Māori.[173] King's admission was not accepted.[174] Pope wrote to Mother Prioress at St Joseph's, reminding her that students would be selected according to living a typical Māori life and for the prospective Māori not to be 'half-Europeanized' or 'almost indistinguishable from Europeans'.[175]

In 1882, James Pope wrote of the two difficulties getting St Joseph's and Hukarere filled with pupils. One was the prejudice of parents; the second was the poverty afflicting those who lived in the remote settlements.[176] An editorial published in the *Hawke's Bay Herald*, weighed in on the issue. It argued that:

> There can be no doubt that education is one of the principal factors for bringing the Maoris into accord with the European population, and rendering them useful citizens and peaceful subjects … One of the principle causes of the weakness of the schools in this district [East Coast] is the removal of children from the neighbourhood of the schools to the boarding-schools at Napier. These boarding-schools could easily be filled with children from districts where there are no village schools … Perhaps the Government would do well to decline to pay a subsidy to any institution that receives any new pupils from any kainga within five miles of a native school, unless such pupils are actually orphans, or are sent to them as scholars by the Government. It seems to me that it is unwise to subsidise institutions that do very much in certain districts to render of little avail the efforts that are being made to diffuse education among the Maoris generally.[177]

The *Daily Telegraph* in 1884 published an editorial criticising the unfair situation that existed between the Roman Catholic schools in Napier and Napier Girls' High School. The editor penned that the 'poor institution' of St Joseph's had a Māori girl's school, an orphanage, and day and boarding schools, with pupils numbering between two and three hundred, whereas Napier Girls: '… is rich with parents able to afford to pay for the fifty girls education but instead rely on the state'.[178] Citing the old state of the buildings and having none of the modern improvements, the Catholic schools were doing 'great work without the goods offered to the pampered State high schools'.[179]

The Catholic schools, argued the *Daily Telegraph*, should be entitled to some consideration as the state provides 'lavish money and endowments' to designated high schools to the 'exclusion of Catholics from the free system'.[180] In conclusion, the newspaper wrote that everything was being done for those who did not help themselves.

The competing *Hawke's Bay Herald* championed a different view of St Joseph's and of Māori boarding schools in general. Although not a direct rebuttal of what the *Telegraph* had written, the *Herald* took issue

James Pope.

with the support lent to Māori boarding schools by the Aborigines Protection Society. The editor focused on the financial inequity between European and Māori schools and stated:

> They [Aborigines Protection Society] might, unwillingly enough, deduce the facts that while European children cannot be provided with even unlined sheds for schoolhouses in many districts, the Maoris only have to ask for a well-built school to get it. They might find that the sum paid for the education of the Maoris is just double the sum paid per head of European. They might find that if a Māori desires to be aristocratic and send his sons or daughters to a boarding-school a benevolent Government will pay all expenses. And lastly, they might learn that Maoris as a rule, do not appreciate education – that their children are as a rule spasmodic and uncertain in attendance, and that when a fine school-house and master's residence have been built some-times no children attend after a little while, and the school-house is turned into a banqueting hall or storehouse, and the master's house into the chief's residence'.[181]

The editorial closed by arguing that only 639 Māori passed the standard examinations, although the papers were 'much easier' than those offered in corresponding European schools, and that to achieve that result over £12,000 was spent.[182]

Over a decade later the *Hawke's Bay Herald* wrote another editorial relating to Māori education. The newspaper referred to the main argument against schooling Māori, which was that they were not reaching the same level of achievement as Europeans and were prone to reverting to the Māori way of life.[183] The editor also cited an 1897 report that stated there were seventy-four village schools and four Māori boarding schools nationwide, and wrote: 'Of this number only nine are in the South Island, and even in these a large percentage of the pupils are not pure Maoris. This shows how in the South the native race is becoming completely absorbed in the European'.[184]

Catholic Church camp.

Native Schools

In 1886, the attendance of Helen Heta at St Joseph's was challenged, as she lived in the Hawke's Bay settlement of Omahu, which had existing native school buildings.[185] Reignier was asked to provide the mileage from Omahu to St Joseph's.[186] The personal circumstances of Heta was that she was twelve years old, had never attended any school, her father had died and her mother was living in poverty within the local pā.[187] The Secretary of the Department of Education, William Habens, wrote to the Mother Superior: 'Through the apathy of the natives the valuable buildings that the Government has provided at Omahu are not used and the Government declines to do anything more in the way of providing education for the Omahu peoples'.[188]

By 1887 Pope clearly conveyed his thoughts regarding the relationship between native village schools and Māori boarding schools. When reporting that St Joseph's is 'a very useful institution' and is stronger in English, he believed it would be desirable that more village school pupils be sent to the school but also opined that it is 'difficult to get them'.[189] The previous year, Pope had written to Habens, saying that admitting pupils who could attend village schools would weaken many of those schools on the East Coast and would act 'against the principle that the road to boarding school is through the village school'.[190] Two years later, following a query from Mother Superior, Habens highlighted that the plan of giving scholarships to village school pupils was to engage with those schools and to give Māori children living beyond the walk of those schools the opportunity of 'becoming acquainted with European language and European habits'.[191]

Catholic Church camp.

Left: Meri Te Tai Mangakahia.
Above: The great-great-granddaughters of Meri Te Tai, who also attended St Joseph's Māori Girls' College, Riria Makareta Lucielle Reihana-Ruka (2006–2009) and Tahnya Zedma Williams (2005–2008).

Māori Leader of the Suffragette Movement

Meri Te Tai Mangakahia
TE RARAWA
1868–1920

On 17 March 1885, Meri Te Tai, a pupil at St Joseph's, was given permission to attend the races in Hastings with friends.[192] Accompanied by her uncle, Meri left the races to go to Pakipaki and then to Waipawa, after which she returned to Pakipaki. She was absent for some weeks. The school sent a senior pupil to Pakipaki to escort Meri back to St Joseph's, with the resident magistrate of Hawke's Bay, George Preece, reporting that she had returned to St Joseph's by 5 April 1885.[193] The event caused some furore. Habens wrote to Mother Superior, stating that the Minister of Education advised her not to allow girls to go on long visits to Māori friends.[194]

Meri's independent attitude would continue after she left school. She became the third wife of Hamiora Mangakahia of Ngāti Whanaunga and Ngāti Huarere. Hamiora was elected premier of the Kotahitanga parliament in June 1892.[195] It was through this movement that Meri would gain national prominence. In May 1893, Meri Mangakahia addressed the Kotahitanga parliament, the first woman to do so.[196] Her words were as follows:

The reason I move this motion before the principal member and all honourable members so that a law might emerge from this parliament, allowing women to vote and women to be accepted as members of the parliament. Following are my reasons that present this motion so that women may receive the vote and that there be women members:

1. There are many women who have been widowed and own much land.
2. There are many women whose fathers have died and do not have brothers.
3. There are many women who are knowledgeable of the management of land where their husbands are not.
4. There are many women whose fathers are elderly, who are also knowledgeable of the management of the land and own land.
5. There have been many male leaders who have petitioned the Queen concerning the many issues that affect us all, however, we have not yet been adequately compensated according to those petitions.

Therefore I pray to this gathering that women members be appointed. Perhaps this course of action we may be satisfied concerning the many issues affecting us and our land. Perhaps the Queen may listen to the petitions if they are presented by her Māori sisters, since she is a woman as well.'[197]

The matter would lapse, but Meri remained involved in the activities of the Kotahitanga Movement through her ongoing participation in 'Komiti Wahine o Heretaunga'.[198] In 1895, the committee met at Te Hauke and discussed the abolition of the Native Land Court. Meri passed away of influenza at Panguru in 1920.

1889

CHAPTER THREE

Exemplary Education

The reports from St Joseph's filed by the Inspector of Native Schools, James Pope, were extremely positive. Often the inspector would remark on the immaculate presentation of both the buildings and the school grounds. In 1890, he wrote that: 'It is difficult to understand how girls after living here for two years, where everything is so orderly, trim and pleasing, to the eye could afterwards live in a Māori kāinga without striving to improve the state of affairs existing there.'[199]

In 1880, Secretary of the Education Department, John Hislop, communicated to Reignier that he was very pleased with the progress of the school but noted that a 'little more attention' should be paid to the pronunciation of English and to arithmetic.[200] The following year, Pope praised the standards of the sisters, stating: 'It would be difficult to speak too highly of the tone that prevails amongst the managers of this Institution. The Sisters are true educationalists exceedingly anxious to promote the well-being and advancement of their pupils. They are always willing to receive and act upon hints that may aid them in carrying on their work efficiently.'[201]

The second report written by Pope for 1881 focused on the pedagogy, noting: 'The methods used are those formerly in use in secondary schools, rather than those that are commonly employed in the modern primary school' but that such methods have 'undergone considerable modifications' in the right direction.[202] The languages taught were English, Māori, Latin and French. Again, Pope was impressed, writing: 'The domestic arrangements are excellent; the literary attainments are not as high yet, but rapid improvement seems to be taking place. At the last examination three girls passed in Standard III, nine in Standard II, and one in Standard I.'[203]

One aspect of schoolwork the department would sometimes call into question was when the pupils worked as a collective, rather than as individuals. It was the strong belief of authorities that working as individuals derives '... real solid pleasure [that] generally accompanies the doing of honest and perfectly independent work'.[204] One of the inspector's reports tracks the great progress being made in the number of student passes.[205] Pope recorded that St Joseph's:

> ... did remarkably well. The girls made great progress in every subject. No one who has seen this school at work can doubt that the girls educated there receive great benefit from their training. It may be, and is often the case, that girls who leave this and kindred institutions do not at once give striking proof of the good that has been done to them, but after a time – after they have settled down and married – the effects of the influence for good that has been brought to bear upon them become plainly apparent, and their dress, their houses, and their children nearly always show that old pupils of these schools have been improved, in many most important respects, by the school training they received.[206]

Such was the standard of the pupils of St Joseph's in 1882 that their work was displayed at parliament buildings.[207] The following year, Pope expressed concern regarding Māori educational arrangements being incomplete.[208] He wrote:

> Granting even that a large number of the children educated at these [Māori boarding] schools will be sensibly benefited by their education, would it not be possible, when so much has already been done, by a trifling additional expenditure to make work begun at the village schools so complete that the young Maoris, instead of running the risk of getting into the way of spending their time in nearly complete idleness, varied by occasional

seasons of drunkenness and debauchery might be fully fitted by it to take their place amongst the workers of the colony, and to be amongst the most useful of our citizens?[209]

A summary of Pope's report on St Joseph's in 1883 was that 'the money could hardly be better spent'.[210] The following year, the same sentiment was articulated by Pope of the providence being 'a very good school'.[211] In 1886, sixteen pupils sat the examination (eleven for the standards, five for the higher certificate and a prize now offered for those who completed their native school course) with 78 per cent passing.[212] The answers in history, elementary science and domestic economy were 'exceedingly good' and the work 'seemed to be of a far higher order than had been previously obtained here'.[213] This was attributed to the school authorities now being aware of exactly what was required and it was observed that one of the striking differences between St Joseph's and other schools was '... that class teaching is to a large extent replaced by constant instruction and supervision of individuals, as the teaching staff being large enough to allow this'.[214]

In 1891, none of the senior pupils, with the exception of two recently admitted students, failed to pass their examinations[215] and, by 1895, the school enjoyed a 100 per cent success rate as twenty-three government and nine private scholars passed their examinations.[216]

Pope discerned that the pupils should now return to sitting written examinations, as the girls had answered in such a way that they left little to be desired.[217] Pope's draft report on St Joseph's for 1885 was an exception. It had been heavily redacted by secretary Hislop. The following passage in Pope's report was marked to be deleted:

> We watched the working of the school for some time, the impression produced was that while all the purely mechanical work was very well done, the purely intellectual faculties of the pupils received but little training – on the whole I am inclined to believe that while the village school pupils that are sent to St Joseph's will learn much that will tend to make them more useful wives and mothers, and to change their tastes and their habits, they will not bring away from St Joseph's much more school training than they took there: perhaps it is not, on the whole, desirable that they should.[218]

It is possible that Hislop was anxious regarding the ramifications of such comments, especially the last sentence. Pope's remarks certainly stand in stark contrast with the view he expressed of the school six years later when he wrote:

> Every fresh visit to this institution confirms my opinion that really good work is done in it. I feel quite sure that girls who have "gone through the mill" at St Joseph's, after completing their village school course, take away with them what will be of great use to them and their people. It is inconceivable to me that girls should spend two years under the kind of training they get here without being benefited by it.[219]

The vast majority of school inspection reports record that the relationship between the sisters and the pupils was exemplary. Very rarely was behaviour an issue; the only problem of note was that, on the odd occasion, a pupil may have copied another in the examinations. Corporal punishment was discouraged (and in the case of St Joseph's there is nothing to suggest that this ever occurred), with the pupils only ever receiving a punishment of writing lines when their behaviour warranted such discipline.

The Importance of Learning English

On every enrolment form for a scholarship to enter a Māori boarding school is a section that reads 'Reasons for this application, or other remarks'. On virtually every form to attend St Joseph's, parents or caregivers wished the girl to receive a good European education (normally to earn a living) and to learn the English language.[220] Euphrasie encouraged the sisters to learn Māori[221] and wrote to Reignier on the subject of teaching English to Māori at the providence:

> With regard to your recommendation not to allow the children to speak Maori, I can assure you that the Sisters do their best to follow your instructions in this. However, you must not be surprised, Reverend Father, if some of these poor children speak in their own tongue, especially those who are slow to learn and who have little or no education. Many of them come to us without knowing a word of English, without any knowledge of grammar, reading or writing, in fact they do not know their A.B.C. These children are unable to carry on a conversation on any subject whatsoever, especially in the English language, which is difficult for foreigners. We ourselves have experienced this difficulty when we first began to learn English, although we had every help and know the basic principle of education, which these children lack. It is good to remind ourselves of this and then we shall be more patient with the children. One can understand that some do not realise this, but you Reverend Father anyone who knows what is needed for the study or teaching of a language will have no difficulty in realising it.[222]

In 1889, Pope stressed the importance of students being taught to speak English 'decently' and that the juniors should 'learn to talk English as rapidly as possible'.[223] By 1891, Pope took notes of a lesson in reading and writing to a junior class by one of the sisters. He observed:

> … it struck one that it would be possible for her to very materially shorten her labour by giving a series of phonetic lessons pure and simple … sounds and their representations should be the sole theme. These lessons should be the nature of drill, perfect pronunciation should be taught and the constant use of the right sound should be secured by practice … I should expect all pronunciation difficulties to disappear under this kind of training in say two or three months. The writing at this school eventually became very good indeed … In the case of Maori pupils complete answers should be insisted on. Elliptical replies are unsatisfactory. I do not think the practice of suggesting an answer by giving the first syllable is a good one. It seems to me better to give a word outright than to give a clear indication as to what that word should be. In the former case the pupil recognises her complete ignorance; in the latter she thinks that she knows some part of what was wanted. The fact is, that if "nominative" is the word dealt with in this way, she merely understands that nom means "nominative".[224]

Later that year, Pope wrote:

> I think the Sisters would find it to their advantage as soon as untaught pupils are admitted to conquest once for all the pronunciation difficulty and not desist from working at this most laudable object until every elementary sound in English is pronounced by pupils with accuracy and certainty. A very good lesson to juniors was spoilt almost by the pupils being allowed to say "tog" "seep" "pegin" for dog, sheep and begin … I am very much afraid that if this matter is not attended to it will tend to spoil the transcription, the dictation, and the composition – If a girl says "poots" or "frower" she is very likely to make these abnormal forms serve her purpose throughout the course and perhaps these very forms will prevent her from passing one or more of the standards as the times for doing so come round.[225]

A focus on the teaching of the English language again became the focus of Pope's school inspection in 1894 when he proposed that the school adopt, for the junior section, F Gowan's system of teaching as it is 'very suitable indeed for young Māori girls'.[226] Pope remarked in 1896 that for senior students '… more attention should be paid to individual peculiarities of intimation and pronunciation …'[227] and in 1899 Pope noted that the fourth formers had a weak spot in their dictation and that 'many errors occurred in spelling of regular past tenses and past participles and of regular plurals of nouns'.[228]

Akenehi Hei.

1. Harata Koopu (1907–1911).
2. Bibi Taapa (1915) and Pauline Haami (1914–1916).
3. Lena Bristow (1910–1915).
4. Katie Nopera.

1. Pine White (1916) and Ruby Haapu (1909–1915).
2. Ema Kura and Joyce Lee (1919).
3. Ada (1909–1915) and Netta Kirkpatrick (1915).
4. Kathleen Maher (1904–1910).
5. Hannah Ropiha (1907).
6. Atareta Ropiha (1903–1908).

Kathleen Harrison (Katerina Mataira), 1947.

Charisma Rangipunga

Te Reo Maori

Dame Katerina Te Heikoko Mataira
NÉE HARRISON
NGĀTI POROU
1946–1949

Te Mihinga Komene
1989–1992

Charisma Rangipunga
NGĀI TAHU, TARANAKI
1991–1994

Despite the best efforts of successive governments to discourage the teaching of te reo Māori at schools, the college has made a significant contribution towards the revitalisation of the language through the endeavours of some of their alma mater. Dame Katerina Mataira went to St Joseph's as Kathleen Harrison. Fellow student, Kaa Daniels, recalls: 'Kathleen Harrison was bright and had a photographic memory.' Born in Tokomaru Bay, Katerina trained as a teacher and art educator before marrying Junior Mataira and having nine children.

In 1976, Katerina began to develop what would become known as the 'rākau method', a system of learning based on using coloured cuisenaire rods.[229] The revolutionary methodology was adapted from Caleb Gattegno's approach to teaching language to second-language learners titled 'The Silent Way', where teachers are to remain silent while students are encouraged to speak in class.[230]

Estimates suggest the rākau method has helped between 30,000 and 50,000 people learn te reo Māori.[231] On her achievements, Katerina remarked: 'The language nests, the language immersion schools, the places that teach, are filled with graduates of Te Ataarangi. The students have achieved whatever mark they have set for themselves.'[232]

In 1985, Katerina assisted with the establishment of the country's first Māori language immersion school, kura kaupapa Māori, at Hoani Waititi Marae in Auckland, and was responsible for co-authoring *Te Aho Matua*, the philosophy and charter for kaupapa Māori schools.[233] Two years later, Katerina was appointed a foundation member of the Māori Language Commission. In 1996 she was awarded an honorary doctorate from the University of Waikato and, in 1998, her services were recognised when she was appointed a Companion of the New Zealand Order of Merit.[234] In 2011, Katerina was appointed a Dame for her services to the Māori language.

With more than fifty books to her name,[235] Katerina was also a prolific writer of Māori children's books, initially to increase the number of resources written in te reo Māori.[236] She also wrote novels in te reo including *Te Ātea* (1975), *Makorea* (2002) and *Rēhua* (2006). The latter was the winner of the 2013 New Zealand Post Māori Language Award. Katerina stated: 'Art is really what I wanted to follow. I found it to be deeply satisfying. Yet strangely enough, when I turned to writing I felt the same passion and satisfaction, it was intense as that which I'd felt in doing art.'[237]

Te Mihinga Komene has built a career from being passionate about te reo Māori:

> Every job I have got is because of having the reo. We were told in the late 1980s and early 1990s that te reo won't get you anywhere. Once I learnt te reo Māori, I found myself. It has got me everywhere, even overseas. If we don't act now about growing te reo Māori, then we will lose it. I've been taught you have to give back what you have been taught and you can't hold on to your mātauranga because it is an endangered language.

Coming from a Catholic Pākehā primary school, 'you could count the number of Māori on one hand and you never felt like you fitted in, especially because I had

Top: Te Mihinga Komene.
Bottom: Ngā Tohu Kaiwhakaako o Te Reo Māori.

a strong Māori name.' Te Mihinga had a cousin who lived not far from her whānau and was attending kōhanga reo, kura kaupapa and wharekura. 'So, by default, we had to learn te reo Māori. My parents started to do night classes and because there was no one to babysit me at home, I tagged along and picked it up.' At St Joseph's, Te Mihinga no longer felt like a fish out of water. '[Te reo Māori] was a compulsory subject at St Joseph's. With it being a School Certificate subject, you could rote learn the language.'

Regarded as a shy girl at primary school, entering the Ngā Manu Kōrero competitions, Te Mihinga developed the confidence to speak publicly in te reo Māori. Once she had won her individual form-class competitions, she went on and won both the junior and senior speech competitions. In the third form, Te Mihinga entered the Junior Māori Regional competition and, in the fifth and sixth forms, she entered the Korimako division. 'In the sixth form, I got runner-up at the nationals and won the impromptu section. My topic was "If you don't stand for something, you will fall for nothing"; it was about your identity and reo, and it was from there that I became a reo "activist".'

Sixth form was the final year for Te Mihinga at St Joseph's and, in order to complete her high-school education, she had to find another school for her seventh-form year. Te Mihinga believes her exposure at St Joseph's was important in preparing her for university life, and she completed a Bachelor of Arts with a double major in Māori and Theatre Studies and then went to the University of Canterbury to do her Honours and teaching qualifications.

A string of jobs involving te reo Māori followed, including lecturing at the University of Canterbury and Waikato University, working at Te Rūnanga o Ngāi Tahu with Charisma Rangipunga to develop television programmes and Kotahi Mano Kaika. Te Mihinga was also part of the Te Panekiretanga programme that developed her language skills. Her first full-time job was at Huia Publishers. 'I applied for the job and on the panel was Brian Morris, my third form te reo Māori teacher from St Joseph's, and Stephanie Pohe, who was a former pupil at St Joseph's. I said "Kia ora, Mr Morris. Just as well I was a good student for you then."'

Her job was to produce Māori resources for Māori-medium education. One of her first projects was working on the *Rēhua* series with former St Joseph's student Katerina Te Heikoko Mataira:

> Brian Morris suggested I should record her, and it was my job to find all of the characters. It isn't until now that I realise how privileged, how lucky we were to have her, as she passed away the following year. Her motivating factor in doing the four-novel *Rēhua* series was being challenged that you couldn't write science fiction in te reo Māori, so she wrote about the post-apocalyptic time on a planet called Rēhua.

Today Te Mihinga is tackling the world of digital technology through her position with CORE Education. 'It's taking me on a whole new world. This is our life now and is one of the reasons I was lucky in being awarded the tohu Māori in 2016. At the forefront of my mind is what I have been taught at St Joseph's. You are representing the past and the future of the kura.'

For part of her working life, Te Mihinga was based at Te Rūnanga o Ngāi Tahu, where she worked with another old girl from St Joseph's, Charisma Rangipunga. Charisma was born in New Plymouth and became part of the mass migration to Australia when she was three years old, as her father searched for better opportunities and pay in the mining industry:

> I remember in Australia; the trophies of our Māori cultural cabinet were cassette tapes of Billy T James and Prince Tui Teka. The other thing we had was the song "Sailing Away" from the America's Cup campaign on vinyl and if you flipped the track over it was "Pōkarekare Ana". Those songs would be thrashed. We

knew we were Kiwis, we knew we were from New Zealand, we knew we were Māori, but beyond that, we didn't really know a lot about it other than Mum and Dad would trash this vinyl and cassette tape and that Billy T James videos were our prized taonga in our whare.

Charisma had constantly been told by her mother that she would be attending a Māori girls' college in New Zealand:

> I had no concept of a boarding school, let alone a Māori boarding school. Mum and Dad split up, and my mother, brother and I came back to New Zealand in the middle of 1989. Halfway through Form 1 in Timaru, Mum kept saying, "You are going to a Māori girls' boarding school", and the original intent of my parents was that I was going to go to Te Waipounamu Māori Girls' College in Christchurch, but it had shut down a year before I started high school and so the thinking was my nanny on my father's side was living in Waipukurau, so let's send her to a school near the whānau. Mum had done some research and St Jo's had a good reputation.

Financially, sending her daughter to St Joseph's was a struggle for Charisma's mother. 'She was a solo mother doing lots and lots of jobs and so our life became applying for scholarships and grants, and we managed to do that for two years. Then in the fifth form, Michael Laws established a scholarship specifically for St Joseph's students, and I was the first recipient for the first two years.' With travel to and from Timaru being an additional expense, Charisma's mother would book her flights months in advance to get the discounted travel.

St Joseph's was where Charisma was first exposed to te reo Māori. That wasn't the only challenge she was subjected to:

> Not only did I not have te reo but I also had a thick Australian accent. It was less than a month at St Jo's and the accent was gone. I still remember the first class that we had that was taught by Mrs Unahi. We were sitting in this classroom and she said, "I'm going to get you girls to introduce yourself." My saving grace was that two girls in front of me, a girl stood up and spoke in English. It was a very harsh way to be first introduced to your own identity and realise you don't have any. I was thrown in the deep end in terms of learning the language, and seeing other girls who were proudly Māori and confident with it was a great motivator for me.

Charisma took to learning te reo Māori, and by the time she left St Joseph's in the sixth form, she had completed Māori at bursary level, had a very high grade for Sixth Form Certificate, and had passed School Certificate twice. 'I was a super geek, and by the fourth form, I was sitting School Certificate Māori.' Charisma went on to complete a Bachelor of Arts (Hons) with a double major in Māori and Sociology at the University of Canterbury. While at the university, there was a reo wānanga at Onuku Marae in Akaroa:

> I had just been learning about my links to Ngāi Tahu, and Onuku is one of my marae. I remember when we were welcomed on, and at that time I had been exposed about the degradation of the reo. When we went to the marae, the pōwhiri was performed by tangata whenua completely in English. It was a manifestation of everything I had been taught about te reo Māori and it was the first time I realised that what I was being told was correct.

Charisma was also a graduate of the first cohort of Te Panekiretanga o te Reo Academy. She is currently a board member of Te Taura Whiri i te Reo Māori, the Māori Language Commission, and has written children's books in te reo Māori.

Not long after graduating from the University of Canterbury, a position was advertised at Te Rūnanga o Ngāi Tahu for someone to support the iwi with their Māori language revitalisation initiatives, which Charisma applied for and got:

> We were still in the stages of developing the tribal strategy, Kotahi Mano Kāika, Kotahi Mano Wawata, so I was exposed to strategic thinking and challenges regarding language revitalisation, not only for the tribe but for our communities. I had become a mum at the end of 1999 and one of the challenges for me was if we [Ngāi Tahu] are going out and telling our people that the language is dying and the only way it will survive is if te reo is spoken to our babies and I'm promoting that message, then I need to role model this in my own home.

Currently, Charisma is employed by Ngāi Tahu Holdings as Chief Values Officer:

> Ngāi Tahu have been fortunate enough that our commercial businesses have been very successful over the past twenty years and have managed to grow our Treaty settlement considerably. Whilst we have been commercially successful, from a tribal perspective we have values and our broader aspirations are beyond making an economic return.
>
> My role is now not about how much money we are bringing through the door, but how we are bringing money through the door. Do they marry up with the expectations with our kaumātua and how do we conduct ourselves in our businesses and what are our broader aspirations with the iwi with regards to our social well-being, our cultural well-being, and the well-being of Te Taiao?

Dame Katerina Mataira and 'protégés'.

James Pope was constantly impressed with the standard of singing at St Joseph's. For the 1882 report, Pope noted: 'It is quite a musical treat to hear the boys at Te Aute, or the girls at St Joseph's Providence, or Hukarere, sing'.[238] Almost a decade later, the inspector observed that the elder pupils sang 'an unseen strand of twelve bars of fairly-difficult music very creditably'.[239] Māori action songs were also performed as part of the school's drill exercises[240] and songs and hymns were sung in English, Latin, French and Māori.[241] The only area for improvement was '... that the Māori voices are invariably low and any attempt to make them go much higher than E must be a failure'.[242] St Joseph's featured in the local press when the end-of-year prizegiving was held. In 1879, the *Hawke's Bay Herald* commented in particular on the displays of fancy work and needlework.[243] Pope decided in 1884 that the government should distribute two prizes annually: one for reading and one for arithmetic.[244]

Of major concern to Māori at the time was the future of Māori as a people and their vulnerability to European diseases. The year 1896 was the nadir for Māori, as the population was recorded at an all-time low of 42,000.[245] This issue would play a central role in life at St Joseph's over the next few decades. It was the responsibility of the inspector to comment on the health of students. Inspector Russell wrote in 1875 that three of the girls were sent home to their villages with consumption and died. This caused Russell to ask: 'From what causes does the rapid diminution of the Native race arise, when brought into close contact with the European?' He observed that, in comparison with village school students, there had only been two deaths among the entire schooling system.[246]

Illnesses seriously affecting the family of pupils at St Joseph's Providence were quite common. In August 1880, following the mid-year holidays, it was recorded that Cecilia and Te Rina Winiata could not return to school on account of their father's illness[247] and that Mary White had returned despite her mother having died.[248]

The Minister of Education in 1894 organised a magic lantern exhibition for schools in the North Island.[249] Included within the exhibition were scenes of England and foreign countries '... to give Maoris a clear idea of social conditions and ways of life altogether different from their own ...'[250] Accompanying the show are illustrations '... of sanitary laws and of the conditions in which health depends.'[251]

In 1895 it was recorded that pupil Wai Manuka passed away after contracting tuberculosis.[252] She had visited Pakipaki with a friend who had the same complaint. Her parents telegraphed for her to return to Te Kaha, where she died. Sadly, it was noted that several children of the same family had died from tumours in their legs.

Another disease that claimed the lives of pupils was influenza, with Hera Kipa succumbing to the illness in 1897 and her body having to be transported by train with three girls in accompaniment.[253] That same year, four girls were unable to sit their final examinations due to influenza.[254] At the beginning of 1899, it was recorded that there had been a considerable 'falling-off presumably through sickness and death having occurred before the holidays'.[255]

The health of the pupils continued to vary into the early twentieth century, with some of the pupils suffering from influenza. Influenza would rear its head again in 1918, with the school being forced to shut its doors before the 'usual time'.[256] Rosalind Stephens, who died from the epidemic, was baptised before her death.[257] In June 1920, Moawai Hepetema, who had been suffering from bronchitis, died.[258]

Ema Mitchell.

Nursing Scholarships for Māori Girls

In 1898 James Pope proposed to Napier Hospital that nursing scholarships of £25 for one year should be offered to the pupils of Hukarere and St Joseph's. Pope broached his desire that '... the girls' work ought to be to a large extent technical and not merely such domestic work as they have been trained to do at their schools'.[259] Motivation for establishing the scholarship is recorded as being that: 'The Department [of Education] has always recognised the importance of directing the attention of the Maori race to the laws of health and the necessity for sanitary reform. It cannot well be doubted that much good has resulted from this but it seems to me that the time has come for making an attempt on external stimuli.'[260] At the end of their scholarship, it was hoped that the girls would be sent back to their settlements to be 'effective preachers of the gospel of health to their people'.[261]

In May of the same year, Napier Hospital responded that they were prepared to trial the plan but that the students would be subject to the same control and would be expected to perform the same duties as the 'probationers'.[262] The first girl to be nominated from St Joseph's was Ema Mitchell.[263] Mitchell was to attend Napier Hospital at 9.30 a.m. daily, to be instructed in nursing, including dressing, attending to the sick and taking temperatures, with her day ending at either 4 or 5 p.m., when she would return to the school. Her scholarship was to be paid directly to the school for board and some money was to be reserved for clothing.

Pope was candid in what he wanted Mitchell to achieve, writing to Mother Superior 'Your nomination is accepted on this occasion in the belief that Ema Mitchell will as a Nursing Hospital Scholar behave herself in such a way as to do her school and the Department credit and pave the way in the Hospital for her successors'.[264] Ema Mitchell became the first registered Māori nurse in 1900[265] and worked for a time at Waipukurau Hospital.[266]

Furthermore, Pope wrote that her appointment should not be seen as an intention of the Department of Education to provide a few girls with the means of earning of livelihood '... but rather to confer on each of the Maori settlements where the girls have their natural home the advantage that ought to flow from the presence of a native woman comparatively skilled in elementary hygiene and able to give (and illustrate) good advice as to the treatment of the sick'.[267]

In July 1899, Pope again wrote to Mother Superior regarding Ema Mitchell.[268] He was happy to hear of her progress but wondered if she should board there for the rest of the term. Pope was keen 'not to lose or loosen our effective hold on our scholars' and that: 'We certainly ought to avoid the risk of introducing these girls to break away from their own people altogether through our lengthening their period of separation from their own people', as he did not want to lose altogether the 'influence for good in Maori settlements to which the scholars belong'.[269] In September, Inspector of Schools and the Secretary for Education, George Hogben, notified the school that Mitchell's scholarship would be extended until the end of the year[270] and the following month he reported that Mitchell had secured a more permanent appointment outside the scholarship scheme, although officers of the Education Department were likely to be disappointed that 'no progress has been made in introducing knowledge of sanitary laws amongst the Maoris'.[271]

George Hogben.

Akenehi Hei.

Pioneering Māori Nurse
Akenehi Hei
TE WHAKATŌHEA/TE WHĀNAU-A-APANUI

Akenehi (Agnes) Hei was born at Te Kaha and arrived at St Joseph's Providence in June 1892 as a government scholar.[272] Encouraged by her brother Hamiora (a leader of the Māori nursing proposal from Te Aute Association), she became an assistant nurse and dresser at Napier Hospital.[273] In 1905, Hei was promoted to probationer (becoming the first Māori to pass all her nursing exams).[274] Three years later, she was appointed theatre nurse, and she completed her midwife training in December 1908.

She worked at Te Kao, Northland, to assist Māori affected by typhoid, before being transferred to Russell, Rotorua and then to New Plymouth in 1909.[275]

Over time, her biggest challenge became balancing her 'Pākehā training' with Māori traditions. An example of this was when she was stationed at Te Kao.[276] With the assistance of the schoolmaster, she persuaded the local people to turn their wharenui into a makeshift hospital. However, when a child died there, the father refused to leave his body, and the patients had to be shifted instead, but the people did not want to return to their homes. They were only persuaded with the threat of being reported to the Department of Health and Education. On the other side of the debate, Hei also wrote despairingly that 'The suspicions natural to my people (especially the old ones) against European

Continuing the tradition of becoming a nurse after having graduated from St Joseph's are a great number of former pupils.

1. Teresa Anderson.
2. Pare Koopu-Marsden.
3. Ani Koopu.
4. Laura Iwikau.
5. Monica Moke.
6. Anne McFarlane and Whina Otene.

doctors and nurses do not exist against me'²⁷⁷ and that Pākehā nurses needed to understand the Māori way of thinking.

In 1910, Hei went to Gisborne to tend to her niece who had contracted typhoid. She eventually also cared for her brother, his wife, her nephew and two other patients. In November that year, she contracted the disease and died after being admitted to Gisborne Hospital.²⁷⁸

Biographer Patricia Sargison wrote:

Akenehi Hei was in every way a pioneer. She faced not only the physical difficulties of travel and inadequate accommodation in isolated districts, but also many administrative hurdles. Her work was regarded as an opportunity to see how these Māori nurses act on their own responsibility. She had to cope with departmental procedures and regulations, and with institutional racism; she had little support from officials concerned with minimising costs and a government not fully committed to Māori health work.²⁷⁹

Māori Doctors

Maia Melbourne-Wilcox	Kiriana Bird	Audrey Robin
NGĀI TŪHOE, NGĀTI KAHUNGUNU, NGĀTI POROU	NGĀTI TŪKOROHE, NGĀTI POROU	NGĀTI KAHUNGUNU, TAINUI, NGĀTI TŪWHARETOA, NGĀTI POROU
1993–1994	1991–1995	1998–2002

Dr Kiriana Bird.

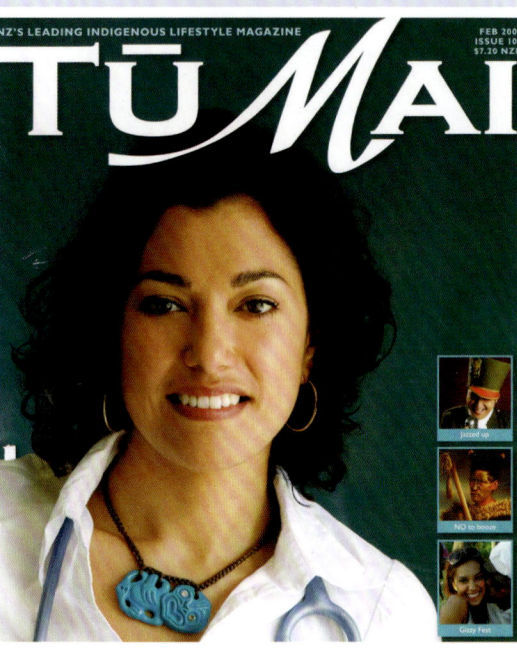

Head Prefect 1994, Maia Melbourne-Wilcox.

Almost a century later, graduates from St Joseph's were not only becoming nurses but also doctors. Maia Melbourne-Wilcox had, as she describes it, 'an eclectic education'. Learning te reo Māori began at home with a fluent father and a mother who was learning. 'Even though Dad [the late Hirini Melbourne] was an expert in te reo Māori, he would be at work or off at hui, conferences, or shows either in New Zealand or abroad. As such, the primary language of instruction in the home was English as my mother had been raised in the era when Māori was not taught.'

Maia attended 'a Pākehā school where you could count the number of Māori on one or two hands' and she had to learn te reo Māori by correspondence because they had no one who could teach it. She was sent to St Joseph's for the fifth form. There, Maia's hunger for Te Ao Māori was satisfied. 'Furthering my experiences with Te Ao Māori happened at St Joseph's. I think that part of those are taught, through things like te reo Māori, through culture, through kapa haka, and some of those things are just the unsaid and the untaught things.' Another important lesson was the practice of studying and coming to the realisation that: 'What you put into life is what you will get out of it. These lessons had a long-lasting influence on my life.'

For her seventh-form year, Maia opted for a local, co-educational school, situated within a poor community. 'For me, it was about preparing myself

Dr Audrey Robin.

for university and getting that real-life experience.' With a father already working in tertiary education, Maia took the next step and enrolled at Waikato University and graduated with a Bachelor of Science. It was at this point that she wanted to specialise in medical research and was awarded a FORST scholarship to do a master's in biochemistry. Still passionate to make a difference in the area of health, Maia was accepted into medical school at the University of Auckland in 2002 but deferred her medical studies for a year to be close to her family, as her father had been diagnosed with terminal lung cancer. He passed away two months before she started at medical school; six years later, she became a qualified doctor.

She is now a general practitioner at a local practice in Christchurch and helps teach Hauora Māori to University of Otago medical students in Christchurch, under Associate Professor Suzanne Pitama and the MIHI (Māori Indigenous Health Institute) team. Maia has always been keenly involved in Mapas (the Māori and Pacific admission scheme) and Te Ohu Rata o Aotearoa, the Māori doctors' association. Maia is grateful for the support, mentorship and positive influence such organisations offered her, both as a student and as a doctor. 'The increase in the number of Māori doctors graduating, including some former pupils from St Joseph's, is really exciting as it is a result of lots of hard work by those gone before us and is part of the solution to addressing Māori health outcomes.' Maia's daughter is now attending the college.

Maia Melbourne-Wilcox and Kiriana Bird are not only of the same year, but they also share a love of their late science teacher at St Joseph's, Maureen Caffery. Maia states:

Part way through the first term in my first year, we did a test and I got 50 per cent. Mrs Caffery came up to me and said, "You did really well in that test," and I quipped, "But it is only 50 per cent." She responded, "Yes you did, but we have been learning fifth form science since last year [when Maia did not attend the school], so if you catch up to where we are now, you can ace School C science." She would come in to our weekend tutorials voluntarily, wanting us to do well, and so I thought "If you are going to give us your Saturday mornings, I am going to make sure I am there!" That was when I realised, in contrast to my previous schools, being at a Māori school, the teachers expect you to succeed.

Kiriana recalls: 'Mrs Caffery stood out for me. She was our science teacher when I was fourteen and she said to me, "You are really good. You should be a doctor." I remember at the time thinking "I don't think so," but that planted the seed, and from there my journey to become a doctor grew.' Not only has the influence of St Joseph's impacted on Kiriana's professional career, but it has also shaped her as a mother and a member of her whānau. 'St Jo's had a huge impact on my life and made me the strong Māori woman I am today.' Another teacher who had an impact on Kiriana was Jan Goudie, the maths teacher. 'In the seventh form, I didn't want to board any more and she offered me her home. That exemplified the special bond you had with your teachers. I stayed with her family for a couple of months until I shifted in with one of the whānau whose daughter attended and who lived close to the school.'

Another similarity in the experiences of Maia and Kiriana is the exposure to taha Māori. Kiriana says:

> My mother is Māori and her parents shifted to Wellington to get jobs. She was raised in an era when te reo Māori was not learnt, and her whānau were scattered around the country. When I came here, the values that I had at home such as the manaakitanga were solidified here. Learning te reo was another aspect of my education. Even though myself and my peers never really spoke te reo, Nanny Rere [Unahi] would always speak in Māori.

Kapa haka was another facet of learning about things Māori:

> We travelled the whole motu, right from the top, to the bottom, visiting different marae that had different kawa and reo. Those experiences I would never have had if I had stayed in Wainuiomata, and they have held me in good stead with my job today. If I am visiting a patient's house or attending a tangi, I know what to do based on what I was taught at St Jo's.

Coming to St Joseph's was a great decision Kiriana's parents made. To pay for the cost of her education and that of her brother, who attended Te Aute College, her father worked two jobs and her mum found a position at McDonald's. Now with a daughter of her own, Kiriana is in no doubt she will attend her alma mater.

Audrey Robin hails from her marae, Kohupatiki, which is near the small Hawke's Bay settlement of Clive. She still lives 'around the corner' and treasures the values of whanaungatanga that have been taught to her from a young age. As the only member of her whānau to have attended St Joseph's (the other women attended Hukarere), Audrey went through her most challenging time when she lost her mother while in sixth form. 'The struggles that I did have here made me a strong woman, and nothing fazes me in the world. I pride myself on being respectful and on dressing a certain way. That comes from the school.' Now Audrey is a general practitioner after graduating from the University of Auckland in 2008, and she can be found practising at Totara Health in Hastings, Hawke's Bay Prison, Directions (a Hawke's Bay Youth Clinic) and the Wellington Campus for Massey University.

St Joseph's Māori Girls' College 1901.

CHAPTER FOUR

The Fight for Survival

The purpose of St Joseph's Māori Girls' College, as understood by school inspector John Porteous in 1920, was to produce good wives. He wrote:

> The aim of the school authorities is to provide the girls with a practical training which in addition to the ordinary school subjects still prove of use and benefit to them when they have left school, and with this object in view instruction in each subject as dressmaking and cutting out, fancy needlework, household duties, cooking and homenursing receive special attention.'[280]

The start of the new century heralded a new attitude among Māori parents, as James Pope observed when writing his inspection report for 1899: 'Parents too are much more anxious to have their children educated than they used to be.' With twenty-five on the roll, the overall impression of the school was 'as usual, very satisfactory'.[281] The next report however, commented that the pass rate had decreased due to the increased stringency in the English examination. The Secretary of the Education Department, George Hogben, wrote: 'The increase here referred to is, in turn, due to the fact that the Department is becoming more and more convinced that the power of writing and speaking English, or spelling correctly, and of understanding the mutual bearing of parts or sentences should be placed in the very forefront of the secular education of Maoris.'[282]

English would, as was the case in the previous century, remain a key focus of successive school inspectors when they visited St Joseph's. In 1909, William Bird, the Inspector of Native Schools since 1903, remarked that more time should be dedicated towards teaching English.[283] The following year, Porteous recorded that reading in the 'lower room' was '... marred by indistinct pronunciation of the final consonants',[284] and in 1912, Bird observed many errors in the pluralisation of the English language.[285]

The use of plurals was a common complaint of the inspectors. In 1913, Bird commented: 'In the written essays the work was characterized by careless spelling, confusion of tenses, want of punctuation and the misuse of the singular for the plural ones.'[286] Bird criticised the written work of the pupils in 1916 and stated that the 'proper form' of letter writing should receive more attention.

He wrote: 'In the first stages of written work in English, the children should be trained to use simple sentences, each beginning with a capital letter and ending with a full stop. This would prevent the tendency to "breathless narration" in the writing of essays later on.'[287]

A discussion emerged in 1902, headed by Pope, that perhaps the time had come to be 'stricter' about the admission of pupils to boarding schools.[288] Pope raised a question of policy: that it was inadvisable to keep young Māori away from their people to such a point that they might lose all interest in home and friends.[289] Clearly Pope still envisaged graduates returning to their settlements to change the behaviour and attitudes of Māori. This prompted the Assistant Secretary in the Department of Education, Edward Gibbes, to write to St Joseph's, informing the school that the

Iriwhiro and William Watson Bird.

Hone Heke.

government was reconsidering the conditions on which children would be recognised as scholarship holders.[290]

The Member of Parliament for Northern Māori, Hone Heke, became involved in the debate, writing to the Minister of Education, William Walker, that he had made some personal enquiries to the Mother Superior at St Joseph's.[291] Heke had learned that the Department of Education intended to discontinue its support for girls sent directly from their homes if those girls lived near a native school. Heke urged the Department to reconsider its position, suggesting that Hukarere was dealt with more favourably by the government.[292] Of particular concern for Heke was allowing parents with Catholic religious beliefs to be able to send their daughters to St Joseph's, as was the case with European girls, rather than a school with mixed beliefs.[293] Walker rebutted Heke strongly, stating that both St Joseph's and Hukarere had been treated the same, other than the fact that Hukarere had not been allowed as many government scholars as St Joseph's.

The alteration that Heke had referred to had '... come about through the Department's becoming more and more convinced that children who are unable to pass Native Standard IV are incapable of profiting by secondary education'.[294] Also in 1902, D T Hamilton, teacher of the Native School in Kāwhia, had written to Pope, stating that the Reverend Mother had offered to take four girls from the school.[295] Hamilton wrote:

> You know the dangers which beset budding womanhood in the kāinga and when that kāinga is surrounded with Europeans of a low type such as are in Kāwhia at present, they are even greater and of a more serious nature than at other times and places ... I am anxious to get away from here so I have recommended my three best pupils ... I am sacrificing the cream of the school but I think that I am right.

In response, Pope responded to Hamilton that he believed he was taking the right course of action.[296]

For the examinations held in December for 1904, Hogben wrote to the prioress that he had found evidence of cheating.[297] Hogben stated that he would leave it to the school to discipline the girl. Apart from this rare case of copying, the results were excellent and Hogben noted that 'If there is a fault it is that the pupils place too much reliance upon their memory ...'.[298]

Inspector Bird conducted the 1906 inspection of the school. He was glowing in his appraisal of St Joseph's:

As is now the case in all Secondary Schools for Maori girls the work in the classes of Standards V, VI, VII is based upon the syllabus work for Public Schools; that of the lower classes following more along the lines of the Native Schools Code. In the case of St Joseph's school, however, the programme of work in the lowest classes really exceeds the requirements, and the children were quite competent to be examined upon the Public Schools Syllabus.

The work throughout the school is in my opinion really excellent, and the degree of proficiency is uniform in all classes – from the preparatory classes upwards. A feature of the work is the excellent reading, in which the enunciation, expression, modulation of voice, and comprehension of the subject matter, are remarkable in the case of Maori girls.

As regards the extra subjects I may state that I have seldom heard more enjoyable singing; it was really a pleasure to listen to.

In drawing, freehand from the flat and from nature is taken and the work is of a very high order of merit, some of the colouring being exceedingly true to nature. Plasticine modelling is also exceedingly well done in the lower classes, the forms of natural objects being reproduced. Drill – which consists of physical exercises, club exercises, and wand exercises, is given 20 minutes daily as well as receiving a special day – a very wise arrangement. The movements were performed with remarkable precision and energy.

In sewing the work is excellent, and I am glad to report that while the girls are taught to do some more elaborate work in which they excel, the practical side receives due attention, and the girls are taught to make the dresses &c of the younger children, and, indeed, to provide these dresses for themselves. Reading, is, considering the time, exceedingly good.

The manners of the girls and the excellent tone and spirit shown by them during the examination call for the highest praise and reflect the highest credit upon the Rev. Sisters and the authorities, who are to be congratulated upon their excellent work.[299]

The first 1907 inspection was undertaken by the chief inspector of technical schools, E C Isaac.[300] His preference was for the pupils to be taught cookery, hygiene, how to care for the sick, sewing and dressmaking, rather than higher arithmetic, for example. From Isaac's perspective, there was little point teaching the more academic subjects in comparison with some of the more home-focused skills that would be helpful for their future home life. The second inspection report for 1907, written by Bird, continued with some of the presumptuous and narrow thinking of Issac. On the subject of drawing, Bird argued that he did not think that the drawing should be extended to include oil painting '… which is of doubtful utility in the case of Maori girls'.[301] A summary of the curriculum is as follows:

SUBJECT	STANDARD OR SUBJECTS TAUGHT
Arithmetic	Public school standards
English	Public school standards
Geography	New Zealand, Australia, British Isles
Physical	Daily rotation, annual revolution, meridians, latitude, clouds
Physiology	Chief bones of the skeleton, muscle, tendons, skin, heart and blood

Technical instruction (cooking by gas stove) was administered by the Hawke's Bay Education Board, which allowed only twenty-four girls to attend from parish schools. Only seven were permitted to attend from St Joseph's. Bird was of the opinion that, as the other girls were taught by the sisters at the school, this type of cooking would be more suitable, as no gas stove could be found at a kāinga.[302] Clothing was also addressed by Bird in 1907, observing that girls were instructed to bring whatever they had and that some arrived at the school with only the clothes they were wearing at the time.[303]

Still in use during this period were the enrolment forms that asked for the pupil's ancestry. In 1908, Ellen Gilroy from Bluff applied to be a government scholar as her parents '… are anxious that she should get a couple of years in a Maori boarding school in order to be of use to her people afterwards'.[304] She was not accepted on the grounds that she was not predominately Māori and she had not gained a Certificate of Proficiency.[305]

The number of government-funded scholarships decreased due to low uptake. St Joseph's was notified in March 1910 that fifteen scholarships had now been allotted to St Patrick's, Wellington, and the Ōtaki Convent School, with thirteen scholarships ordinarily available to St Joseph's now being transferred to those schools.[306] The memo from the Education Department also noted: 'Several of your nominees come for places where public schools are available and I remind you of the old rule that this is not allowed'.[307] In May that year, Prioress Mary des St Martyn responded that, for some years, the number of government scholars had been set at thirty-three and that the reason why this number had been unable to be filled was due to the Department sending a 'limited number of scholarship holders', mainly because of the restriction that scholarships could only be awarded for those who passed Standard IV.[308]

Secretary of Education, George Hogben, responded in October that year, stating that the number of scholarships available to St Joseph's stood at twenty-five, as five were transferred from the Ōtaki Convent School by Father Deloch. He also noted that in the previous year the regulations for scholarships had been amended for Māori children, so the requirement for pupils to have attained Standard IV no longer applied if they had come from native village schools.[309]

Although the rules had been relaxed to accommodate pupils below Standard IV in 1910, by the following year, Bird in his school inspection strongly recommended that the authorities of the school decline any pupils below Standard III, as the school with a roll of sixty-three was considerably full and the accommodation of the senior room was 'overtaxed'.[310]

Presidents of the Māori Women's Welfare League

Dame Whina Cooper
TE RARAWA
1908–1910

Kataraina 'Kaa' O'Brien
NGĀTI AWA, NGĀTI PIKIAO
1954–1956

Dame Whina Cooper.

Kataraina O'Brien.

Hohepine (Josephine) Cooper, otherwise known as Whina, was born at Te Karaka in northern Hokianga to Heremia Te Wake and Kare Kawatihi.

Her father was a catechist for the Catholic Church and, after having attended Whakarapa Native School, she was sent to St Joseph's from 1908 to 1910 through an arrangement with her father's friend, the Native Minister Sir James Carroll. As Whina recollected: 'My father said to the minister, "I want to send my girl to college more than anything else. I just wish I had the money …" "Look here," he said to my father. "Let me have your girl. Let her be my girl too. I'll pay for her education. We'll send her to St Joseph's."'[311]

One year after she had started at St Joseph's, Sister Bernadine wrote to Heremia:

> ... I must put you straight about our school. First the Government do not give us anything for our Maori girls until they have passed the Fourth Standard and we have nothing of our own. You therefore see how hard it must be for us to feed the children if their friends do not help a little, many of them do most willingly I am glad to say. Six pounds a year to help us buy food is all we ask, we teach them for nothing.[312]

The obvious misunderstanding in relation to the funding for pupils led to Heremia corresponding with Carroll to send him 'a note to remind you of what we discussed at Te Kohukohu'.[313] In June, 1908, the Under-Secretary of Native Affairs wrote to Sister Bernadine to say that £6 would be granted for the education of Hohiwhina, the daughter of Heremia Te Wake, until his daughter passed Standard IV.[314] The costs were again paid by the Department the following year,[315] and for 1909 a voucher of £5 was sent for her maintenance, with the Department noting that it would not be 'permanently committed to this expenditure' and that 'In the future, the father should make payment.'[316]

Whina had not been to a township bigger than Rawene during her childhood. She travelled to St Joseph's by boat to Onehunga and then to Napier, an experience lasting three days, with many tears on the way. The distance meant she only returned for one set of holidays during her time at the college.[317] As 'the most mischievous person' at school, Whina accepted a dare to jump from the highest diving board at the Napier swimming pools and enjoyed playing hockey, women's basketball and tennis. Another vivid recollection of her time at St Joseph's was witnessing Halley's Comet in 1910: 'Maoris believed it was a bad omen, and some Catholics thought it was a sign that the end of the world was near ... There were earthquakes too, at about the same time ... The nuns just told us to pray.'[318] Whina also learnt how to dance at St Joseph's, including the quadrille, waltz, lancers, schottische, heel and toe polka.[319]

Although later in life Whina would claim that she learnt everything of value outside school, her biographer, the late historian Michael King wrote: 'Nevertheless the assurance with which Whina approached her adult life, and her ability to keep records and accounts and to conduct correspondence, were all skills inculcated and developed at St Joseph's. They were skills that were not available to Maoris in general, and they were considerable ingredients in the success of many of her subsequent ventures.'[320]

Whina continued to have a relationship with the school in her later life, sending some of her daughters to attend and going to reunions. Her first trip back, however, was not a happy one. Not long out of college, Whina had decided she would like to become a nun. Her father was concerned and, through him, she met pupil Ruby Wawatai, who was in tears and told her she had been expelled from the college. Whina exclaimed later: 'Ruby was a lovely girl. How could anybody be so cruel ... They didn't understand Māori things.'[321] Whina decided, to the relief of her father, that she would not become a nun.

Ruby Wawatai

After having been heavily involved in a number of leadership roles within her community of northern Hokianga, eventually Whina shifted to Auckland in 1951 and, at the inaugural conference of the Māori Women's Welfare League in Wellington, she was elected foundation president. In this role, Whina and her executive were instrumental in devising programmes 'to improve the circumstances of Māori women and children' by focusing on issues involving education, housing, crime, employment, health and racial discrimination.[322] Awarded an MBE in 1953, Whina stepped down from being the League's president in 1957 with the organisation having three hundred branches, eighty-eight district councils and over four thousand members. That same year at the annual conference, Whina was anointed 'Te Whaea o te Motu' (Mother of the Nation).[323]

During the 1960s Whina helped spearhead the raising of funds for Te Unga Waka, a Māori Catholic Centre in Auckland, which opened in 1966.[324] In 1974 she was awarded a CBE and the following year, a coalition of groups formed Te Rōpū o te Matakite to protest over the alienation of Māori land. Whina was asked to lead the group, and she proposed a hīkoi from Te Hāpua to parliament. In 1981 Whina was awarded a DBE, and a decade later, she was made a member of the Order of New Zealand.[325]

Kataraina 'Kaa' O'Brien, President of the Māori Women's Welfare League 2012–2014, can recall Dame Whina Cooper speaking about her time at St Joseph's. 'She thought that the Sisters were very strict during her time. She was a very staunch Catholic person.'

1. Dame Whina Cooper and Sister Crescentia cut the cake at the 125th anniversary of St Joseph's.
2. St Joseph's Māori Girls' College Māori Women's Welfare League 1994. Manager Miss Tapine.

Baptised as Catholic and following her mother's faith, Kaa's father was Ringatū, which was prevalent in the community of Te Teko were she was raised as a child. After her first year of high school at Whakatāne High, it was suggested that Kaa be sent to a Māori boarding school.

Memories of the college include the only lay teacher, Api Smith, being in the marching band as a 'stick twirler' and the then principal, Sister Crescentia: 'I can recall one incident when four of us went to the *Glenn Miller Story* at the movies at Taradale. It was our Saturday afternoon walk and we weren't supposed to go and we were reprimanded. I always recall her [Crescentia] saying to us "Birds of a feather, flock together".' Another observation Kaa made is that former pupils keep beautiful homes: 'That was taught to us there. We had to polish the floors until we could see our reflections on them.'

Her father also imparted some career advice. 'He said, "We have enough teachers in the whānau, so don't do that."' However, after working at a paper mill and starting a family, O'Brien didn't heed her father's advice and enrolled at Auckland Teachers' College, becoming a teacher by profession. Her association with the League dates back to 1967 when she joined the Aotea branch and became a very active member. 'We had role models and women like Dames Whina Cooper and Mira Szaszy and you couldn't help but be impressed,' states Kaa. When becoming the president, the focus of O'Brien and the League was '... what the League was founded on, the well-being of whānau, the upskilling of our women and encouraging them to go as far as they can, and te reo Māori me ōna tikanga'. Such was the impact of the education Kaa received at St Joseph's that she sent her daughter Yvonne O'Brien (former deputy CEO of Te Whare Wānanga o Awanuiārangi and current Programme Director of the Atlantic Institute at the University of Oxford) to the school.

Evie O'Brien.

Māori Purposes Fund Board

In 1925, the Māori Purposes Fund Board (MPFB) decided to grant an additional £10 per student on top of the £20 per annum that government scholars were receiving, for other costs involved with their schooling.[326] In providing advice to the MPFB, the Department of Education wrote that the usual practice at the school was for parents to pay money, which was held by the principal who disbursed it and the scholars kept a record of expenditure.[327] The department wanted a similar process to remain in place, as they did not want the scholars to receive the money without supervision. When informing the school of the payment, the Board explicitly stated that it was for the purpose of providing additional clothing and other incidental costs and to relieve the parents financially.[328]

Five years later, the amount of the scholarship had been reduced to £6 as an allowance for equipment, with just over £3 of that coming from the Māori Trustee.[329] The scholarship scheme was also discussed between the Director of Education and the Inspector of Native Schools, John Porteous, in 1933.[330] The genesis of the scholarship scheme, explained Porteous, was that at the end of 1870 no provision for the secondary schooling of Māori established by the government existed and so scholarships were made available with Ministerial authority.[331] A decade later, the funding was altered to 'enable the clever Maori children that have gone through the village school course' with an opportunity for two more years of schooling; the idea was that these pupils would be able to do good among their own people 'to whom they should always return'.[332]

MĀORI BOARDING SCHOOLS	SCHOLARSHIPS AVAILABLE IN 1900	SCHOLARSHIPS AVAILABLE IN 1926
St Stephen's	30	30
Te Aute College	10	25
Hukarere	20	25
St Joseph's	33	22
Queen Victoria	-	10
Turakina	-	4
Te Waipounamu	-	5
Total	93	121

Over time, demand increased for Māori secondary education, and the schemes that did exist were superseded by '… a large number of Government Junior Scholarships or Free Places for suitably qualified Maori scholars'.³³³ In 1919, the value of each scholarship rose from £20 to £30 and they were available for a two-year period at approved schools that had been established for Māori children. By either ministerial or cabinet approval, the number of scholarships increased as necessity grew. As Porteous wrote: 'The ordinary schools did not provide a sufficiently practical training of a kind desirable for the Maori youth, and consequently, in the absence of suitable Government schools advantage was taken of existing denominational schools for Maoris which provided a good practical training – domestic duties, sewing, cookery, nursing and hygiene and first aid for girls, and woodwork, agriculture for boys.'³³⁴ The schools where the scholarships were available and the number of scholarships is shown below:³³⁵

The expenditure of scholarships resulted in £4,500 being spent. The three types of senior scholarships were:³³⁶

1. Industrial scholarships or apprenticeships (carpentry, saddlery and railway workshops)
2. Agricultural scholarships (farmers)
3. Nursing scholarships (placed under the Department of Health at £35 per annum).

In addition to the senior scholarships, two university scholarships (£40 each) were available each year for males or females who had passed the matriculation examination and who were prepared to be employed in a profession that would be of benefit to Māori.³³⁷

In 1931, secretary of the MPFB, Henare Balneavis, disclosed that the funder of the scholarships (£20 with £15 for fees and £5 for equipment) was the Native Trustee and that the decision makers of the scholarships were the head teacher and the inspector of schools.³³⁸ The Native Trustee was responsible for the administration of Māori reserves.³³⁹

St Joseph's Māori Girls' College 1925.

In 1922 the staffing personnel consisted of Mother Mary St Rosalie as the charge teacher, Sisters Julius and Domitille teaching literary subjects, Sister Athanasius taking music and dressmaking, and Sister Fabian teaching cooking.[340] Two pupils were sitting the Trinity College Examination for book keeping and, in history, the 'Maori side is taken with a focus on Maori figures'.[341] As for the buildings, the playing area was asphalted and the girls slept in well-ventilated dormitories, with a number of them sleeping in an open balcony.[342] Two years later, school inspector G M Henderson, wrote: 'Sewing, or dressmaking, is excellent in quantity and is a special feature of the school and deserves a special commendation.'[343]

In 1925 and 1926, dressmaking was a standout subject. The inspection observed one of the older pupils instructing Standard III (two students) and Preparatory Class (four girls), commenting that: 'She is quite a promising beginner as a teacher; but, through inexperience and want of knowledge of methods of teaching and the requirements of the syllabus, she has not achieved the results in reading and arithmetic in Class P (preparatory) and Standard I that are desirable, otherwise these classes have been well taught and managed.'[344] The reliance on older pupils to take the younger classes may be that there were not enough staff. In 1927 Porteous criticised the 'understaffing' and observed that a 'Maori assistant' cares for girls below Standard IV.'[345]

In 1928, Standards VII and VIII were renamed Forms I and II, and the issue of understaffing was again raised in the 1929 report, with Sister Mary Julius taking all the classes in practically all the subjects.[346] The only exception was in music, which was taught by Mihi Walker.[347] In a memorandum to the Director of Education, Inspector Douglas Ball focused on what he perceived to be the major deficiencies in the teaching at St Joseph's. With a school roll of fifty-four, Ball wrote that, even though 'At this school the girls receive a good grounding in English and in subjects which will be helpful to them when they take up house-keeping (sewing, cooking, etc.)' there was much room for improvement in the pupil's oral composition.[348] The teaching of history had a strong focus on New Zealand and Māori history, yet 'English history, its social aspect, might be undertaken.'[349]

Problems with Arithmetic

By 1929, problems with arithmetic had surfaced in the inspection reports. Ball wrote to the Director of Education that 'mental and speed work require more attention'.[350] In 1931, arithmetic was again highlighted. The average test score was 19 per cent, with the pupils having little idea of how to work out problems. 'In the Bankruptcy sums, most of the pupils put liabilities over assets in order to find the dividend, and in fact all of the work showed lack of appreciation of basic principles.'[351] The following year, inspector Tom Fletcher was alarmed at the weaknesses in arithmetic:

> Particular attention should be paid to mechanical accuracy and to the practical aspect of the work. Plenty of practice should be given in weighing, measuring, shopping, etc, so that the terms used are fully comprehended. It will be found that the practical work greatly increases the ability of the girls to tackle problems in the proper way. At present they have little idea how to set about the work.[352]

In 1934, Form III students taking arithmetic were divided into two groups. One was given a written test and the other sat a mental examination. The results of the mental test were poor, and the results of the written test were considered 'very disappointing', with three scores of zero, one who achieved one mark and the other picking up two marks. Ball lamented: 'There appeared to be a complete lack of understanding of what was required with the practical problems and no knowledge of methods to be employed.'[353]

Four years before this, Ball had been more forthright in his assessment of what was required at St Joseph's, suggesting structural change when looking at the curriculum. He wrote to the Director of Education that two parallel streams of courses be provided: domestic and academic.[354] Domestic '... should include, for the greater number of girls, sewing, dressmaking, cookery, hygiene and physiology, infant welfare, nursing and first aid as well as English, Arithmetic, Music, Art, History, and perhaps Geography.'[355] The academic course should cater for pupils who wished to sit Matriculation, Public Service Entrance, and Intermediate Examinations.[356] In order for the latter to be achieved, a science laboratory with a qualified secondary assistant was recommended.

Science at St Joseph's 1950s.

Accountants

Tineka Hall
NGĀTI KAHUNGUNU, NGĀTI TŪWHARETOA,
TAINUI, NGĀTI MANIAPOTO
1992–1996

Grace Allen
NGĀTI KAHUNGUNU
2008–2011

Since the late 1920s and early 1930s, St Joseph's has made huge progress in results for mathematics. Accountant Tineka Hall is currently a senior manager at Price Waterhouse Cooper in Napier. Tineka was attracted to St Joseph's after she had attended her older cousin's powhiri to the school the previous year. 'I thought it was awesome. I was blinded by the whole charade. That just drove me and I told my parents and they agreed with me. They just worked their butts off to make sure they could provide so we could have the things they couldn't growing up.' One teacher Tineka had a special regard for was Dermott Kelly:

> I had him a lot of the time for accounting and economics. I left in sixth form and I went to another local high school for seventh form. You could only do seventh form by correspondence and even though I was at another school, I would drag myself back to St Joseph's. It was such a different environment being co-ed and so I asked my mum and dad if I could go back to St Jo's.

Grace Allen worked under Tineka as an accountant at Price Waterhouse Cooper after graduating with a Bachelor of Commerce at the University of Auckland. A turning point in Grace's life was when Miss Kingi stopped her with one of her friends when they were leaving the school gates on the last day of term and said:

> "Girls, Ngā Manu Kōrero." I said, "What's that?" Miss Kingi told me what they were and that we needed a junior entrant but

Tineka Hall and Grace Allen.

because I was in the third form, I argued that a fourth former should do it. She said, "No, you'll do it." My whole homework for the school holidays was writing a speech. I came back, handed it in, and she ripped it apart. I had to have writing lessons at the time because it was in English, and I had attended kōhanga reo. She pushed and pushed me, and I said, "Miss, I don't want to do the speech because I didn't write it." It didn't feel believable and okay saying someone else's words. We had a discussion in her office and I said, "Okay, how can we work together?" So, we used bits of her speech and my speech. As a young Māori woman, my thoughts are important and she made me feel that.

Grace also feels a deep connection to her teachers at St Joseph's:

There was this general attitude amongst staff here that you knew they would do more for you than at other schools. I never felt like I hated my teachers here, that they were bad or that they didn't care. They teach you after school or on the weekend and you feel more like whānau than being in a teacher–student relationship. I've never felt that kind of connection with teachers elsewhere. I owe a lot to the school, now I am so proud, so happy, that I was forced to come here, and it has become part of my pepeha.

The 1931 Napier Earthquake

On 3 February 1931 at 10.47 a.m., disaster struck Hawke's Bay. The Napier earthquake would cause destruction, injuries and death on a scale never previously seen in New Zealand or since: '... the ground in the Hawke's Bay region heaved sharply upward and swayed. A deceptive half-minute pause was followed by a downward motion and violent shaking and rocking. In all, the quake spanned two and a half minutes.'[357] Of the 256 deaths, 161 died in Napier, 93 in Hastings, and 2 in Wairoa.[358]

At the Catholic schools on Napier Hill, which included St Joseph's Māori Girls' College, the schoolchildren were in the playground at the time:[359]

I didn't know what had thrown me to the ground with such fury until someone shouted "Earthquake", the ground heaving beneath us, huge trees appearing as if they were about to fall on us, screams, crying, heartfelt acts of contrition. I don't know how I got there, but there was a bank of geraniums with a friend underneath me, and we were praying as we had never prayed before … "Oh, my God I'm sorry …" I really thought it was the end of the world.[360]

Napier after the earthquake.

Following the quake, the sisters made their way out to the playground and took the children to the highest part of the grounds. Luckily only the laundry collapsed, as it was constructed out of brick, with the rest of the school being built from wood. The sisters then went into the chapel and prised the tabernacle from the altar. 'Those Sisters not occupied with the children knelt before it [the Blessed Sacrament] in prayer, pleading for mercy and protection for all and for pardon for those people in the town who had been killed.' St Joseph's, which had just undergone repairs, was so severely shaken by the quake that it was estimated that it would cost more than it was worth to make it habitable again.

The furniture, statues and crockery were all destroyed.[361] Sister M Vergine recalled that there were only about eight Māori pupils from St Joseph's present when the earthquake hit, with those girls preparing the meals during the days following. 'The Māori girls were very devoted, lighting fires and peeling potatoes, and doing all they could to help the sisters.'[362] The playground of St Patrick's school was used as a morgue, as parents identified the bodies of their children as they were brought from the nearby Technical School. Teachers and pupils of nearby Napier Central School came and used the school after the earthquake. At Greenmeadows, Sister Mary St Ignatius had died at the convent on Guppy Road after being struck by falling bricks. At the seminary, more deaths were registered, with two priests and seven students losing their lives.[363]

> Later, from our vantage point on the drying green outside the mass of concrete and mortar that had been the laundry, we could see the port area ablaze, to the left of us, billowing clouds of bright colours coming from the town, now flattened and burning. The earth never stopped shaking, but now and then there'd be extra big ones, and we'd all scream and pray – how we prayed! The sisters were marvellous, keeping us calm, supplying drinks, erecting sheets between clothes lines to keep the blazing sun off us, and leading us in the rosary.[364]

'Many of the day pupils remained all night at the convent as their homes had been destroyed. All slept outdoors and sisters and pupils took turns together to keep watch before the tabernacle under the trees and to say the rosary.'[365]

View of Hastings Street, Napier.

Hastings St Napier

Rebuilding St Joseph's Māori Girls' College

In 1927 representations were made by the Māori members of parliament to the Prime Minister, Gordon Coates, to rebuild some of the Māori schools. The erection of a new building to replace the existing St Joseph's Māori Girls' College building on Napier Hill was first broached by Prioress Venatius to the Māori Purposes Fund Board (MPFB) in 1928.[366] She wrote: 'The present wooden building was erected in 1866, and is not only lacking the modern conveniences necessary for the working of such an establishment, but is altogether too small and almost unfit for habitation.'[367] At the time, the building housed sixty pupils with the cost of a suitable building being estimated to be approximately £40,000, of which the school asked for a grant of £13,000 from the MPFB.[368] The Board responded that assurance could not be granted until the government made a further grant.[369]

The principal of St Joseph's wrote to the MPFB, stating that they hoped to receive one-third of the estimated cost from the MPFB for the rebuild of the school. They intended to borrow the remaining £6,000 from a bank or another local body and that, 'We are assured that once the work is begun it will not be held up for want of monetary assistance as the need for sufficient and up-to-date accommodation is so very urgent'.[370] The principal wrote to Apirana Ngata in 1934 that the school had accepted the lowest tender submitted to rebuild the school for £5,487 and that they were now applying for the grant promised some years earlier.[371]

Attempts to secure funding from the MPFB for rebuilding the school were rejected, with the MPFB saying all the money allocated for the rebuild of Māori secondary schools had been exhausted. Father James Riordan, the priest charged with the responsibility of having the government contribute financially toward the new building, labelled the decision 'outrageous' in a letter written to the Acting Minister of Native Affairs, Robert Masters.[372] Masters' response to Riordan was that all the MPFB could do was '... keep up the payments of interest on the unpaid balances of the grants voted ...'[373] Masters also assured Riordan that: 'I think the Board's decision is not a refusal for all time to making any grant to your institution, but is merely an indication that the present position of its finances will not permit of any grant being made.'[374]

In a memorandum from Ngata for the Minister of Native Affairs, George Forbes, he pointed the finger at Treasury for the accounts of the MPFB being empty. He wrote that in 1936 an approach was made to Treasury for the sum of £11,500 in annual instalments of £3,000 as a reimbursement for the money paid towards the Māori secondary school rebuilding programme. Treasury advised that:

> The state already provides a free primary and secondary education, and also contributes largely towards the cost of the universities, all of which facilities are open to any pupil in the Dominion. The Education Department has not provided special Maori secondary schools because firstly, Maoris are free to attend the ordinary State Schools, and secondly, certain denominational interests have built schools of their own. St Joseph's Girls' School is of the latter character and is thus a private venture for which the State should not assume any capital liability.[375]

One major bone of contention was whether or not a promise from Apirana Ngata was made for the school to be funded. Ngata himself commented that: 'When the sisters waited upon me in 1930, I informed them that in respect of other schools the Board had authorised grants up to one third of the cost, but no promises were made.'[376] An infuriated Father Riordan wrote to Prime Minister Michael Savage that he would be prepared to swear on oath that Ngata had made such assurances, as he had done with Mother Venatius who was in charge of the erection of the new building.[377]

He wrote: 'For over seventy years our heroic nuns have borne the burden of building, staffing, and equipping this institution, giving any profit that resulted from the working of the college to further scholarships for deserving pupils. Never have they received more than a bed and board and the most meagre supply of dress.'[378] Then, in a letter to the acting Native Minister, Frank Livingstone, he wrote:

> The treatment meted out to us in the matter of assistance for re-building, is a little short of sheer callousness. I must point out, Sir, that our sisters, for whom no forty-hour week exists or could exist, have heroically and practically alone carried out the duty of educating the Maori girls of the country since 1867, for seventy years. Every penny over and above the working expenses of the school has been put back into scholarships for indigent girls of intelligence. No personal gain or pecuniary profit has ever come to the nuns all

Top: Sir Apirana Ngata.
Bottom: Father James Riordan.

those years. No rich endowments helped them to carry on their arduous task ... We naturally applied for help similar to that given similar, but highly endowed institution.

The years roll on and all we hear is a monotonous rendering of the refrain of "Kathleen Mavoureen" [a popular Irish song of endearment]. Please do not think me rude when I tell you it is awfully raucous and out of tune when sung by a Labour Minister. You are aware, Sir, that the sisters suffered frightfully during the earthquake. Their new convent was demolished and one of their brilliant young nuns killed. Surely you will understand the bitterness of my disappointment when our repeated requests for bread bring only a stone in response.[379]

In response, an enraged Livingstone wrote:

I hope you will pardon me when I say that I am bewildered and astonished ... suggest that you "remove the mote from thy brother's eye, you extract the beam from your own" ... I would like you to understand that I will take second place to no one – not even yourself – in my desire and ambition to improve the well-being and happiness of the Maori people. Tens of thousands of pounds are required to be spent on behalf of the Natives. In addition to the ordinary money provided for assisting them on to their own land, over £200,000 was taken last year from the Unemployment Fund, towards which the Natives contribute very little, and made a free gift to pay the wages of those employed in Native land development work. Not one penny of this amount is loaded on to the land for the improvements effected.[380]

Prime Minister Peter Fraser.

Despite Livingstone's inability to secure funding for the MPFB and thus, St Joseph's, he sent a memorandum to the principal of the college to congratulate the school on celebrating seventy years and stated: 'Your institution and other denominational schools are to be praised for so successfully carrying on the duty of educating the Maori youth of the Country …'[381] Riordan took the opportunity to air his grievances when the soon-to-be Prime Minister and current Minister of Education, Peter Fraser, visited the school in April 1939.[382] In his welcoming address, Riordan stated that the school had seventy-five girls but could have two hundred, if the money permitted. He continued:

The Church had given very little help and the Government had given less … The premises would soon have to be enlarged. Former Ministers of Native Affairs had given Kathleen Mavoureen promises that they would assist. On the strength of those promises buildings costing £10,000 had been put up. They had this debt over their heads. They scraped money from music lessons and put back into scholarships anything they made over and above. At present, they were faced with serious difficulties …[383]

Fraser responded that: 'If promises have been made, they should be kept.' He promised to make enquiries with Ngata, the Department of Education, the MPFB, the Prime Minister and the Minister of Finance.[384]

A briefing note from the Private Secretary of the Prime Minister stated: 'It is clear that an intention to assist existed … The obstacle is Treasury, which considers that the State provided sufficient educational facilities for the Maoris without also assisting private ventures.'[385] Riordan was clear that the school was unable to meet added demands unless they received the aid that had been promised and upon which heavy commitments were made.[386] His final plea was that at present the school buildings required enlargment to provide better accommodation and facilities for teaching, in line with the wishes of the Department of Education.[387]

In 1941 Riordan met with the Prime Minister, Peter Fraser, and the Minister of Education, Rex Mason.[388] Fraser relayed that there was no challenge to the validity of the claim, that it was only a question of money, with Mason adding that St Joseph's was the last school to be funded but that '... the axe fell before anything could be done'.³⁸⁹ Fraser remarked that: 'I think we can all forget about the promises and deal with the case on its merits ... The thing is to consider what can be done, whether we will give you the grant straight out or give a grant through the Maori Purposes Fund Board.'³⁹⁰

Mason then recommended that a grant of £2,400 be made to the school with the only procedural matter being an opinion from the MPFB whether it should come from their funds or Vote Education.³⁹¹ However, there would be one final hurdle: following the meeting between Riordan, Fraser and Mason, the under-secretary of the Native Department registered his displeasure at the deal, stating that assistance should only be granted if the MPFB had recouped the outstanding £11,500 it had paid on the promise of funding from government and that other schools might have to be funded that had not received any money, such as Queen Victoria, Wesley College or Te Waipounamu Girls.³⁹² Finally, in 1943, the decision was made to fund the £2,420 directly from Vote Education, instead of from the MPFB.³⁹³

St Joseph's Māori Girls' College 1949.

At the end of 1931, a school inspection was carried out by Ball and Fletcher. The report stated that when the school reopened in March 1931, the school roll was sixteen and at present, the number had increased to twenty-one.[394] As could be expected, the inspectors report that: 'The school work was seriously disorganised and the roll number depleted by the severe earthquake in February.'[395] In a departure from historic policy, perhaps as a result of the earthquake, it was recommended that all girls should receive instruction in the Māori language.

In 1932, the school re-opened with six girls present, and a new teacher, Sister Mary Elphege. By the end of February another eight pupils joined the college.[396] Also at the beginning of 1932, the pupils were divided into three whare (Papura, Koura and Kākāriki). The distinguishing colours of each whare were displayed with two poi hanging from a bow of ribbon made in the three whare colours: purple, gold and green. Each prefect was also awarded a medallion with the word Prefect etched on it with background colours of the whare they were responsible for.[397]

A clear focus of the 1932 school year was on entering the various provincial shows around the country: at Wanganui in the embroidery competition, where Pare Koopu won the first prize, with Toma Koopu coming second; Julia Tapsell won the second prize at the Waikato Show for her Stocking Bag entry; Pare Koopu came second in Fancy Work in Palmerston North; pupils won both first and second in the Knitted Vest, Knitted Pullover and Princess Slip competitions at Hawke's Bay; and at the Christchurch Show, St Joseph's students won the School Tunic and Dress-Making Notebook categories, with a second place being gained in Tāniko Weaving.[398]

Accumulating prizes from the provincial shows was not the only accomplishment for 1932. In October, four pupils of Bella Renata sat the Elementary Book-Keeping Exam of the Southern Cross Commercial College, Sydney. In November, the school was notified of the impressive results, with Pirihira Waititi achieving 100 per cent and Toma Koopu, Lena Haerewa and Mana Manuel each receiving 99 per cent.[399]

In English, inspectors pointed out that 'Maori errors' were still noticeable and suggested that a dramatic and debating club would greatly enhance speech, ennunciation and expression, and, in history, the teaching of civics was urged. Inspector Fletcher echoed the sentiments of Ball from 1930 that courses offered in the first year should be regarded as exploratory to 'discover which girls are sufficiently of bright intellect to go on to higher studies ... The others, except those preparing for commercial life, should continue with general Courses, which is quite suitable in character for the great majority of the girls'.[400] The inspection also recorded that sleeping porches were available for girls with 'tubercular trouble' and that 'an isolation ward' was also provided.[401] At the end of 1933, the report was scathing of arithmetic, with pupils not gaining a good knowledge of the basic rules and were unable to relate the processes to everyday life. Under the topic of instruction, Ball wrote: 'No instruction is given in Mathematics, Science or a language other than Maori.'[402]

Top: St Joseph's Māori Girls' College building 1935, before it was demolished.
Bottom: St Joseph's Māori Girls' College 1911.

Kylie Tiuka with her award-winning entry worn by Melanie Chase.

The art of Kylie Tiuka that hangs above the Tūhoe Boardroom.

Māori Artist

Kylie Tiuka
NGĀI TŪHOE
1996–1999

Much like the pupils of St Joseph's in 1932, Kylie Tiuka has always been interested in creating. When she reached St Joseph's it was her art teacher Ann Raphaelov who nurtured her artistic streak by suggesting she enter the local Wearable Arts Award, which Tiuka ended up winning. 'After sixth form, I knew I wanted to be an artist. I was going to EIT but following a conversation between Miss Kingi and my father, I enrolled in a Diploma in Computer Graphic Design from the National College of Design and Technology in Wellington.'

Despite having 'zero' experience on a computer, Kylie successfully completed her diploma only to discover that she still yearned to 'experiment with painting, sculpting and glass blowing'. Back in Hastings and working at Watties, she spotted an ad to enrol in a Bachelor of Māori Visual Arts. She quit her job and was taught by the Māori artist Sandy Adsett at the School of Māori Visual Arts, Tomairangi. Furthering her studies in art, she graduated from Massey University with a Master in Māori Visual Arts.

'I like creating work that acknowledges my Ngāi Tūhoe identity and expressing the narratives that are held within the written, oral and visual histories of my people.' Kylie has generated art for a variety of forums: from set design for television productions, and postage stamps for the 2015 New Zealand Post Matariki Kōwhaiwhai Stamp Series, to art for the boardroom of the headquarters of Ngāi Tūhoe, Te Kura Whare, in Taneatua. She has shown nationally at Te Manawa, Palmerston North, the Suter Gallery, Nelson, and at Pātaka Museum in Porirua. Kylie attributes her expectation of producing a high standard of work as coming from St Joseph's. 'I never give up or let myself fail. I expect the best from myself, and the school definitely installed pride in yourself in being a Māori woman and striving for success in whatever you do.'

The first pupils at St Joseph's Māori Girls' College, Greenmeadows, 1935.

CHAPTER FIVE

Growing at Greenmeadows

In 1934 the Prioress received a memorandum from the Director of Education that the school must achieve a roll higher than eight pupils to remain open.[403] In February, the following year, the same threat was relayed. Sister Athanasius responded to the memorandum by asking that an extension be granted, as 'we are just beginning to get the pupils back here again'.[404]

The department consented to the request but noted that there were only two pupils of school age attending St Joseph's and that the department intended to omit the school from the list of 'registered primary schools'.[405] From 1934, not only would St Joseph's need a new home following the earthquake. The school also, desperately, needed more pupils.

Following the Napier earthquake of 1931, St Joseph's not only had to be rebuilt but also had to be relocated because the old site on Napier Hill was too dangerous. Once the sisters had purchased nine acres of land at Greenmeadows and a cottage of six rooms from the trustees of the late Patrick McCormick in 1933 for a total of £2,400,[406] work was underway for the new home. In the interim, the students remained on Napier Hill and were taught by two sisters and a pupil teacher until 12 March 1935.[407] The 1935 school diary reads: 'The old site had served its purpose with many past pupils now being trained teachers and nurses.'[408]

Before the earthquake, just under 100 students attended the college.[409] Many students left the school, fearing a repeat earthquake. However, it was not long before the school roll improved: the school re-opened after the earthquake with six pupils, by 1936 there were thirty-nine pupils, by 1937 there were fifty-six pupils and by 1939 there were seventy-five.[410]

The first entry of the school diary for 1935 reads: 'The year 1935 marked for St Joseph's an event which should have lasting effects on the progress of the school. Talks of a new school have been heard for many years but the opening of this scholastic year saw the fulfilment of our dreams.'[411]

Despite the anticipation of the pupils to relocate to a new school at the start of the school year in 1935, the girls would have to wait a further month until they could take residence, as the top floor that housed the dormitories had not been completed. Then, on 12 March, the school diary reads: 'Amid much rejoicing we moved to our new home. The girls were greatly impressed by all that confronted them and were sure they had the best school in Hawke's Bay. The workmen still had a little to do on the building and were laying the foundation for the chapel.'[412] The architects of the new St Joseph's were Finch and Westerholm from Napier, who, following the 1931 earthquake, banded together with another three architectural firms to rebuild the city.

Finch and Westerholm were known for building in a Spanish Mission Style and were also responsible for building the Scinde and the Logan and Williams Buildings on Tennyson Street, as well as the State Theatre on the corner of Dickens and Dalton streets. The school was built by E Perrin, and J Rockwell was credited for his 'fine interior joinery work including the chapel and altar'.[413]

As one newspaper article reported: 'The building is one of the largest wooden buildings in Hawke's Bay with the interior being constructed with heart rimu and tōtara and the internal colouring being chocolate and cream.'[414] Downstairs were three classrooms and an assembly room, as well as a refectory, kitchen and servery on the ground floor. Upstairs housed three dormitories with accompanying bathrooms and lockers. The total cost of the project was £10,000.[415]

The Opening of St Joseph's Māori Girls' College in Greenmeadows

The official opening of the new school and chapel took place at 2.30 p.m. on 23 June 1935. It was a large gathering with the Reverend Dean Holley officiating and Archbishop Thomas O'Shea opening and blessing the building. O'Shea's address stated:

> The girls sent out from the college have carried with them the blessings received at this institution and in their districts and settlements they have had a beneficial effect in uplifting the Maori people of this country. I have first-hand knowledge of the good effect they are having in the remote parts of New Zealand … We whites have a great debt to the natives because they were the original owners of this fine country. Early missionaries brought with them religion to the natives but the white men were not always just. They put material things before spiritual well-being. In this fine building we are extending the privileges which our own children enjoy to the children of the natives. The policy that has been followed has not brought material prosperity to the people, as we can see to-day. At present we have poverty and unemployment … After the great earthquake and when the depression was at its height, the Sisters saw their numbers were diminished and sought a fresh place to carry on their activities of the city. They set about the work and the result is this magnificent block of buildings which would do credit to any Pakeha Dominion.[416]

Pupils of St Joseph's Māori Girls' College, Greenmeadows, 1939.

The Labour Member of Parliament for Napier, William Barnard, rose to address the crowd following O'Shea's words. Barnard acknowledged '… speaking for the whole Protestant community, we have always appreciated the work that these fine women [mission sisters] have carried out on all occasions … I agree with His Grace [O'Shea] in that the Maori people have not received anything like a square deal from the whites.'[417]

With other prominent local residents, the crowd inspected the building to music played by the Napier Citizens Band, and proceedings were brought to an end with a pontifical benediction given in the new chapel.

Walker Whānau

Edith Sainsbury
NÉE WALKER
NGĀTI KAHUNGUNU, RANGITĀNE
1935–1937

Lady June Mead
NÉE WALKER
NGĀTI POROU
1944–1947

Hineatatu Dorset-Paewai
RANGITĀNE, NGĀI TŪHOE
2012–2017

Henrietta Kawhia
NÉE WALKER
NGĀTI POROU
1939–1941

Kaapua Smith
NGĀTI POROU, NGĀTI AWA,
NGĀTI APA
1994–1998

Edith was the eldest living former pupil of St Joseph's before she passed away in 2017 in her mid-nineties. Upon her arrival at the college, Edith remembered a few of her relatives from Tikitiki already being there and feeling homesick. 'I felt like running away, but I didn't.' Her lasting memories of the school were the teachers, with:

> ... Sister Crescentia taking the education part and Sister Athanasius taking the dressmaking. We used to call Sister Athanasius grumpy and she was fairly old. [For] the weekends, we would be in Napier. They would take us for a ride in the bus and they took us to Cape Kidnappers and the teachers got caught in the tides coming in but there was a tractor handy that went out to get Sisters Athanasius and Crescentia. I said to the girls, "Oh well, she'll [Sister Athanasius] be in bed for a few days and we will have peace."

One aspect of life in a dormitory also relates to the sisters:

> Night time was hard in bed because you didn't know how to settle down. [Bedtime was at 8.30 p.m. and the mattresses were made of straw.] We weren't allowed to speak or we would get a detention. When the sisters went on retreat, that was when the fun started when the girls would get up and have a pillow fight.

The opening of the college at Greenmeadows is one event that Edith remembered. 'We had to get ready for the opening with Bishop O'Shea opening it. He had a beautiful white beard and we used to say, "Wouldn't it be lovely to be swinging on it."' Edith left St Joseph's in 1937 because she wanted to play hockey, which was offered by Dannevirke High School. At St Joseph's, it was 'all basketball' (netball). 'I got tired of playing basketball and so I said, "I'm not coming back next year."' Edith was also grateful to the school for being taught how to cook. 'That's one thing I'll give them credit for. We all took turns to help the sisters cook the meals.'

Henrietta Kawhia and the late Lady June Mead are two of fourteen Walker siblings from the Mangaporo Valley near Ruatōria and are the 'cousins' Edith referred to from Tikitiki. The elder sister, Henrietta, still lives in the family homestead that overlooks her former primary school, which also operated as shearing quarters. Once their father, Raana Walker, passed away, the school was closed and the Walker children then had to attend Whakawhitira Native School 'down the line' that taught pupils to the level of Standard VI.

The eldest sister attended St Winifred's in Gisborne, as there was no local high school. Some of the siblings had to support the family by milking the cows. Paving the way for the sisters in attending St Joseph's was older sister Hiria (she was engaged to Moana Ngarimu, who was postumously awarded the Victoria Cross for his actions in World War II). She attended with her cousin, Edith. As Henrietta comments: 'It had a reputation as a finishing school and there were a few tomboys that were sent from this area. However, I never became a lady.'

For June:

My mother was a dedicated Anglican but she sent three daughters to St Joseph's and the fourth to another convent and she told the nuns not to convert us. There were many non-Catholic girls who attended St Joseph's. We had Mormon girls from Bridge Pā, most of the East Coast girls and from the Bay of Plenty were not Catholic. Mum went to Hukarere, and on the hill was St Joseph's before the earthquake. She said she couldn't help and observe how differently the girls from the convents were treated compared to them in the early 1900s. It was the church schools that were taking Māori children.

Lady June Mead and Sir Hirini Moko Mead with daughters Aroha and Linda.

On one occasion, June asked Kereni (Sister Crescentia) if she could become a Catholic after witnessing a confirmation ceremony for one of her peers. 'She said, "And have your mother after me? Run away, child!"'

Henrietta received a two-year scholarship 'and if you were clever, you got another two-years continuation scholarship. For me, my last year was not paid for.' June, who would become a teacher, remembers the scholarship scheme both as a student and an educator:

The government had scholarships for Māori boarding schools for those who could not go to a high school locally. The church schools, such as St Stephen's and Queen Victoria in Auckland and St Joseph's, Hukarere and Te Aute College in Hawke's Bay, took Māori students and the only state schools that took Māori scholarship pupils was Dannevirke Boys' High and Auckland Girls' Grammar. Years later when my husband [Sir Hirini Moko Mead] and I were teaching in primary schools, we used to travel around the state schools to see if they would take Māori pupils and they wouldn't.

June had vivid memories of arriving at St Joseph's:

My sister was dying and passed away one year after Moana Ngarimu, so my mum kept me at home until one month after she was buried. After arriving in Hastings and staying one night with my mother's sister, they took me to St Joseph's. It was a Sunday night and we walked in the main school area and met the principal, Sister Crescentia. She said, "Go down the passage and the Ngāti Porou girls are in a room." I said to her, "Aren't they all Ngāti Porou?" A girl marched up to me, and said, "No! I'm from Te Arawa." Next minute, Emma Kawiti rescued me and said, "Come with me." I have three articles of faith: one tribe, Ngāti Porou; one church, Anglican; and one political party, A T Ngata's.

Henrietta did not like school and took no joy in learning Māori:

I couldn't put it all together. I could understand it because our parents spoke Māori but they didn't speak to us and we spoke English all the time. I had a friend who I would sit with and she said, "I will write you something if you can draw for me." She got better marks for drawing than I did for Māori!

Henrietta also remembers Grumpy Garry (Sister Athanasius). 'She couldn't bear you doing nothing and would repeat "Idle hands make the devil's work."' Henrietta also remembers the sisters finding out when the young priests from the seminary were going for their walks and the pupils of St Joseph's wouldn't be allowed out. 'We used to visit the seminary and sing, way up in the balcony, and all we could see were the top of their heads. There were two Māori boys, one from Rotorua and one from up north, and all you could see were these two black heads.'

Unlike her sister, June enjoyed her time at St Joseph's and remembered being taught social etiquette:

You had to take a bus to get into Napier, and you only went if you had to go to the dentist or doctor. The sisters would give us enough for a bus fare and enough to buy an ice cream and the rule was don't eat in the street, go sit on the chair, that's how you should be seen in public. It was a social rule … There was the odd girl who tried to push the boundaries, and they tended to be the senior ones. We had a gardener who mowed the lawns and looked after the grounds, and he had a wheelbarrow. He used to come from behind the convent where there was a two-storied barn and fruit was stored upstairs. There was wine there also, and the senior girls persuaded him to bring him a bottle of wine in his wheelbarrow. They didn't get away with it.

Henrietta remembers 'praying for peace' when World War II broke out. There were 'prayers before school, during school, and after school, and we got sore knees'. The war also played a role in the only time she got into trouble at the college:

The Māori Battalion had their final leave, and they were travelling back to Palmerston North with a lot from the coast. We were allowed to go to the station and see them, and my brother was one. Our friends from Taupō said, "We have family too", although they didn't, and the sisters got all emotional, telling them they could also go. So, there were a whole lot of us, and we went to the railway station. We saw them off, and the

Hukarere Girls were there. We "paled up", decided we weren't going back to school and missed the bus. Instead of returning to school, we got a taxi and went to Hukarere School to take a look around, and those girls got into trouble. We got back to our school, and the sisters wouldn't have known if the girls had served us lunch – they didn't leave it on the table. The sisters came in and said, "Who is supposed to be here?" The coast girls were the ringleaders, and we were punished.

After leaving school, Henrietta returned to Mangaporo and started working for the local dairy company:

The Government was subsidising the butter fat and subsidising the company and then they stopped the subsidy, so the company closed. In 1943, I joined the WAAF [Women's Auxiliary Air Force] and was trained as a telephone operator in Wellington before being transferred to Ōhakea. There were oodles of Māori women involved in the WAAF. The skills I had acquired came in handy because I then came home and worked as a telephone exchange operator in Ruatōria until it closed in 1986.

June embarked on a teaching career:

In our time, to go to teacher's college, you had to have an interview by the local education board and pass a medical test. In my third year I became ill when at St Joseph's and contracted a heart condition. I applied to go and I failed my medical, so I had a fourth year at school. The Department of Education said I could teach as a junior assistant at the local school. I attended for a year, as a trial, and that's when I met Hirini [her future husband], and he wrote a letter to the authorities that I was not to engage in any physical activity. I then went to Auckland Teachers' College.

In the 1960s, both Hirini and June Mead finished teaching in primary schools, as the government closed the Māori schools:

We [Hirini and June] have a strong belief that the government may have incorporated them into the state system because nearly all of them had Māori husbands and wives in charge of them. In Hawke's Bay, for example, Raupunga had a couple, Tangoio had Whare and Maud Issac [another old girl who attended St Joseph's], down the road at Waimārama was Hirini and myself, further down at Te Hauke was John Bennett and his wife and up at Rātana Pā was Vernon and Mary Penfold. We were sending the pupils we taught off to boarding school.

Kaapua Smith is enrolled to complete her PhD in political studies at the University of Auckland and is currently the sustainability manager at Contact Energy. Her name may also be familiar from her foray into national politics when she stood as a list candidate for the Māori Party in the 2011 elections, and she is now a co-leader of the party. 'Part of the reason I went to St Joseph's was due to my nan [June Mead] and her sister [Henrietta Walker] and also because the school promoted the attitude that girls can do anything.'

Smith was only eleven years old when she attended the college, straight from kura kaupapa:

At the time, there was no year 7 or 8, and I was the youngest by two years in my form. The first form is when you learn to survive. My dad [Professor Graham Smith] would say, "If you can last a day, you can last a week. If you can last a week, you can last a month. If you can last a month, you can last a year. And if you can last a year, you can last five years."

Much like other pupils, Georgina Kingi made Kaapua compete in Ngā Manu Kōrero. 'It was through that, that I developed my confidence and public-speaking skills. The school gives you a strong sense of self as a woman, and you don't tolerate nonsense in the working world or your personal life.'

After having heard of her great-grandmother's experiences at St Joseph's (Edith Sainsbury) and knowing that she was the fourth generation of her family to attend St Joseph's, Hineatatu Dorset-Paewai is very proud of the family connection to the school. She shared that, if she has a daughter, she will most likely send her to St Joseph's. For Hineatatu, whose sister Marewa also attended the school, her first impressions of St Joseph's were not favourable. 'It was too strict, and I was naughty when I started because I liked doing things my way, but I'm glad I stayed.'

Hera Black winning at Ngā Manu Kōrero.

Alana Broughton with the Jock McEwan Trophy, Ngā Manu Kōrero 2013.

St Joseph's Māori Girls' College 1939.

The inspector's report for 1938 recorded a teaching staff of five (sisters Crescentia, Athanasius, Petronius, Carmel and Theresa) with one lay staff member who was responsible for teaching first aid, Miss Norman.[418] Forms I to VI were offered, and of the forty-eight pupils, thirty-five were government scholars. The courses included Christian doctrine, English, arithmetic, geography, history, Māori, hygiene, first aid, dressmaking, physical drill, singing, drawing and crafts. Students undertaking the academic course (in 1938, this was just one student) also took Latin, home science and mathematics, and those doing commercial (two students in 1938) were taught typewriting.

Inspector Fletcher recorded that the girls had trouble 'assimilating' in the subject of English and that for the younger years they struggled with Shakespeare, with a suggestion being that the pupils should be exposed to more modern plays. Arithmetic was recorded as being 'uneven in all forms' and for hygiene it was proposed that infant welfare instructions should be provided to the students.[419] The previous year, Apirana Ngata wrote to the Minister of Education, Peter Fraser, informing him that the college had raised the need for more Māori literature in Māori high schools:

> There is a need for an intermediate work containing selections of prose and poetry with annotations, and of a Reader in English containing extracts from the writings of Best, Buck and Percy-Smith. If you think the Government should take the matter up I suggest a Committee consisting of Messrs [Douglas] Ball, Bishop Williams, W [William] Bird (a very good Maori scholar), and myself to prepare the textbooks.
>
> I feel the time is opportune for a practical follow-up of one of the matters emphasised in the conference last September.[420]

One obvious observation about the school calendar for St Joseph's during this period is that it was littered with Catholic religious days of observation, commemoration and celebration. The most important days are listed here.

DATE	OCCASION
17 March	Saint Patrick's Day
19 March	Saint Joseph's Day
46 days before Easter	Ash Wednesday and the beginning of Lent
April	Easter
15 August	Feast of the Assumption of Mary
24 August	Feast of Saint Bartholomew
8 September	Feast of the Birthday of Our Lady
11 October	Feast of the Divine Maternity of Our Lady
1 November	Feast of All Saints Day
25 December	Christmas

Sister Marie Chanel (Dawn McNicol), Mother Crescentia (Kathleen Gibbs), Sister Mary Joseph (Martha Keogh) and Sister Mary Katarina (Theresa Mariu).

Saint Patrick's Day was often hailed with an assortment of green decorations being placed at the school, followed by an annual hāngī. In 1952, preparations for the hāngī began the day before, with pupils offering prayers to saints Patrick and Joseph for fine weather.[421] The following day, their prayers were answered with pork, mutton, potatoes and pumpkin in the hāngī, and bacon, corn and watercress boiled in the copper.[422] Following their meal, the day was followed with sport and capped off with ice creams and lollies.

Two days later came the biggest religious day in the St Joseph's calendar. The day of Saint Joseph. On this day, the students would have a picnic at Windsor Park and view the wallabies or go to Cornwall Park to ride on the boats. Form V pupil in 1963, Lillian Taylor, recalled in the school magazine how the school travelled to Windsor Park and the girls either went swimming, swinging, played tennis or read in the shade.[423] At lunchtime, pies, sandwiches and cakes were served and 'As soon as the shed was opened, there was a mad scramble and soon the stream was alive with fast moving "war canoes" and slow "chug boats".'[424]

At Easter a hāngī would normally be put down, with the possibility of an excursion to Wairoa or Waimārama, attending the local Catholic Church or performing the Passion Play to local Māori communities. For occasions such as the Feast of the Birthday of Our Lady, the pupils would often participate in a service at St Mary's at Meeanee.[425] On All Saint's Day, pupils would visit the Puketapu Cemetery. The school would also celebrate the feast day of the saints after whom the sisters were named. For Sister Athanasius, this was 2 May, and for Sister Crescentia, it was 5 April.

Children of Mary 1949.
Front row: Teresa Anderson, Rita Peni, June Bluett, Queenie Brosnahan, Yvonne Hawkins, Madeline Morrison, Ina Tuta, Jean Kelly.
Middle row: Lily Poutama, Mihi Hiini, Bunty Nuku, Katarina Manaiapoto, Monica Moke, Francis Box, Roha Stewart, Mary Anderson.
Back row: Molly Collier, Mei Kelly, Monika Marr, Teresa Mariu, Maria Martin, Sadie McDonald, Lizzie Peters, Victoria McDonald, Reginia Bidois.

A constant source of delight for the pupils was seeing an old girl become a sister of the Sisters of Our Lady of the Missions. Rita Rainsfield became Sister Mary Carmel in 1942, with Father Carmine writing: 'She is the first representative to enter the religious order (founded by the bishop for Māori women).'[426] Others included Sister Katarina Mariu (Theresa Mariu), Sister Mary Joseph (Martha Keogh), Sister Mary Chanel (Dawn McNichol), Sister Marie St Andre (Betty Otimi) and Sister Mary St Adrian (Marina Palmer). Another big event was when other students were either baptised or had their first communion. In 1948, Kataraina Maniapoto, June O'Brien and Beatrice Makiha were baptised and made their first communion with their saint names being Regina, Cecilia and Carmena.[427]

In the 1950s, four selected pupils would visit another region to participate in the annual speech competition known as the Catholic Secondary Schools Competition. In 1951, they were held at Hastings Hall.[428] Forms V and VI left for the debate, with Effie Edwards delivering the Impromptu Speech, Janet and Betty Hakaraia competing in the Oratory and Religious Doctrine category on the topic of mixed marriage, and Te Ao Tamihana in the Elocution category presenting on 'The March of Te Rauparaha'. The speeches doubled as an opportunity for other activities, including going to the swimming baths, having sandwiches, cake and drinks, and then meeting some boys from Te Aute.[429] Significant religious occasions were also observed, such as listening to the Coronation of Pius XII on the radio in 1939[430] and the canonisation of Peter Chanel in 1954.[431]

In 1951, former student Rora Iwikau visited the school to share stories of her trip to Europe, which included meeting Pope Pius XII.[432] After having seen the Pope during one his sermons, Iwikau, dressed in a piupiu, had an audience with the Pope with five fathers at the Gondolfo Castle, where she received one of his holy medals.[433] Before Iwikau returned to New Zealand, she was able to send small bottles of water from Lourdes to people back home, as well as go to the cemetery at Beach Head Ancio to find the grave of Sergeant Tionga Waaka, where she took a little soil to give to his parents.[434]

Chores such as cleaning, polishing, washing shams and counterpanes and weeding the potato patch were titled 'employments' at St Joseph's. Pupils were even expected to clean the septic tank, which was 'some job' and remembered as the 'day of days'.[435] Within the school, the teachers and pupils created their own practices to observe aspects of the Catholic faith. From 1930, the school instituted annual three-day spiritual retreats,[436] and, in 1941, a Catholic sodality (sisterhood) was formed. The president was Lovey Walsh, the vice-president Edie Kumeroa and the secretary Elizabeth Te Wake.[437] A Children of Mary group also operated and at monthly meetings it discussed matters around the Catholic religion and issues involving Māori.

The Children of Mary celebrated what the diary described as Memorial Day, when Father Frank Wall received a pledge from twenty students to abstain from all intoxicants for life.[438] The school diary recorded: 'May their voluntary sacrifice of reparation reap for this great work, many blessings to help overcome the terrible scourge of kai wai piro among our Maori people, and Pakeha brothers.'[439] Wall was of the opinion that 'At least one of three things will come into their lives when they leave school. Either they will take jobs of some sort, they will get married or they will follow a vocation into the religious life ... The abuse of drink will spoil any one of these three careers.'[440] He continued:

Passion Play.

A girl who drinks will gravitate from job to job, eventually becoming unemployable, and a burden on the community from which she comes. Drink poisons marriage … It ruins parenthood and dooms the children to years of misery. Bad as it is in a husband and father, in a wife it is the gateway to despair … As regards to the Maori race it is possibly the greatest evil; at least it is a never-failing introduction to all the others. Many of our Maori people find moderation in this matter extremely difficult … The girls who leave St Joseph's every year are good girls; they wish to become good women. In a very few years they will be amongst the national leaders of the Maori race.'[441]

In other years, sermons and religious instruction explored issues around adultery, mixed marriage, the 1951 Waterfront Strike, Marxism, Henry VIII, Martin Luther and birth control.[442]

Another aspect of religious life at St Joseph's was promoting the Catholic faith among the Māori community. In 1949, the students went to Moteo and participated in mass, as many of the people had converted to the Rātana faith. The school diary recorded: 'We prayed hard for the conversion of the people.'[443]

Perspectives on various social issues were also discussed as part of the curriculum and speakers were invited to promote discussion. In 1949, the pupils prepared essays in Māori on 'How Māori boys and girls can best fit themselves for service to their race and country'.[444] The Minister of Māori Affairs, Ernest Corbett, visited the school in 1951, stating: 'Here you have the opportunity of becoming great leaders in your Maori race. What is needed by your people is a good leader.'[445] At the 1962 prizegiving, the former Secretary of Māori Affairs, Jack Hunn, encouraged the pupils to adapt Māori culture to modern life, as it would enable Pākehā to acquire the culture also.[446] Hunn stated: 'Then it would become the national culture of two and a half million New Zealanders, not just that of 180,000 Maoris.'[447] He proposed that Māori carvings in stylised form could be incorporated into architecture and furniture and that tukutuku and taniko patterns could be used for wallpaper and floor coverings. Choral festivals could have Māori oratorios. 'If you cared to introduce and explain Maori phrases and words in ordinary conversation they would become popular with the Pakeha and pass into the vernacular of New Zealand.'[448]

Hunn continued to argue his case by advocating that a culture survives by changing and that 'If you young people freely accept the "winds of change" and welcome the modernisation of Maori life and arts you may live to see the fulfilment of a prophecy that in 50 years' time the people of New Zealand will call themselves Maoris, not Pakehas.'[449]

Entertainment and presentation of gifts.

St Joseph's Māori Girls' College Chapel

In 1956 the old school chapel was shifted[450] and was relocated to behind the Marian Block. An extension was added, so that it could be converted into an assembly hall and it became known as Rangimarie.[451] The foundation stone of the college's new chapel was blessed by the Apostolic Delegate, Romolo Carboni.[452] The welcoming entourage of the school had painted a large placard that read 'Haere Mai' with Josephine Toma chanting a Māori welcome.[453] The Head Prefect, Matilda Martin, gave the welcome speech in te reo Māori, followed by a translation provided by Leata Scanlon, with pupils singing 'Vivat Pastor Bonus' before Carboni was presented with a spiritual bouquet and a gift of poi.

Carboni spoke of being aware of the school before he arrived and that 'The Maori Priest and Sisters here present prove what excellent vocations can be hoped for from among the Maori people.'[454] Carboni's speech was summarised by Eileen Duggan in the 1957 school magazine. She reminded readers that:[455]

1. Opening of the chapel, 1958.
2. Prime Minister Walter Nash addresses the crowd.
3. Archbishop McKeffry and Prime Minister Walter Nash, led by the head boy of Hato Paora, Maurice Tito.
4. Entering the chapel.

A HISTORY OF ST JOSEPH'S MĀORI GIRLS' COLLEGE 135

Interior view of the chapel.

There is no pure race: that, by God's will races mix and mingle; that, following inclination or an instinct for self-preservation, they emigrate, reaching other countries, and become assimilated into them. This integration must not be pushed and must not be stopped. Here races, he said, mix in a natural, a supernatural, and a beautiful way … The next chapter will be titled Age of Transition.

The new chapel was unveiled on 13 July 1958.[456] The Mangatu Incorporation in Gisborne contributed £50 towards the new chapel.[457] The school diary records: 'In the afternoon, everyone assembled and waited in silence as the Archbishop [McKeefry] assisted by other Priests and Brothers blessed the Chapel. Immediately after the blessing, the Prime Minister Walter Nash arrived and all formed a guard of honour.'[458] Following this was benediction, then the entertainment given by the special party of girls, and also by the Māori Boys of Parorangi College.[459] The school magazine also notes that the head boy of Hato Paora, Maurice Tito, welcomed the official party with the head girl of St Joseph's, June Barnes, also extending a welcome in Māori that was interpreted by Teresa Wirori.[460]

Following the formalities, Nash announced the appointment of Charles Bennett as the High Commissioner to Malaya. Also in attendance was old girl Ani Konuke from Wairoa. Then in her eighties, Konuke had addressed Euphrasie during one of her visits to New Zealand. The following year, the Steiner family of Meeanee gifted a crucifix that was carved in Oberammergau, Germany, where every ten years the Passion Play is performed.[461]

Wives of Anglican Bishops

Kathleen 'Kaa' Bennett	Lady Doris Vercoe
NÉE CLARKE	NÉE EIVERS
TE ARAWA	NGĀI TAI, WHAKATŌHEA
1940–1941	1941–1943

Kaa Bennett was born in 1927. She had obtained a scholarship to St Joseph's from Te Matai Native School. 'They were wonderful times. I stayed with the Scott family from Porangahau because Mum couldn't afford to send me home for the holidays. I remember the A&P show that we went to once a year. We also used to go to the Tūtaekurī River.'[462]

Kaa also enjoyed playing basketball (netball) and tennis. Later in life, Kaa met her husband, Manu, who was to become the Anglican Bishop of New Zealand.

From Ōpotiki came the late Doris Eivers who left home in tears with Ruby Bluett (née Hughes), Pauline Koopu (née Ngamoki), Ewa Winder (née Edwards), Edith Sorenson (née Williams) and Teowai Collier.[463] Doris had to quickly adjust to a new routine. She, along with her peers, had to rise at 5.30 a.m. for the 6 a.m. mass. Friday was polishing day as well as laundry day. During the day, students were not allowed to enter the upstairs dormitories and parcels from home were opened in front of Sister Athanasius. Any money was handed to the sister for safe keeping, the food was shared with friends, and the rest was placed in the dining room cupboard below the staircase. Quoting the sister, there were times when 'a little black devil sat on one's shoulders' and the naughty girls were read out on Fridays.[464] After leaving St Joseph's, Doris became a junior teacher at Waiohau Māori School, before completing her teacher training. Doris taught at primary, secondary and tertiary level in New Zealand and Malaysia. She married Whakahuihui Vercoe, who became the first Māori Archbishop of New Zealand from 2004 to 2006.

Top: Manu and Kathleen (née Clarke) 'Kaa' Bennett.
Bottom: Doris (née Eivers) and Bishop Whakahuihui Vercoe.

McCormick's farmlet.

Girls in the old chapel (now Te Rangimarie Hall).

St Joseph's Māori Girls' College 1943.

With the outbreak of World War II, world events featured strongly at the school. Like other New Zealand schools, they expressed their support for Mother Britain and their allies in conquering Germany and its axis supporters. *The Marist Messenger* printed a feature written by St Joseph's student and member of the Apostolic Group, Queenie Higgins, in which she argued:

> At the Battle of Trafalgar Nelson cried to his men, "England expects every man to do his duty". He trusted his men, and they fulfilled their duty. So it should be with us … Fervent prayers should continuously rise from every home, morning and night, for the pagans and their faithful pastors … It is a thrill for young men to enlist as soldiers to defend our country, but what a greater thrill to enlist as soldiers of Christ, and defend the souls purchased by His Blood … We Maoris have a glorious past to look back on … During the battle of Orakau, a famous event in the contest between Maori and Pakeha, the brave chief Rewi Maniapoto, even amidst the overwhelming of his followers, cried to his enemy "Ka whawhai tonu matou mo ake, ake, ake!" ("We will fight on for ever and ever"). That should be our motto: Fight on for ever, fight on for souls, for God.[465]

In August 1941, the pupils visited Pakipaki, where a requiem mass was held for the deceased Māori soldiers of the area and memorial gates were unveiled with a Union Jack being hoisted and then saluted, accompanied with Māori Battalion gunfire.[466] The school was also host to several visits from Polish children stationed at the camp in Pahiatua, with the college diary recording: 'When the bus pulled up there was a mad rush for the gate as all the Maori girls want a Pole. The little Polish boys were frightened of the brown faces and ran away but the girls went after them …'[467] In September 1946, the students were following the developments of the Peace Conference, noting that the world was nearing a dangerous crisis as the conference was in its seventh week with no decision having been made and Russia acting as an obstacle to progress.[468]

During the war, St Joseph's took part in a concert at the Greenmeadows Hall to help raise patriotic funds[469] and, in 1942, the girls knitted scarves and mittens for the soldiers.[470] Life during the war disrupted schooling at times, as in 1942, when allowances were made for two members of the Māori Battalion to visit their East Coast kin at the college or when wartime restrictions prevented the pupils from an excursion to Haumoana due to a petrol shortage.[471]

At the end of the war, the Māori Battalion canteen named Rau Aroha visited the school. The truck was a gift from native schools and was described by the battalion as 'their best friend'.[472] With bullet holes on the side panels, Rau Aroha had endured multiple battles in the Middle East. Captain Charles Bennett and Padre Wi Huata explained that Rau Aroha would be permanently stationed in Rotorua as a memorial to the Māori Battalion.

Rau Aroha.

Royal New Zealand Air Force

Linda Mastny
NGĀTI KAHUNGUNU, NGĀTI TAMATERA
1979–1982

Jill Cotter
NÉE BLACKMAN
NGĀTI RAUKAWA
1997–2001

Linda Mastny

Jill Cotter

St Joseph's has produced trailblazing Māori women in areas where men have historically dominated. One example is in the Royal New Zealand Air Force. The relationship between the school and the air force dates back to World War II, when the Women's Auxiliary Air Force (WAAF) was formed. Initially, women in the WAAF were employed as cooks, mess hands, clerks and typists, but, by the end of the conflict, women were also performing a number of trades.[473] In total some 4750 women were involved with the WAAF.[474] At least two past pupils of St Joseph's, Kahu Koopu[475] and Henrietta Walker, were members of the WAAF.

Linda Mastny, along with her three sisters Donna, Tracey and Tina, attended the college in the late 1970s and early 1980s. A member of the concert party, Linda credits the discipline she learnt at St Joseph's as holding her in good stead. 'We were drilled and we practised and practised and that carried through to our other subjects. You felt like the whole school was like that in a good way.' The Dux of St Joseph's in 1981, Linda's love of the sciences boded well for her career path as an engineer. After completing her degree at the University of Auckland and, being only one of three female students in the course at that time, Linda had bigger dreams. She explains: 'When I was little, I thought I wanted to be an astronaut' and, aged twenty-two, Linda applied to two universities in America. 'I wanted to go to NASA and I wanted to do more study in aerospace. I was accepted but I didn't have enough money to go unfortunately.'

Undeterred by the financial setback, Linda still wanted to work with aircraft and so applied to join the Royal New Zealand Air Force in 1988. 'When I started the process of applying to join the air force, women were not allowed to be pilots.' Armed with her degree in engineering, Linda became the first woman engineer in the air force and climbed the ranks to become a squadron leader from 1995 to 1997.

She helped promote the air force to women and them becoming engineers. Nowadays Linda is an investment officer for Taupō Moana Funds, a subsidiary of Lake Taupō Forest Trust.

Following in Linda's footsteps is Jill Cotter (née Blackman), who has reached the same heights as Linda after being appointed as a squadron leader. Raised in Taumarunui, schooling options were limited and her determined mother knew that her daughter would attend a Māori boarding school. 'Mum grew up not learning te reo Māori and so she wanted me to go and learn it,' explained Jill. In the seventh form, Jill applied for the Royal New Zealand Navy and the Royal New Zealand Air Force.

A logistics officer, Jill's plan had always been to gain an education while in the air force, and fifteen years later she has a Diploma in Business from the Auckland University of Technology and has completed a post-graduate qualification at the University of Auckland. When asked whether she had been involved in any conflict, Jill tells of her seven months working for the United Nations, being in charge of 'Conference Row' (the demilitarised zone between North and South Korea). 'I think that was the making of me. I was in an 800-man camp and I was the only female there.' The ratio of women to men in the air force currently is approximately one to six; however, its leadership is working hard to address this imbalance. The ratio is even less when comparing Māori with other ethnicities. However, Jill is noticing a culture shift: 'When I came through, no one would ever do the haka. Now we have a Royal New Zealand Air Force haka and our Tūrangawaewae opened at RNZAF Ohakea in 2016.'

Jill's long-term goal is to become wing commander and then group captain. Perhaps under her command, there might be two other former pupils from St Joseph's, Jess Thornbush and Jody Toatoa, who joined the Royal New Zealand Air Force after Jill. Whatever the case, the contribution by St Joseph's to the air force has been etched in history.

Kapa haka 1982.

SJMGC Women's Basketball Team 1935.

Women's basketball (netball) matches featured prominently at St Joseph's, and the games were often reported in the local newspapers. In 1932, the school played against Scinde (Napier Hill) and won 28–6. The local paper printed: 'The match resulted in an easy win for St Joseph's, Scinde being outclassed right from the commencement of the game. The passing displayed by St Joseph's was very fast, every player keeping in position to receive the ball, and getting rid of it almost immediately.'[476]

St Joseph's regularly featured as competition winners. As of 1940, the St Joseph's basketball team had won the school's grade competition six years in a row.[477] One constant basketball rival over the years has been Hukarere, as this entry from 1946 proves: 'A sad day. Huk [Hukarere] comes out and walks over us. SJ where is your pride.'[478] Tennis was another popular sport. Concrete enclosures replaced the grass tennis courts in 1957,[479] with it being noted later that year that 'Tennis is the fever now.'[480] Another popular sport, introduced to the college in 1954, was softball, which '… is very similar to American baseball, the chief difference being the method of pitching employed'.[481] During the 1950s, sport was coached by Mr Bygate and former pupil Api Smith.

1. Netball Team 1952.
2. Senior B Netball Team 2000.
3. Senior A Netball Team 2015.
   Back row: S Clark, M Cashell, M Hoepo-Scott, R Keepa, M Houkamau, Coach Miss Prentice.
   Front row: J Smith, V Houkamau (Captain), K Bartlett, J Curry.

Quadruple New Zealand Representatives

Ramona Belmont
2000–2004

Tammi Wilson-Uluinayau
NÉE WILSON
TE RARAWA
1987–1989

Ramona Belmont.

Tammi Wilson-Uluinayau.

Tammi Wilson-Uluinayau and Ramona Belmont not only share the same high school, but they also have represented New Zealand in four different sports. Ramona has represented New Zealand in all cue sports: billiards, snooker, 8-ball and 9-ball, and Tammi has represented New Zealand in sevens, touch, rugby league and rugby.

Having attended a school on the North Shore, Tammi longed for a school that offered more to her culturally and she pushed to go to St Joseph's, with her brother going to Hato Petera. Her mother, Dr Jenny Te Paa, was the first to instil the importance of education in Tammi and, despite belonging to the Anglican faith, she sent her children to Catholic schools for their education. Tammi describes St Joseph's contribution to her understanding of taha Māori as being 'immeasurable'. 'We had a two-pronged attack: Nanny Rere [Unahi] taught the oral component and used whakataukī, whereas Mrs [Patricia] Fitzgerald taught the grammar.'

Tammi wanted to go to university, so, during fifth form, she looked for a school closer to her family in Auckland so she could 'acclimatise' rather than just spending her final year at another school. Tammi settled on Auckland Girls' Grammar, as she knew one of the girls there through netball:

It was a massive culture shock. Auckland Girls' is significantly larger than St Jo's, and we were sitting in an auditorium and there were well over one thousand girls. Seeing girls with blonde hair just freaked me out, and at Auckland Girls there were probably forty-seven different cultures, and the school is nowhere near as regimented as St Joseph's with the three hours' study in the evening. I somewhat lost my way at Auckland Girls' Grammar because I went sports mad. I attribute quite a lot of my academic success to the stringent regime at St Joseph's.

Once Tammi had completed her schooling, she enrolled at Auckland Teachers' College and Massey University because 'I thought that being a PE teacher would be cool.' It was at this time that Tammi's sporting prowess was starting to flourish, playing for New Zealand Women's Touch, runners-up in the Touch World Cup, and New Zealand Rugby League sides in 1995. In league they played seven matches undefeated in Australia, including three tests against the home side. 'In 1997 I was encouraged to play rugby because of the amount of money some of us were paying to play touch and league, and being a student at the same time was tough.' Once Tammi had completed her Bachelor of Education and graduated with a teaching diploma, she taught physical education at Ōtāhuhu College and, as they needed a science teacher in their bilingual unit, she taught junior science.

Tammi, who plays fullback, was named in the Auckland Storm for the women's national competition and was then drafted into a Black Ferns (New Zealand Women's Rugby Team) training squad for the World Cup competition the following year in Amsterdam:

> We had set the standard in 1998 – no one knew about New Zealand women's rugby. The first game we played [was against] Germany and we won 136–6. We did change the way women's rugby was played. England had dominated, and it was ten persons' rugby and so Darryl Suasua, the coach, set the standards in terms of fitness and skill sets, but we had to keep raising the bar because other teams had caught up.

Tammi continued to play for the team until the end of 2002 when they played another Rugby World Cup in Barcelona. All told, Tammi has never lost a match in sevens and rugby league and when playing rugby for the Auckland Storm. After over a decade in sport, Tammi encountered a few physiotherapists. 'I took a leap of faith for four years and did a Bachelor of Health Science, specialising in physiotherapy.' Currently Tammi is continuing with her studies at master's level and is lecturing a first-year physiotherapy paper.

For Ramona Belmont, her journey to St Joseph's involved her mother's sister, Tini, who teaches information technology at the college. Arriving in 2000, Ramona's family lived in Napier at the time and she attended as a day student. Somewhat of a child prodigy at cue sports, Ramona remembers:

> There were rules however. I had to do well in my sport and in my academic studies, so I used to do much of my study during the school holidays. When I was twelve and before I started school, my Dad suffered a brain haemorrhage and he nearly passed away. I spent four weeks away from school and hoping that Dad would survive. My attitude changed from that time on. I didn't want to let my parents down, because they were paying all this money towards my education.

On her attraction to snooker, Ramona recognises her father. 'I picked up a pool cue at the age of five. Dad put me on a beer crate because I was too short, and I played pool on the whānau table in the garage in Wairoa.' From age twelve, Ramona entered competitions and tournaments. 'I won my first tournament, but I had to cope with losing and getting thrashed. You had to be a good loser and handle the jandal.' Ramona was also a talented badminton player, and at the age of fifteen she had to make a choice between the two sports after she represented the central region and trialled for the New Zealand Junior Development Squad:

> What swung it for me with snooker was that Dad and I played together, and we played at the Cossie Club. When I won my first tournament, I wanted to know what was in the envelope. It was $100, and I said,

"That's $50 each." Dad said, "No that's your envelope, you can make some good money off the sport."

It was six years ago that Ramona last played competitively, wanting a 'normal' life. Her long list of achievements includes winning her first national billiards title at the age of fourteen, winning six Oceania women's snooker titles, representing Oceania at the World Snooker Championships and making the semi-final in two of the championships.

In pool she won the World Valley Pool Competition and won six New Zealand 8-ball titles. When opposing men, she has qualified in several ranking men's tournaments and has been placed in the top four on more than one occasion, including as the winner. After having played for seventeen years as a top New Zealand cueist, Ramona has travelled the world, including England, the Netherlands, India, China, Jordan and Thailand.

Nowadays Ramona lives with her partner in Huntly and drives a truck at the Drury Quarry, with a wheel bigger than a person standing next to it. Ramona attributes the way she is to her parents, and Georgina Kingi. 'I'm very close to my parents, and recently I donated my kidney to my mum, Maku, due to her having diabetes, and now she is no longer hooked up to a machine all the time. I also thank the school for the way I am.'

Music class 1999.

1. Senior A Basketball Team 2015.
   Back row: Ereti Kingi, Mrs Murphy.
   Middle row: Mrs Taufale, Marama Herewini-MacDougall, Phoebe Puru, Sage Butler, Areta Crawford, Mr Taufale.
   Front row: Waimihi Paki, Marjorie Cashell, Analeah Taufale.

2. St Joseph's Hockey A Team 1976.
   Back row: Gloria Winterburn, Ethel Parata, June Parata, Teresa Ngawati, Sandria Johnson.
   Front row: Vera Rameka, Louise Paurini, Amiria Tibble, Cheryl Marino, Adella Perenara, Jean Beech.
3. Tira Holland at Mission Cup, 2010.
4. Softball Team 1981.

A HISTORY OF ST JOSEPH'S MĀORI GIRLS' COLLEGE

1. Tennis 1952.
2. Swimming sports 2019.
3. Waka Ama 2018.

1. Estelle Sword competing in the javelin, 2010.
2. Athletics, long jump, 2010.
3. Athletics, running, 2010.
4. Athletic champions 1964: Ann Greatorex (Junior), Billie Wilson (Senior) and Ngaire Hape (Intermediate).

Apart from sport, another reason for leaving the grounds of St Joseph's was to attend the Napier Municipal Theatre. Students would attend the theatre to hear either the National Orchestra or plays by Shakespeare, such as *Twelfth Night* or *A Midsummer Night's Dream*.[482] Exposure to such entertainment was a first for many who attended, as the diary entry records: 'Although we cannot boast of having many real fans of classical music, all were enthralled by the beautiful music of Mozart, Dvorak, Elgar and Britten.'[483] In 1951, Forms IV to VI attended the Gilbert and Sullivan opera *Iolanthe*, with the diary reflecting: 'As it was the first real opera many of us had seen you can imagine with what expectancy and indeed curiosity we experienced the play.'[484]

In 1955, the girls attended a performance by the von Trapp Family from Austria, on whom the musical and film *The Sound of Music* was based.[485] The following day, the fifth form were invited to a Napier Catholic Women's League gathering where they were hosting the von Trapps, and the pupils were taught an Austrian dance, the Landler. In response, the girls taught the von Trapps some poi actions.[486] On the Sunday, the touring family visited the school, where again they were entertained with action songs, poi and stick games.[487] Such was the fascination with the poi that the von Trapps decided to introduce the routine to their shows in America, with one of the daughters, Hedwig, writing: 'Annette and Barbara do the small poi on the stage sometimes, when we feel that the audience will understand what we want to convey with it ... keep it up, but be sure and do not water it down with false elements and helps like piano substituting your beautiful singing.'[488]

One destination the pupils visited was the National Tobacco Company in Napier, where they were shown the process of manufacturing tobacco and where they were presented with a sample packet of tobacco as a memento.[489] There were annual visits to the Watties' cannery, trips to Westshore Beach, walks around the nearby Napier Racecourse (now Anderson Park), swims at Puketapu and walks at Sugar Loaf: 'We all enjoyed an invigorating walk up Sugar Loaf's formidable heights, and even though we all puffed and blowed, the view on reaching the top, was worth it. This hill is a landmark to all at S.J.C. for we know not far from its base is our beloved school.'[490]

Fruit picking was a common pastime for pupils. Hawke's Bay provided plenty of opportunities for the pupils to pick fruit, whether picking blackberries by the Tūtaekurī River or eating apples at an orchard. June Mead remembers plenty of Catholic orchardists and growers who would supply the school with produce. The school dairy of 1954 recollects:

> Some of the fortunate Form IV girls went to Pākōwhai fruit picking – I can imagine how many fruits went in the bag!! The rest of Form IV girls picked potatoes in our vegetable garden and seemed to enjoy it immensely. I should imagine they enjoyed the ride on the cart, more than they did picking potatoes. There appeared to me (as I watched them from the classroom door) more girls on the cart, than potatoes.[491]

Another escape from academic work at St Joseph's was seeing a movie. During the 1930s through to the 1940s, pupils would visit either the State Theatre or the Mayfair in Napier, seeing films such as *Little Women* or *Snow White and the Seven Dwarfs*.[492] With the new acquisition of a Bell and Howell Film Projector, students were able to watch films at the college.[493] They viewed movies such as *Men of Boy's Town*,[494] *Oliver Twist*[495] and *The Great Caruso*.[496] One film the girls particularly enjoyed was *Green Dolphin Street*, as '... much of the story takes place in New Zealand and concerns Maori life'.[497] Often educational films were shown, such as *Deficiencies caused by Food Nutrition*[498] and on one occasion, pupils were filmed performing the stick game.[499]

In 1950, the school upgraded the movie projector, which cost £85, thanks to the generosity of parents and friends.[500] In 1953, they noticed problems with the sound quality on the films. The problem was solved after an investigation:

> The mysterious behaviour of the sound box during the showing of a film has been solved. A family of mice found the sound box an ideal home and built a nest therein.
>
> Mama mouse settled down busily to raise her young family of five, free of taxation and rent problems, with visions of a cosy and peaceful old age. Alas for her rosy dreams! The nest and its occupants were detected ... The fate of mama mouse and her little family is too sad for contemplation. One can hardly forbear to notice however, that tabby, the feline member of our household seems uncommonly contented with his lot in life these days.[501]

During this period, it was very rare for the girls to venture much further than Hawke's Bay. One example of travelling further took place in 1950 when nine pupils and two sisters went to the South Island, sailing on the *Hinemoa* for Lyttelton, where they visited Te Waipounamu College.[502] Three years later, students were asked if anybody had been outside New Zealand, with one response stating: 'I was down the South Island only about a month before I came back.'[503]

Three members of the Vienna Boys' Choir.

Margaret Walsh.

Rangireremoana and Aleeta Hau.

From the Country

Margaret Walsh
NÉE BROUGHTON
TE ĀTIAWA, TARANAKI,
NGĀTI RAUKAWA,
TE ATI HAUNUI-A-PĀPĀRANGI
1951–1954

**Rangireremoana
Bernadette Hau**
NÉE HATA
TE WHĀNAU A TE HUTU
1954–1956

Aleeta Hau
TE WHĀNAU A TE HUTU,
TE WHĀNAU A APANUI,
NGĀTI WAI, NGĀPUHI
1984–1986

Margaret Walsh (née Broughton) came from Te Horo, near Ōtaki. As the only secondary school in the area was in Levin, the local priests, Father Wall and Father Durning, suggested to her grandparents that she should go to St Joseph's. Education was important to Margaret's family. 'My koro was Mormon and he used to say English was our bread and butter language. Therefore, we had to go and learn it properly. We could always pick up Māori, as they [her grandparents] were fluent speakers but it is too hard for us. I was taught Māori at school.'

Margaret's sisters, Betty Werata and Mei Broughton, followed her to Greenmeadows. They lived in Pātea with her parents and they faced a similar dilemma of having to commute to Hāwera by bus to attend high school. As Margaret explains: 'That was part of my journey. I had to catch the train and then a bus. It was scary travelling through the Manawatū Gorge when the slips came down. There were girls from Ōtaki, Levin and Wellington who travelled with me to the college.' Others who came from Ōtaki at the time included Betty and Janet Hakaraia, Janet Marino and Makuini Ransfield (née Johnson). 'Margaret Murray came from near Manukau and Hilda Parata was from Waikanae.'

Rangireremoana Hau (née Hata) was born at Te Kaha in 1937 and, although Te Kaha is predominately Anglican, Rangireremoana would later discover that her first cousins went to St Joseph's. They travelled by boat, dressed in their uniforms and were seasick. 'A lot from the coast went there [St Joseph's] because there was no local high school.'

Rangireremoana, however, was raised in a Ringatū household and as the youngest of nine children was told she was going to St Joseph's, which came as a complete surprise when she asked who the packed bags were for. After threatening to run away, she changed her mind after hearing that Major John Waititi was travelling thirty miles from Whangaparāoa to pick her up. 'I felt guilty because our people lived off the cream cheque and had no money. We only went to Ōpotiki once a year for a bag of flour and sugar. Other girls would get a penny for an ice cream; instead our money went into a pot that was never touched and was put towards food.'

The financial sacrifice for Rangireremoana's family was significant:

> Years later I went through Mum and Dad's papers that included their bills. I came across how much it cost to send me to St Joseph's and it was a small fortune. My mother went without and she had osteoarthritis and couldn't walk for a while. She wanted linoleum on the floor boards and she never got them. She didn't get new curtains or furniture and the family went without new posts for the fence and the roof needed doing.

Coming from the country, Rangireremoana found going to St Joseph's a culture shock and that screaming down passageways was frowned upon. 'The sisters would say "Ladies don't run around in buildings, they walk." "It is uncouth to see girls from the country running around, and you need to walk with decorum," they would say. They had girls from all walks of life, like the Home of Compassion, with children who were orphaned, and a couple of them were quite rebellious.'

Life in a dormitory was also strange. At the family home in Te Kaha, she slept in a single bed next to her parents:

> I was always frightened of kēhua and so my parents always had a light lamp. The Marian Block, at night, was quite scary and all the counter panes were white and you're lying there and there are all these rows of people breathing. Then the sisters go through, and it was worse with those habits that float out and all you would see were the white parts. We had steel mattresses. They were comfortable, but it was cold because there was no heating, so what we used to do was put our beds together, share our blankets and pile in together.

> You would get up early before the sisters came and you learnt to bring extra blankets when you went home for your one holiday a year. You would place your gym frock underneath your mattress and laid newspaper in the pleats, so they would look ironed.

Teaching social etiquette was another focus of the school:

> They taught you how to dress properly. There was a wash house and we had basins where we washed our clothes in cold water. You had to hang your clothes out properly so you didn't have to iron them because we didn't have any irons. You also didn't waste anything and would darn your stockings on a Saturday morning. Sundays were for going out and we wore two-piece black suits, a silver and grey tie, and a black felt hat. If we visited another convent or attended a concert, you took a black handbag and wore polished shoes and gloves. The worst job was cleaning the septic tanks. We would have to push everything

down. There was this long stick from the bush and you had to push it up and down until it cleared the pump, twice a day.

Dress inspections were carried out when playing sports:

> When we played basketball [netball], we had gym frocks and purple bloomers down to our knees, and before we left for our game, we were inspected. As soon as we left, the girls would pull up their bloomers. If we were caught or not to the satisfaction of the sisters, we would be reminded that ladies don't flaunt themselves. It was about being modest.

Bathing was also an experience at St Joseph's for Rangireremoana. 'We were allowed one bath a week and the water was heated with coal. We had to go outside and wash in those copper basins, even in winter. It was tough. There were over one hundred girls there.'

Kēhua continued to feature when Rangireremoana was dared by a collection of girls to creep into the pantry on the convent side of the school at night.

> Girls knew where the key was and when I was told it was my turn, I said no because there was a kēhua there. You had to go through the quadrangle, down the second floor (I also didn't like heights). When I said I wouldn't, they said I wasn't in their group any more. So I did it and it was the most horrible experience, thinking you would either be caught by the sisters or the kēhua. I put the loaf of bread I had stolen in the bottom of my wardrobe and one of my mates pinched it and ate it and I was caught by Reverend Mother [Sister Crescentia] who said, "What do you have to say for yourself?" I said, "Nothing, Reverend Mother." She said, "We were told that you went and stole some bread." I said, "How do you know?" and she said it was found being eaten by this person, and she said that Rangi Hata had stolen it. I couldn't look at the Reverend Mother for a long time, and that was awful.

> Sister Crescentia said, "Why don't you ask sister for some more food?" And I couldn't say anything because we didn't ask Sister Agnes, who we called Sister Scrooge, because there wasn't enough food.

Rangireremoana remembers Sister Athanasius when she would growl at the girl's for looking at the jockeys who trained on the racecourse opposite the school. 'Sister Athanasius would be at her window, calling us "hussies" and waving her stick. They were little fellas anyhow.' For fun, the girls would sometimes dance to the latest music over the airwaves. 'You could try and get a sister's radio, either in the morning or at night, when they went to church. You would go to the library, turn the radio on, and Elvis Presley would be playing. We would all be jumping around, with one girl being on the lookout for the sisters in the chapel.'

Rangireremoana departed St Joseph's with the acronym AMDG (All My Work is Done for God) at the forefront of her mind. She had passed all her exams for the commercial course and remembers that the sisters pushed the pupils to not just qualify but to pass in the 90 per cent range. Wanting to fly planes, she joined the air force and worked for the camp commander in a secretarial role before becoming the aircraft woman leading hand who looked after women in the barracks. After having had her family, Rangireremoana became the chair of the Old Girls' Association in Wellington with Piki Anderson as the secretary.

Following in her mother's footsteps was Aleeta, who attended St Joseph's from 1984 to 1986. After she left school, Aleeta worked for the Ministry of Education and had several dealings with Georgina Kingi. 'She [Kingi] was seconded to the Ministry of Education a few years back and one of our juniors who had also attended St Joseph's, Helena Davis, was in her team and Helena kept calling her Miss. Miss said to her, "Call me Georgina," and Helena said, "OK, Miss".' Aleeta was responsible for the new scholarships for Māori boarding schools, Te Puawaitanga, which was a privilege. 'My manager gave it to me because I was an old girl of St Joseph's, and the first year, we had a reception for the recipients in the Banquet Hall at parliament. I was happy to make her [Georgina] proud.'

	DUX		C.D.
1944	EMILY ERU	1944	SUSAN PALMER
1945	LYDIA TAWHAI	1945	DULCIE MIHINUI
1946	JESSIE MOORE	1946	MARIE PARAIRE
1947	ELLEN GOLDSMITH	1947	ROMA HEALY
1948	BELLA PAUL	1948	EMMA HAMILTON
1949	API SMITH	1949	MEI KELLY
1950	JUNE BLUETT	1950	QUEENIE BROSNAHAN
1951	EFFIE EDWARDS	1951	DOVEY MAKIHA
1952	LUCY CROSS	1952	CECELIA HODGES
1953	MEI UTEMATE	1953	PATRICIA KELLY
1954	ALICE WHAKAMOE	1954	DIANNE BIDOIS
1955	GABRIEL WALLACE	1955	POLLY NGAWATI
1956	PHOEBE SADD	1956	HARATA HOTERE
1957	ADELAIDE NGAROPA	1957	BETTY WERETA
1958	JUNE BARNES	1958	NGAIRE AMOHIA
1959	GEMMA IWIKAU	1959	IVY HEPI
1960	MARLENE WEBSTER	1960	EDITH WIPERE
1961	GEORGINA KINGI	1961	MIRIA TITO
1962	GEORGINA KINGI	1962	MARTHA MARIU
1963	GLORIA KAIPUKE	1963	CECILIA WHATAPUHOU
1964	CECILIA WHATAPUHOU	1964	GEORGINA O'BRIEN
1965	GEORGINA O'BRIEN	1965	VERONICA HURIWAI
1966	VERONICA ROLLESTON	1966	AGNES MORUNGA
1967	SUZANNE SMITH	1967	AGNES MORUNGA
			HEAD PREFECT
1968	SUZANNE SMITH	1968	NGAIRE EDWARDS
1969	LUCY KOOPU	1969	ALICE BISHOP
1970	ANI TIHI	1970	ANI TIHI
1971	SHARON LAWTON	1971	DERNA RICHARDSON
1972	SHARON LAWTON	1972	SHARON LAWTON
1973	LORNA O'SULLIVAN	1973	LORNA O'SULLIVAN
1974	SHARON BEAMSLEY	1974	HELEN ANI ROSE
1975	SHARON BEAMSLEY	1975	MICHELLE JACOB
1976	RACHAEL TINIRAU	1976	DEBRA TIBBLE
1977	MOANA MANIAPOTO	1977	DEBRA MARAMA MARSHALL
1978	{TANGIWAI TAPIATA / NANETTE WEHIPEIHANA}	1978	BERNICE REREKURA
1979	LOUANA FORSTER	1979	TANGIWAI TAPIATA
1980	RANGIMARIE WILLIAMS	1980	{LOUANA FORSTER / NGAHINA TAIAKI / GERARDINE RICHARDSON}
1981	LINDA MASTNY	1981	{LUCIA HOTERE / DONNA POMANA}

Dux Board 1944–1981.

Kaa Daniels.

CHAPTER SIX

Producing Quality Teachers, Nurses and Typists

Father Pat Cleary wrote of how he thought others perceived St Joseph's when he left the Hawke's Bay Province in 1951:

> From St Joseph's have emerged nurses, teachers and typists. Girls at St Josephs have been taught cooking, dressmaking and the care of homes and families. They have been fitted to take a leading place in Maori or Pakeha society. The culture of their own people has been maintained in the Maori language, arts and crafts, poi and song. St Joseph's basketball teams have won an enviable reputation and of recent years they have become famous for their mass marching and their drum band.[504]

The type of student produced by St Joseph's during this era was very much as Father Cleary described. The school roll continued to increase and, academically, nothing was lost with pupils continuing to excel in the subjects offered at the college.

Typing class 1954.

Clothing class 1954.

Api Hemi.

Mere Roha-Stewart.

Teachers

Api Hemi
NÉE SMITH
NGĀTI POROU, NGĀTI KAHUNGUNU
1946–1949

Kaa Daniels
NÉE MANIAPOTO
TE ARAWA, NGĀTI TŪWHARETOA
1947–1949

Heni Henderson
NÉE PAENGA
NGĀTI POROU
1937–1940

Mere Roha-Stewart
TE WHĀNAU A APANUI, NGĀPUHI,
NGĀTI POROU
1946–1949

Erana 'Bunty' Bricknell
NÉE NUKU
NGĀTI AWA, NGĀI TŪHOE
1946–1949

Api Hemi (née Smith) made quite an impression as a pupil and as a teacher at St Joseph's. As a student, Smith flew the Union Jack as a member of the marching squad in Wairoa, won the Red Cross Prize in 1947, won the Prettiest Costume award as the Snow Queen at the 1949 Fancy Dress Day, and came first in a writing competition for her poem in the same year.[505] As a teacher, Api was held in high regard by students for her skill in sports and in 1953 introduced the girls to the new sport of softball.[506] Kataraina Millen, whom Api taught, remembers her: 'I thought she was such a gentle, beautiful lady. We thought she was just it, a real model and she was groomed by the sisters. She could relate to our generation.' Api now lives at Temple View, Hamilton, where she has taught for many years at nearby Church College.

The choice of being a Mormon was made early in life when living in Nūhaka, as Api's kuia took her to the local Anglican church, which she found boring and instead gravitated towards the church attended by her neighbours.

Such was the dedication of her kuia to the Anglican Church that Api received her last hiding for not attending the Anglican Māori girls boarding school of Hukarere. As Api explains: 'I had seen the girls who went to Hukarere and they were tomboys. I was already a tomboy, and I wanted to change because I already got wood from the bush, helped to dock the lambs, milked cows, ploughed fields and bailed hay.'

Api remembers knowing when the school bell would ring to wake up the girls 'because the Taradale Clock was loud and it would chime at six'. A bright student, Api was awarded Dux at St Joseph's in 1949. 'I went straight to teachers' college at Ardmore. I always knew I wanted to teach ever since I was at primary school, and in my last year the principal wrote: "I hope she takes up teaching".' Once she had been awarded her Teacher's Certificate, her first posting was to Kōkako School at Waikaremoana, followed by a new school at Pukekohe. 'I then went back to see the teachers who taught me at St Joseph's and Crescentia and Reverend Mother asked, "Would you consider coming back here to teach?" I thought that was most unusual because they knew I wasn't Catholic, but because I knew the run of the school and enjoyed my time there, I said yes.' Api remained teaching at the school from 1953 to 1957 and was responsible for teaching te reo Māori and all sports at the school. Api was a natural sportswoman, representing Napier in what was then known as women's basketball (later in life Api became the manager of the New Zealand Women's Basketball Team).

In 1956 Api was approached to be Pania of the Reef in the Hastings Blossom Festival. Her recollections of teaching at the college include being the only kapa haka teacher and imparting routines that were taught to her as a young pupil at Nūhaka. 'I taught them the rākau and the Tūtānekai and Hinemoa poi.' Api loved teaching at Greenmeadows and would have remained if she hadn't been approached to teach at another school. Following her time at the college, Api taught at Te Awamutu College. Today, Api is a retired grandmother of twenty-five and a great-grandmother of twenty-six.

Raised Catholic, Mere Roha-Stewart was a whāngai by her mother's uncle and aunts, the Stewarts, from Ngāpuhi. 'They taught me te reo, and we were allowed to speak it at school, especially in the grounds.'

Original dining room, Greenmeadows.

Left: Monty and Kaa Daniels.
Right: Kaa Daniels at her debutante ball.

Attending a little school called Pōtaka, Mere's principal was John Bennett, the son of Bishop Bennett. 'He asked the ones who were going to secondary school if we wanted to apply for scholarships, and if we were successful, we would get two years of assistance from the government to go to Hato Hohepa. I got four years because if you worked well in your first two years, you got another two years free.'

For Mere, 'It [St Joseph's] was a different world. We lived in houses with dirt floors, and I was raised by a bush feller.' Living in a dormitory was also a new encounter for Mere. 'There were a lot of people living in a dorm compared to our house. You had blankets and all of these up-to-date things. Getting changed, you had to learn how and when, not to disturb people with loud talking and you learnt to change your behaviour.' An avid reader, Mere would receive a little magazine for girls called *Girls' Crystal* in the post from one of her pen pals, Joan Stephenson from Ramarama. 'I also wrote home quite a bit because we had time for writing. They couldn't afford to visit.' Mere sings the praises of those who taught her at the college, who had a high standard when it came to discipline. 'Every month we would have a little talk with the teachers. It wasn't a judgment day type of thing. It was a quiet talking to of people who could behave in a better fashion.'

Career-wise, Mere wanted to be a dressmaker but was told she wasn't good enough. 'I went to Ardmore Teachers' College with some of the girls from St Joseph's and became a teacher. My probationary year was at Hiruharama, and after that you could apply where you wanted to go. I ended up going to Ruatāhuna, Murupara and Minginui, all of the Māori schools.' Later in life, Mere joined the Volunteer Service Abroad and went to Papua New Guinea for two years, and she became an advocate for teaching Māori in schools. When the Education Review Office opened in 1990, Mere, along with John Hunia and Anita Moke, was responsible for primary schools and kōhanga reo. Given the role St Joseph's played in giving Mere an education, she sent her two daughters to the school in the 1970s.

Kaa Daniels (née Maniapoto) comes from Whakarewarewa in Rotorua. She spent time as a child between the farm at Horohoro with her koro and at 'Waka' with her father. With her koro not being able to speak English properly, Kaa would try to help him read. 'I would say c-a-t, cat, and he would pronounce the vowels in Māori. I would go into the bush with him and we would chop wood together. But when I was back in Waka, it was back to civilisation and you would dive for pennies and buy your kai.'

Kaa's mother was an Anglican and her father a Catholic. 'At Waka, the people on the right-hand side became Anglicans and the people on the left-hand side became Catholics, but we were all one family. My brother became a Catholic and I became an Anglican because we lived on different sides of the road. During my second year at St Joseph's, I became a Catholic.'

When living at Horohoro, Kaa had to catch the bus to get to school at the local Anglican convent:

> We'd get to school at 10 a.m. and would have to leave at 2 p.m. The bus driver had to pick up and drop off all the high school kids at Horohoro and then do the same for the workers at Waipa Mill. It wasn't my fault I was only at school for four hours a day; it was the system's fault.

Seeing others from the village going to Māori boarding schools, including her brother who went to Te Aute College, evoked a sense of how lucky they were:

> My stepmother was Guide Kiddo [Kiri], a tourist guide at Whakarewarewa, and she saw how I wasn't ladylike. I was a tomboy, hanging out with the boys and wearing trousers with a rope around my waist and hobnail boots. So, she said to my father: "We have to get that girl right because she's a bit too rough." My father spoke to me and asked if I wanted to go, so I thought I'd go there and see if I could transform from being a tomboy.

To afford his daughter's education, Kaa's father applied for funding assistance from Te Arawa and Tūwharetoa Trust Boards. 'So, I got an overcoat from Ngāti Tūwharetoa and a pair of shoes from Te Arawa and away I went.'

Luckily for Kaa, eight of her cousins from Waka attended the college, which helped her along the way. 'After my first year, I did well and then I thought for my second year, I had better stick my head down, do my work and get School Certificate.' For her final year, in 1949, Kaa arrived a few days late at St Joseph's because she stayed back at Waka to celebrate the twenty-first birthday of her cousin. Hoping that someone would save her a bed, one of the girls came out from the college and welcomed her back:

> We went upstairs and she put my luggage on a bed. I said, "That's where the head prefect sleeps," and she said, "That's right, you're the head prefect." That changed me again and I think the sisters chose me because they knew I was a rogue and could probably catch the girls. As a prefect, you had to accompany the girls to the dentist or the doctor in town. The rule was that there were always two of you.

After finishing her schooling, Kaa observed that many of the former pupils went to parliament as typists. 'St Joseph's had a good reputation, and they expected the girls from St Joseph's to go there. Most of the girls I went to school with became typists, teachers or nurses.' Kaa had always wanted to be a teacher, and she chose to go to Auckland Teachers' College. 'Erana Nuku and I went to Auckland, and the others went to Ardmore or Wellington. I went back to Horohoro School where I was taught and gained my teacher's certificate there.' Kaa ended up marrying Monty Daniels, and they

Back row: Ashley Blatch (2003–2004), Riaana Rameka (1990–1994), Elizabeth Taurima (1961–1965), Kiri Rameka (1960–1966), Whakiao Taurima (1992–1996), Anesia Taurima (1987–1990).
Front row: Irihapeti Tuhura (2008–2011), Heni Henderson (1937–1940), Charlotte Thomas-Taurima (2013).
Inset: Stephen Kolyvas (1969–1972).

returned to Christchurch where Monty (Ngāi Tahu) was from. While teaching at a home for 'naughty kids', Kaa was approached to teach te reo at Christchurch Polytechnic and had to develop a teaching programme by herself.

Erana [Bunty] Nuku followed her older sister to St Joseph's:

> I hated my first year because I was homesick, but I'm glad I stayed because I ended up thoroughly enjoying my years at St Joseph's. It was a family tradition going to St Joseph's, with plenty of Merito relatives going to the school. Coming from the country at Waiohau, it was a bit of a cultural shock for me, and Father Gabeours arranged for me to go.

Bunty recalls the pupils participating in 'area competitions' and loving her sports. 'The only sports we had were netball (nine-a-side), marching and Phys Ed. Sister Kereni [Crescentia] was the coach for netball, and I carried on marching after I left school.' For punishment, Bunty remembers a 'black day'. 'One day sister would tell us what we had done wrong. We had to confess our sins. You would get a black mark, and sometimes you had to polish the floors.' While at St Joseph's, Bunty completed both her School Certificate and Continuation Certificate before going to Auckland Teachers' College with Kaa Daniels. 'Kaa is one of my best friends. Sister Crescentia said, "Why don't you two go to Auckland because nobody is going there? I've already arranged board with the nuns," so I responded, "Great, we'll go there."' Bunty continued to teach until the age of seventy.

A HISTORY OF ST JOSEPH'S MĀORI GIRLS' COLLEGE

Chapel redecorated to meet post-Vatican II needs, 1970s.

Heni Henderson's father was a lay minister in the Anglican Church and, on the advice of one of her teachers who was a former pupil, she was sent to St Joseph's. Heni, the second eldest of sixteen children, was only twelve when she first attended the college. Not having seen a sister before, Heni's first reaction was: 'Ooh look at that lady! They were all dressed in black, all the time, but they weren't going to a tangi.'

Heni returned to St Joseph's as a teacher of te reo Māori during the 1950s. After some encouragement from the sisters, she trained as a teacher in Hamilton in 1975. Heni taught at Havelock North High School, Colenso High School and St John's College, before returning to St Joseph's and retiring in 1992. She has also been president of the Old Girls' Association. Heni also sent her daughters, Liz, Bernadette and Stephan, to her alma mater, who have also returned as teachers, with Kiri (Bernadette) currently teaching at the college. 'Sometimes it took me a long time to pay my bills and if I was going to pull my daughters out [because of the cost], they [the sisters] wouldn't let me. They never hurried me, and I just paid when I could.' In order to make ends meet, Heni sold tomatoes she grew in her garden and gave her family benefit book for the sisters to administer. Her three granddaughters have also attended the college. In 2015, Heni received the Benemerenti Medal from the Vatican for long service to the Catholic Church.

Ngaroma Ngamoki, Bridget Rika, Anamarie Rika and Ngaroma Rika.

Healey – Ngamoki – Rika Whānau
Te Whānau a Apanui

Ngaroma Ngamoki
NÉE HEALEY
1944–1947

Bridget Rika
NÉE NGAMOKI
1973–1974

Anamarie Rika
1999–2003

Ngaroma Rika
2008–2012

Ngaroma Healey had a big year in 1947: she won the senior Christian doctrine prize,[507] came second for the speeches at the Catholic Secondary School Conference in Palmerston North,[508] and, along with three other girls, went to Napier to learn how to classify a library and then started doing exactly that when they returned to school.[509] Ngaroma Ngamoki (née Healey) ended up at St Joseph's 'by accident'. After having attended Te Kaha Māori School, Ngaroma wanted to follow her friend Jean Corbett (née Walker) and was awarded a scholarship. Born a Catholic but having attended the Anglican Church during her childhood because 'they had more fun', Ngaroma won the first Christian doctrine award at St Joseph's in 1947. 'I didn't get Dux. I got the Christian doctrine award and I was disgusted because I wanted to be the Dux. I'd had enough of being the most religious person there.' One of the first activities the pupils had to do was 'mattress ticking'. 'Each one of us had to fill our own mattresses with straw. It had to last a whole year, and when we left for Christmas, we had to empty our mattress, so it would be ready to be filled again when we returned the following year.' As for returning after the holidays, Ngaroma distinctly remembered encountering a foul odour when she returned to school. 'My mum had made pāwhera – fish that has been hung out to dry in the sunlight – and it smells. She had wrapped it up in my bag with my clothes, and it smelt bad for ages. I never took pāwhera again!'

Ngaroma remembers that every Wednesday Māori was the language of the day:

> We had to speak it. We tried to stick to that, but there were times when we lapsed and went to English because a lot of the girls couldn't speak Māori. It was only girls like us from the coast, from up north, and the more rural areas, who spoke Māori. A lot of the girls from Rotorua couldn't speak Māori. Māori was my first language before I went to school, and St Joseph's reinforced my reo with the grammar.

The thrust of her education at St Joseph's was, for Ngaroma, to gain a vocation in life:

> The vocations available were teaching, nursing and commercial work. A lot of us had no say really. They [the sisters] would say you are going to be a teacher, a nurse or a commercial worker, according to how they saw us. They said to my friend Jean, you are going to do nursing, and she was placed in the nursing stream. A lot preferred the commercial area.

Ngaroma was made head prefect in 1947:

> By that time, I was at the stage when I could be a junior assistant, and I helped with the teaching of English with the new girls and was offered work there after my training. She [Sister Crescentia] offered me a job a couple of times, but I didn't take it on. As a head prefect my responsibilities included being in charge of the houses and more the religious sides of things. For example, we answered the mass in Latin in those days and we were called the servers. We had our favourite priest, Father Keane, a nice man, and we would see him walk in and think, "Oh good! We will be out of here in ten minutes!" Once a year, we did the broadcast that went to the Pacific Islands with mass sung in Latin. One of our great singers was Peggy Scott, and there is a memorial award for her.

Ngaroma remembers a 'kangaroo court' that operated every Wednesday in the assembly room. One of the sisters would scroll down the roll:

> The priest would stand up, and I was accused of pinching prunes out of the refectory because I was one of the girls assigned to do the breakfast. It was true – I spotted some prunes and collared them. My crime was I was accused of stealing, pilfering, some blimmin prunes! We were held up in front of everybody and we took our punishment, just the humiliation of standing in front of everyone.

On leaving the school, Ngaroma remembers having a rise in her self-confidence:

> I wasn't very confident as a person. It was sort of a racial thing in reverse as a child. Some of the Māori children would say, "Punua Pākehā". I didn't even realise I was so fair and that was the sort of thing I had to contend with going to school. I do feel that at St Joseph's I got a big boost in my confidence and realised where I was going.

Ngaroma then went to Ardmore Teachers' College, and her first posting was at Te Kaha.

After retiring, Ngaroma still received calls from whānau who would ask her to take care of their class while they either trained or had children:

> Then I was called to Te Whare Wānanga o Awanuiārangi when it was a seed. There were two classrooms, an ablution block, a one-room office and staffroom. I was one of the first five teaching staff including Matt Te Pou and Ruihi Richards. I was there for seven years and was responsible for the distance education for a couple of years.

However, as retirement yet again beckoned, Ngaroma was offered a contract to translate the Ngata Dictionary, and she developed a Māori language course for seven local schools.

Ngaroma's daughter Bridget attended St Joseph's for two years, 1973 and 1974. For Bridget it was exciting as her mother, aunts and older sister had also attended. 'I went with my cousins. There were huge numbers of girls going from the coast, mainly from Ōmaio to Whangaparāoa. It was like going with your whānau.' Luckily Bridget was able to make connections with those from the coast, as well as from Ngāpuhi:

> Mum and Dad didn't have a lot of money, and 99 per cent of us from the coast went exactly there with what was required and we got $1 per week for the tuck shop. There were four of us at boarding school: my sister Wai, myself and my two brothers. Ngāpuhi were like those of us from the coast, pohara. Mum and Dad couldn't come to the school events like the gala because they couldn't afford it. The girls from Te Arawa seemed quite rich to us, so they would buy lollies and we would buy toothpaste and soap from the tuck shop. If a parcel arrived, we would always share it, no matter how small it was. If you had money, you could also catch a bus from netball, but some of us would have to walk back.

Bridget has a strong belief that the Progressive Achievement Tests (PATs) the girls sat upon arrival may have predetermined who was in what course. 'When I was at St Joseph's, I didn't know you could carry on to university or that if you did, you had to do certain subjects. I thought our options were to be a nurse, a teacher, the armed forces or something commercial.'

Bridget's first day was memorable for all the wrong reasons:

> I got into a punch-up with a girl from Whakatāne. I had never been on a top bunk, and she had her name on it. I asked if I could have it, and when she went to the shower, I took her bed. She pulled me out, and it was all on. The sisters came running in and

separated us. Then we had to sleep in the corridor for a week, and it was scary. We were out there with our mattresses for five nights, on opposite sides of the corridor, and we could hear all the squeaking. I said to her, "Are you awake?" and she responded with a grumpy "No!" I then asked, "Are you scared?" and if I could sleep by her, to which she said, "No!" on both occasions, but I moved my mattress by her anyway, and we ended up best of friends, even though we called her Hoha [Gaylene Hohapata]. The sisters knew exactly what they were doing.

Although Bridget only spent two years at St Joseph's and completed her secondary schooling at Te Kaha District High School, she took away an understanding of the value of education. After having spent some time doing factory work and realising that she was smarter than her manager, she decided to become a teacher through the Auckland College of Education. She had her mum as a teacher, as Ngaroma was responsible for teaching about the Treaty of Waitangi. Bridget is currently the principal of a small Catholic school in Whakatāne named St Joseph's in Matatā.

There was no doubt where Bridget would send her daughters for their secondary education. 'My three girls, Katarina, Anamarie and Ngaroma, went there for the whole five years. The hostel hasn't changed since I went there, and even the carpet is the same; it's just been worn right down. I've often asked God if I can win Lotto because I will buy the college new carpet.'

Bridget remembers going back to the school for one of their reunions:

My cousin Trudy took back this big bag of munchies because we remembered what it was like to have treats while we were there. Trudy would say to the pupils, "Excuse me, are you from Te Whānau a Apanui?" After having asked several of the girls, she said to one girl, "Where are you from?" and she said, "Ngāti Porou". "That will do!" said Trudy and she asked the girl to wait there while she went to her car and pulled out six big plastic bags of chippies, chocolate biscuits and everything else under the sun. She gave them to this girl from Ngāti Porou, and she told her to share them with the rest of Ngāti Porou!

Granddaughter of Ngaroma and daughter to Bridget, Anamarie remembers not getting an option as to where she would study for high school. 'I was asked if I wanted to go to Whakatāne High School or St Jo's. I chose Whakatāne but was told that wasn't happening, so I don't even know why I was asked!' Anamarie was largely raised by her aunt and her grandmother, Ngaroma. As Ngaroma comments:

I was amazed how good she was at speaking Māori, and I was wondering about how she became fluent and knowledgeable. I realised I failed as a role model with te reo Māori because the thinking of my era was: "It's of no use to you, and it won't provide you with a living." It was instilled in the children that after gaining an education, away you go and make your way in life. When my kids were younger, with my vocation being an English teacher, and despite my husband and I being fluent speakers of Māori, we only ever spoke English to them. The only time we ever spoke Māori in front of them was when we didn't want them to know what we were saying. I feel I failed them so miserably, as my own first language was Māori.

Bridget's youngest daughter, Ngaroma, was going to follow in her eldest sister Katarina's footsteps and become a pharmacist. 'I got my certificate in health science at the University of Auckland and I was going to become a pharmacist, but I decided to go to Victoria University and graduated with a Bachelor of Commerce, majoring in accounting and management, in 2018.' Ngaroma became the head girl in 2011.

'There were two of us and she was fluent in Māori and I was supposed to be her equivalent with the English language. I was in the sixth form and some of the seventh formers didn't like it, but they got caught going to a party and were de-badged.' Ngaroma explains: 'St Jo's taught you to be proud, to have faith, and about being Māori. It also taught us that whatever you do, do it to the best of your ability.'

Te Ao Marama 2003.
Back row: R Rota, C Olsen, K James, T Metuamate, R Fellerhoff, A Grant, C Carlson.
3rd row: E Whaanga, C Campbell-Tawhara, L Paenga, G Wipaki, E Te Huna, E Keelan, S Togiatama, J Waihua.
2nd row: T Lenden, J Smith, N Pomare, E McDonald, W Taumaunu, S Carlson, M Savage, K Epiha, S Gardiner, F Harris.
Front row: T Graham, T Bruce, C Brown, M Kahu-Kuranui, T Nicholls-Olsen (Prefect), M Paku (D Prefect), T McCarthy, M Komene, J Maxwell.

Opening and blessing of the Marian Wing, 1954.

Statue of Our Lady.

Each year began with a familiar noise, as the 1951 school diary records: 'Once again the walls of Hato Hohepa echo with the cheery greeting and shouts of merriment. Introductions all round and the meeting of old friends. Suitcases were unpacked and new girls were given a helping hand. A few but a very few need an extra day.'[510] The next accustomed sound was that of bells, to which the new girls took some time to adjust.[511] In 1952, it was recorded that Sister Lucia knew how to wake the lazy girls – by rolling them out of bed![512] One of the first tasks the girls performed was to write letters to their anxious parents on Sunday.[513] (Two telephone lines were installed in 1952, one for the sisters and the other for the pupils.)[514] The first important decision of the school year was to appoint the prefects.[515] Their role was to be a 'formidable group of officers of Law and Order'.[516]

After almost a decade since the opening of the new complex on Osier Road, there was a flurry of building projects to accommodate a growing roll. Discussions began in 1941 after the roll had increased to eighty-two.[517] By 1947, temporary accommodation had to be found, and, by the following year, the school roll had reached an all-time high of 108, with authorities wondering where to place the overflow of students, as work had not yet commenced on the new dormitory.[518]

Built by Natusch and Sons for a cost of £1,512, a new science laboratory and dormitory were unveiled in 1944, with 250 people arriving to view the new addition.[519] (The government granted £2,400 one year earlier for the project and the Māori Purposes Fund Board contributed £500 in 1945.)[520] In 1948 a wash house was completed;[521] in 1950 the dining room was extended;[522] and a new dormitory with thirty new beds was finished in 1952.[523] In 1953 construction began for the new Marian Wing at a cost of £20,000 and was opened for Forms V and VI at the beginning of the first term of 1954, with rooms designated for homecraft (with modern equipment for cooking and sewing), commercial studies and dormitory facilities for an additional thirty-two students.[524] The outside dormitory had now been renamed the assembly hall.[525] The wing was opened with much ceremony.

Archbishop Peter McKeefry declared the wing open, with a number of the clergy making a formal speech, one of whom was Father Te Awhitu.[526]

Another speaker was the Inspector of Māori Schools, W A B Goodwin. He sang the praises of the college, commenting: 'We believe that the progress of a people depends on its womenfolk. The teachers of St Joseph's can have pride in knowing that they are contributing in no small measure to the progress of the Maori race ... Whereas more than 90 per cent of European children receive post-primary education, the Maori figure had been a great deal lower.'[527] His measure of success was Māori schooling having the same reach as for European children.

Eileen Duggan reflected: 'The Maori students are of all creeds and the domestic instruction received is shown in their homes when they marry ... Its teachers encourage the students to keep their racial pride and have themselves specialised knowledge of Maori lore and customs.'[528] Students from St Paul's (Hato Paora) formed part of the choir, and the girls assisted with the action songs. Following afternoon tea, the marching girls gave a display, and a dance was held between St Paul's and St Joseph's, with the diary noting: 'We are greatly obliged to Father Gupwell for

Home nursing, 1943.

allowing the boys to remain for a while after tea ...'[529] In 1963 the old barn was dismantled and work began on the new convent block and, three years later, a modern kitchen and steam laundry were added, along with a new hockey field.[530]

In 1944, the school had been granted provisional registration as a secondary school.[531] The move allowed the school to award Higher Leaving Certificates. It also gave the school the right to access a boarding allowance.[532] In a 1946 inspection, the inspector describes the 'real aim' of the school as being '... to give all pupils good training in English, Homecraft and Clothing',[533] reflecting the view girls from St Joseph's should be directed towards careers in nursing and primary school teaching.[534] This view was reinforced by vocational officers who would speak '... on the importance of girls occupying jobs that they are most fitted for'.[535] One pleasing development in 1946 was that an electric stove was now in the science room so students didn't need to travel to the Naper Manual Training Centre. The Aga stove had been supplied by Justice O'Regan after he made an appeal to readers of *Zealandia* and *Tablet*.[536]

In 1949 the roll numbered over one hundred and the boarder accommodation was full beyond capacity.[537] All eight students undertaking Form VI achieved School Certificate and were now sitting Endorsed School Certificate.

The objectives of the school were stated in this way:

> This school sets out to give Maori girls a sound post-primary education to School Certificate level, with adequate provision for a further year in Form VI to Endorsed School Certificate standard. Apart from its academic work, it aims at teaching pupils a good standard of living, dress and general deportment. For this reason, the girls take a very active part in the running of the House – they take turns at helping in the kitchens, the gardens and the laundry, they are responsible for their own personal washing, and they do all the housework.[538]

Of particular interest to the inspector in 1949 was the attention paid to social studies, or Māori culture, throughout the curriculum, leading the reviewer to remark that he was unsure where social studies began and ended.[539] 'So much of the work done in singing, when Māori action songs are taken; in art, where Māori designs and draft are studied; in outside activities, where stick games and poi-dances are part of the regular activities.'[540]

He also noted that senior pupils were researching their ancestors' canoes from the great migration and that the library had a good nucleus of reference books about Māori history and customs. On the subject of te reo Māori, and while noting the absence of an excellent Māori textbook (reminiscent of what Ngata had written about in 1946), the inspector penned: 'This subject is taken by most of the pupils and the treatment is liberal and interesting, being far more than a mere study of Maori grammar and vocabulary.'[541] Finally, regarding Māori, the inspector believed the school had made a wise decision to make the subject one of the most important for School Certificate.

On mathematics, the inspector encouraged the teaching of simple money calculations, the giving of change and the calculation of simple profits. The inspector was clear that he felt such skills would assist the pupil in later life, such as '... working out a family budget; the checking of accounts'.[542] Overall the inspectors were pleased with the school, commenting: 'The inspectors feel that this school must have, and will continue to have, a very profound influence for good on Maori people whose relatives and friends attend there.'[543]

Kataraina Millen remembers the school curriculum:

> The first thing you had to sew in dressmaking was the rompers for PE. They were ugly, and we didn't know what they were. They had elastic and looked like balloons. Fancywork was about how to crochet, how to tack, how to make doilies, and everyone made tāniko with the seniors teaching the juniors. Home nursing was taught by the Red Cross, and with mothercraft, you learnt how to bathe babies with dolls.
>
> We enjoyed it, and we thought it was preparing us for life. We had cooking classes, and we learnt how to preserve and we made the Christmas cake for our Christmas dinner before we left at the end of the year. We also learnt how to cook with electric stoves, yet we didn't have electricity up the [Whanganui] river. We had to help the sisters cook, and we would steal the eggs out of the outhouse and put them in the copper to cook when we boiled the sheets. We would eat the boiled egg, with someone watching the door.

One aspect of the school curriculum was the focus placed on the annual Māori speech competitions that were first held in 1945. In 1949, Father Gupwell from Hato Paora came to adjudicate, with twelve speakers in the junior section arguing the merits of 'The Value of Maori Education'.[544] Fifteen speakers participated in the senior section with the topic being 'The Part Maori Men and Women Should Play in the Development of the Country'.[545] The following year, the judge was Rangi Royal, with the junior section focusing on 'A Prominent Maori Figure Who I Admire', and the senior section speaking on 'What Role Do Maori Women Play in the Development of the Maori Race?'[546] The competitions in 1951, with Father John Durning as the judge, saw the pupils speak on 'A Maori Legend or a Stirring Event in Maori History' for the juniors, and 'Tell the Story of the Life of a Saint' for the intermediate section and 'The Evils of Drink' for the seniors.[547]

The speech delivered by May Utemate in 1953, which won the senior competition, was on 'The Maori of New Zealand'. An excerpt from Utemate's speech reads:[548]

With amazing aptitude, he has been able to keep pace with his pakeha neighbour who, nearly a century ago, prophesised that the Maori was a dying race. The years have come and gone, and with the passing each year we have seen the Maori advance more and more into the fore of the ranks of the civilised and cultured peoples of the world. We have seen him give in abundance to his country splendid teachers, nurses, farmers, and carpenters, and public servants. In fact, there is hardly an occupation in New Zealand in which the Maori has not entered.[549]

One speech, delivered by Lillian Taylor in 1963, sparked such interest that she was asked to repeat it on the radio, at the Christian Family Movement Symposium in Hastings. A number of papers and magazines also printed it. An excerpt of her speech reads:[550]

But when I see a mother with her little Maori baby, my heart is sad, as well as happy. It is sad because I wonder what the future holds for that little child. Have you ever stood outside a North Island hotel at 6 o'clock on a Saturday night?

Have you ever watched the crowd pouring into the TAB? Too many of my people have accepted the evils of pakeha ways – ways that lead, too often to borstal and prison … To you it is the Maori problem, but to me it is OUR problem – and to all the girls at St Joseph's Maori Girls' College who kneel at the same altar rails, as you do, and who pray to the same God, this sordid problem of drunkenness, gambling, and ever-increasing crime is an inescapable problem which dominates our lives … Yes, it is called the Maori problem because we have inherited it, not because we have caused it … If only our people could be inoculated against the TAB … This problem of excessive drinking is a new problem. It is only of recent years that Maoris were given equal drinking rights. Before that, liquor was seldom seen in the Maori pas and homes …

We could fight the armies of Hitler and they could not destroy us, but we shall be destroyed by the enemy within our own country unless all that you can do and all that we can do immediately … Do not ridicule us for having large Maori families. Help us to obtain and appreciate better housing. Do not allow Maori streets or ghettos to develop in the cities … How many times have you had Maori guests in your homes? There is no colour bar in New Zealand, but one is being created. I would not like to think that one of you would shift away if I came to live in the house next door. That sort of thing is happening in Auckland today … The Maori mother who fears for her child's future has real fears that a pakeha mother never knows – and I pray will never know … This is more than a speech competition. It is an appeal coming from those of us who have been given enough education, if not to overcome the evils that surround us, at least to see and realise their danger. We do not want the shadow of the prison darkening our homes and haunting our future.

Patrick Hickey.

Lillian Taylor.

St Joseph's Debating Coach
Patrick Hickey

The debating coach for St Joseph's during the 1960s was Patrick Hickey. After he opened a bookstore in Hastings, Hickey was spotted by Sister Augustine, who said to him: 'What about coming and coaching the girls at St Joseph's?' 'So I did and the team won the O'Shea Shield!' Describing the win as a 'great feather in the cap of the school', Hickey recalled the team defeating some of the larger schools such as St Patrick's and Silverstream colleges. Two members of the debating team were fifteen-year olds Georgina Kingi and Lillian Taylor.

Kingi did a narration on Lord Cobham, the then Governor-General, who visited the school and heard firsthand a performance of the speech delivered by the pupil herself. Taylor won the narration, defeating Bill Jeffries, who would become the Minister of Justice. 'In essence I wrote it, but she had to learn it and handle it and put a bit of life into it.' Hickey has seen both Kingi and Taylor in recent years. 'For years, I wondered what happened to Lillian. I eventually found where she was in Whakatāne and I wrote a letter. A couple of days later, I got a telephone call. It was Lillian, and she said my letter arrived on her sixty-fifth birthday, fifty years after she had delivered her speech!'

Debating team 1960: Georgina Kingi, Marlene Webster, Hariata Rewi and Anita Mitchell.

Member of the Debating Team

Hariata Rewi

NÉE TE AO

NGĀTI WHAKAUE

1957–1960

One former member of the St Joseph's debating team is Hariata Rewi. From Maketū, Hariata's parents wanted a better life for their daughter:

> My mother and her sisters were all old girls of the college. They had come from up north and Mum got to Taihape when the ground started shaking from the 1931 Napier earthquake. When she arrived, the sisters were waiting at the bottom of the hill to walk them up to the school and she said, as she was walking up, she could see the cracks in the road and the stones going down to the bottom.

Hariata can remember the cost of her education in 1957 being £75 per year:

> We were well taught. The top shorthand typing exam when I was there was government public service, junior and senior. You aimed for that and you could get any government job. We had commercial or general streams. I was in commercial, and it was totally different. You did the commercial exams, and if you were in general, that was for nursing and teaching.

Hariata also recalls being in the Passion Play, singing in the *Mikado* and playing Hinemoa with Marlene Webster playing the role of Tūtānekai. A memorable sister for Hariata was Sister Agnes or, as the pupils would call her, Scrooge. 'She worked in the kitchen, and we used to pinch food from the kitchen. We would pinch the loaves of bread and hide it from her in the copper.'

The best lesson St Joseph's taught Hariata was not to feel inferior to Pākehā and that Māori were on the same level. 'Being articulate and being able to express yourself was important. The sisters brought you up to a high standard as to who you were as Māori and as young women. They stepped us up from our homes.'

Going to and leaving St Joseph's also proved to be a traumatic experience for the young student. 'I had never left Maketū, and so it was overwhelming being put on the bus for the first time. But leaving St Joseph's was just as bad. The sisters looked after us well and the thought of having to go into the big wide world from "home", what we called St Joseph's, was traumatic.'

Lucy Cross, Dux of St Joseph's 1952.

St Joseph's excelled academically, and the school also won many national prizes. One piece of artwork from a St Joseph's student was noted in several newspapers in 1934. It was described as: 'A splendid example of youthful Maori craftsmanship and art work – a portfolio of drawings, photographs, water colour sketches, pen and ink sketches, even replicas in embroidery of the convent uniforms.'[551]

The piece was a combined effort of several pupils and was submitted as a nationwide entry to be part of the International Red Cross Conference. Of particular note were a pen and ink sketch of a Māori village, a miniature korowai, examples of kōwhaiwhai panels as examples of reed work, an elementary lesson on the Māori language and an essay on Māori medicines from various plants, which were all included in the submission.[552]

In 1940 the college completed two posters for the Centennial Exhibition: one on the history of the sisters and another on Māori missions. The Education Department sponsored a Regional Survey Competition among the schools in New Zealand, and the college submitted 'A Survey of the Catholic Church in Hawke's Bay'.[553] In recognition of their efforts, the Minister of Internal Affairs, William Parry, classified their work as Class A.[554] This was the highest class for 'work of outstanding merit faithfully carried out and ably presented'. The £4 award was used to purchase eleven books for the library.

Inspector reports constantly record the pleasant demeanour of the school environment and that, academically, St Joseph's continued to excel. The visits by school inspectors were often described as 'an ordeal', second only to the annual flu injections. Comments found in the diary leave nothing to the imagination. In 1952 the diary reads 'None of us can truly say we are dreadfully sorry'[555] when it was reported that the inspectors were staying only one night instead of the planned two, and in 1959 the diary records the 'pain' of a visit by the inspectors.[556]

The room where the girls sat their exams became known as the 'execution room'.[557] Studying for exams was a focus for pupils, with some rising as early as 5 a.m.[558] The following passage refers to home nursing exams: '... the period before school started for the day was employed in last-minute cram "refreshers", and the school corridor looked very much like a casualty ward with heavily swathed "patients" in the last stages of life, and blessed Florence Nightingales administering, none too gently, however, to their sorely afflicted persons.'[559]

A HISTORY OF ST JOSEPH'S MĀORI GIRLS' COLLEGE

Pupils sat a number of exams, ranging from First Aid Certificates, Public Service exams, Trinity College London exams, Maori Interpreter's Licence and School Certificate. In 1933 Lilly Boyce finished top of the Hawke's Bay in first aid, with all girls passing and sixteen of the eighteen honours falling to pupils at St Joseph's.[560] The same year, those sitting the Junior, Preparatory and Higher Local Theory Music Examination achieved high honours.[561] Two of those students, Agnes Goldsmith and Peggy Scott, received 100 per cent.[562]

Pupils who excelled were awarded various prizes: the local Napier Chamber of Commerce presented certificates for commercial exams;[563] Te Arawa Trust Board awarded £25 to Lucy Cross for obtaining the highest marks in the 1951 School Certificate results among Te Arawa descendants;[564] Ngaire Makoare won the Ngarimu Essay Competition among all Māori schools in 1955;[565] and in 1957 the Red Cross presented the school with the Sybill Nathan Cup for having the highest average of honours in their examinations for the third time in the previous five years.[566] All 135 pupils who sat the Red Cross exam passed, with Wiki Kapu receiving 100 per cent in both the oral and written examinations.[567]

At times, St Joseph's admitted girls who were not of Māori descent. One example is Esther Fonofehi, who arrived from Tonga in 1955.[568] The girls found her background of great interest and she fielded many questions, the pupils speaking the few Tongan words they knew,[569] with Esther reciprocating by entertaining with some Tongan songs and dances.[570] Esther's only complaint was the cold weather, and she found it fascinating that girls did not wear their blazers. Esther would later comment that, being so far away from home, she spent her term breaks with Marian Heke.[571]

Past pupils 1956–1960 at the Jubilee.

Lexia Puna and Winnie Spooner.

Pupils from Ngāti Kahungunu

Winnie te reo Spooner
NÉE RIKI
NGĀTI KAHUNGUNU, RONGOWHAKAATA,
NGĀTI TŪWHARETOA, NGĀI TAHU
1949–1952

Lexia Puna
NÉE KAUKAU
NGĀTI KAHUNGUNU
1953–1956

Winnie Spooner attended school at Puketapu before going to St Joseph's:

> During those school years there was a Marist Priest, Father Cleary, who visited our home. I was with a friend and all these girls came out on Marine Parade. I asked my friend, "Where are those girls from?" and she told me: "St Joseph's". I thought I wouldn't mind going to that school and so when I next saw Father Cleary, I asked him if he knew about the school, which he did of course, and he then said, "Let's do something about it." A few weeks, later I met him, and he asked if I was still interested in going. I explained to him that I wasn't a Catholic, to which he said, "That doesn't matter. We don't look at things like that." My mother knew nothing about it until a prospectus arrived in the post.

As Winnie would learn, her grandmother, Amiria Raihania Waipapa, attended the school when it was on Napier Hill. With aspirations of participating in the school marching squad, Winnie recalls never having enough to eat and being cold due to the lack of heaters, with girls either dancing or performing hand games to keep warm.

> Early morning on certain days the baker would turn up in his van to the door, and he would put the bread into these big baskets, and we would say to him, "Have you got a

spare one?" and he'd look at us, laugh, and say, "Why not." He would throw us half a barracouta, and he would cut it all up while we were working.

Getting up at 5.30 a.m. to be ready by 6 a.m. was a struggle, with Winnie, along with twelve girls who were also non-Catholic, fulfilling the morning duties while the other girls attended mass. 'Some of us protested from obeying the rules. Their parents were called in and when they came out of their meeting with the sisters, we all enquired what had happened. Their response was that you do as the Romans do, otherwise go! The mothers had pleaded with the sisters to give their daughters another chance.'

Describing her time as a 'life of learning', Winnie thought that the sisters were better than public teachers because they had the time to listen to you. When asked about expectations from attending St Joseph's, Winnie comments: 'You were more or less born to produce children, to be a good wife, a good mother and your duty in life was to look after the house and the home. You had only ever had three careers in the college: teachers, nurses and administrators.' Another profession was becoming a sister, and three students did so after they had completed their schooling, which Winnie described as 'quite a shock'. Winnie was able to achieve her dream of being a marcher, and she travelled to Palmerston North and Napier. In 1994 Winnie's granddaughters, Michelle and Sheridan Spooner, attended St Joseph's.

Lexia Puna, like Winnie, also undertook her primary schooling at the local Puketapu School. 'I thought I would end up going to Napier Girls' High, but Mum told me I was going to St Joseph's. I didn't even know where it was, and when I got there, I'd watch the traffic go by and looked for trucks that may have been driven by my dad or my uncles.' Lexia, like Winnie, was not a Catholic, and her grandmother, Waimiraka Nepata, had attended St Joseph's when it was on the hill.

> Home economics really interested me, and I learnt a lot of things about cooking. One of our puddings that we didn't like was called frog legs, and I soon learnt it was sago. Working in the kitchen prepared me later in my life because I was involved in a lot of catering, cooking for the hospitals, and the skills I picked up all stem back to here. All I remember was "Wow!" when I become a mother and I am going to be a good mother because I had learnt all these things.

Another skill Lexia developed at St Joseph's was caring for the elderly. 'In the winter evenings, I would fill up Sister Athanasius's hot water bottle and I would follow her and stand at her bedroom door. That was my job, and I enjoyed looking after her. When I left school, I went to the Waikato to train as a nurse there.' Such was her experience at St Joseph's that Lexia sent her daughters Monica (1974–1976) and Delwyn (1975–1977) to the college:

> My husband at the time was suffering with cancer and died. One of my daughters left abruptly, with Georgina [Kingi] saying to me that she felt the sister in charge didn't understand the stress she was going through. The sisters brought my daughters and their friends to the tangi and eighteen months after that, my third daughter died suddenly, and still the school supported our whānau through that trying time.

Marching, 1959.

Marching

Marching was a regular feature of life at St Joseph's, with the pupils being taken for practice, displays and competitions with their marching instructor and one of their 'best friends', A D Lynch.⁵⁷² Dressed in scarlet tunics with white-peaked caps and gauntlets, the girls performed in front of six thousand people at McLean Park for the North Island Championships. A newspaper wrote:

> The girls, to the accompaniment of their eight drum majors and the Technical Band, gave a faultless display of rhythm and precision, the 80 taking part moving as one identity. Perfect dressing when marching, both in column and in line abreast, a brisk marching pace and a swing of the arm to please the eye of the most exacting regular Army Sergeant-Major were some of the characteristics of the impressive sight.⁵⁷³

The departure of Lynch from Hawke's Bay to Palmerston North did not prevent the marching tutor from continuing to lead the girls in 1947,⁵⁷⁴ and in 1951 the marchers travelled by railcar and the drummers by private car to Palmerston North to perform.⁵⁷⁵ Such was the standard performed by the St Joseph's Marching Girls that Lynch at one stage brought with him two American women to film both their marching and some action songs with the poi.⁵⁷⁶ In 1955 the marching squad performed at the Blossom Festival and in Wairoa to help raise money for the local swimming baths.⁵⁷⁷ After taking the railcar to visit Wairoa, the squad took part in the Trooping of the Colour Ceremony with the Wairoa Girls' Marching Team and the Wairoa Cadet in front of 15,000 people. A newspaper reported that the school was 'remarkably well trained' and '… were undoubtedly the attraction of the afternoon'.[578] In April 1964, 'Papa Lynch' died after twenty-four years of service to the school, with Bernadette Henderson of Form VI writing in the school magazine: 'To the girls of the college he was more than just a marching teacher. He was an adviser to whom all looked for guidance.'[579]

Mere Roha-Stewart remembers marching as a pupil under the guidance of Mr Lynch. 'He was marvellous. He taught us how to get in line, how to listen to the different instructions, how to turn around, how to form patterns. Mill on the floss was one such pattern, and it was like a moving wheel.' Amiria Tapa retells one incident that has stayed with her ever since. 'I can remember one of the pupils having an epileptic fit while we were marching in a figure eight. We just marched over her. She was from the coast. Then the sisters just dragged her off.' Papa Lynch's son, Lynch Junior, took over the marching training after 1964.

1. 'Papa' Lynch.
2. Marching, 1950s.

Show Day, 1950s.

Life at St Joseph's was not all work and no play. One humorous incident took place in 1953 when one pupil put salt in the tea urn rather than sugar. Much to the pleasure of the students, the tea was poured down the drain and they were given cocoa. The diary records: 'A mishap is so unusual at St Joseph's that I have a sneaking feeling that many of our more adventurous comrades are quite delighted and are filled with wicked glee when incidents such as the one here told, occurs. Girls will be girls!!! – a salt will be salt!!!'[580]

Pupils always looked forward to the annual fancy dress balls. In June, 1959, the school diary reads:

Everyone is hustling and bustling about. Someone has pricked her finger with a needle and given a lovely howl. Paper is flying all over the place and material lying all over the clothing room table. What is the cause? Have you guessed? Yes, it is the Annual Fancy Dress Ball. Sister Katarina [Mariu] is supervising the decoration working bee in the hall. By 6.30 p.m. everyone is ready. Oh! The array of costumes and colours! They are simply marvellous. Some would make you cry with laughter, especially Dolly Niania's. We have an audience too. Sister Chanel played "The March" and the girls played for the dances. Prizes for costumes were won by Dolly Niania as a box of Roma Tea, Yvonne Cribb as a gypsy, Martha Mariu as Blossom Queen, Bibiana Marshall as the Daily Telegraph and Maureen O'Carroll and Kathleen Seymour as Twins in Towels.[581]

As far as balls were concerned, formal interaction with the opposite sex at St Joseph's was restricted to other Catholic boys' secondary schools and Māori boys' boarding schools. In 1945, the First XV from St Patrick's visited, with the girls entertaining them with the poi.[582] The school that visited the most was clearly the brother school to St Joseph's, Hato Paora, called St Paul's or Parorangi. The excitement of students of St Joseph's could hardly be contained when they visited Hato Paora when it opened in 1947.

The diary reads: 'A great day at last! Seniors leave very early for Parorangi. St Paul's is a beautiful school and the grounds are simply marvellous. Although it rained, we all enjoyed ourselves immensely and we were quite popular with all. We were a little sorry to have to leave but all good things must come to an end.'[583] A visit from the Hato Paora First XV in 1952 was a memorable occasion for the girls '… and although there was little trouble about getting to know each other, it wasn't long before everyone was quite at home'.[584]

The following year, pupils visited Hato Paora for the opening of a new block. The school magazine reflected: 'For days the fortunate seniors were preparing for the outing and it was an over-excited group that went to bed the night before the appointed day.'[585] St Joseph's girls also attended debutante balls. One example was in 1951, when the debutante ball was held in Napier.[586] Fortunately for the pupils, one of the old girls, Dolly Tawaroa, came to the school before going to the event, which the students were 'thrilled with', and she was dressed according to tradition – in white with a fur jacket draped over the dress.

The Blossom Festival, or the Hawke's Bay Spring Show (forerunner to the Royal Agricultural and Pastoral Show), was another event students looked forward to. In 1952 the girls were excited at the prospect of wearing civvies and enjoying the sideshows such as stalls, dodgems and the 'Octopus' ride.[587] The wearing of summer frocks was welcome.[588] Wini Spooner recalls: 'When you get a bus full of St Joseph's Māori girls parked up to the Te Aute bus, Hukarere would get jealous because they had to wear their uniforms.'

June Mead also had fond memories of going to the Hawke's Bay Show:

> You didn't go in uniform, you went in mufti, and at the beginning of the year the girls would plan and design their dress and then sew it in the sewing classes. Sister Garry [Sister Athanasius] would say, "Well today, girls, enjoy yourselves. You will probably meet your future husbands from Te Aute College!" That was a big event. Hukarere and Te Aute would be in uniform.

For country bumpkin Rangireremoana Hau, the girls from the country didn't have stockings or nice dresses for their first Blossom Festival:

> We knew what to wear the next year. We were lined up and the sisters inspected the clothing. If the dress was too short, you would have to lower it. You had to wear gloves and shoes and our nails, faces and hair was checked to ensure they were tidy and in place. Some of the girls were trying to make a favourable impression with the Te Aute boys and some of those girls would be pulled up because they were flaunting themselves too much.

Hariata Rewi also remembers the 'outing'. 'That was the one time we would dress up and wear high heels and put on lipstick. The girls were stunning and we would get all the Te Aute boys looking at us.'

Another occasion to celebrate was when one of the girls' birthdays fell in the school year, as it would be acknowledged with a party or a concert. Jacky Gillies's birthday party was held at lunchtime and 'The tables were beautifully set, and the fare presented was like "Mum's home cooking".'[589]

Mother Athanasius.

Mother Crescentia.

Athanasius and Crescentia

Mother Athanasius
BRIDGET MORAN
1871–1967

Mother Crescentia
KATHLEEN GIBBS
1900–1997

As Sister Sarah Greenlees verifies:

> After the earthquake, our province leaders wanted to close St Jo's, and the parents didn't want to send their girls because of the earthquake. Sister Athanasius and Sister Crescentia went and pleaded with the powers that were, for starting up the school at a new place and if they hadn't gone and made that strong protest about closing St Jo's, the college would have closed. Those two women had such wonderful foresight for this place here.

The impact of Mothers Athanasius and Crescentia cannot be understated in the history of St Joseph's. They ensured the school continued to survive and flourish after the disastrous Napier earthquake of 1931. As the years from the 1930s to the 1960s demonstrate, the two main authorities and teachers at the college were Athanasius and Crescentia.

Bridget Moran, otherwise known as Mother or Sister Athanasius, and known as Sister Garry by the pupils, received an MBE in 1956 for her work at St Joseph's.[590] She taught at the Napier Hill site and transferred with the college when it was rebuilt at Greenmeadows in 1935. When she died in 1967, she had dedicated seventy years of her life to the school. The 1956 school magazine wrote of Moran:

> A West Coaster, she has the simple, salty wisdom of the Coast that goes straight to the point without preamble. Right or wrong, no way out of it, no watered down excuses! But with it all infinite patience, and love arising out of her long knowledge of the race … The greatest reward of her and her kind has been to go to the homes of married past students and to see them clean and orderly, with the children neatly clothed and happy and healthy.[591]

Athanasius seems from all accounts to have been the school's main disciplinarian, which may explain why some of the former pupils remember her as being 'grumpy'. June Mead recalled Athanasius as an elderly sister:

> There was a sad story about Sister Garry. She was engaged to a young man, I think it was World War I, and he went overseas. She got word that he had been killed in action and she became a sister. Sometime later he returned. He hadn't been killed, and he found her family and found out she was a sister and he decided to become a priest. One of the old girls told us that.

Both Lexi Puna and Kataraina Millen remember Athanasius taking them for dressmaking, a subject she was in charge of at the school. Lexi recalls: 'She taught us how to sew and that came in handy because I learnt how to sew all of my children's clothes, and they all remember how their mother made all their dresses with the same pattern.' Kataraina remembers a funny incident in sewing class. 'We had to measure our busts and Sister Athanasius would say, "That's why girls are fainting, they are pulling them too tight!"' Kaa Daniels also has a funny memory of the sister: 'She would look outside her window, and we would be sitting on the concrete. She would clap her hands and say, "Girls, get off that concrete. You'll get piles." We would say, "Piles of what? Money?"'

During the first term of 1954, principal Sister Crescentia was promoted to Reverend Mother,[592] and, in 1960, Mother Crescentia was appointed delegate for New Zealand to the General Chapter of Our Lady of the Missions. She was invited to pen the foreword for the centenary magazine of the school in 1967.[593] She wrote:

> In the annals of St Joseph's there are records too, of many notable exploits of former pupils, and while neither overlooking nor belittling any of these, my thoughts go rather to those noble hundred over the years from Cape to Bluff, often amid hardships and sufferings, but encouraged and profiting from the lessons learned at Hato Hohepa have raised Christian families where home life is a treasured heritage and where the search for happiness is not measured in material possessions … May St Joseph's go forward happy in the assurance of a dream fulfilled and into a future beckoning to even greater achievements without the loss of the characteristic culture that is best in Maoritanga but which can yet absorb the best of what these changing times have to offer.[594]

Sister Crescentia, Kathleen Gabriel Gibbs, also affectionately known as 'Kereni' by her pupils, was born in Oamaru and, shortly after, her family shifted to Christchurch. After having been

Mother Crescentia receiving her QSM in 1982.

educated by the Sisters of Our Lady of the Missions, Crescentia attended Teachers' Training College.[595] In 1933 Crescentia was appointed principal of St Joseph's and would remain in the position until 1960.

Both the Walker sisters, Henrietta and June, were taught by Crescentia. Henrietta states: 'Crescentia taught everything, including English and Māori. After the show in Hastings and if you lost or misplaced anything, she would say, "Your head is all mumbled up with those red cap boys" and that you had gone behind the buses with them. She called the boys from Te Aute "red cap boys" because they all wore red caps!'

On the topic of her qualities as a teacher and principal, Lexi Puna states that she found her to be strict. 'I would see her and the matrons that used to look after me during my lifetime. I used to sit there and think such and such she reminds me of Kereni, the way she used to hold herself and explain things. That was exactly who Kereni was. As you walked in the room, they commanded your presence.'

Hariata Rewi remembers sneaking out to the shops to buy biscuits and being caught by Mother Crescentia:

The shopkeepers used to phone the college and let them know we were down there. One night we came back and we jumped the wall. On the other side was Kereni and she stood there and said, "Go to my office!" We used to call her "the bomb" because she was short and because of her shape. When I first heard her called that, I was in the third form. We were fast asleep in our dormitory, and the next minute the girls said, "Here comes the bomb." I dived under my blankets thinking it was a bomb, but it was Crescentia returning from Christchurch.

Kaa Daniels and her husband Monty would take Sister Crescentia out for lunch and would visit her in hospital in her later years in Christchurch. 'I used to go and visit her at the convent. The day she died, they wouldn't let me in, and one of the sisters said, "This lady used to always come in and see Mother Crescentia." Eight old girls came down and saw her off.'

Sister Sarah, who knew Crescentia well, remembers:

She was a trained teacher before she entered, so she had those qualities that made her a good teacher, and she was very committed to the Māori people. She was firm but fair, and she was a very knowledgeable person. She was so effective with the girls, and whatever she was doing she was doing in the best interests of the girls. Crescentia and Athanasius were fired by the zeal that Euphrasie had for St Joseph's.

Another regular feature of the school year was when famous visitors would call and visit the school, often with an expectation that they would be entertained with a kapa haka performance. In 1950 two busloads of overseas parliamentary delegates from Canada, South Africa and New Zealand arrived, with the pupils performing the march 'Tripoli', some action songs and 'Po Atarau'.[596] That same year, the touring British Lions rugby team was playing Hawke's Bay at McLean Park, with the school being called on to perform a small concert. The girls performed songs of welcome, poi, haka and a marching display.[597]

Following the drill, two members of the side, Bill McKay and Grahame Budge, both former army commandoes, grabbed the drums and began to beat them. Before the bus drove away, the girls were positioned down one side of the road, asking for autographs and photos and singing 'Now Is the Hour'. A newspaper reported: '"It seems worthwhile to have come 12,000 miles just to hear you girls singing" stated Surgeon-Captain L B Osborne, the manager. "There is a beauty and grace to Maori singing that transforms many songs that otherwise might sound ordinary." He called on the team and they responded with Welsh songs, concluding with "Good Night Ladies".'[598]

Nine years later, the team toured again and was ushered into the assembly hall, where they were presented with poi by the head girl, Ivy Hepi, and the deputy head girl, Caroline Kingi. Many of the rugby players took photos of Indiana Kuru performing the long poi before the school marched in their squads of Rauhina, Te Aroha and Matenga, with the school band playing the English favourite 'Sussex by the Sea'. Reciprocating the performance, the Lions sang 'He Pūru Taitama E' and 'Haere mai', the latter being heard sung by the college to Ngāti Pōneke at the state reception at parliament.[599]

In 1951, the Fijian team visited St Joseph's.[600] The school diary also observed the relationship between All Black success and the mood of New Zealand in 1956 when New Zealand defeated the Springboks for the first time in a test series. The diary recorded that the pupils had followed the second test on the radio, writing: 'The N.Z. disease – rugby, has even contaminated the fairer sex, especially here at school.'[601] When the All Blacks won the third test and the series, the diarist wrote of the school's fundraising efforts for a new swimming pool: 'Several pairs of girls went selling raffle tickets around the district today and found the people most cooperative and generous because of the radio news!'[602]

In 1954, St Joseph's pupils were excited to attend a concert in Hastings given by the world-famous Vienna Boys' Choir.[603] The school diary reads:

> The morning's classes couldn't go fast enough, but however we managed to persevere, and when the buses finally arrived, the girls were out of school in a shot. The Vienna Boys were just what we had imagined them to be (small) but however we did not think that these small boys could sing as they sang. Every minute of that concert was thoroughly enjoyed, but (as usual), not long enough. Whoever applied the name of "angel's voices" to these youngsters certainly applied it well, for it suited them to perfection.[604]

Ten years later, the choir toured again and performed at St Joseph's. Form VI student Cecilia Whatapuhou wrote: 'Within seconds we were listening spellbound to the indescribably beautiful notes of the world-famous Vienna Boys' Choir, singing in our own hall.'[605]

Alamein Shoulten with Guide Rangi.

Pioneering Māori Air Hostess

Alamein Shoulten

NÉE PITAMA

NGĀI TAHU, NGĀ RAURU

1957–1958

Alamein Shoulten was the first air hostess from Ngāi Tahu and quite possibly one of the first-ever Māori hostesses. 'I worked for national airways and initially I wanted to work in ticketing. The guy there said, "Go for an air hostess job", and I didn't think they would accept me. I had about four interviews, and then I was accepted.' Highlights of Alamein's career include flying on the inaugural flight to Rotorua after the airport had been renovated and having her photo taken with fellow air hostess Maureen McEwen and the Prime Minister of Australia, Robert Menzies, which appeared on the front page of the *Sydney Morning Herald*.

Alamein's uncle and the eldest of that generation, Te Ari Pitama, became a Catholic in later years, even though her family were Rātana. 'He formed Te Whetu Ariki o Kahukura at the Catholic Centre in Christchurch and was well known for kapa haka.' Father Wall from the Catholic Church befriended Te Ari Pitama and was instrumental in the recruitment of girls from the south. 'Our whānau were the one whānau he wanted from Tuahiwi to be Catholic because my parents didn't drink or smoke.'

Alamein's uncle worked for Māori Affairs and said that the best Māori girls' college in the country was Hato Hohepa and Te Aute was the best Māori boys' college. Accordingly, Alamein was sent to St Joseph's and her brother to Te Aute. Her parents were fluent in te reo Māori, but she wasn't, and she remembers being criticised at St Joseph's:

You go up to Hohepa and they all speak te reo Māori and you'd be bullied because they would say we are like Pākehās. You copped it both ways, especially living in Canterbury. Mum's attitude was the Māori was not going to pay the bills and get us work. She was right in those days because if you had a brown face you were crucified in those days. Growing up in the Māori pā, the Pākehās used to say, "That is where the dirty Māoris live." It was terrible and it is embedded in the people here in Canterbury.

With the jibes Alamein received at St Joseph's, she only lasted two years at the college. Unfortunately for Alamein, she was also on the receiving end of some disapproval when she came back home to Tuahiwi. 'Out at the pā, some of them would say, "Who do you think you are, travelling up north to go to boarding school?" The neighbouring kids used to think we thought we were better than everyone else because we went to boarding school.' Alamein was not the only pupil to have come from the South Island; Hine West came from Bluff and was a girl who was 'white and who had been on the Muttonbird Islands', and there was Jaynie Solomon and Susan Reid.

The next school Alamein enrolled in was St Mary's and, after leaving school, she worked for an accountant in Christchurch before being placed at Māori Affairs. The skills she had acquired in the commercial stream at St Joseph's had come in handy, as she was employed as a shorthand typist and worked for Māori welfare officers such as Don Mananui, Fred Katene, Ann Delamere, Whetu Tirikatene, Frank Dormer, Buddy Nikora and Joe Hakaraia.

Alamein then became an air hostess and, after finishing with the airline industry, she became a psychiatric nurse at Oakley, Auckland. After having lived in Australia for twenty years, Alamein returned to New Zealand and was voted deputy chair for a Māori-owned farm at Rākaia, which won the Ahuwhenua Trophy for the best Māori farm in 2015.

St Joseph's performing for Queen Elizabeth II, Napier Wharf, 1962.

Queen Elizabeth II, 1970 tour, with
St Joseph's pupils in the background.

The coronation of Queen Elizabeth II brought much excitement to St Joseph's in 1953. The pupils decided to have their own coronation. With paper cut from the publication *Coronation Procession* and skilfully arranged greenery, they recreated the scene with a stool from the science room as a throne.[606] As Coronation Day dawned, buses transported students to McLean Park. 'With our own band looking magnificent in their scarlet and white uniforms, and our squad leaders strikingly and colourfully arranged, S.J.C. was turning out in traditional style to celebrate the Coronation of Her Majesty, the Queen.'[607]

A decade later, the students performed for the Queen on the Napier wharf and were among the crowd of 16,000 people at McLean Park to see the presentation of colours.[608] The Mayor of Napier, Peter Tait, thanked the school for its involvement commenting: 'I have already heard that Her Majesty was most pleased with the singing and was deeply touched by the farewell.'[609] During her visit, senior prefects from St Joseph's were able to join other prefects from Hawke's Bay schools to have afternoon tea with the Queen and the Duke of Edinburgh at Hastings Boys' High School. Form V pupil, Elizabeth Paraire, recalled being on the wharf with 3000 people to say their goodbyes to British royalty: 'Then came our moment – for six unforgettable moments we sang our Māori action songs and twirled our pois as the Queen and Duke of Edinburgh swayed to the rhythm of our singing and moved their hands in time with our twirling pois ... The memory of that glad day will be with us for many years.'[610]

A HISTORY OF ST JOSEPH'S MĀORI GIRLS' COLLEGE

Ani Konuke and Emily Walker.

Emily Walker

At the end of 1959, former pupil Emily Walker died.[611] She had arrived at St Joseph's when she was two or three years old in 1877 and she was eighty-five when she passed. 'Mother St Ignatius loved to tell how Father Reignier brought her in his arms to the Providence and how her father's people did not forget her (her father was in the armed forces) and would send her parcels of beautiful clothes from England.'[612]

Aged ten, Walker lost her sight and remained at the convent on Napier Hill, helping in the laundry where the introduction of the electric iron caused her some confusion. It would be during one of the visits made by the Mother Foundress that Euphrasie instructed the order to give Walker a home at the convent for as long as she wished.[613] Every Saturday, two of the girls would take her for a walk and, after dinner each night, the girls would read to her.

When St Joseph's shifted to Greenmeadows in 1935, a room was set aside for her, but she decided to stay in Napier, as she knew the place well and was frightened of falling over at the new college. One regular feature of the school diary from around 1940 was the annual visit by twenty members of the Blind Institute. Just before the Institute first came to the college, Walker commented that everybody else had somewhere to take the blind, whereas she had nowhere. Mother Mary St Therese replied, 'Well, the girls will invite them out here and that will be your visit.'[614] Walker was gifted a wireless, a gramophone and records from the Institute when the girls left their old site in 1935.

I Ō MAHI KATOA, MAHIA

St Joseph's annual radio broadcast began in 1932 when the pupils sang half an hour of Māori songs during 'children's hour'.[615] Held at the studios of 2YH or 2YZ in Napier, the pupils would sing songs such as 'Sancta Maria', 'Te Haami mo nga Tupapaku E Hehu i te Tapanakara' and 'O Sacrum Convivium'.[616] In 1955, the rosary was given over the radio in Māori for the first time, with Matilda Mariu providing an explanation.[617]

The St Joseph's Concert Party began initially as an attempt to raise funds. In 1939, £20 was made from a recital[618] and, during World War II, pupils performed at the Napier Municipal Theatre to a crowd that contained 'only a few Māori'.[619] At the end of the war, a newspaper article reported that the college performed at the Hastings Municipal Theatre with other artists assisting.[620]

The article observed that the girls had already been heard over the air, as almost a full house was ushered into their seats and with the proceeds of £80 being donated to the Catholic Māori mission. With the usual poi and action songs, the contralto voice of Rubina Kingi stole the show with 'well-merited applause'. The newspaper article also stated: 'The college girls naturally provided the lion's share of the entertainment and their brilliant part-singing and poi dancing were big features, but it is safe to say that the most appreciated of their contributions was the clever and fascinating stick game which literally "brought the house down".'[621]

This period also saw the sound of St Joseph's being recorded. Pupils would often become excited over seeing new technology, such as a gramophone[622] or a radio. The latter brought great joy to students as they listened to Kiri Kaiwai, an old girl, sing from Wellington the waiata 'Pōwhiritia' and 'E Pari Rā'.[623] In 1959, the school's first record, *Māori Love Songs*, was released and, in 1965, a second album was recorded that combined Hato Hohepa and Hato Paora.[624] The following year, Flora Edwards and Pukehuia Cotter won a New Zealand-wide competition for a poi composition.[625] Such was the reputation of the school at singing that in 1961 St Joseph's was part of an official visit of Australian reporters, who were part of a programme to promote tourism from Australia.[626]

From the late 1940s through to the 1950s, the girls were trained in Gregorian chants by the blind Mr Papesch. Girls were taught 'The Plain Chant', and he also provided the only records of the Benedictine monks singing in New Zealand.[627] Kataraina Millen remembers Papesch and that the Gregorian chants were 'lovely because they flowed sweetly and were more attuned to the Māori ear'.

At this time, the students' health and well-being was of primary concern to the school authorities. In 1937, owing to cases of infantile paralysis (polio) among Napier schools, the opening of St Joseph's academic year

Flora Edwards and Pukehuia Cotter who wrote 'Tenei Au Me Taku Poi' won the first New Zealand-wide Māori action song poi tune competition sponsored by the NZBC, 1966.

A HISTORY OF ST JOSEPH'S MĀORI GIRLS' COLLEGE **193**

was delayed until March.[628] Influenza reared its head in 1939, with thirty-six cases being diagnosed within the space of a fortnight.[629] In 1957 it was reported that many girls were unable to return for the start of the third term as they had contracted the flu, and those at the school who had the illness were put in the fourth dormitory, which became known as Ward Four (this was the first year the school adopted the term holidays, to align the holiday periods with other secondary schools in New Zealand).[630]

The routine for pupils at St Joseph's during this period was for girls to be taken to Napier Hospital early in the school year to be x-rayed for tuberculosis. During the same time of year, a doctor and nurse would visit the school to administer a series of injections, much to the dread of the pupils. Amiria Tapa remembers being given 'dreadful cod liver tablets'. Doctor Lee visited during 1953. The school diary reads: 'We are happy to supply the information that no deaths through pain have occurred'.[631] At times, the school would take a proactive stance on health care, such as organising lectures on DDT, penicillin[632] and tuberculosis, including screening a short film on the effects of the disease on the community of Wairoa.[633]

In 1935 twenty-one pupils sat and passed 'home nursing', with twenty going through with honours.[634] On the odd occasion, the students would encounter former pupils who were nursing at Napier Hospital.[635] One such student was Pare Koopu, who became a sister and worked at Napier Hospital, much to the pleasure of the pupils who saw her when they visited the hospital.[636]

The process for becoming a teacher involved being interviewed by a selection committee for entry into Teachers' College.[637] One of the first pupils from St Joseph's to become a teacher was Annie Lawson, with the girls praying for her on the day she sat her examination for her Teacher's Certificate in 1939.[638]

Te Uta Murphy and Rita (Marr) Coster.

Sunrise at St Joseph's Māori Girls' College.

CHAPTER SEVEN

A New Dawn

In December, 1964, *Te Ao Hou*, the Maori Affairs magazine, reported on a visit it had made to St Joseph's Māori Girls' College:

> ... like most of the famous Maori boarding schools, St Joseph's Maori Girls' College is a long-established institution with a very considerable history behind it. It is so old, in fact, that already there are at the school some great-granddaughters of early pupils, while the next reunion of past pupils, to be held in 1967, will celebrate the school's centenary. How does a school with such a long pioneering tradition behind it, cope with rapidly-changing modern conditions: with pupils who are in many ways so different from their elders, and with the modern emphasis on academic attainment?[639]

The magazine recorded that in 1963 ten pupils sat School Certificate, with all students passing.[640] For 1964, nineteen pupils were sitting School Certificate, four were participating in University Entrance and one was attempting Higher School Certificate. On the subject of music, the magazine wrote '... St Joseph's Maori Girls' College is best known for its magnificent choral work, and the excellent recordings it has made.'[641]

Te Ao Hou noted that, on leaving school, former pupils obtained good office jobs or became nurses, including dental nurses, or entered the teaching profession.[642] The magazine also recorded that head prefect Cecilia Whatapuhou was going to study at Victoria University, with former pupil Georgina Kingi in her second year of study at the University of Auckland. The article concluded that the latest Education Department report highlighted that Māori church boarding schools were more effective than state schools and that pupils at boarding schools were 'less likely to leave soon'.[643]

For the best part of twenty-five years, the Department of Maori Affairs and then the Department's successor, the Ministry of Māori Affairs, kept records of their visits to St Joseph's. The purpose of these visits was to report on the physical condition of the school, to comment on the 'nature' of individual students, and to keep a record of the study or employment the students embarked on once they had left school. Comments made on the 'nature' of students could include that the pupil was conscientious, suitable for university, a good leader, diligent, easy going, apathetic, unambitious, had poor English or a background that impeded their education.[644]

For those assessed in 1965, vocational options included clerical work, teaching, nursing or becoming an occupational therapist. For the following year, the list of potential opportunities was expanded to include general community work, missionary work, being an air hostess, working in either the air force or the police, and working in broadcasting.[645] From the notes compiled by the Department of Māori Affairs, Miss N P Witana, recorded about one student:

> ... this lass seemed to "have a chip on her shoulder". Of the careers discussed, the clothing trades seemed to appeal most though she was not particularly keen on the length of training in a factory, should she not be successful in acquiring a position with a private dressmaker. Her questions on air hostessing, beauty culture and stewardessing indicate that she is still to pass the glamorous phase which is typical among third and fourth formers. Other careers discussed included hairdressing, office machinist work and radiography ... [she] was actually more interested in finding out about the "pay" than the actual work, training or abilities required.[646]

Witana also noted that another pupil: '... has a longstanding interest in veterinary science work but realises now that this could probably be beyond her scope because of the average academic ability and subjects required. She would prefer outdoor work but after a discussion of the limited opportunities, e.g. research and field work, farm work, horticulture, herd testing and seasonal work, the interest slightly waned.'[647]

As late as 1990, the government, through the Iwi Transition Agency, was still keeping tabs on the families and career paths of pupils.[648] Records were kept on the occupation of the parents or guardians, the pupil's tribal affiliations, their fluency in te reo Māori, any convictions against the law, career interests and what subjects and grades they held.

Until 1962, swimming lessons were held at the local Tūtaekurī River or the swimming baths at Taradale.[649] One school diary entry records a typically hot day in 1956: 'The cool clear waters of Tūtaekurī, proved an irresistible urge, and many that afternoon enjoyed an invigorating swim or just the coolness of which they enjoyed sitting on the river's shallow depths, or on the banks.'[650] Later that month, one entry read that the girls are 'fish' and that 'Perhaps in future years we might see an old girl from Hato Hohepa in the Olympic Games, and when asked where she developed so well she will reply "In the Tūtaekurī River, Taradale, when I went to S.J.C."'[651]

Swimming competitions were held annually. Some competition categories in 1933 included the 'biggest splash', a 'tub race', an 'egg and spoon race' and a 'Maori canoe' race.[652] For many years, the focus of St Joseph's fundraising was on building their own swimming baths. In 1955 Mother Provincial presented £150 towards the cause[653] and that same year, Shelley Mann, the future gold medal winner at the Melbourne Olympics, and Pat McCormick, the diver who won four gold medals at the 1952 Helsinki and 1956 Olympics, participated in an exhibition in Napier to which the school's best swimmers were invited.[654] So inspired were the pupils that it provided added motivation to have their own swimming baths.

The St Joseph's Queen Carnival of 1958 was another attempt to raise money for the pool, with 'Princess' Adrienne Semmens winning the coveted crown. On Gala Day a coronation was held as 'The procession set off, led by two standard bearers who were followed by court attendants, lord chancellors, and heralds. Next in the procession, came the official bearers of the Crown, Sceptre, Orb and Sword. Behind them were the princesses with their respective attendants.'[655] In 1962 the swimming baths (75 feet by 35 feet or 23 metres by 11 metres) became a reality at a total cost of £5,000.[656] Parents, pupils and benefactors had contributed just over £3,000.[657] The Māori Purposes Fund Board provided £250 towards the baths[658] with the Golden Kiwi Lottery providing a grant of £1,500.[659]

Fundraising events generally took the form of either a bazaar or a garden fête. In 1939 the fundraiser was held at the local Greenmeadows Hall and in 1946[660] at the school grounds and raised £220.[661] Initially the garden fêtes were held with all local Catholic schools in the area before being hosted by St Joseph's alone. In 1943, there were many sideshows at the fête, including lucky dips, skittles, a spinning wheel and an art gallery.[662] Despite the war-time rationing of sugar, there was a sufficient supply of sweets. A decade later, the offerings included ice-cream and soft drink stalls, horse and donkey rides and a puppet show.[663]

The organisation that was principally responsible for fundraising was the St Joseph's Old Girls' Association. During the mid-1940s old girls of St Joseph's began having regular reunions during the mid-year holidays in June. The first was held in 1945 with thirty former pupils attending, where it was decided to have an 'old girls' badge' and to establish a scholarship fund titled the Mother Annunciation Memorial Scholarship.[664] Reunions would include a visit to Sacred Heart to see the old site of the school, having an 'annual tangi',[665] playing college students in a game of netball and hosting a fête. In 1949, the reunion was formalised and an Old Girls' Association was formed.[666]

Thirty former students attended the reunion: 'With very few exceptions, every tribe from Ngāpuhi in the far North to Ngāi Tahu in the South Island, and every age group of girls in their teens to great-grandmothers, was presented.'[667] Hosted by Father Riordan, the Old Girls' Association appointed Archbishop O'Shea and Bishop James Liston as joint-patrons, with the Reverend Mother Provincials of Sacred Heart and St Mary Provinces of the Institute of Our Lady of the Missions to be vice-patrons. Elected officials included president Ani Konuke, secretary Ruby Wawatai and treasurer Lena Wairea, and they formed a vice-president and a management committee for each district. The reunions became an annual event and funds were sought for an Old Girls' Scholarship.[668]

The aims of the Old Girls' Association were:

1. To foster and maintain a spirit of loyalty towards St Joseph's college, pupils and teachers.
2. To assist in preserving, reviving and maintaining the teaching of Māori arts and crafts, the Māori language and to perpetuate the ethics of Māori culture and tradition.
3. To provide assistance, financial and otherwise, to the college.
4. To maintain and develop a deep sense of Christian faith and love within their homes and families, and to provide a Christian education for their children.

By 1954 the school magazine wrote that the reunions were '... now tradition and many districts arrange for representatives ...' with active branches found at Panguru, Gisborne, National Park and Raupunga.[669] Two years later, the reunion celebrated the careers of former pupils and listed sixty certified teachers, two homecraft teachers, one dental nurse, twenty-seven certified nurses, twenty-two shorthand typists and Bernadette Mariu who had joined the police.[670] (It was noted in 1964 that Martha Mariu was stationed at Army Headquarters, Singapore).[671] Branches had expanded with divisions in North Auckland, Taranaki, Wellington, Taupō, Whanganui, East Coast and Hawke's Bay. That year, £1,080 was raised at a 'bring-and-buy' sale at the school grounds. One novelty was the outdoor wireless that provided a progress report of the match between New Zealand Māori and the touring Springboks (with the hosts being trounced 37–0).

In 1964 the Association donated a large statue of St Joseph, which was erected on the college grounds in 1967. Wawi Paraire donated a carved shield called the Lynch Shield, named after the marching coach Mr Lynch, which was to be competed for annually.[672]

The year 1960 saw the appointment of a new principal, following the long service of Sister Crescentia. Sister Mary St Eugenia stepped into the role, but her reign would be short-lived with an illness seeing her replaced in July the same year by Sister Mary St Augustine.[673] Sister Augustine was no stranger to St Joseph's, having arrived to teach at the college in September 1950.[674] Patrick Hickey remembers the strong relationship she had with the pupils:

> She was sitting in a chair and there were five kids kneeling around her, another five standing behind them, and they were all talking to her. They all had to have a piece of her. Georgina [Kingi] has a photo of her on the wall of her office and when she has a problem, she will ask her, "What would you do?"

As in previous years, it was still a challenge to accommodate a growing roll. In February 1962, the Reverend Mother Provincial had to restrict the roll to 158 students due to the cramped accommodation.[675] In October 1963, the old barn was dismantled to make way for the new convent block and, at the beginning of the third term that year, a new administration block and offices were opened.[676] In 1965, a new cool storage room with a deep freeze was built, and in June, the sisters

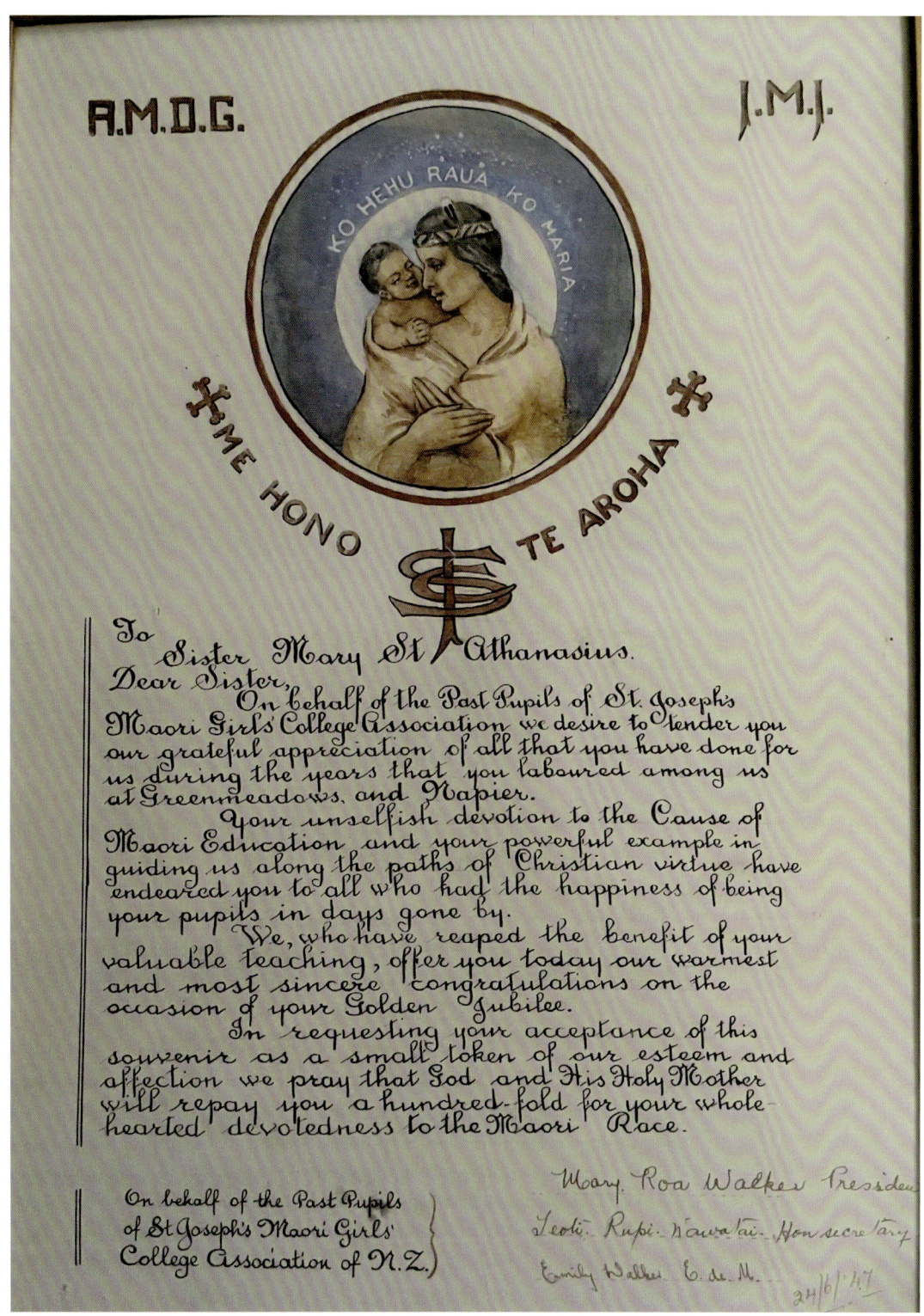

purchased a block of land next to the college for £2,000. In 1966, a modern kitchen and steam laundry were installed and a new hockey field laid out.[677] During 1966 and 1967, a new commercial block consisting of three classrooms and upstairs dormitories for senior pupils were built. Another complex that included the sixth form classroom, the principal's office and staff rooms was built to accommodate the growing number of students who wished to gain University Entrance.[678]

The 1967 centenary celebrations were significant for the school. Bishop Owen Sneddon said a mass of thanksgiving and unveiled the statue of Saint Joseph that had been donated by the Old Girls' Association.[679] St Joseph is holding the baby Jesus inside his korowai, the cloak symbolising the protection of the Māori people. In his right hand, he is holding a greenstone adze as a symbol of his trade, and at his feet is a gourd and a basket of kūmara to signify his role as a provider.[680] The statue was carved by J Gown from Wellington.[681] One guest speaker was Member of Parliament Whetu Tirikatene-Sullivan who commented that her late father, Sir Eruera Tirikatene, had worked happily with stenographers from St Joseph's during his two periods as a cabinet minister.[682] The evening celebrations included a banquet, a ball, a hāngī and entertainment provided by pupils from St Joseph's and Hato Paora.

Former pupil Mary Kereopa remembers the centenary well:

> I was in Form VI at the time and a prefect. It was a big celebration. I remember all these wonderful old girls turning up, and I can remember Ruby Wawatai who was the oldest living pupil at the time, cutting the cake. We had to prepare; we had to have marching practice, we had kapa haka and the whole school learnt waiata in preparation of the people turning up. Hukarere, Hato Paora and Te Aute, all sent contingents to help us celebrate.

Erica Herangi recalls:

> It was a huge undertaking. We had to perform because the old girls were coming to the school, and the college had to be impeccable from top to bottom. We cleaned, we scrubbed and we polished. The school was absolutely spotless and you could see yourself on the floors. The old girls were coming, and the expectation was we had to present the school and we had to be presented as well. The old girls were our aunties, mothers and nannys. You didn't necessarily have to be an old girl to come to the centenary. You could also be connected by family, and it was wonderful to see your family come, and if they did, you were given the responsibility of taking them on a tour of the school. It was run with military precision, considering the number of the pupils at the school. The seniors were in the front, and the third formers were not seen or heard.

Outside the school, St Joseph's girls were still called on to do performances. In 1964, Thelma Hape was crowned Miss Aotearoa by the Raukawa District Council, which was raising funds for a memorial hall for the Māori Battalion. Thelma Hape raised £1,740, which included proceeds from a concert performed by the college at Dannevirke Town Hall.[683] In 1966, the school performed alongside Hukarere and the Waipatu Club at Waipatu Marae for a Māori Battalion Reunion[684], and in 1968 the college performed at the consecration of the new Anglican Bishop of Aotearoa, Manu Bennett, at Napier.[685] In 1966, the New Zealand Broadcasting Corporation held a Māori action song and poi tune competition. Charles Tuarau of the Dominion Museum carved the winning trophies, with Flora Edwards and Pukehuia Cotter from St Joseph's winning the poi section.[686]

1. Sam Paenga leads Bishop Sneddon at the centennial celebrations. The chairman of the centennial committee, Mr Tane Nikora, is seen to the right of the bishop, 1967.
2. Whetu Tirikatene-Sullivan addresses the centenary.
3. Centenary celebrations, 1967.
4. Haka tautoko.

Mothers and daughters 1956.
Back row: Margaret Jones, Mrs Jones, Percyna Jones, Queenie, Mrs Hodges, Maria, Patricia and Mrs Seymour.
Front row: Mrs Maxwell, Jean, Mrs Te Amo, Christine, Mrs Healey, Irene, Alva, Mrs Te Tomo, Angelina.

Mothers and Daughters

Kathy Bates
NÉE MCMAHON
TE ARAWA
1960–1963

Sharon Melrose
NÉE LAWTON
NGĀTI KAUWHATA
1968–1973

Kim Wetini
NÉE TUARI
TE WHĀNAU A APANUI,
NGĀTI POROU
1975–1979

Katrina Bates
1986–1989

Unaiki Lawton
2008–2012

Te Atamarie Wetini
2010–2014

Kathy Bates was one of eleven siblings and, even though her family struggled to make ends meet, her mother insisted that she go to St Joseph's. 'I was lucky because I had a year for nothing with Mother Aileen giving me a year of free board to help me. It came at a time when I was going to have to leave because Mum couldn't afford to have me there.' Sports was a feature in her teenage years:

I was into athletics and basketball, and we were the top in basketball. We had marching around the netball court as well, but that was a joke. Sister Katarina was the only one who could speak Māori and teach te reo. Whenever she was around us, she would never listen to us until we got it correct, and that's how I got my pronunciation right, otherwise she would just turn her back to us!

Sister Frances had the memorable moniker of 'Tank'. Kathy, along with other pupils, used to stay awake at night to see when and where the sisters went to the toilet. 'They were in their habits, and we would stay up all night waiting for one of them to come out. One particular night, a sister came out, and she was wearing a long white nightie and a cap and carrying a candle. We finally found out where and when they went to the toilet, and it made our night!' Another recollection relating to the sisters was the annual picnic the girls enjoyed on St Joseph's Day. 'If it looked like it was going to rain, the sisters would put the statue of St Joseph out on the lawn.'

Kathy's daughter, Katrina, first attended St Joseph's in 1986 with her brothers going to Hato Paora. Although the sisters were not as prominent during Katrina's education during the 1980s, they continued to have a presence at Greenmeadows. 'Sister Monica would go through all our letters before they were sent. We had made a tape of ourselves singing and making fun of the sisters. Unfortunately, the tape was intercepted, and we were told off.' Marching was used as a punishment during Katrina's time at St Joseph's. 'If we didn't get to sleep at night, they would get us out in our nighties and have us march around the tennis courts.' One incident Katrina remembers is at a game of soccer:

> Myself and my friend came off at half-time. We went over to the van and noticed the car keys were in it, so we thought what if we just backed it. Everyone looked and stopped the game to see what was going on. We said, "Well it's too late now," so we took off, drove around, and it was hilarious.

However, rather than being made to march around the netball courts, this time the punishment was more serious. 'Mum and Dad got their letters again. Our punishment was that we weren't allowed to go to any of the school dances with St John's and Te Aute, and we had to stay behind for one school holiday. We had our own ball because we had the whole school to ourselves!'

Like her mother, Kathy, sports featured prominently in Katrina's school life. 'There weren't a lot of opportunities to travel. You weren't allowed to play more than two sports a term, and most of the time we played as much sports as we could to get out of the school grounds.' Katrina also remembers her Sunday afternoon walks as another opportunity to leave the school grounds. 'We got $2 each, and everyone put their money in. You'd buy those potato fritters because they were the cheapest and a tub of ice cream.' After leaving St Joseph's, Katrina became a qualified teacher.

The Lawton whānau have a long association with St Joseph's. Janine Lawton (1966–1970) was the eldest of the Lawton girls, followed by Sharon (1967–1971), Roimata (1972–1975), her daughter Zoe (1996–2001), Rahera (1979–1982) and daughter Punanga (2004–2008). Sharon explains: 'I did some research [on] when my nanny attended St Joseph's on the hill. Their education was about being good housewives and maids. They would also do all the laundry for the Pākehā girls at Sacred Heart College.' Apart from the family connection to St Joseph's, another reason she and her sisters attended was the reputation of the local high school where the Lawtons lived:

> My generation went because we lived in Feilding, and the local high school had a particular reputation when it came to educating Māori. All the Māori kids were put in the bottom stream, regardless of what they wanted to do or what they were capable of. Our parents challenged the school over a period of years, and the Member of Parliament for Southern Māori, Whetu Tirikatene-Sullivan, became involved. Dad's sisters had gone to St Jo's, so my older sister went and our cousins followed.

Cost was a major challenge for her parents, who managed to put a total of six children through

1. Katrina Bates (1986–1989) and Kathy Bates (née McMahon, 1961–1963).
2. Unaiki Lawton (2008–2012) and Sharon Melrose (1968–1973).
3. Kim and Horowai Wetini (2000–2005).

St Joseph's and Hato Paora. 'We got a uniform grant in our first year and some help from the Porirua Trust.'

The Dux for two years, 1971 and 1972, and the head prefect in 1972, Sharon developed a close relationship with one of her principals, Sister Margaret Purdie. 'I became a close friend of Margaret and she is the godmother of one of my daughters, Roimata. She is pretty cool, and she made some great relationships with people in the community. They would do things for the school like some of the building that took place.' On the subject of building at St Joseph's, Sharon recalls: 'One of the builders was this little Scotsman, Donald McPherson, and he had a romance with Charmaine McEvedy in the sixth form. It was hilarious, and one night we woke up and his car was on the hockey fields. They ended up getting married!'

Even though Sharon flirted with the idea of joining the convent, on leaving school she went to Palmerston North Teachers' College. After completing her study, she taught at two primary schools and then ended up at Timaru Boys' High School where she is employed as the kaiako Māori.

Sharon's daughter, Unaiki, attended St Joseph's from 2008 to 2012, with her cousin Hinenui Tipoki-Lawton attending from 1999 to 2001 and becoming head prefect in 2001. The Head Prefect in 2017 was Paretao Tipoki-Hansen, Sharon's great-niece. Paretao's aunt, Mereana Lawton, attended between 2002 and 2006. In 2001, a newspaper article reported that a company owned by seventh formers at St Joseph's, including Managing Director Hinenui Tipoki-Lawton, was voted 'the most successful Māori Young Enterprise Company in the world'.[687] The company, Cre-a-Toa, decorated wooden frames with Māori motifs, and the frames were supplied by Onekawa Disability Services. The enterprise was awarded a carved trophy from the Pounamu Trust.

The powhiri for Unaiki's first year at St Joseph's was unforgettable as she fainted three times in the hot Hawke's Bay weather. 'I told my older sister that Mum said she was going to send me to St Jo's, and she said, "Don't worry about that. She threatened me with that my whole life!'" After completing her secondary school education, Unaiki completed a Bachelor of Arts in Māori and Indigenous Studies at the University of Canterbury in 2015.

> In 2016, I did my honours degree in te reo Māori, and the Head of Māori and Indigenous Studies at the University of Canterbury approached me to be the project manager for a new initiative, Maui Lab, that brokers and manages intern projects, provides consulting services and develops research projects. As well as that, I am lecturing in te reo Māori over the summer.

Kim Wetini (née Tuari) is originally from Tolaga Bay. 'We moved to the South Island on the *Wahine*. My father worked on the steam trains, and we moved to Otira.' Aged twelve, Kim's mother told her that she would be attending a boarding school. Kim's older sister Robyn had been to St Joseph's and described the college as a prison. 'I was the only pupil from the West Coast, and there were only two others from the South Island. Three pupils came from the Chatham Islands, and we also had girls from the Nauru Islands and Australia. If you came from Te Waipounamu, there was this perception that you were rich and that it was more exotic.'

When talking about Hato Paora: 'We were supposed to have this relationship with HP [Hato Paora], and if we had a ball either there, or with us, we would be on one side and they would be on the other. It was a waste of time and effort to get all glammed up.' Kim especially remembers 1978:

> We did a record in 1978, and it was the first year they had a seventh form intake, but we still had to go to Taradale High. The following year, myself and Tangiwai Tapiata went to a radio station and did the news in Māori for Te Wiki o te reo Māori, as service to the community. We didn't get to see television or hear the radio, only when we were on it.

In her final year, Kim was the deputy head girl, which resulted in her being given the responsibility of the pastoral care of the younger pupils. 'Miss [Kingi] would place more responsibility on us to lead the school and the girls.' Eventually, Kim worked for Māori Affairs and is still employed in Christchurch as a senior advisor for Te Puni Kōkiri.

Kim knew that if she had daughters, they too would attend her alma mater. 'My oldest daughter, Te Horowai, went there, and we told her when she was seven. Even though she didn't want to go, she ended up the head girl in 2005. As a result of our whānau going there, my husband's niece, Stephanie Nuku, went there also. We also have three grand-nieces who are going there, the Raihania girls.'

As for Te Horowai, she is now teaching at the local school, Te Pā o Rākaihautu. Kim's youngest daughter, Te Atamarie, also attended St Joseph's. Te Atamarie recalls: 'The only way we could get out of study was to read. We would stack up our books to hide what we were really reading and then Nanny Collins cottoned on and we were only allowed our school book.' Like her mother, Te Atamarie was recorded 'singing with Hinewehi Mohi in the chapel'.

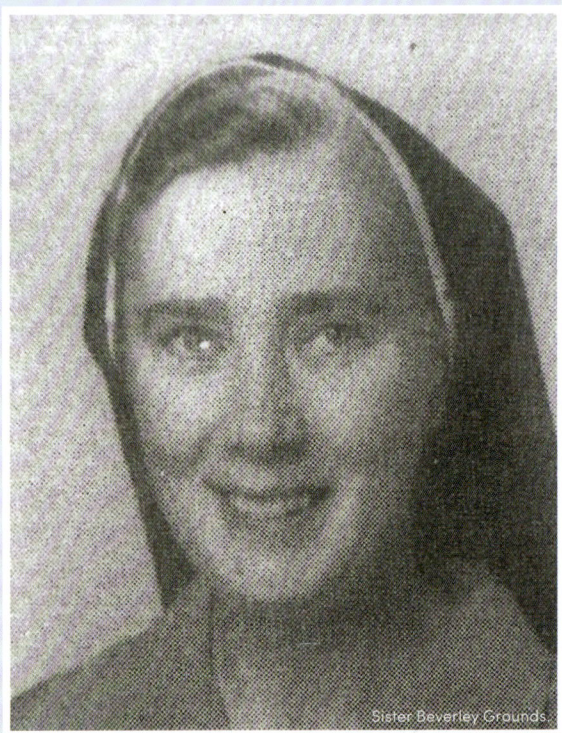

Principal of St Joseph's Māori Girls College 1964–1969
Sister Beverley Grounds

PRINCIPAL	TEACHER
1964-1969	1978-1984

The late Sister Beverley Grounds vividly recalled the moment when she knew she would devote her life to God. 'I was in the sixth form and I attended a play written by Shakespeare that was performed by the University Drama Society. During the intermission, I heard a voice that said "Beverley, I want you for myself."' For Sister Beverley, deciding on how she would best serve her calling wasn't a difficult choice.

'Since the Sisters of the Missions had taught me, I chose them, and when I was at Sacred Heart, I thought I'd like to be a teacher, even though at one stage I was sweet on one of the boys.' After having gained School Certificate and University Entrance, she attended the novitiate for three years before teaching in Christchurch and Nelson. Already teaching French, Sister Beverley completed a science degree, so she could teach chemistry, biology and geography.

Sister Beverley was told by Mother Provincial in 1964 that she was going to Greenmeadows to be the principal at St Joseph's Māori Girls' College. 'In those days, you were sent where you were told. I had never met a Māori in my life except when I was at school and we played Te Waipounamu in netball. My biggest concern was how was I going to remember all their names?' Her first challenge after arriving was when some of the pupils had been caught smoking. 'One of them said to me, "Sister, is it because we are Māori that you are growling us?" I said, "Look here, lady. I don't care if you are Chinese, Indian or Pākehā. If you disobey the rules, you will be spoken to." I never had any trouble after that.'

She was puzzled about why the school was teaching French rather than Māori. 'Then I discovered that you were not supposed to teach Māori. The powers that be in the government had decided that it would only muddle the children up.' Through experience, Sister Beverley strongly disagrees with the sentiment of the government of the day towards the teaching of te reo Māori. 'The younger they are taught Māori, the better.'

At the end of 1969 Sister Beverley returned to Christchurch to finish her arts degree, majoring in French and German. After a stint at Sacred Heart at Lower Hutt, she jumped at the opportunity to return to Greenmeadows. With her love of languages, Sister Beverley was approached by Georgina Kingi to teach Māori in 1978. A disbelieving Sister Beverley responded, 'C'mon, Georgina, you know how much Māori I know.' But Georgina was undeterred, encouraging her to learn the language. Sister Beverley enrolled to study Māori at University Entrance level by correspondence, and the pupils that year were surprised to see one of their teachers sitting at the back of the hall for the examination. The following year, she taught te reo Māori to the third and fourth formers.

Sister Beverley also recalled the help provided to her by Rere Unahi. 'She was a wonderful person and highly respected by the girls, and I got this sense of why is a Pākehā teaching us Māori from the girls.' Mrs Unahi helped Sister Beverley combat any misgivings held by the girls after the new Māori teacher was approached by Mrs Unahi during one morning tea. Mrs Unahi explained that she had received a query in class and knew the right answer, but couldn't explain the reason why and believed that Sister Beverley would be the teacher to help them understand the rationale. 'In English, you and your, are just two words. But in

Sister Patricia Huckle.

Māori it is koe, kōrua, koutou, and then when you make the participial phrases and adjectival phrases, you also have the masculine and feminine endings. I think in total you have about fourteen possibilities. After I had explained the rule, I never had another bit of trouble.'

The following year Sister Beverley found herself back in a leadership role as the deputy principal, and in 1983 and during the first term of 1984, she was the acting principal while Patricia Huckle was overseas. 'Up until that time, I had been called Sister Annetta, but when a school inspector asked the girls in the playground, "Where is Sister Grounds?" and they didn't know who he was referring to, I thought this is stupid, and we were allowed to change back to our family names, so I did.' Sister Beverley's passion for languages was put to good use after she finished at St Joseph's. Following a decade in Rome as an archivist, she spent three years in France translating the many letters and documents associated with the order's foundress, Euphrasie Barbier. The annotated book is *Missionary Beyond Boundaries* and is considered the authoritative text on Euphrasie.

Toia Lucas-Walden.

Being a Pupil in the 1960s

Toia Lucas-Walden	Veronica Huriwai-Hawkes
NÉE BROWN	NÉE HURIWAI
NGĀTI TŪWHARETOA, NGĀTI RAUKAWA KI TE TONGA	NGĀPUHI
1960–1962	1961–1966

Toia Lucas-Walden (née Brown) came from Auckland and went to St Mary's in Ellerslie before attending St Joseph's. Out of her fourteen sisters and brothers, her mother proposed that Toia go to the college in Greenmeadows when her mother's brother, Pā Te Awhitu, wanted one of his nephews to attend Hato Paora. 'It was during the time of rock 'n' roll, and I was really into that, so going to a Māori girls' college was a real shock for me.' Toia remembers that going to St Joseph's always meant that she found work. 'I never realised how many people knew about St Joseph's even though they weren't Māori. If you went to St Jo's, you always got a job.' Since leaving school, Toia has been a member of the school's Trust Board.

Both sides of the late Veronica Huriwai-Hawkes's family went to St Joseph's. They have included cousins and aunts on her mother's side and a cousin and daughter on her father's side. Veronica's sister, Rosina, also attended. Both parents were Catholic; her father was a convert and her mother hailed from Ngāpuhi. Recalling the cost of her education, Veronica remembered her mother saying to her, 'You had better get a good job when you get out because you owe us!' Veronica regarded herself as a 'mozzie' (a Māori Aussie), having lived in Australia for some time. Clearly the education that Veronica received was good as she worked for ministers of the government in Australia and was asked to work for ministers in New Zealand.

'For me, the best thing St Joseph's taught us was how to be articulate, to have an opinion, and if you had something to say then for goodness' sake, say it.' Memories of the school include being taught gymnastics by one of the sisters. 'When we did the horse, one sister would stand there with the biggest scowl on her face and would say, "One leg to the west, one leg to the east, and everything else in-between!"' Veronica also recalled:

> I was one of the naughty ones and was described by one English teacher as a fair rebel. They had the tradition of getting up for mass every day at seven. That's fine if you respect your church in that way, but no way was I going to get up every day at that early time, so I used to whinge, groan and be difficult. So, when Mother Annetta announced I had won the prize for Christian doctrine, she said, "And we have done a recount because they couldn't believe it!"

New school uniform 1963.

Pupils from Ngāti Awa

Hana Gulliver
NÉE MERITO
NGĀTI AWA
1956–1959

Maria Maui
NÉE MERITO
NGĀTI AWA
1963–1967

Erica Herangi
NÉE MERITO
NGĀTI AWA
1967–1968

Cynthia (Taini) Hudson
NÉE KINGI
NGĀTI AWA
1965–1969

Te Arani Barrett
NÉE LORRAINE [PEEP] JARAM
NGĀTI AWA, TE WHĀNAU A APANUI
1967–1969

Marama Cook
NÉE HARAWIRA
NGĀTI AWA, NGĀTI PŪKEKO,
NGĀI TE RANGI
1988–1991

Frances Te Kani
NGĀTI AWA, NGĀTI POROU
1988–1991

Marama Studer
NGĀTI AWA
2003–2007

Zoe Studer
NGĀTI AWA
2008–2012

Courtney Reneti
NGĀTI AWA
2006–2010

Erica Herangi (née Merito) treasures the two years she had at St Joseph's after she successfully sat a scholarship exam at Poroporo Primary School that was 'easy as'. As older sister Maria Maui (née Merito) reminisces: 'I sat the same exam and during the year I got a letter from the mayor of Whakatāne, Mr Warren, to congratulate me. I was so buzzed, and I showed it off.'

In total, four of Erica's sisters, Hana, Maria, Ivy and Waina, attended St Joseph's from a large family of seventeen when her father 'couldn't possibly afford to send us to boarding school'. Erica states:

[Receiving the scholarship] depended on how far you lived away from the nearest high school and before they cut our [Whakatāne] River off, we lived quite a distance away from Whakatāne High School so all the students from Poroporo School were eligible to go to the schools of Hukarere, Hato Petera, and Hato Paora, Queen Victoria, Turakina, Te Aute and Tipene. I only went to St Joseph's for two years because funding from the Maori Education Foundation ceased. It cost our family about $100 per term. My heart broke to leave but my dad could not afford to send me.

Erica says, 'My years at St Joseph's were the happiest of my life. We studied when we woke up, we would study in-between meals, before dinner and after. If you didn't succeed, it was totally on you because they gave you every opportunity, and the sisters were very strict about classes and attendance.' Her memories of St Joseph's are in stark contrast to attending high school in Whakatāne:

Going to secondary school in Whakatāne was absolutely traumatic. There were boys in my class for a start, and they are nasty. At St Joseph's, every time a teacher would enter the room, we all stood as students, regardless. Sister would say, "Be seated" and we would all sit down. So, at Whakatāne High School, this is what I did in my St Joseph's uniform. The other students were all in their black and yellow uniforms, and everyone is looking at me because I'm standing up. I took no notice and just looked at the teacher. The teacher knew what was going on, looked at me,

Back row: Frances Te Kani, Marama Cook, Zoe Studer, Courtney Reneti, Marama Studer, Tira Ruru.
Front row: Stella Marr, Cynthia Hudson, Maria Maui, Hana Gulliver, Erica Herangi, Te Arani Barrett.

and said, "Thank you. You may be seated." Sometimes you did things automatically until my cousins said, "Please don't do that." That's how ingrained some of the values are, the respect that they [the sisters] installed in you, and sometimes I find myself checking what I am doing and saying to myself, "Sister Katarina [Mariu] would not approve of that, so I won't do it."

Such was the positive experience of St Joseph's for Erica, she sent her two daughters, Joanne and Bianca, to Greenmeadows.

Marama Cook is the third generation of her family to have attended St Joseph's. 'My grandmother, Theresa Rapana [née Merito], went there as did my aunt, Tina Whaitiri [née Rapana]. The reason I went was because of our family history with the school, but I had also attended St Joseph's Primary School here in Whakatāne.' Nowadays, Marama works at Te Whare Wānanga o Awanuiārangi, where she has worked for twenty years after having started as a nineteen-year-old. 'What I have gained at the Wānanga and at St Jo's is that whatever I do, it has to be about serving the people.'

The younger sister of Georgina Kingi, Taini (Cynthia), attended the college during the 1960s. Taini recalls: 'The sisters were good teachers. We had action songs that were taught by Sister Katarina during the lunchbreak.' The idea of an outing at St Joseph's during Taini's time was going out to Pakipaki or Te Aute College. 'It was wonderful!' The connections made with her wider family within the school also stick in her memory. 'I can remember the first day Peep [Te Arani Barrett] came to school. She was running up and down the stairs, and I said to her, "Look here, where are you from?" and lo and behold, she was my own relation!'

Te Arani 'Peep' Barrett's (formerly known as Lorraine Jaram at St Joseph's) mother attended St Joseph's because she was an orphan:

It was quite sad for her, and the place offered security and safety, which is what she wanted for me, so she sent me there against my father's wishes. My father worked as a Māori Affairs welfare officer and refused to pay for it because he thought that going to a single-sex Māori Catholic boarding school was practising separatism. So, my mother became a toll operator in Hamilton to pay for myself and my five siblings to go to boarding school. By the second year, Dickie [Georgina Kingi] had straightened me out, and so Dad enrolled my sister and started paying the bills.

For Te Arani's father, Wishie Jaram, having his daughters at St Joseph's changed his mind about the value of Māori boarding schools:

Also, at the time, he did a study of it as a Winston Churchill Scholar, and from that, he could see how it helped. It changed the way he engaged at Māori Affairs and so instead of focusing on welfare, he looked at engaging and creating more positive ways for young Māori. He was involved in the Māori Trade Training Scheme and became quite instrumental in the Tū Tangata programme. That's an outcome of me having gone to St Joseph's.

According to Te Arani, there was a dual value system underpinning St Joseph's. 'Catholicism was one, and the principles associated with being valued human beings was two.' Te Arani was in the general stream because she liked it:

Dad wanted me to do the commercial course at the fifth form so I could learn shorthand and typing. I said to him that I wanted to stay in the general stream because you learnt te reo Māori. Te reo Māori wasn't just "sat down and learnt", it was imbued in the entire schooling system, through church, through waiata, and it was contextualised learning. He said, "You won't get a job learning te reo Māori." I lost the argument, but my education

Wishie Jaram.

has put me in good stead for the rest of my life, and because of that foundational learning I received at St Joseph's, I have never been without work as a result.

As for extra-curricular activities, Te Arani can recall catching one of the three buses that travelled to Wairoa in the middle of the night for the dawn opening of Takitimu Marae. 'You hardly got out! We even looked forward to going to the dentist in Taradale!' She also thinks fondly of the French rugby team that visited the school in 1968. 'That was a big event. I was working in the laundry with Kura Mason, and she took the "n" off her surname because she fell in love with the French player Joe Maso!'

After having completed her high school years at St Joseph's and having taken the commercial stream as her father had wished, Te Arani had a job waiting for her in the Justice Department as a judge's stenographer. Afterwards Te Arani became a teacher:

I just keep reinventing the skills I had learnt at school, and I was at the cutting edge of word processing when it first came out. I went back into teaching at a local high school. I was head of computer science and information technology and was part of developing the unit standards and then later the achievement standards for NCEA as a member of some of the working groups. I then came to Te Whare Wānanga o Awanuiārangi and developed the E-Wānanga that is here, the beginning of the distance learning module for the Wānanga.

Frances Te Kani is part of the Kingi whānau, having had four aunts attend the school (Caroline, Georgina, Cynthia and Mere) and two older cousins (Hana and Tinaka Merito). 'We just naturally attended the school gala and different performances, and, although I'm not Catholic myself, I wanted to attend.' Having her aunt, Georgina Kingi, as the principal was not easy for Frances. 'She was one of my favourite aunties before I left. It was hard because often I'd be bleeped over the loud speaker as a third and fourth former. I guess the standards she set for her niece were a bit higher than others, but across the board, the expectations to achieve and behave were really high.' Frances also remembers her teachers. 'They all stand out, and I compare the teachers at my son's high school to them, because of the passion and drive they had at St Joseph's.'

Marama and Zoe Studer attended St Joseph's in the 2000s. Marama remembers going to a Paerangi Ball that included Te Aute, Hato Paora and Hato Petera. 'We all came together, which was very, very rare. However, it was the first and the last time we had a ball because some of the Te Aute boys were caught sneaking in our dorms.' A highlight for Zoe was going on the numerous kapa haka tours around New Zealand and going further afield such as when a school group of twelve travelled to Hong Kong and Guilin in China in 2009.

As she comments: 'For most of the girls, it was our first time being on a plane. We had security guards and were escorted by the police when we performed. We received the royal treatment.'

Courtney Reneti is currently a legal executive and works for a law firm in Whakatāne. 'I wouldn't know how to study if I went to another school. I now know how to work my way through a bunch of law books.' That same dedication to learning also helped her research for her rōpū Hinemarie for the cultural festival at St Joseph's. 'There is a lot of pressure to research and have your whānau watch you perform.'

6M class 1991.
Back row: Charlene Peita, Tania Henry, Olive Prince, Raina Hiki, Shona Walker, Pia Pohatu, Maata Ratana, Mr Perry.
Front row: Belinda Katene, Rose Parker, Rozanna Mclean, Tania Sword, Delilah Messent, Angela Te Haara, Barbara Emery, Christine Nepe.

CHAPTER EIGHT

Te Wero

The building programme established during the 1960s under Sister Beverley Grounds would flourish under new principal, Sister Margaret Purdie. Georgina Kingi reflects on Sister Margaret:

> She didn't blow in like a breath of fresh air; she blew in like a tornado. It was out with the old and in with the new, literally, with some of the old textbooks and band uniforms being disposed of. She had a clear vision for the school, and she wanted the girls to pursue careers outside of nursing, teaching or the social services. She also encouraged the girls to be more outspoken, to think for themselves, to be independent.

Sister Margaret can also be credited with the strong relationships formed with Ngāti Kahungunu iwi and all Hāhi, not just Catholic. Former matron Sister Maureen Richardson says: 'Margaret Purdie was the principal, and she encouraged the girls to stand up and take their place in the world. In those years, the roll was growing, and a lot of building was going on. The painter got the stencil, and we painted all the tukutuku panels.'

It was during her era as the prinicpal that the building programme would be titled 'Te Wero' (The Challenge) as the roll continued to grow. As school historian and teacher Maria van der Linden writes:

> Student numbers continued to increase steadily, because of the greater awareness of parents to encourage education at the fifth and sixth form levels. This increased the school roll to 192 boarders, putting pressure on the hostel facilities, which led to the existing hostel amenities being upgraded. More showers were installed and plans were made for an erection of more classrooms and an extension of dormitory space.[688]

Te Wero was officially launched in conjunction with St Joseph's brother school, Hato Paora, which faced similar challenges, and a combined goal of $100,000 was set to be reached in order for the building to take place at both schools.[689]

Apart from the launch of an extensive building campaign, the school also implemented the annual mid-winter cultural festival in 1970 and, in 1972, control of the school was transferred from the sisters to the Board of Governors.[690]

Board of Governors 1987.
Standing: Mr A Lawson, Sr M Rose Holderness, Mrs D Greene, Mr R Curham, Fr M Mariu, Mr P Pene, Mr D Lanigan, Sr Lorraine Evans.
Sitting: Miss G Kingi, Mr S Hepere, Mr H Ngaia (Chairperson), Mr P Edmonds, Mrs R Wiki.

Hine Mato, Corinthia Dunn, Anne Nicholls, Helen-Ani Rose.

Te Wero: The Waiata

Stella Marr says: 'I was the original leader for Te Wero. It was composed by Miss Kingi and Helen-Ani Rose, who sadly died two years after leaving school from an asthma attack.' The waiata has, over time, become very popular and is often sung by Māori.

Te reo karanga o te rā	There is a challenge (ahead of us)
Te wero, te wero, te takinga	Let us unite (in order)
Mā tōu rourou, mā taku rourou	That we iwi Māori can move forward
Ka ora e te iwi e	(survive)
Hikitia, manaakitia!	Let us embrace
Āwhinatia te wero!	(the kaupapa)
Hikitia, manaakitia!	Let us support
Āwhinatia te wero!	(the challenge of Te Wero)
E rapu ana i te ara	Our pathway to success is built on our
Te mātauranga o te Pākehā	strong foundation of tikanga Māori
Me ngā tikanga Māori	with mātauranga Pākehā
Ā ō tūpuna e	(to widen the perspective on life)

When the Minister of Maori Affairs, Duncan McIntyre, opened the new wing in 1971, he spoke about the government's policy of 'integration':[691]

> This [school] surely is integration at work, and the point is that the girls, enter life as confident, educated responsible women ... For a long time we have coasted along in the belief that the Church, the Maori people, and the public were well aware of their value and that they were quite safe from being closed down. But in recent years we got quite a shock. We found that the Church was not necessarily going to give full support or assistance. We found that the number of Maori parents sending their children to these schools had dropped. And we also found that the public increasingly could not see the reason for supporting the schools ... I am here today because I believe that there is an important place for the type of people who are coming from these schools.[692]

In 1972, 71 per cent of Form V qualified for Form VI, giving the school their largest intake ever of girls for Form VI.[693] Sister Margaret Purdie noted in her report that the school had two students wanting to stay and study for Form VII: Cheryl Christy and Charmaine Duff. In response to the request, Sister Margaret stated that:

> I think that a girl preparing to enter university could well benefit from exposure to a much wider section of society, and a much greater range of competition than a seventh form year spent at St Joseph's could provide. For this reason (somewhat reluctantly I must admit, for we realised that a seventh form would add prestige to our school) we enrolled the girls at Napier Girls' High School, where they would be part of a large class and a large school, where all their subjects including Maori are taught and where the school is already committed to an active interest in its Maori pupils, catering as it does for the girls from Hukarere. I think it can be said that the experiment was an unqualified success. Although Charmaine lived with a Napier family, Cheryl continued to board at St Joseph's.[694]

Sister Maureen Richardson recalls:

> By the end of Margaret's reign as principal, we had a very small seventh form. It was Margaret's initiative, and she thought it would be a good idea for the girls in seventh form to live at St Joseph's and they would have exposure to co-education. She approached Mr Twaddle, the principal at Taradale High, and he was simply delighted. He said, "Sister, I would love it. I can't get my Māori students past the fourth form."

Another concern for Sister Margaret was the growing roll and that in order to keep pace with demand '... an extensive building programme has started, thanks to the initiative of the Board of Governors and my own Provincial Superior'.[695] More building work was planned.[696] Sister Margaret recognised the lofty goals of the programme stating that it was 'brave' as, in comparison with Te Aute and St Stephens, St Joseph's was not well endowed and charged lower fees.

Acting Principal, Sister Mary Raphael, reported in 1974 that the school continued to grow, with an increase of thirty in the roll, bringing the school roll to just under two hundred. At the start of

Above: Minister of Maori Affairs, Duncan McIntyre.
Right: Building the new classrooms of H Block in the 1970s.

the year, the school used a new block of six new classrooms with the original classrooms being transformed into sleeping quarters for thirty-nine girls. The new dining room had been completed, and the reception room and offices were nearing completion. At the end of 1974, two new classrooms and a hall were being built.

With the momentum of a flourishing roll and new buildings being erected, Raphael believed the school could cater for 250 pupils, as they had turned down 120 applicants because the school could only receive an additional fifty pupils per year. She stated: 'We believe we must go on because we have seen the evidence in our pupils that St Joseph's Maori Girls' College helps girls grow into young Maori women with a pride in their race and a concern for others.'[697]

In sport, the school excelled with four of the five hockey sides winning their grades and, in basketball, three of the four teams won their grades.[698]

The 1974 year began with a 'prefects' initiation' led by Sister Margaret Purdie.[699] Once the prefect badges had been blessed in the chapel by Father O'Hagan, Sister Margaret drove the eleven girls to Waimārama. The prefects composed a waiata, lit a fire and discussed what it meant to be a prefect, before going to bed at 3.30 a.m.

St Joseph's lifted the O'Shea Shield for public speaking in 1976, and the coveted trophy departed Wellington for the first time in sixteen years.[700] Also in 1976, the dining room was decorated under the direction of Para Matchitt[701] and Sandy Adsett. However, the most significant development for the college that year was the blessing and opening of a major building extension in October.[702]

Building at St Joseph's in the 1970s.

Current buildings at St Joseph's.

Winning O'Shea team 1976.

Over 700 people attended, with Cardinal Reginald Delargey presiding. The extension included a library, sewing, music and typing rooms, science and physics laboratories and a new classroom block. A special tribute was paid to Gill Trower, who received the Papal Decoration for his efforts in overseeing the buildings at St Joseph's, and $4,000 was raised during the event; in 1987 Gill Trower retired as the hostel manager after twenty-two years.

Speech competitions were a feature of 1977.[703] Debbie Marshall won the regional speech competition and held the Anthony Eden Cup aloft, with the school magazine singing her praises for battling a sore throat and winning the contest: '… Debbie, with a raging sore throat, rose bravely from her sickbed to hold her own in front of an attentive audience. Our heroine!' The school was placed in all categories for speeches, and the choir distinguished itself.

The principal's report for 1978 signalled that within the near future the school would be 'integrated'.[704] 'This means, in very simple terms, that the government will pay for the school's operating costs provided we keep our special character … Putting it as concretely as possible, I think there are three aspects to look at: St Joseph's is Catholic, it is Maori, and it is a boarding school.'[705]

Thirty girls travelled to Christchurch as part of the concert party.[706] The three buses that took the students were named The Red-Hot Rod (lent by Sacred Heart Napier), The Yellow Flying Banana and Blue Streak. The ferry crossing did not go well, with several students falling ill, but, once in Christchurch, highlights included visiting a women's prison and giving a concert at Te Rangimarie, the Māori Catholic Church in Christchurch, with old girl Wiki Baker and a former pupil of Hato Paora, Tommy Ruakere.[707] Another excursion was travelling to Auckland to help celebrate the seventy-fifth jubilee of Queen Victoria School, where students made a hole in the floor while performing.[708]

In 1979, an arson attack occurred at the college, with a 14-year-old girl appearing in court for wilfully setting fire to the altar in the chapel.[709] The young woman had placed newspaper under the Māori carvings and had also written on the walls with oil paints, following a severe argument at her home.

Sister Margaret Purdie with the 1972 prefects.
Back row: Theresa Rahui, Nancy Koroheke, Mere Koopu, Angela McCauley, Stella Marr, Cheryl Christy, Charmaine Luff.
Front row: Maria Anaru, Sharon Lawton (Head Prefect), Sister Margaret Purdie, Roasanna Murray, Melda Dewes.

Principal of St Joseph's Māori Girls' College 1970–1976

Sister Margaret Purdie

TEACHER	PRINCIPAL
1962–1963	1970–1976

Sister Margaret Purdie has a clear memory of when she was told she was leaving St Joseph's as principal:

> I got a letter from my boss that said I had been appointed to Ferry Road in Christchurch, and I can remember sitting at the back of the chapel, crying my eyes out. I was very, very sad. We went where we were sent. We had a council and a Sister in Charge. You had not much input into decisions in those days.

Born in Christchurch in 1935 to a Catholic mother and a Scottish Presbyterian father, Sister Margaret can't remember a time when she didn't want to be a sister. 'My mother wasn't too happy about it and thought I should wait until I was twenty-one. My father said, "Let her go. She could do a lot worse."' Sister Margaret became a teacher by studying extramurally through Massey University and was posted to a number of schools in Nelson, Christchurch and Kaikōura, before arriving as a teacher at St Joseph's. Mother Augustine (principal at the time) says she was 'an outstanding teacher who was real clever and an intellectual'. Georgina Kingi was the head prefect. Sister Margaret says: 'Georgina ran the school. She was a huge influence and a help to Sister Augustine in terms of being Māori. She had tremendous authority amongst the girls, the girls respected her, even in those days. It was very new to me and a great learning curve because I had little experience of things Māori, but I loved it there.' The school, run solely by the sisters, 'had a little trouble with the meals not being so good. Complaints were lodged to the sisters who had to serve the meals, and it got better.'

One significant development of the school during her time as principal between 1970 and 1976 was the comprehensive building programme. Sister Margaret credits Gill Trower, the builder who oversaw the scheme, as being instrumental in ensuring its success:

> He was the father of one of our sisters ... He did all the detailed plans, and he built that big classroom block that enabled him to turn the old classrooms into dormitories. He was great. Prior to that, all the girls had slept upstairs, and they were quite crowded with no privacy at all. Once it was built, they had much more space and privacy with their own cubicle, a built-in bed with drawers underneath, and a wardrobe.

She continued:

> One of the things that I was happiest about during my time at Greenmeadows was the commissioning of the altar in the chapel and the tabernacle in 1976. Moni Taumaunu from Gisborne carved them for us, as it was his idea. Hato Paora gifted us the lectern, and we placed tukutuku panels around the walls with the girls having done those under the tutelage of Sister Patricia Huckle. I was happy to introduce Māori art into the chapel. It was a Māori College and a very, very Pākehā chapel. I wanted it to be Māori friendly.

When asked about the type of graduate the school attempted to produce, Sister Margaret responds:

> I think we aimed to produce an all-round woman, not just an academic. Someone who would go on and be a wife, a mother and a leader in her community, and many of them became academics. We tried to give them as much freedom as possible and make things as homely as possible, rather than be strictly regimented. They could find enjoyment in small things that gave them pleasure. I loved their enjoyment of life, and they were great kids.

Following her years at St Joseph's, Sister Margaret spent time in Samoa, Rome and Winnipeg in Canada, before retiring for good to the place of her birth, Christchurch.

Moni Taumaunu and the chapel carving.

Maru Karatea-Goddard and daughters, Rangiora (left) and Ripeka (right).

The Tibble Sisters

Ngāti Porou, Ngāti Tūwharetoa, Te Whānau ā Apanui, Ngāti Raukawa

Amiria Arapere
NÉE TIBBLE
1972–1976

Debra Williams
NÉE TIBBLE
1973–1977

Puhiwahine Tibble
1974–1977

Maru Karatea-Goddard
NÉE KARATEA
1975–1979

The Tibbles grew up in a devout Catholic home. The second eldest of ten children, Amiria, says, 'I think for our parents it wasn't really about religion. It was more about their love for God. Mum first learned about God through her paternal grandmother Rihi Gotty [née Iwikau] who espoused that God came from Waihi [near Tokaanu, Lake Taupō].'

Younger sibling Maru Karatea-Goddard retells the family connection to St Joseph's: 'My mother Taruke went to Hato Hohepa in the late 1930s because of the Marist fathers.' For the Tibble whānau during the 1950s and 1970s, like many Māori Catholics, they prospered from a relationship with Father Frank Wall, a Marist priest. Amiria states: 'He was the most darling of priests. He would turn up to our house; sometimes our parents weren't home. He would grab a tea towel or sleep on the couch for a short break. He had a pair of boxing gloves too.'

Puhiwahine was ecstatic about attending Hato Hohepa:

At home, I was always helping Mum and Dad with the boys, the cooking, the cleaning, while the boys seemed to play all day. It never seemed to end. Our house was not conducive to study either; we were loud and typical of many Māori homes where older and younger siblings shared bedrooms, so Hato Paora, for our brothers, and Hato Hohepa, for myself and my sisters, were the perfect option for us.

Financially, sending their children to boarding school was a struggle for Olive and Waho Tibble. Puhiwahine recalls:

> When I was in the fourth form, Mum and Dad came to St Jo's to take me home because funds were all but depleted. Tiwana was at Hato Paora and Debbie and Amiria were at Hato Hohepa with me. Mum and Dad arrived at Greenmeadows; Mum got out of the car and cried … Sister Margaret [Purdie] happened to come around the corner … pulled up and put her arm around Mum and asked what was wrong. Mum explained that they no longer had the funds to sustain four children at boarding school. Sister Margaret replied that the school had just received a grant from the Catholic church for a student from our school. I was the recipient of that grant for three years.

Puhiwahine loved her time at St Jo's. 'Whakapapa, te reo Māori and Tikanga Māori were and are still my passion. We learned to read and write in te reo Māori, but we arrived and left still orally incompetent.' Maru adds: 'We were raised in Māori-speaking homes, where adults spoke Māori to adults, but children were not supposed to speak the language. Children were definitely not part of the conversation, and it wasn't encouraged …'

Sister Margaret Purdie remains large in the memories of the Tibble sisters. Debbie remembers:

> During Sister Margaret's watch as our principal, the school roll surpassed two-hundred pupils, and that meant improved educational and living facilities. Sister Margaret was responsible for opening up the new wings. A modern science laboratory, fully fitted out sewing room, a new library and small music rooms with pianos were just some of the additions. Previous classrooms were transformed into dormitories or bathrooms, and in 1974, the dining room of today was built and opened. Overnight, we went from being squashed sardines in the old dining room to being able to choose which table we sat at in the spacious, modern eating facility.

Reflecting on the school curriculum, Puhiwahine remembers:

> When I began at St Jo's, the curriculum didn't help us become doctors, lawyers or accountants – those sorts of people … but nurses, teachers, maybe principals, secretaries but not the general manager. However, when I was in the sixth form [1977], we were the only New Zealand secondary school that had sex education, and when Sister Margaret was asked why, she said, "Because my girls will grow up to be mothers and they need to know their options." Sister Margaret certainly thought outside the box.

When Puhiwahine left St Joseph's, she trained as a teacher at Loreto Hall Catholic Teachers' College in Remuera:

> One of the sisters in my class, who was of the Order of Our Lady of the Missions, once told me that it was every novice sister's dream to teach at St Joseph's. Of all the schools where they taught, our school did something wonderful to them. I asked her why she thought that was the case, and she told me,

"Because Māori are so open with love and generosity, whereas in the traditional Pākehā culture, you keep a stiff upper lip and you don't let people know what your true feelings are in case you get hurt."

Debbie remembers:

At the beginning of 1976, I was elected head prefect, and it was our watershed year because we won the prestigious O'Shea Shield. Before that, we were known by the locals in Taradale as "those Māori girls down the road who sing beautifully and steal our oranges". But once we won that shield, there was a shift in the atmosphere. The local and national papers, even national television, wanted to know who we were. Suddenly, we were famous because we had done something never achieved before – an unknown Māori Catholic girls' school had just won the top, cultural prize off the top Catholic boys' school [St Patrick's, Silverstream]. Some of the girls who came from that team include Moana Maniapoto, Debbie Marshall-Lobb, Laura Hond [Erana Hond-Flavell], Frances Goulton, Shona Gardiner and myself. Really, Sister Margaret Purdie and the rest of her band of sisters and staff – in particular our speech and drama teacher, Shirley Duthie, are to be congratulated because they believed in us when no one else knew we even existed.

Debra Williams, Puhiwahine Tibble and Amiria Arapere.

Moana Maniapoto-Jackson.

Hinewehi Mohi.

Maisey Rika.

Divas

Wiki Baker
NÉE BROWN
NGĀI TAHU
1958–1959

Hinewehi Mohi
NGĀTI KAHUNGUNU
1978–1981

Moana Maniapoto-Jackson
NGĀTI TŪWHARETOA
1974–1977

Maisey Rika
TE ARAWA, WHĀNAU-Ā-APANUI
1997–2001

St Joseph's has a long and proud history of producing exceptional singers who have gone on to illustrious careers. Frances Te Kani explains: 'I think our sound is unique. In comparison with other schools, it is really sweet. Georgina [Kingi] makes us hit those high notes, and they go higher every year. Today with kapa haka, you see quite a masculine performance from females, and I think St Joseph's maintained that lady-like performance.' For Stacey Hape, who would become the head prefect in 1993, the sound of St Joseph's made her want to enrol at the school. 'I was at the opening of Te Papa o te Aroha at Tokoroa where St Joseph's and Hato Paora had come to perform. I remember saying to Mum, "I want to go to that school" because they had the voices of angels.'

Wiki Baker is regarded as 'the first voice' of St Joseph's. A soprano, Wiki was taught firstly by her mother and then by Sister Chanel at the college:

We were asked if we wanted to be trained to sing properly. I said yes, and so I went to Sister Chanel. After three months, I was asked by her if I wanted to learn some opera songs, and I said no. I couldn't see any future in it – it wasn't Māori. I enjoyed doing the

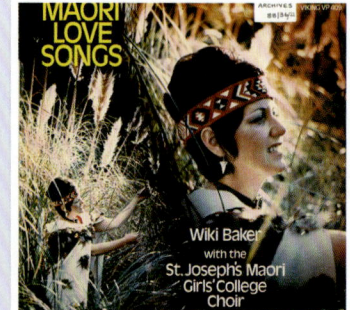

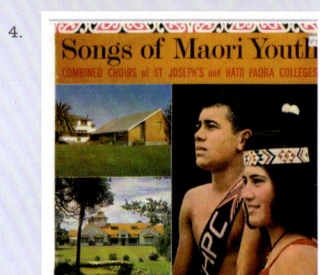

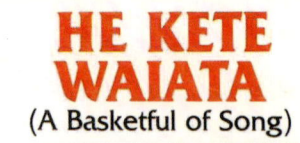
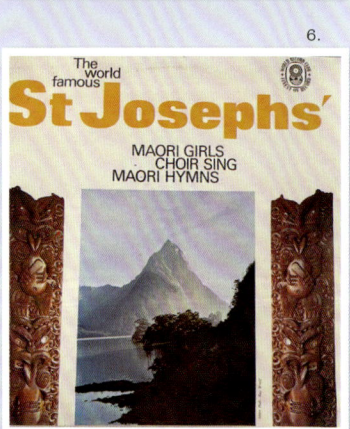

1. *Pokarekare: The World Famous St Joseph's Maori Girls' Choir.*
2. *Maori Love Songs: Wiki Baker with the St Joseph's Maori Girl's College Choir.*
3. *St Joseph's Maori Girls' College Sydney Tour 2005.*
4. *Songs of Maori Youth: Combined Choirs of St Joseph's and Hato Paora Colleges.*
5. *The Beauty of Maori Song: St Joseph's Maori Girls' College Choir and Concert Party.*
6. *The World Famous St Joseph's Maori Girls Choir Sing Maori Hymns.*
7. *He Kete Waiata (A Basketful of Song): St Joseph's Maori Girls' College.*
8. 1997 Mana Reo 'Tui' Award.
9. *He Koha Waiata: A Gift of Song: St Joseph's Maori Girls' College.*
10. *Maori Songs of Enchantment: St Joseph's Maori Girls' College Choir.*
11. *E Hine: An Anthology of Maori Love Songs* with Maisey Rika.
12. Gold disc – certifying 100,000 sales of *Maori Songs of Enchantment: St Joseph's Maori Girls' College Choir.*
13. Certifying 2,000,000 sales of *E Hine: An Anthology of Maori Love Songs* with Maisey Rika.

8.

9.

10.

11.

12.

13.

A HISTORY OF ST JOSEPH'S MĀORI GIRLS' COLLEGE   231

action songs and singing in the choir, but I couldn't grasp reading music. Everything I have ever done has been done by ear.

Wiki remembers the first time she heard her own voice:

> In 1958, the school was approached by a record company. We were told it was to raise funds for the new chapel. We decided on fourteen songs and Sister Katarina said to me, "You sing 'Pōkarekare Ana'", so I did. I was walking down the street by the Cenotaph in Wellington in 1961 and passed Beggs, a well-known music shop. As I walked past the door, I could hear the music coming out, and I got goosebumps. I thought to myself, "That sounds like us from the school and that sounded like me!" I went in and asked the manager of the shop, "Can you tell me who the singer was singing those Māori songs?" He said that is a new record that has just been released by Viking and that it was the St Joseph's Māori Girls' College. I was stunned! The manager continued, "I tell you it is going to be very popular, and there is one singer there that is singing 'Pōkarekare Ana'." I asked if I could have a look at the record, and I looked at the cover to see if my name was there, but it wasn't. The manager told me that I could take the record home with me for free, and I cried.
>
> He said, "Why are you crying?" and I told him it was because that solo person singing "Pōkarekare Ana" was me! My name wasn't on it because the money was going to the school. I walked out, and I have treasured it ever since.

In 1976, Wiki was presented with a gold record by the Minister of Maori Affairs, Duncan McIntyre, as the recording had sold over a hundred thousand copies. 'I asked for two; one for the school and one for me.' The school magazine wrote:

> In 1976, twenty-three girls, Sisters Margaret and Raphael, and Georgina Kingi, travelled to Wellington, under the pretences of making a record. Believing they were there for a publicity photo, the pupils dressed in their costumes. However, instead of a photographer walking in, the Minister of Maori Affairs, Duncan McIntyre, walked into the studio with two gold discs; one for the school and another for Wiki Brown. The gold discs were for an earlier recording of "Pōkarekare Ana" that had sold more than 100,000 copies (the equivalent of one million copies overseas at the time). After the presentation was made, they recorded a new album with Wiki titled Māori Love Songs from which the girls also appeared on television.[710]

Wiki was raised next to her marae at Arowhenua, on the outskirts of the South Island town of Temuka. After two years of schooling at Temuka District High School, her Uncle Te Ari Pitama came to visit her mother to talk about whakapapa. He said:

> "I am here to talk about Father Wall who happens to be a Māori missionary priest from up north, and he has been visiting me and asking if I know of anybody from the south who can send their girls here to St Joseph's Māori Girls' College." Mum met Father Wall at the marae, and after a short discussion, he said that St Joseph's Māori Girls' College would be the best place. I asked, "Where is St Joseph's?" and he said it is in Hawke's Bay, but I didn't even know where Hawke's Bay was. Mum asked how much it would cost, and Father Wall said, "Don't worry, we will find the money."

In 1958, aged fifteen, Wiki left home to go to her new school and, when she had arrived at her new school, she had never seen so many young Māori girls in one place:

> The sisters called us into the assembly room and said, "We want you to stand up and say who you are and where you come from." I watched the girls' faces, and I could see them giggling and laughing, and I heard them saying, "What is that Pākehā doing here?" [Wiki's skin colour is more white than brown] and I felt uncomfortable. We had to sing a waiata after we introduced ourselves, and I had never done that other than with the kapa haka group at the marae. I stood and said my name is Wiki Brown from Temuka, recited my whakapapa and sang "Pōkarekare Ana". Well, they kept giggling until I started singing, and then everything just hushed, and then I sat down and the girls were all blown away.

After school, Wiki continued singing. 'When I was living in Wellington, I was in Ngāti Pōneke and we would sing in the overseas liners.' Wiki was also in a television singing competition in the 1970s:

> I got into the finals and Howard Morrison, who was one of the judges, said, "I remember you and you are going to win." I didn't win; I got second, but everybody said, "You were the winner!" I was then very much involved with my own band. In those days, you could go to the hotels and sing for two to three hours and you were paid, so I set up the Phoenix Show Band. We travelled from one end of the island to the other, and because people knew me, it was easy to get bookings.

In 2008, Wiki was awarded a Queen's Service Medal for services to Māori, music and the community.

Moana Maniapoto-Jackson's name has been synonymous with the New Zealand music industry for the past quarter of a century, ever since she released her first single 'A E I O U' with her band, The Moahunters. The track featured on her first album titled *Tahi*, which earned Moana and her band its first gold record.[711] 'Black Pearl' was another song on the album that would become an anthem for Māori women, reaching number two on the national charts.[712] 'Rebel in Me' was sung to President Nelson Mandela when he was hosted at a church service in Auckland and 'Peace, Love & Family' also featured the famous Neville Brothers from America. Her second album, *Rua*, was released in 1998.[713] The song 'Moko' was crowned the winner of the 2003 International Songwriting Competition, and Moana became the first non-American to win a major American songwriting

Wiki Brown and Indiana Kuru with members of the Lions rugby team.

A HISTORY OF ST JOSEPH'S MĀORI GIRLS' COLLEGE   233

competition. The closing track features St Joseph's singing 'Ave Maria' with Moana. Moana now has five albums, and in 2016 she was inducted into the New Zealand Music Hall of Fame. She was appointed a Member of the New Zealand Order of Merit in 2004, and at the 2008 Māori Waiata Awards, she received a Music Industry Award for her positive contribution to Māori music.

Moana decided she was going to St Joseph's when her best friend from Rotorua Intermediate, Marina Johnson, decided she would go there. Unfortunately for Moana, Marina wasn't accepted to the college, so she arrived not knowing anybody. 'My parents scrimped and saved, and the whole neighbourhood came to say goodbye as money was thrust into my hand,' recalls Moana. She remembers really taking a liking to the church aspect of her schooling:

> The singing was so beautiful. It was very romantic for a young girl. We used to go to the church down the road that was run by Pākehā, but it was boring because they couldn't sing. The brothers used to come down from the seminary and practise their sermons because they had an appreciative audience. A lot of them were only a couple of years older than our senior girls.

It was at St Joseph's that Moana developed her skills as a public speaker:

> My public speaking skills came from the school. The brothers from the seminary would come down and take our debating team, so I joined the team. Last year, I was at a hearing for the Waitangi Tribunal, and the main judge turned to me and said, "We have met before, but you won't remember. We debated against you at the O'Shea Shield and you whipped us, so I'm not going to argue with you here today."

For Moana, who had lived in Invercargill during her childhood for a decade, as her father, along with other men from Te Arawa, shifted to the far south in search of work, learning Māori at St Joseph's was important as part of her cultural identity. 'I was part of a big Māori family, and we were involved in our marae at Waitetoko, Taupō. We learnt the written part of te reo Māori from the Waititi books.'

Her final year at St Joseph's was in the sixth form, with the seventh form option not being available. 'I wanted to go home and lose some weight. We all ended up like tubs of lard, podgy as, because we would just eat food and there was no nutritionist.' Going to the school that her sisters attended, McKillop College, Moana realised she was the only pupil doing te reo Māori in the entire Bay of Plenty region, and her friend, Erana Hond, was the only student doing Māori in the Waikato province, both by correspondence. Developing study habits at St Joseph's is one skill that Moana has maintained her whole life. 'I was so conscious of my parents' investment that I studied, and I ended up being the Dux, and my grandfather described me as being the "Duck". I'd just study, study, study, and the Sisters would have to drag me off the study.'

Equipped with the ability to swot, Moana entered university. 'There wasn't any consciousness or encouragement of going to university. It was all about becoming nurses, secretaries or teachers. Erana Hond's mother told us that we were going to varsity. I thought universities were for rich Pākehā. We [she and Erana] ended up going with Donna Awatere, who was studying to be an educational psychologist at Waikato University.' From Waikato University, Moana enrolled at the University of Auckland to study law.

It was at St Joseph's that Moana learnt how to harmonise and play the guitar:

> I am the chinga-chinga guitarist, and the only time I've played the guitar at a concert was at the Sydney Opera House. I didn't know

then that I wanted to pursue music as a career. I was useless. I was in the second or third row of the concert party; in fact, I wasn't even in the back row! I wasn't a star singer at school; Hinewehi Mohi was [Hinewehi was also a member of The Moahunters for a time]. There were heaps of people who could sing at St Jo's. I was just another one, one of a dime a dozen. It is songwriting that makes a difference. I started to write music at St Joseph's but nothing too flash because I could only play about three chords, which is about my repertoire now.

It wasn't until Moana was at law school that she started to contemplate becoming a musician. 'I started doing talent quests with Aroaro Hond and playing in pubs. Then I met Dalvanius, and with my husband of the time, Willie, we began to plot my career and started my own band.' Moana has returned to her old school to record the girls singing 'Ave Maria'.

Hinewehi Mohi is probably most well known for transforming New Zealand's national anthem. In 1999, she sang 'God Defend New Zealand' in Māori before the test match at Twickenham between the All Blacks and England at the Rugby World Cup. Her act caused controversy at the time, with politicians declaring that the convention would be for the first verse of the anthem to be sung in Māori, followed by the English equivalent. That same year, Hinewehi released her first album, *Oceania*, the first Māori language album to be released internationally, followed by *Oceania II* and *Raukatauri – Te Puhi o te Tangi*. The latter is named after her daughter, Hineraukatauri, who was born with cerebral palsy in 1996. In 2004, Hinewehi opened the Raukatauri Music Therapy Centre as a musical haven for those with disabilities. Hinewehi herself faced a personal struggle in 2011 when she was diagnosed with breast cancer, which led to a double mastectomy. Two years later, Hinewehi was a semi-finalist in the New Zealander of the Year Awards, and in 2008, she was named a Member of the New Zealand Order of Merit.

Hinewehi was raised on a farm in Flemington in central Hawke's Bay. 'We were a long way from Waipukurau, so most kids after primary school knew they were going to boarding school.' Getting into St Joseph's was not straightforward for Hinewehi:

> I'm not Catholic, but I really wanted to go to St Jo's. For the first term and a half, I went to Hukarere and won the local Korimako speech competitions. My dad approached Georgina to see if I could get in halfway through the year, and because I had shown some level of achievement with the speech competition, I was accepted.

Describing herself as a 'goody two shoes', Hinewehi has fond recollections of the sisters:

> Sister Maureen 'Doc' Richardson took care of pastoral issues, doled out the medication and was very much the mum of the hostel, a really wonderfully warm and kind-hearted person who embraced us as her own kids. Sister Maureen was the cook, and the food was really awful, so we survived on getting food from family. Our mate Barbie [Erana] Keelan had the best food parcels that contained rewana bread.

Other members of the clergy included Father Bernie Atkins. 'Father Atkins was another favourite. We adored him so much, and he was a real father figure to us, like a koro.'

Another recollection Hinewehi has of the Catholic clergy was when one 'hard-case girl' said: 'When the brothers come in today, let's see if we can turn them! Let's see if we can get them to leave the seminary!' Hinewehi is full of praise for her former te reo Māori and concert party teacher:

As a singer-songwriter, I just adored St Joseph's, and it was what set me in good stead for recording and performing music because Georgina [Kingi] was really strict, and I liked that firmness. A couple of months ago, I did a recording with Maisey Rika for her new album, and we had the St Jo's girls performing with us. Georgina was right there, scolding Maisey and I for not trying to reach the high notes. I think she is amazing. I know a lot of girls found her very confronting in terms of being a disciplinarian and the matriarch of the school, but they also have huge respect for her. I've never been in the same sort of environment. I loved the purity of the voices and the sweet singing because Georgina had a way of getting the right tone.

Hinewehi compares her personal experiences with some of the schools of today: 'I see some schools really focusing on kapa haka rather than the academics. Georgina was very clear – first was academic and everything else was second, third, fourth and fifth to that.'

Maisey Rika has now produced four albums: *Maisey Rika* (2009), *Tohu* (2009), *Whitiora* (2012) and *Tira* (2016). Her first taste of music success came when she was at St Joseph's in 1998, aged fifteen, when her song 'E Hine' went double platinum and won the Best Māori Language Album at the New Zealand Music Awards and she was awarded Best Female Vocalist.[714]

Maisey and friends.

In 2010, Maisey won four out of the four nominated categories at the 2010 Waitata Māori Music Awards, including Best Māori Female Solo Artist, a category she had won the previous year, Best Māori Pop Album and Best Māori Songwriter.[715]

Maisey, whose nanny is former old girl Ngaroma Ngamoki, came from the small settlement of Ōmaio in the Bay of Plenty. As Maisey's mother wanted her to go to Greenmeadows to receive a better education, she worked three jobs to pay the fees, with Maisey also receiving a scholarship. 'I was really against going because all my friends were in Whakatāne. I had never been to a Catholic school before, and around Whakatāne and the coast, it is all Ringatū. We were quite tomboyish. We liked our hats and big jeans. I had never worn togs in the pool or high heels before.'

Life at a boarding school was a new experience:

> There were no washing machines, so everything was hand-washed, and when you ate, you don't make clattering noises on your plate. Our jobs were called employments, and you had your houses and your name under the list of employments. It was mainly our seniors who were the disciplinarians. We didn't get an EFTPOS card until you reached fifth form. You had to earn your money card, and it felt good to earn it.

Maisey still keeps in touch with her friends from St Joseph's:

> I've met some wonderful friends who have become sisters. Everywhere I go, even in Rarotonga, they are at every show. When I recorded the latest album, *Tira*, some of the girls jumped into the studio to help. We've had our twenty-firsts, our children and our weddings together. Now we make excuses to see each other. It's like you haven't left, and you have that bond together. You grow up together in those turbulent adolescent years. We know when someone's hurting and when someone's happy.

Rites of Passage

Most high school pupils will, at some time stage, try smoking, drinking alcohol, dating, perhaps getting a tattoo or tā moko or, these days, smuggling a cellphone into class. As former principal Sister Margaret Purdie remembers:

> We had the old hall when the new church at Greenmeadows was built. It was cut into two and moved onto our property. There was an old storage loft above the entrance way, and we had to keep an eye on it because that would be a spot where the girls would go smoking. I used to think "God help us, things could be a lot worse!" Smoking was a particular issue Whānau Whānui discussed during the 1980s. In 1985, it was identified as a problem at the school and a letter had to be sent to parents,[716] and three years later, it was noted that some girls were smoking in the hostels at night which was a very dangerous practice.[717]

Taini Hudson, a student during the 1960s, states: 'If you were caught smoking during my time, you were expelled, just like that. It was quite sad because a lot of them were quite bright and they were gone, no questions asked.' For Te Arani Barrett, it took her forty years to make a confession to Georgina Kingi. 'I told her it wasn't me smoking in her room because I had never smoked. Tina Mitai did it!' Tania Jacobs remembers being caught smoking. 'We had to pick the prickles out of the field, and we thought that was great because we could take our smokes out on the field and keep smoking! We were just being typical teenagers.'

Theresa McAlister remembers almost being caught. 'One of the sisters came towards us, and one of the girls shoved the cigarette in my ice cream!' She also remembers trying to get a cigarette off pupils at Hato Paora:

> My friends and I used to write to a group of boys at Hato Paora. They had come up and managed to get a smoke off us, so they owed us a cigarette. They had sellotaped it to a page, and there was a letter to say, "You have been discovered" signed "The Scarlet Pimpernel". We thought, "What the heck?" For a while, we were really stumped, and then I got a letter from my brother and on the bottom, it said, "Hi Theresa. How are you going? Hope things are going well. Father Max". It was the same bloody handwriting who had caught us out!

Rawinia Higgins admits to being a smoker at St Joseph's. 'I used a lot of Impulse, and I got caught in my fifth form. I had to ring my parents and tell them, and it didn't go down very well.' Beth Dixon smoked in the caretaker's, Uncle Bill's, shed. 'It used to cram eight of us, at the back of the kitchen. Another spot was the roof. One of the girls unpicked the lock, and we had a smoke on the roof. The seniors found out, raided our tuck boxes and took us into the hall. We didn't get to go to Nūhaka that year.' Kimiora Kaire-Melbourne remembers quite a few in her year smoking. 'One year, the smokers lost one week of their holidays. Miss Kingi got all the parents behind her, and we had to do a course to quit smoking that week.'

Nadell Karatea can remember being caught with alcohol. 'One year, I was naughty and indulged in a few liquid beverages, and to this day, I am gutted I participated in those beverages. My grandmother came to the school and swore to Miss Kingi that her grandchild would not do that again.' Pania Newton faced the Board of Trustees when she sneaked alcohol into the college. 'One of the girls' mums brought it in. I had a cellphone, and the Board read all the text messages of the girl getting her mum to bring the alcohol.'

Tattooing with Indian ink is one forbidden activity that Noreen Pakinga remembers. 'Sometimes you'll see girls with SJC tattooed on their skin. We would get the ink out when the sisters went for their dinner.' Moana Maniapoto-Jackson confesses: 'I think I'm responsible for a whole lot of terrible tattoos on girls! I was the school artist, and I would do all the graphics.' Mere-Kingi Harvey-Brewster confirms that tattooing has gone to another level in recent years. 'A few girls in my form had a tā moko, and one of them was in kapa haka. I would have to spend ages with the concealer trying to cover her up, and another one had it up her thigh and she had to put a bandage on it.'

On the subject of boys, Michelle Hoko recollects:

I had a boy cousin at every boys' boarding school. I would get letters from them, and the girls would want to know what they said. Some of them would give me their pictures and say, "Can you give this to this girl?" and I would tell them, "You have to do my art work." We also used to go to the seminary up the road. There were two boys from Hato Paora who were training. We used to think, "What are you doing you crazy people. You are just too spunky, you can't be a priest!"

Georgina Kingi has clear opinions about balls. 'Balls are a hōhā! Do you know, I can't remember ever saying the day afterward we have been involved in a ball, "That was marvellous!" It was just a headache, and they are just expensive and a distraction to their schoolwork.' Rather than a ball, seniors and school leavers have a graduation dinner with their parents at the end of the year.

Nowadays, cellphones are a distraction for pupils. As former student Mere-Kingi Harvey-Brewster states:

No cellphones are the rule, and I don't think we should have them. When I was a year 11, I snuck my phone in, and it was just a distraction with Facebook and contacting boys. Miss Kingi caught one girl with a cellphone, and she put it in a bucket of water. The girl said, "That's not going to work, it's waterproof!" Then Miss said, "That's okay, I'll just back my car over it."

Board of Trustees and discipline committee member Tuterangi Nepe-Apatu remarks that the school has a zero-tolerance policy on drugs. 'If we find drugs, the girl goes home. If you drink, you'll be suspended and return to school on some very tight restrictions. When it comes to fighting and bullying, there is zero tolerance, and we have been known to call in Youth Aid because of lessons needing to be made.'

Senior dinner 2015.

The Green Nun

The 'ghost' story at St Joseph's is the story of 'the green nun'. Noreen Pakinga tells the story.

> Some seniors used to tell us about the hostel being haunted to get us to go to bed. I was told that the green nun was a clumsy nun who fell down the stairs and broke her neck and then died in the laundry room, so all these rooms are haunted. Looking back, it was to stop us wandering at night because we were scared we would see her. There was also a "blue nun".

Riria McDonald remembers trying to pour cold water over the ghost theory:

> The lights went out, and I said, "Nah, there is no such thing as a ghost here."
>
> Letitia Hawkins goes, 'I'll prove it to you. I'll go down to the toilets. Sister Annetta [Beverley Grounds] was coming up the stairs. She was quite tall and slim and very fair, and she freaked Letitia out so much so that she had to go and sleep in Doc's office because she believed the dorm was haunted. So, no one ever went to the toilet.

For Kimiora Kaire-Melbourne, she was told about the green nun in the third form:

> The seniors would take study and would tell us the story. There is a mattress room, and it is quite scary. I was in B dorm and the toilets were down the other end, next to D dorm. As you are walking there, there are the stairs up to the fourth form dorm, and there is a white statue of St Joseph. Then you pass the mattress room. The story goes that a nun died in there, and she used to haunt that hallway. The college has an intercom system, and the seniors would breathe into the intercom during the night, and then you would get to seventh form and you would continue the practice.

Hikurangi Edwards didn't like walking over the manholes on the lino floor when she had to go to the toilet or use the shower in case a hand came out. 'I used to get bad rheumatics, and the sisters used to say to me to go back to the dorms and have a hot shower and go to bed. When you are the only one in there and it is steaming up from the shower, it can be a scary place.'

Sometimes the pupils took it on themselves to act as the ghost. Maureen Rogers remembers: 'In the fourth form, Carla Kereopa had a key, and some of the girls got dressed up in white sheets and put powder on. They ran through the third form dorm and freaked the daylights out of them! That was a dishes punishment.'

Sister Katarina and others reliving their youth at the 140th celebrations.

CHAPTER NINE

Being Bicultural

The period from the 1980s and 1990s at St Joseph's can be described as the point when the Sisters of Our Lady of the Missions became more 'biculturally aware'. As historian Susan Smith observed, between 1982 and 1994 '... various Provincial Leadership Teams were responsible for several initiatives aimed at conscientising them to this issue'.[718] Examples of such activities including sending sisters to work with Māori in Ruatōria and Kaikōura and researching the titles of congregation-owned land to ensure that it was not confiscated Māori land or purchased at unjust prices. These investigations led to an apology to Ngāi Tahu in 1992 and money being given by the order to help establish archives. In 1988, two hui were held at St Joseph's to promote biculturalism within the Church.[719]

A trio of sisters died during late 1979 and early 1980. Sisters Mary Lawrence and Mary Constance, who both taught at the school during the 1940s, passed away in late 1979. Sister Mereana (Martha Keogh) died on New Year's Day, and a requiem mass was held before her body was returned to Kaikohe.[720] Sister Beverley Grounds was the acting and deputy principal when Sister Mereana died:

> We had two elderly sisters staying at the college at the time and she said she would stay during the Christmas holidays with them. I was travelling to my brother's holiday house at Okarito on the West Coast of the South Island when she died, and the police were trying to locate me. Eventually Father Foot told me. I met the cortege in Auckland after I managed to catch a plane. It came as a terrible shock to us as she was still so young.

Tuterangi Nepe-Apatu also remembers Sister Mereana's passing. 'I got to carry her into the chapel, and I carried her out, and then we took her down the road to the church in Greenmeadows. We then took her home to rest in Te Tai Tokerau.' St Joseph's also grieved for former old girl and sister Dawn Mokomoko McNichol, otherwise known as Sister Marie Chanel, who died suddenly in Sydney in November 1986. McNichol attended the college between 1953 and 1956 and was laid to rest at Tūrangawaewae.[721]

Left: Ann Knox.
Right: Sister Mereana (Martha Keogh).

Marlene Wilkinson at the opening of Te Maori exhibition in New York. To the left is Lady June Mead.

Sadly another staff member at St Joseph's would also pass away during the 1980s. In February 1984, teacher Ann Knox passed away after being ill with lung cancer.[722] Ann had been associated with the school for sixteen years, initially as School Certificate supervisor and secretary of the college. After having joined the teaching staff as a member of the Commercial Department, she became the senior mistress, head of the Commercial Department and the careers advisor. A trophy was presented by her husband, Gordon, to be awarded to the pupil who has achieved general excellence in commercial studies and shorthand.[723]

In 1980, the school achieved its best-ever results for School Certificate and University Entrance.[724] In 1981, two Māori carvings were presented by two inmates at Paremoremo Prison, whose mother and grandmother had attended the school, in appreciation of the counselling they had received from Sister Maureen Duncan. The carvings now adorn the entrance way to the old hall, Te Rangimarie.[725] On Easter Sunday 1982, the school performed a play 'Te Maramatanga – The Light of the World' on the television show *Credo*, which played on TV One.[726] Described as a Māori response to Easter, the play was written by Father Tim Gordon with Georgina Kingi as musical director. The play focused on the last four days of the life of Jesus Christ, with waiata and dance, and, impressively, was filmed in just one day.

For Marlene Wilkinson, March 1986 would be memorable, as she represented the school at the opening of the Te Māori exhibition in Chicago.[727] Marlene's observations of the Native American dawn ceremony in Chicago was that: 'The ceremony was similar to our pōwhiri: Where tāne use taiaha, the Indian man used knives and the women stood behind supporting with song ... The first whakairo I saw was Pūkaki, a ray of light shining on his face'.[728] Another recollection for Marlene was assisting Hirini and June Mead, who were taking night tours of the exhibition. One evening, a

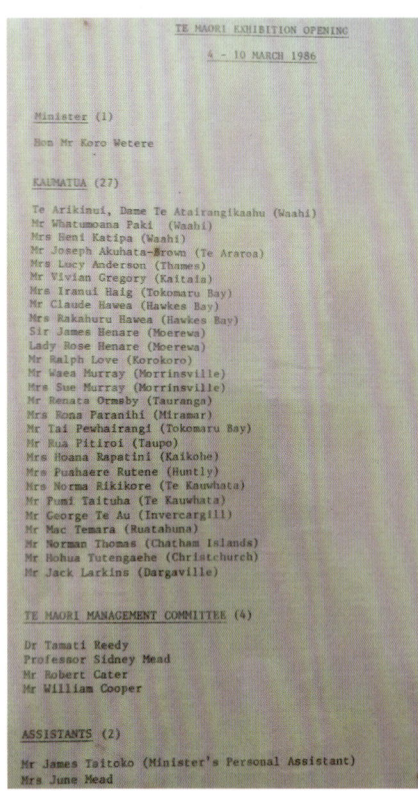

List of Rangatira attending Te Maori exhibition.

group of two to three hundred teachers asked, 'How come you speak English so fluently? Are you a Māori? I thought they were all dark.'[729]

The biggest event of 1985 would be the unveiling of large carvings that would become a school landmark.[730] The carvings that now stand on the Marian Steps arrived at 7.30 a.m. on 12 August. Accompanying the carvings were Pā Henare Tate accompanied by Kuia including Ka Corbett and Tui Campbell-Swannenbeck. There weren't enough men to unload the carvings and some last-minute phone calls had to be made to gather some help. With Father McGowan and Pā Tate having blessed the carvings, they were erected on the Marian Steps on the following Thursday in preparation for Saturday's unveiling. Carver Robert Koko, along with 100 visitors, arrived at 1 p.m. and Koro John Koko, with pupils from Hato Petera, helped unveil the carvings. Koro John then placed the eyes in the carving, with a puhi walking underneath the figurine. Following an explanation of the carvings, a hākari was held.[731]

Phyllis Peni was involved in taking some of the pupils to Paremoremo Prison:

> When Robert Koko had almost completed the carvings, a few of us went up there to the prison, and we took the senior girls. Some of them were a bit iffy about going into a prison, but it was an awesome experience. We stayed at the Māori mission, and that night, the late Zac Wallace [the Māori actor who is probably best known for his role in the 1983 film *Utu*] spoke to the girls about his life, which was a bit shady, and he openly spoke about the things he had done and the consequences. He was telling the girls to make something of themselves.

Integration agreement.

The Integration of St Joseph's Māori Girls' College

On 13 September 1982, St Joseph's became integrated into the New Zealand state education system. With the roll being fixed at 237 boarders, the special character of the school was preserved through the agreement the Catholic church had reached with the government: that the school would remain an educative centre of the Christian Catholic community, and that it would preserve its distinctive Māori ethnic character.[732] The agreement meant the school was entitled to state funding.[733]

Sister Beverley remembers the need for the school to become integrated and the relief the move offered the sisters:

> Sisters and brothers were becoming fewer, with most of our membership being in Asia, Vietnam, India and Myanmar. Services to the Western world were dying out a bit. It was really a help because we had to get more and more lay staff, and it was good to get government help. It didn't change things the way the school ran; that aspect was seamless. The school had the full support of the bishop of the diocese, and we were glad to get the help.

Kimiora Kaire-Melbourne reporting live from Waitangi.

Media

Iulia Leilua
NGĀTI HAUA, NGĀTI HEKEĀWAI, SAMOAN
1981–1984

Mereana Hond
TARANAKI
1983–1986

Stephanie Tibble
NÉE POHE
NGĀTI RONGOMAIWAHINE, NGĀTI KAHUNGUNU
1984–1986

Kimiora Kaire-Melbourne
NGĀI TŪHOE, NGĀTI KAHUNGUNU, NGĀPUHI
2006–2009

Iulia Leilua is a familiar face in the media, having appeared on TV for the past thirty years. Born in Taumarunui, Iulia was educated at St Patrick's before joining the Māori girls from the area and being sent to St Joseph's. 'The Pākehā students were sent to either Sacred Heart or Silverstream in Wellington. I was a little different at St Joseph's because I am part Samoan and my name is Samoan. There were two or three other part Samoan/Māori students who went to St Joseph's, as well as a girl from American Samoa.'

Iulia remembers being very homesick. 'I was the first of my immediate family to have gone there, and my aunts and uncles would say, "Don't waste your parents' hard work. Go and do well." I knew that going there cost a lot of money. Some kids got a Māori Education Fund scholarship, but we didn't qualify, and so my mum had two jobs.'

One experience that Iulia credits with giving her the confidence to foot it in the world of media is having succeeded in the Ngā Manu Kōrero Competition

Iulia Leilua.

Ani-Piki Tuari.

in 1983. 'I entered the Korimako section and won the regional competition for Hawke's Bay, even though I was really shy growing up and not forthcoming.'

As there was no seventh form at St Joseph's, Iulia had to finish her schooling at Taumarunui:

> That was a culture shock, and my careers advisor said, "You're a hothouse flower, and having come from St Joseph's, you need to be in certain conditions to flourish." During the holidays, he introduced me to the Waiariki Māori journalism introductory and booster courses. That's when I decided to become a journalist. It was a natural progression from having done Ngā Manu Kōrero, and I had my first story published in the sixth form, a poem, for the *Tū Tangata* magazine. It was awesome on the journalism course, being around other young Māori. That's when I realised I had been conditioned to thinking in a Māori way.

After having completed the journalism course at Waiariki Polytechnic, Iulia returned home to Taumarunui to work at the *Taumarunui Gazette* for a few months. One day, she received a phone call from Pere Matai after she had expressed an interest to go on a television course:

> He said that I could go with six other Māori on a special course at the end of 1986 and work for the Māori Department at TVNZ in Auckland that was going to be established in 1987. I was with Erana Reedy from St Joseph's, George Stirling, Temuera Morrison, Fiona Murchie, Eliza Bidois and Bradford Haami. We didn't have Māori Television or Iwi Radio, but we were populating the first Māori Department at TVNZ, being trained by Whai Ngata and Ernie Leonard, and I've been in TV ever since. The choices of programmes were *Te Karere*, *Waka Huia*, *Koha* or *Tagata Pasifika*.

I chose *Tagata Pasifika* because I knew very little about my Pasifika side, and I was there for ten years. I went on to work for Aotearoa TV, then did news producing for *One News* and had a PR company for a decade.

Ask Mereana Hond about her time at St Joseph's and she says she's certain about one thing: she would not have achieved many of the things she is most proud of without the strong foundation she got from the school. 'I left with lifelong friends, confidence on a stage, on the sports field, as well as gaining that innate understanding of the give and take of living with others. And thanks to the regimented study regime that St Jo's old girls will remember well, I got good grades, which set me up for what lay ahead.'

What lay ahead was a career in academia, involvement in the settlement of Treaty claims for Taranaki and then a switch to journalism. The common thread to it all was a passion for te reo Māori and tikanga:

> Our parents instilled in us a strong sense of self: as Māori, as followers of Parihaka, as members of Te Hahi Katorika and as young Māori with an identity squarely around Taranaki and the muru me te raupatu (confiscation). It was a positive childhood. But there were gaps. The gaps come from a childhood in the 1970s, well before the kōhanga reo and before the recognition that speaking Māori at home is fundamental, not only to its survival, but to the health and well-being of the next generation.

It was at St Jo's that she discovered a love for subjects she'd shown little interest in before, like chemistry and maths:

> I put that down to the teachers. They were so incredibly dedicated. As a student, you pick up on that in many different ways. Mrs Rafaelove putting on extra classes for us when the going got tough. The sisters letting us stay up late to study in the old hall before School C exams. Mr Curham with his long spidery writing across the blackboard, sparking that burning interest in history and encouraging us to find meaning in our past.

But St Jo's wasn't all about study. Mereana says it was about friendships formed and having a good time with your mates. Movie night on the weekends watching *The Terminator* and *Conan the Barbarian*. Devouring chips and dip, chocolate and biscuits sent in care packages from home and coming up with imaginative ways of keeping themselves entertained. 'We'd go to the fields out back and pretend to be commandoes. It was mad but hilarious.' By the time Mereana left St Joseph's, she was joint head girl and Dux of the college. Unable to do seventh form at the school, she had the opportunity to go to Brazil on the Rotary Exchange Programme for her seventh form year.

Mereana has benefited from being able to follow in the footsteps of her siblings. Her sisters Erana and Aroaro attended St Jo's. And she followed her mother, Pat, her sister Erana and her two brothers Ruakere and Tama to Waikato University. 'I wasn't entirely sure

Mereana Hond.

what to study back then. So, I took Ruakere's advice and enrolled in law and, of course, Māori studies.' Mereana completed her studies at Victoria University with an LLB and a Bachelor of Arts (Hons) in Māori studies and linguistics. 'I started teaching te reo Māori at Victoria while I was studying, and in my third year I took up a lectureship at Te Kawa a Maui [School of Māori Studies] at Victoria. A few years later, I went on to lecture at the law faculty.'

The switch in professions from academia to journalism came in 2003:

> I was always a bit of a news geek. I loved the law, but I would find myself drawn to journalism yet again – political commentary in particular. My sister Aroaro is a great journalist in her own right, so I was inspired by her and the Māori she worked alongside at the time, people who paved the way for all of us.

Mereana went on to win a Qantas Television Award for her journalism, including her coverage of events at Waitangi, and she became known for her work as one of the few journalists covering Māori issues in mainstream media.

Then, in 2006, she moved to London to broaden that knowledge base. She worked for the international news agency Associated Press and balanced out the office job with work that took her around London and throughout the UK and Europe, performing with the London Māori Club and for Manaia, a Māori Performing Arts Company based in London. Mereana says the highlight was performing the karanga at the memorial service for Sir Edmund Hillary at St George's Chapel at Windsor Castle. 'There I was in this gathering place of royals for centuries, a stunningly beautiful church, with the most incredible acoustics I'd ever encountered. It was absolutely packed – a veritable who's who of royalty and New Zealand dignitaries, including the Queen and then Prime Minister Helen Clark. And all of it broadcast live back home.' Four years later, Mereana moved to the Middle East to work for Al Jazeera English at its headquarters in Qatar.

Stephanie Tibble (née Pohe) comes from the small Hawke's Bay town of Wairoa. Both of Stephanie's grandmothers helped pay for her education, with her mother working in the kiwifruit orchards in Nūhaka to help subsidise the cost:

> St Jo's was the making of me. I came from a community where being Māori was a problem, a deficit, and the schools were dominated by gangs. When you are from a certain area, you were affiliated with a gang, even though you're not. I was smoking and going to parties, and it was hard to be different. I wanted to take Māori at college, and because it was streamed and I was in the higher stream, you couldn't, and all the dummies took Māori.

Being able to take Māori at St Joseph's was a major attraction to attend the school. 'My best friend's brother who attended Te Aute would come home and could understand *Te Karere* and that was cool. At St Jo's it was cool to take Māori.'

The final year for Stephanie at St Joseph's was the fifth form, as the money to support her education had dried up:

> My parents thought that if you had School C, you had the main qualification. I went to Nelson where my parents were living and went to a mainstream school with all Pākehā, where it was a culture shock. When I went into the sixth form, there was no Māori, and it had to be done by correspondence. That was quite lonely, and I didn't hang out with kids at school. I hung out with Māori who

Tihini Grant, Miki Apiti, Stephanie Tibble and Orini Kaipara.

were not at school. I left halfway through my seventh form and went on an access scheme at the local marae.

Looking back at her schooling at Wairoa, it provided some inspiration in Stephanie wanting to become a teacher. 'Friends I went to primary school with were leaving, and yet academically we were all the same, and they didn't get School C. That cemented for me that I wanted to be a teacher and that Māori kids needed support to reach their potential.' Stephanie ended up at Wellington Teachers' College with two other former pupils from St Joseph's: Nessa Gotty and Vicky Peni. 'They were in their second or third year of teachers' college, and they looked after me. It was the early days of bilingual education, so I did that, and then I went straight into teaching at an immersion school in Porirua.'

Following her foray into the teaching profession, Stephanie went to Japan for a few years and taught English. 'I then went to Huia Publishers. I didn't know anything about publishing, but I had some ideas about education publishing.' Stephanie managed the resource team. 'My idea was that we could come together and make really good resources for kura.' After Huia, Stephanie returned to teaching at Te Kura Māori o Porirua and was the deputy principal for two years:

I then went to Auckland and saw a job at *Waka Huia*. I had watched the programme since I was a kid, and I had boxes of VHS. I ended up being a director, a reporter, a jack of all trades. My first shoot was with Te Rangihau Gilbert and Miki Apiti with the Ngāi Tūhoe tohunga, Hohepa Kereopa, and I was sold.

From *Waka Huia*, Stephanie transferred to presenting *Marae* under Whai Ngata. 'He is a significant person, and he went to Te Aute, so going to St Jo's and having those whakapapa connections meant something to him.' After five years in television, Stephanie returned to Wellington, doing a range of media consultancy roles for the Ministry of Education, Te Taura Whiri, Te Puni Kōkiri and Māui Productions. One of her more recent projects has been working with former St Joseph's pupil and friend Celia Joe, doing the St Joseph's Oral History Project.

Kimiora Kaire-Melbourne and her cousin Wikitoria Day presented 'Rereata', midday news bytes that were broadcast online by Māori Television. Kimiora's grandmother, Maria Melbourne (née Martin from Mitimiti) attended St Joseph's, as well as her mother's first cousin, Maia Melbourne-Wilcox. Kimiora was raised in Ruatoki and, having attended kōhanga and wharekura, her mother was keen for her daughter to focus on having a Pākehā education.

Being away from Ruatoki gave Kimiora a different perspective on life:

> When you are in Ruatoki, you think everybody else is like that. You are quite sheltered and not aware of how different everybody is, like having a different mita and girls not growing up where they are from. Some girls during my time had grown up in Australia and had not known where they were from tribally. Ruatoki was a Māori school, and knowing te reo Māori was the norm. There were a few girls at St Jo's who knew te reo, but not many girls from Ngāi Tūhoe went there. When I did Ngā Manu Kōrero in the third form, they started picking up my mita such as dropping the G's.

It would be through doing the Māori speech competition in 2006 that Kimiora gained confidence. 'I was very shy and hardly spoke.' At prizegiving, Kimiora was awarded the Rāwhiti Ihaka section:

> When I went back to school, I was picked up from the bus stop. Instead of going down the school's normal driveway, I went down the chapel driveway. They did a haka pōhiri for me, and that was overwhelming. Even the prefects came up to me and congratulated me. If she [Miss Kingi] hadn't pushed me into it, I would not be in this industry.

Kimiora also reflects about coming from the community of Ruatoki. 'Girls were not given the opportunity to speak Māori. Our men would speak Māori. If I didn't go to St Joseph's, I wouldn't have known what I was capable of. The school gives you that confidence.'

For her final year of high school, Kimiora attended Epsom Girl's Grammar. During her last term, Kimiora had a part-time job working the autocue at Māori Television and had heard of an opening as an online reporter, so she applied.

'I was twenty-one and was interviewed by Julian Wilcox. He asked me what job I wanted, and I told him the reporter position, and I've now been doing that as a presenter and reporter.' Kimiora also worked there with Ani-Piki Tuari, who had been the head girl of St Joseph's when Kimiora was in the third form.

Mereana Hond and her sisters.

Ivan Emia, Cyril Gotty and Tom Tuhura.

Whānau Whānui

The first hui to form a national parent and friends association for St Joseph's took place in July 1982.[734] Paul McAlister remembers the chain of events:

> I used to go over on a Saturday, and I can remember saying to Sister Jo, "Why isn't there something organised for the girls to do?" She said, "You do it." So, we started "Top Town" for the girls in 1980. It was a success, and it helped introduce the new third form to the girls because it was always held at the beginning of the year.

From there, 'Mr Mac' was approached by Sister Patricia Huckle to help organise the local Parent–Teacher Association (PTA):

> The first meeting was held in the dining room. It was well attended, and I was appointed interim chair. All the money raised was to be for the benefit of the students or the school. The PTA was a really strong group of people, and they were very devoted to their daughters and the school. We would meet monthly, and from there, because we had shown such strong ties and our fundraising was really good, the other regions saw what was happening. The main person who suggested that we form a national PTA in 1982 was Tui Campbell, who became Tui Swannenbeck.

The AGM held the following year attracted fifty people and saw the election of Ben Hita as the Chairman.[735] Over the years, branches were formed in Taranaki, Wellington, Whakatāne, Horowhenua, Bay of Islands, and the smaller centres such as Dannevirke, Tokoroa, Kawerau, Murupara and Moerewa. It became known as the Whānau Whānui, and AGMs were held biannually at the annual cultural festivals that were held in July, with other meetings being held at the school's gala and prizegivings. In 1990, the organisation identified the following aims:

1. To foster and promote mutual interest and fellowship among staff, parents and friends of St Joseph's College
2. To assist the college staff in their work and welfare
3. To provide means whereby there may be closer relationships between the parents and staff
4. The promotion of college activities and the provision of necessary facilities for the use of pupils
5. Formation of sub-committees
6. To encourage membership of all parents and friends.[736]

In general, the issues discussed by the Whānau Whānui fell into five categories: fundraising (normally in the form of the annual gala with the proceeds going towards the long-awaited gymnasium), holding debutante balls, organising the Top Town event, the costs of attending St Joseph's and disciplinary matters. As long-serving Board member John Bishara explains, 'The role of the Whānau Whānui is, for example, getting the Wellington whānau to turn up one weekend and paint the dorm toilets because the Board can't afford to do it. The gala money goes to the Whānau Whānui, and they decide how it is to be distributed. The Whānau Whānui keep St Joseph's going.' The amounts received for the gala have been impressive: $12,000 (1986[737] and 1987[738]), $20,000 (1988[739]), $16,000 (1989[740]) and $17,000 (1990[741]).

In November, 1987, $90,000 had been raised for building the gym.[742] It was finally built in 1997. In 1985, the Wellington Whānau Whānui held a debutante ball at Pipitea Marae.[743] They also held a ball in Auckland at Te Unga Waka in 1989,[744] but due to a lack of response from former pupils in 1990, it was cancelled for that year.[745] Senior dances were also organised by Whānau Whānui, such as in 1987 when the Hawke's Bay branch held a dance with Hato Paora, with chair Paul McAlister observing that plants seemed to go missing whenever there was a function.[746]

From 1985, a significant issue for Whānau Whānui was outstanding accounts. A range of solutions were discussed, including parents applying for loans to the Catholic Credit Union and having girls from the north of Auckland applying to the Sister Mereana Trust Fund.[747] In 1987, Sister Mary Martin reported that the hostel had a debt of $120,000 in unpaid fees. The sisters continued to state that even though the parents of the child had not paid their fees, the hostel could not stop looking after the child and feeding them.[748] They decided to quietly remind parents.

Whānau Whānui Memories

Julia Pomana, Huia and Peter Borrell, Makareta Paku, Moana Beveridge, Meriama and Talalelei Taufale, Derek Bartlett

Julie Tangaere has nothing but praise for the local parents who contribute to St Joseph's:

> My father Peter would be here every Sunday afternoon with these humongous bags of apples from the orchards. The influence the Whānau Whānui who live in the Hawke's Bay, on girls who don't come from here, is huge. They would be here every weekend cooking us lamb tails because we wanted them, driving the girls and taking them to Mission Cup or taking them on tour. For every generation of girls who come through the college, there is always going to be a group of local parents who took the time to be with them when their parents could not. For the generations of kids, they were the stabilisers in our lives, and I don't know that they realise how important they are to all of us.

Julia Pomana managed a farm with her husband, Noni, at Patoka:

> We had three boys at Hato Paora and three girls at St Joseph's: Donna, Lorraine and Gina. Girls in their year would ask if they could come up the farm for the weekend. One year, Noni had invited the boys from Hato Paora for a weekend, and he didn't know that I had agreed that the girls from St Jo's could come. They slept in different rooms, and there was no funny business going on because we were up all night! That was a weekend and a half, and we never did that again!

Another set of parents who lived at Pātoka were Huia and Peter Borrell, who had shifted from South Otago. With no high school options available in the small settlement, Huia and Peter had to contemplate sending their daughter, Te Rina, to a boarding school:

> Our daughter was very shy, and she struggled when she first came here. In those days, there were a lot of social welfare girls at the school, and our daughter had come from a protective home. Hearing about what the social welfare girls would talk about, like abuse from their parents, our daughter knew nothing about it, and she really struggled.

The cost was another struggle for the Borrell family. 'I think we got $120 a year from the government to contribute towards her education. You learn to live on plenty of sausages and spaghetti!'

As a member of the School's Whānau Whānui, Huia remembers 1981, when they first became involved with the college:

> Our first meeting was with total strangers who were to become lifelong friends, and I can still remember that night when we met. We needed a chairperson, and this guy, Ben Hita, put his hand up really fast. Then we needed a secretary, and Phyllis Peni volunteered. We needed a treasurer, so another volunteer, Reg Sellwood, offered.
>
> Then the rest of us formed a committee that consisted of Julie and Noni Pomana, Waina and Cyril Gotty, Olive and Sam Sydney, Bella and Joe Broughton, Colleen Sellwood,

Peter Peni, Josephine Hita, Lorraine and Harry Dixon, Julia and Bob Beamsley, Pauline and John Barber, June and Tom Collins, Paul and Hiria McAlister and ourselves. Many people have now passed on. I can still remember to this day when our good friend Noni died, the day Peter Peni died, when Jo Hita died, and I think of young Carla Rewi who was the head prefect in 1983.

Makareta Paku's grandmother, Harata Te Kao, and mother, Lovey Roberts, attended St Joseph's, and the latter continued to be heavily involved with the school as a president of the Old Girls Association:

> As a little girl, I was staying there a lot and I always knew I would end up at St Joseph's. I remember stories about my grandmother coming from Waikaremoana in the early 1900s. She attended St Joseph's when it was up on the hill and was pulled out of school to return to Te Urewera to receive her kauae moko. Even my father's side came to the college and when my daughter came, she was the fourth generation to attend St Joseph's. It is a family tradition and a proud one.

Moana and Martin Beveridge, the parents of Meriama Taufale (née Beveridge), were heavily involved with the college when their daughter attended as a student during the 1980s. Such was their dedication to the school that they remained as members of the Board of Governors and then the Board of Trustees until the late 1990s. Moana's decision to send her daughter to St Joseph's was facilitated through Father Bob Lee, the principal of Hato Paora at the time:

> My late husband Martin was a devout Catholic, so I converted to the Catholic Church and Father Bob married us. I was pregnant with Kelly, our eldest son, and Father Lee asked if we wanted to send him to Hato Paora. Because neither myself or Martin could speak te reo Māori, we sent our children to either Hato Paora or St Joseph's.

Meriama and Talalelei Taufale [also known as Mr & Mrs CrossFit, as they take pupils at the school for CrossFit], like Meriama's parents Moana and Martin, are both involved in the school. Meriama recalls: 'I was supposed to go to Te Waipounamu Girls' until it was looking to close, so I came here.' Her husband Talalelei states:

> We knew where our girl Analeah was going when she was born. As a Samoan, we grew up in the church and so that's what I liked about St Joseph's. The hardest part is realising that she is going on the day you have the pōwhiri. You see that they mature as they progress through the school. It's been a really good experience for us as parents.

As a member of the Whānau Whānui, Talalelei cites fundraising as the organisation's primary objective. 'There are also plenty of parents who chip in and take them away on school trips, train them in waka ama and selflessly give themselves to the kura. When Meriama's father, Martin, passed, some of the old girls came along and said, "I remember Mr B. He would give us a couple of dollars here and there."'

Like Talalelei, Derek Bartlett '... got involved with the Board of Trustees because Miss Kingi told me to'. His daughter, Kelsey, was a pupil from 2011 to 2015:

> When my girl first got involved with St Jo's, she was a day student, and when she got to the fifth form, she wanted her to become a boarder. I asked Miss Kingi where the money was going to come from, and she awarded my daughter a Te Puawaitanga Scholarship. That was a godsend for us, and we give back to the school as much as we can.

Paul McAlister flanked by Larissa Hanara, Karen Ratana, Kiri Tahana and Ngawaiata Scott at Government House for the Duke of Edinburgh Awards.

McAlister Whānau

Hiria McAlister
NÉE MOKE
TAPUIKA, TE ARAWA
1960

Paul McAlister, Theresa McAlister
1979–1982

Hiria McAlister believes she was sent to St Joseph's because she was naughty. 'My last year was at Hohepa. I had been at Te Puke High School, and I wish I had been sent there from the start. I had the opportunity to go, but I said no because I had a boyfriend.' The McAlisters had two daughters, Theresa and Vicky, and both attended St Joseph's. 'Our daughters went to convent schools but they weren't exposed to being Māori. Paul worked for the air force at the time and was posted in Christchurch and Wellington. I felt like they were missing out, especially our eldest daughter Theresa. She wanted to learn as much as she could about her Māori side.'

Paul 'Mr Mac' McAlister got involved with the school as a founding member of the Whānau Whānui. 'Because we shifted to Napier, I felt a strong obligation to do what my parents did for my son when he attended Hato Paora.' Although they now live in Te Puke, the McAlisters have attended every gala and cultural festival until 2015. 'Even though some of the girls who went to seventh form went to Taradale High School, our home became a stop-off point for them because we lived not too far from the school and we told everyone where the key was. If it wasn't one of the priests lying on our couch, it was one of the girls.' Paul, who had represented New Zealand and played a lot of hockey and softball, helped with coaching at St Joseph's. 'I also used to take the Duke of Edinburgh [awards] and take the girls through the bush. The awards were presented at Government House and was presented by the Duke himself!'

Gala day at
St Joseph's Māori Girls' College.

Whaea Atawhai

June Collins
NGĀTI KAHU, TE RARAWA

Eileen Transom
NGĀTI MANIAPOTO, TE RARAWA

A critical aspect to the success of St Joseph's is the support offered by the staff known as the Whaea Atawhai. Jill Cotter remembers the pivotal role they played in her first year:

> The first year, you are away from your family, and so they really take on that mother role and their door was always open. There were eighty of us and we had one, Auntie Christine Love, and everyone loved her so much that we would line up and get a kiss and a hug before we went to bed. It settled everyone down.

The Principal's Message for 2009 was that 'Their [Whaea Atawhai] care, their thorough knowledge of every girl and their relationship with whānau ensures that our students are able to take advantage of every opportunity that is presented to them.'[749]

Nanny June Collins has been a Whaea Atawhai for many years. June was initially a pupil from 1962 to 1966. 'When I came back as a Whaea Atawhai, Sister Annetta [Beverley Grounds] saw me and spoke to me about the shortage of sisters that was becoming a worry for her. She said she would like to see more ex-pupils and if I had a couple of hours a night, would I mind coming in?' Having begun as a fulltime Whaea Atawhai back in 1986, June recalls ringing the late Pā Henare Tate to discuss the role:

> He said to me, "Number one, you are Māori; you respect and you love all hapū and don't think you are special because you are Ngāpuhi!" I asked him, "What's number two?" He said, "I want you to manaaki and keep the spirit of the sisters in your heart." My inspiration for becoming involved as a Whaea Atawhai was Miss Kingi. I just knew she had the expertise and the passion to carry it, and I was very safe under her reign, and that is why I have remained here all these years. I also knew I could do a good job because nothing had changed since I was a student; the standards that need to be upheld, the wairua of the college and working with the spirit of the sisters is the same.

When asked what being a Whaea Atawhai entails, June responds: 'It's like being a parent. For me it's making our kura home, a safe place, for the students. There is a lot of love in what we have to do and a lot of discipline.' June is also appreciative of the role men have played over the years. 'We have had some great men and they haven't been Catholic. When I came in, they were dynamic, and you could call on them at the drop of a hat, and they could put a nail here and there.'

Eileen Transom's daughter, Ngahina, attended St Joseph's from 1985, and it was then that she first became involved with the school. Eileen now works at St Joseph's as a Whaea Atawhai. 'My children attended a public school at Taihape, and I said to my husband that I wanted her to go to boarding school because it was pointed out when she went to primary that she could excel in better schools.' After a discussion with her daughter, Eileen asked if she would think about going to St Joseph's, to which her daughter agreed, and she was accepted after being interviewed. Eileen then had to inform her husband of the choice that had been made, to which he responded, 'But I am a founder of Taihape College!' Eventually, he accepted the decision but didn't realise then that Eileen would follow their daughter. 'I said to my daughter, "If I shift back to Napier, I am going to ask Miss Kingi for a job." I rang Miss Kingi, and I have been here ever since 2002!'

1. June Collins.
2. Eileen Transom and daughter Ngahina.
3. Whaea Atawhai 1993.
   Standing: Daphne Nicholls, Wiki Shailer, Erana Te Pou Konui.
   Seated: Mere Paku, Rita Tapine.

Peni Whānau

Phyllis Peni, Julie Tangaere
NÉE PENI
1980–1984

John Tangaere
NGĀTI POROU

Jade Tangaere-Tuhua
NÉE TANGAERE
2002–2006

Varni Carson
NÉE PENI
1984–1987

Vicki Peni
1984–1987

Lisa Ropiha
NÉE PENI
1987–1990

Fonz Ropiha
NGĀTI KAHUNGUNU, NGĀI TŪHOE

Pirihira Ropiha
2014–2018

The Peni whānau have been involved with St Joseph's since the 1950s. Following in the footsteps of her aunties, Julie Tangaere attended the college in 1981 after the local Catholic girls' high school, Tennyson College, closed in 1980. Julie recalls: 'We were raised Catholic and went to St John's College during our holiday for Catholic camps. Our local priest was Pa Brennan, and he would visit our house regularly to see my parents.' Julie also remembers the humble beginnings of her whānau:

> We lived on Bledisloe Street in Hastings, a low socioeconomic state housing community, two houses away from the Mongrel Mob. Coming to St Jo's got me School Certificate and University Entrance, and I think I was probably one of a very few from my age group who did so from our street. Some of the kids we hung out with growing up were the children of mob members. It was cool to one day catch up with one of those boys at a college event when Jade was there and to find out that his own daughters were at St Joseph's at the same time.

Phyllis, Julie's mother, admired the school's ability to educate her eldest daughter. 'We watched Julie's progress here and then decided, well we have three younger daughters and they can come too, whatever it takes to get them through.' Financially it was tough for the Peni whānau when, on two occasions, three daughters were attending the college at the time, with spaghetti becoming the staple diet in the household. Julie reflects:

> There were points in the year when an aunty living in Christchurch would help with paying some of my school fees to help my parents out. Our parents never owned their own home, and I think that was one of the reasons they didn't because they sacrificed those sorts of things in order for us to get an education. That was the driver for me when I was here because of what they had sacrificed.

Joining older sister Julie, in 1984, were twins Vicki and Varni. Vicki regards herself as 'the naughty one' for being suspended twice. 'The first time a big group of girls went outside at night, and because I was told you don't nark on your friends, I didn't and was sent home. On the second occasion, Sister Sarah thought I swore at her, but for the record, I didn't!' The youngest of the Peni sisters, Lisa, considers herself to be the opposite of Vicki and describes herself as being 'a model student'. Nicknames remain top of her mind when thinking back to when she was a pupil at the college: 'I saw some

Peni whānau: Fonz and Lisa Ropiha, Jade Tangaere-Tuhua, Pirihira Ropiha, Varni Carson, Vicki Peni, John and Julie Tangaere. Children: Te Kahui Tuhua, Teina Ropiha, Grace Carson and Kamaea Tuhua.

mates from school who I hadn't seen for a while, and I said to one of them, "Teko!" My mate responded, "It's Ngaire! No one calls me Teko any more!"'

Daughter of Julie and John Tangaere, Jade, also attended St Joseph's, as did the two daughters of Lisa and Fonz Ropiha, Avelon and Pirihira. Due to the sixth form getting into trouble constantly, fifth former Jade was appointed a prefect and was made a group prefect the following year. Then, in her final year as a seventh former in 2006, she was made head prefect along with Ani-Piki Tuari. Jade states: 'I knew I was always going to boarding school, but I didn't know how much of a big deal it was to my whānau. I can't imagine life without St Jo's. It is still a part of us and who we are.'

Jade's father, John, recalls when his daughter was born. 'Julie's father, Peter, was on the Board [of St Joseph's], and when he came to Wellington to see us he said, "Just so you know, she is already enrolled in St Jo's."' Jade's younger cousin, and daughter of Lisa and Fonz, Pirihira, has just completed her schooling at the college, after her older sister, Avelon, attended from 2009 to 2013. Listening to the whānau connection to the school, Pirihira admits to not realising how strong it was.

Phyllis also played a pivotal role in supporting the school through the Whānau Whānui and remembers the harakeke a collective of local mothers planted at the back of the school:

In the mid-1980s, Father Rob McGowan was having discussions with Georgina [Kingi] about the lack of piupiu here, and in his wisdom, he got a group of local parents to come. We started off with fifteen mothers, and then, for whatever reason, that group was whittled down. Eight of us started making a piupiu, and only five of us were able to complete one. Every now and then, I'd go to where the harakeke is planted and have a little tangi because out of the eight of us that started a piupiu, I'm the only one left. I find that hard coming into the college and remembering those who have gone on from when we first started being involved in St Joseph's.

For Vicki and Varni, neither have children who attend the school, but they are still involved, with Varni coaching netball and Vicki coaching hockey for a number of years. Husband and wife Fonz and Lisa are still involved with the school, the former as a netball coach and the latter as the voluntary sports co-ordinator. Lisa recalls:

> Having our niece Jade attend St Joseph's was really neat because it brought us back as a whānau to the college. To have that connection to St Jo's, it is hugely important because it is what our parents started. For me, it was just seeing all the mahi they did. It felt like for years we would be here until midnight doing the gala hāngī. It is about giving back. It is what our parents did.

Fonz also served one term on the Board of Trustees.

Julie and John Tangaere are long-time waka ama coaches at the school. Julie comments:

> Even though Jade was here a decade ago, we are still the coaches of waka ama. We started waka ama when she was in year 10, and in year 12 we took them to their first nationals. We act as support mechanisms, which is the same thing that I saw my father do with my friends. I'm the way I am about this school because of my dad.

John also served on the Board of Trustees and can relate to Fonz's experience. 'I was going to finish serving on the Board when we shifted to Wellington two years ago, but I was told I was to continue by Georgina Kingi.' As for John's role on the Board of Trustees, he observes:

> You are only focused on the education. It is understanding why this school exists and is prominent in terms of what the principal's focus is. If you understand that, then it is all about achievement and making sure that everything is in place, making sure that the staff are on the kaupapa. This school does not have the issues that other Māori boarding schools face. They have a waiting list which, for other Māori boarding schools, is a dream to have, and the key to that is about leadership. Because of that leadership, they know where they are going; this is the standard and if you buck the standard, then there are other options for you. If you are here at St Jo's everybody performs this way. Some families have withdrawn their children from the college because there are more options at other schools. Having said that, it's proven that the base subjects taught at St Joseph's, together with the values and principles, provide a foundation that enables a student to pursue any career pathway they want.

The late Peter Peni.

Beth Dixon.

Riria McDonald.

Being a Pupil in the 1980s

Charlie Mackey
NGĀTI POROU
1979–1982

Beth Dixon
NGĀI TŪHOE, NGĀI TAHU,
NGĀTI KAHUNGUNU
1982–1985

Taria Tahana
NGĀTI PIKIAO, NGĀTI MAKINO,
TAPUIKA
1983–1986

Te Aranga Rolleston
TAURANGA MOANA, NGĀTI POROU
1982–1984

Caroline Roberts
TE TAI TOKERAU, TE TAIRĀWHITI
1983–1986

Riria McDonald
NGĀPUHI, TE ARAWA
1982–1986

Charlie Mackey was sent to St Joseph's because her mother said the local high school on the East Coast wasn't good enough:

> Being an Anglican, when I went to St Joseph's that was the first time I had seen a nun in my life. I thought we all had to dress like that, so I was crying to my father to take me home. I've since found out that our great-aunt, Emily Walker, went to the college and was raised by the sisters. It was through her that a lot of the Walkers and Mackeys went to St Jo's, and we are all Anglicans!

Charlie also remembers the memorable nicknames her peers gave each other. 'Robin Vincent's nickname was Scab, Jackie Puru was Bulldog and Nessa Gotty was Fish.'

Te Aranga Rolleston hails from the small settlement of Bethlehem near Tauranga. Having grown up in an Anglican, Rātana and Catholic family, Te Aranga recalls being reminded that she was part of the 'small per cent' of girls who attended St Joseph's who were not Catholic. 'At Tauranga, Father Delpha didn't even let me come in the church, but all my sisters would be going. I had to wait outside because I wasn't Catholic. But when I got to St Jo's, Father McGowan

A HISTORY OF ST JOSEPH'S MĀORI GIRLS' COLLEGE   **265**

was there and he was awesome! He even gave me communion!'

Not initially being Catholic would also feature in the journey of Caroline Roberts, who was sent to St Joseph's, aged twelve, after her father had died at the age of forty-eight. 'I was naughty, and it was quite a traumatic time for me. My dad was a staunch Catholic, and all my aunties from Tolaga Bay went to St Joseph's. They pulled me aside and said, "You're not Catholic, so we had better make you a Catholic before you go."'

Unfortunately for Caroline, her start at the high school was rocky to say the least. 'Within ten days, Sister Patricia [Huckle] caught me smoking. I didn't know you couldn't smoke at St Jo's! I was told if I didn't apply myself in this environment, then I wouldn't last.'

Another memory was being taught te reo Māori at St Joseph's. 'My dad was a native speaker, and he never spoke Māori to us. Both my parents were adamant that being in a Pākehā environment and speaking English was what you needed at the time. I was surprised when you are raised only hearing the language, how much you actually know.'

Beth Dixon attended St Joseph's between 1982 and 1985. 'I had no choice. My grandmother had paid for my first year's tuition. I thought I was going to Havelock High, and I didn't want to come to St Jo's. I got tragically homesick, even though I lived down the road!' After St Joseph's, Beth went to Waikato University. Working now in Māori medium education, Beth is envious that other old girls have had the opportunity to work at their alma mater:

> As an educator, dare I say it, I'd like to come back and teach before I die. For all my naughtiness, I absolutely have no regrets that I was sent here. Now look at us; we are

Top: Te Aranga Rolleston.
Middle: Taria Tahana.
Bottom: Charlie Mackey with her daughter Hinematererangi Mackey-Pasene (2014–2018) who was the prefect of Hine Ngakau.

all successful. We can all handle life and whatever it throws at us, and you can pretty much guarantee if a St Jo's woman walks into a hall of people, there will be a way about her. I sent my girl, Tyler, here as a day girl. She gained so much strength from coming here.

Taria Tahana's father was the President of Hato Petera Old Boy's Association, so she spent many weekends at a Māori boarding school. The contrast with the mainstream school she was attending in Auckland inspired her to ask her dad if there was a girl's college like Hato Petera. He said, 'Yes, it's in Napier', and six months later, Taria found herself starting at St Jo's. Despite missing her mother's cooking, Taria found the transition to boarding life a liberating experience. 'It fostered an independence as well as a close bond with fellow students.' She also comments that being locked up with sixty other girls created a shared journey into womanhood with lots of teenage talk about boys, periods, smoking and their own hopes and dreams. Taria states: 'At the time, the discipline of class life felt tedious. However, I now believe that the structure and rigour of learning at St Jo's provided a strong foundation for higher education and future achievement.' Taria's positive experience at St Jo's soon saw her joined at the school by her younger sisters Ngaroma and Kiri, further expanding the close community of friends.

For her seventh form, Taria joined her parents in Rotorua and attended the local high school. Like many St Jo's girls, the first year out of boarding school became more about boys, nightclubs and earning money than 'I ō mahi katoa, mahia'. However, after a year of indulgence and the inevitable dip in academic performance, Taria returned to more serious matters and began a business management degree at Waikato University, graduating in 1993.

After spending time as a manager and consultant in large corporations, Taria brought those skills to Māori development, running her own consulting business and working as general manager for a large Te Arawa post-settlement entity. She is now a policy manager at Te Puni Kōkiri, focusing on ensuring that Māori economic rights and interests are front and centre of government priorities. 'I love contributing to better futures for whānau and supporting Māori to determine our own futures in our own way,' exclaims Taria. Two current areas of responsibility for Taria are the reforms of Te Ture Whenua Māori Act and *He Kai Kei Aku Ringa* – the Crown's Māori Economic Development Strategy.

Riria McDonald was raised Catholic. She was the youngest, and her parents wanted her to receive the best education she could. 'Mum booked me in early for St Joseph's, and there was a big waiting list then.' Riria loved her time in the St Joseph's concert party:

> We, the juniors, found it quite competitive to get into kapa haka, to get in there and knock out the seniors. Miss Kingi had to put a kapa haka group together, and I remember walking in the hall and thinking, "Who is in trouble now?" She said, "Right I've got no choice but I have to use you and try and make something out of you in order to put this on." We were chuffed to perform for an end-of-year function, and we were forever making CDs.

One of her favourite recollections of St Joseph's was when she collected songs from her iwi as part of the Group Comps (at the cultural festival):

> That was fun because you had to go back to your iwi. You would take the senior girls from your iwi, and you would sit down with a kaumātua. My grandfather, Hamuera, took us, and all my mates were crying at the end of it. Mum took him aside and said, "You need to calm down and not be so strict." He came back the next day a little bit better. The tawhito songs he gave are cherished now.

Kaumātua on the paepae: Ivan Emia, Joe Northover and Waru Cooper (with Michael Laws seated behind).

CHAPTER TEN

Rangatiratanga

In 1987, a 120-year tradition at St Joseph's Māori Girls' College came to an end. The resignation of Sister Patricia Huckle was the last time a Sister of Our Lady of the Missions was principal of the college. The Provincial Superior stated that 'The sisters recognised the growing awareness among the Māori people of their rights for self-determination, so we believe it is the time to step back and assist that process.'[750] For her farewell, eight prefects took Sister Patricia to dinner at the DB Heretaunga, Hastings, and, in August, a poroporoāki was organised in the dining room with over 400 people present.[751]

In April 1987, the Whānau Whānui discussed the qualities they wanted to see in the new principal. Joe Mason (Ngāti Awa) was of the opinion that priority needed to be given to preserving the special character of the school and, as such, the successful applicant should be Catholic and have the Māori language.[752] It was also suggested that the principal should be a Māori woman and be able to be interviewed in te reo Māori. After some intense correspondence between the Catholic Education Office and the Department of Education, Georgina Kingi was appointed principal of St Joseph's in September 1987.

One reason for objections to Georgina Kingi's appointment centred around the fact she was unmarried but was living with her partner Jim Donnelly. There was also a sense that she was a little outspoken. During her time teaching at the college, she said that she had witnessed chauvanistic and patronising treatment of the sisters, especially by some involved with the education of Māori. She found this to be in stark contrast with the respect, admiration and support given to the sisters by kaumātua, by marae, by Kahungunu iwi and by iwi Māori. Board member Tuterangi Nepe-Apatu remembers:

> It was our old people who came in behind her, not only Catholics such as Paul and Jane Mareikura, John and Nanny "Wa" Koko, Ivan and Tere Emia, but every iwi and hāhi. She [Georgina] had been at St Joseph's as a student, then as a teacher, and she was well-versed in Te Ao Māori. She understood what the sisters were about and would continue the vision they had for the school.

Witnessing Bryan Kora, Chair of the Board of Trustees, signing the deed are Sister Muriel Kivell, Sister Claire Murphy, Trust Board Chair John Bishara and Tuterangi Nepe-Apatu.

June Collins recalls the process:

> The proprietors' representatives on the Board were quite difficult. We were told specifically that we should not have meetings at the school about the issue, and so the first meeting we had was at Waina Gotty's. We then branched out and went to the marae at Pakipaki. There were about three hundred people there, and the talk was to push Miss Kingi to apply.
>
> Some Catholics said she was not suited for the position, and that really upset me, so much so that I thought, "Well if this is the Catholic Church, then I am going to become Ringatū!" To make matters worse, they decided to interview her when we were on a marketing tour in Tainui, and we had to hurriedly return back to school.

Kaumātua Mary and Enoka (Togi) Waitoa.

Georgina remembers that day well:

> Because of the revised schedule, Jim was not able to be at the interview having already committed to caring for our horse Dana who was running at Te Rapa that day. He was to worry about this for some time. I think he felt guilty that he had put the interests of a horse before mine! However, it was the sight of the kaumātua and Whānau Whānui that brought about strong mixed feelings – on the one hand, I was humbled by the iwi who had arrived in numbers at such late notice and annoyance towards the proprietors' representatives for what I perceived to be arrogant treatment of our iwi.

The interview did not go well, with Te Ao Peehi Kara giving Georgina a dressing down. He felt she could have handled the situation with more dignity. It was a lesson that remains with her today, and consequently, the kāhui kaumātua are never far from her side. Despite the fraught process, Georgina was offered the position. However, this came with conditions. It was clear, however, that the Sisters' Council did not know of the proprietors' representatives' decision, because within half an hour of being told of the added conditions, Georgina received a phone call from Mother Provincial telling her to disregard them. She was principal, and that was to be the end of the matter.

On 26 September, Georgina Kingi was formally introduced to the school as the principal, with a pōwhiri that included over 1000 people.[753] Georgina was welcomed by Ngāti Kahungunu and brought onto St Joseph's by her iwi Ngāti Awa. To commemorate the occasion, she was

Kaumātua
Te Ao Peehi Kara.

gifted taonga including a korowai from Ngāpuhi. Every iwi was represented, including delegations from the Māori boarding schools of Hato Paora, Hato Petera, Tipene, Te Aute, Hukarere, Turakina, Queen Victoria and local schools.[754]

After the commotion surrounding her appointment had settled down, Georgina moved into her office just after Christmas. 'I sat there surrounded by paper with my PA Margaret Orbell, both of us wondering where to next, when Sister Valerie Lawson, then principal of Sacred Heart, Lower Hutt, breezed through the door. She told us to leave things where they were and to go to lunch with her.' The sisters had closed ranks around Georgina, letting her know that they were there for her. Today, the whanaungatanga between all the mission schools persists and endures. However, the drama didn't end there for Georgina.

Only months after her appointment, rumours began to circulate that the school's religious education curriculum was not being taught well, that the college was about to close and that the hostel was in debt. Georgina could not understand the reason behind the rumours. The religious education curriculum was no different from before, and she knew the financial state of the hostel and had complete trust in Sister Margaret Irwin's fastidious approach to accounting. Georgina recalls:

> The sisters were prudent with their spending and frugal when it came to their own personal needs. Moveover, they were convinced of the place of St Joseph's in quality education for Māori girls and were committed to ensuring that the college continued, so Sister Margaret's contribution to a healthy financial position was a key element to this. In the two years since Sister Margaret had left St Joseph's, it seems that the hostel management did not factor in that they would now have to pay all their employees (the sisters did not claim any wages – giving of their service for free). They had also not followed the policy of ensuring the hostel fees were regularly paid, and that a set budget was followed, so the income was considerably less than the expenses, resulting in savings being eroded to such an extent that the hostel was in debt.

Board member John Bishara was shocked when he first became involved in the governance of the college:

> When we opened the books, the hostel was in dire straits. We were acting insolvent, because there was less money coming in than going out. One of the critical meetings we had was the pressure to close the college. My phone went, and it was Brian McKee,

the accountant who was involved with Sacred Heart in Lower Hutt and who served on the Catholic Education Board. He said, "John, I hear you have some issues." I said, "Yes" and the next day we met. What I learnt was that the Catholics have got this network that helps, and he rang the creditors. I also found that our creditors supported the church and the sisters, and there were all these people who were not going to let the college close. For about five to six years, we were living hand to mouth. It would have been easier to increase fees, but Georgina wouldn't allow that. The insistence was on the payment of hostel fees by all parents and caregivers, and not a sudden hike in fees that whānau were not prepared for.

Malcolm Mitchell, a Board of Trustees member, along with John Bishara, offered to mortgage his house. 'That's how much faith we had in Georgina Kingi. We could have lost our houses. We fought a good fight to keep the college afloat. Throughout their years of mission, the sisters had established a wide network of people who could be called upon to lend a hand whenever they were needed.'

Another problem that Georgina encountered was that she wasn't able to have a say in the management of girls in the hostel. Tuterangi remembers: 'The structure was that you have the Board of Trustees and the Hostel Management Board. Georgina was sitting over there at school, and she didn't get a say in what happened in hostel.' This problem was rectified when management was given to Māori. As Tuterangi recalls: 'The sisters came to us and said, "We think it is time to hand the college to iwi Māori. We no longer have a role, not only in this college but in all our colleges.'

Sister Muriel organised the transition from the colleges being run by the Sisters of Our Lady of the Missions:

> I was asked by our leadership team to set up our trust deeds. We had a national meeting of all of our sisters and one of the proposals stated that we were a missionary congregation. That means we go where there is a need for women in education and where the disadvantaged are. If we are truly missionary, we move in, we work with the people, we move over, and then we move out. The question being asked was, "Is it time we move out from all of our colleges here in New Zealand?" There was unanimous agreement, and the answer was "Yes". The query the sisters raised was to ensure that in handling the properties, the special character in terms of our education and what we are about remains. I passed that on to our international leadership, and that was accepted. I had to work with civil law and church law, so I was working with canon lawyers and civil lawyers, to put the deed together. I was living at Greenmeadows, and a crisis arose in the hostel before the trust deed was finalised. What we already had was a proprietors' committee, a local committee that kept in touch with what was happening, so that group preceded the trust board, and wherever we had a hostel we had a hostel board. So, the hostel committee met and asked me if I would take over the management of the hostel, and so I set up a number of structures when working with staff.

An example of the divide between the school and the hostel was, in October 1988, when a representative of the Director-General of Education wrote to Sister Mary Martin, who was in charge of the hostel at that time.[755] A student had been suspended from the hostel as a result of being caught smoking and leaving the school grounds without permission. However, a student expelled from the hostel is not automatically expelled from the college.[756]

Sister Muriel remembers:

> In setting up the trust board, I worked with Peter Callinicos, who was the chair of the proprietors' committee at the time. He understood what was needed in the trust deed. He moved on and his brother, Kevin, took over, and we had a basic set of clauses for each school the order owned. As well, each college had clauses that were appropriate for their own college.
>
> We had a big hui with the old girls. The place was full, and we had a discussion. From there, we decided if we were going to consult with the Whānau Whānui, we would need to have hui throughout the country, which we did. We went to Taranaki, Gisborne, Rotorua, Auckland, Nelson, Christchurch, Dunedin and also Panguru because Whina Cooper insisted that we go there as well. There were some very good discussions and some tension also because there was the sense of "You are leaving us". There were some serious questions asked about how we would keep our special character as Māori and Catholic. One of the essential points that came through was that the hostel management board was to be a sub-committee of the trust board and that's in the deed. That is essential, so that what the college is about cannot be changed and what the hostel is about cannot be changed.
>
> At the same time, we were also shifting out [of] the convent at the college and the question was, "Where do we go?" There were mixed opinions among the sisters. Some said we should buy our own place and some said we stay on the site. My gut said stay. I came to the school, and there was Georgina, Rere Unahi and Heni Henderson. I asked if they could help me with what we should do, and one of them said, "Ahi Kā". "You leave here, your flame will be extinguished, so stay." There was a sigh of relief all round. With those two little houses opposite the school, we've kept that section of land in the name of the sisters, and everything else is in the name of the trust board. With the land being transferred to the trust board and as long as the school stays, it stays in the trust. If the school is wound-up, it would go back to the order because under church law, it is the patrimony of the order. On 19 March 1995, we signed the trust deed. There was a big hui, and all the old girls and parents were here.

Sister Sarah remembers being supportive of the handover of St Joseph's to Māori:

> We wanted Māori to run their own show and for us to be there as a support for them and if they need us, they know we are there. I said to the sisters, "This is exactly what was supposed to happen. Māori won't do it our way, so we have to stand back and let them do it their way, but I bet you they get the same result."

Dame Georgina Kingi receiving her damehood with the Governor-General, Dame Patsy Reddy.

Principal of St Joseph's Māori Girls' College
Dame Georgina Kingi
NGĀTI PUKEKO, TAIWHAKAEA, NGĀI TAI, NGĀTI AWA

STUDENT	HEAD OF DEPARTMENT MĀORI	DEPUTY PRINCIPAL
1959–1962	1969–1974	1985–1987
ASSISTANT TEACHER	SENIOR MISTRESS	PRINCIPAL
1969–1974	1983–1985	1987–

Dame Georgina Kingi is known as a firm disciplinarian and as someone who expects the very best of every pupil. As a student, Georgina was known as a formidable character, being head prefect in 1961 and 1962, as well as being awarded the Dux of the school for those same two years. The 1963 college magazine records the efforts of Georgina and Indiana Kuru, who were representing the school in the Catholic Debating Competition (for the O'Shea Shield) against St Patrick's Silverstream. 'The moot was "Should decimal coinage be introduced into New Zealand?" However, the climax of the argument was reached when Georgina, in her summing up, tore a legal five-pound note in half to stress the absurdity of abolishing our present monetary system. The audience was astounded, the judge astonished and our opponents somewhat shaken. We won our argument.'[757]

Born in 1943, Georgina Kingi was raised by her parents Romana and Kani (née Maui) in the small settlement of Poroporo near Whakatāne. She was one of twelve children, eight girls and four boys. 'From an early age, the importance of education was impressed upon us by our father, strengthened by the fact that our uncle was Mohi Hotene, the headmaster at Poroporo Native School where we all attended, except for one sister.' Not only was Georgina's uncle the local headmaster but her father was the chairman of the school committee. 'My father had attended Wesley College as a student and then St Stephens.'

Her mother's whānau were Catholic, and one of her cousins was Sister Walburga, a Sister of Compassion. 'My older sister Caroline was raised by my mother's uncle who was Catholic.' Georgina's father's whānau were Anglican (her father in later life became an Anglican minister). 'We were not allowed to talk about religion at home. It was banned because we would have these slanging matches with our sister who attended the convent. Caroline was a "Catholic dog sitting on logs eating frogs out of bogs!!" She would retort: "Primary cats sitting on mats, eating rats out of vats. Aue!"'

Te reo Māori was used in the home. 'I learnt te reo Māori well by listening to my parents' conversations, talking about stuff that they didn't think we should know about.' Georgina's nickname was Dickie. 'I think they expected a boy, but they got a girl. I had two uncles who had gone to war, my mother's brother Dick and her cousin George.' As for her high school options, Georgina's father was offered a scholarship to send her to the Anglican Te Waipounamu Māori Girls' College in Christchurch, 'but my older sister, Caroline, who was Catholic, was sent to St Joseph's. My father was friends with the local Catholic priest, Father McCarthy. He also valued the teaching and discipline of the nuns.' His daughters were to become 'convent' girls. Georgina converted to Catholicism when she returned to St Joseph's to teach.

Enrolled at St Joseph's, Georgina's father had to borrow a car for the journey to Napier and accompanied his daughter and one of the Merito girls to St Joseph's:

> We drove up the driveway to the convent entrance. I had never been taught by sisters, and the first face I saw through the 'grille' was Sister Adrian [Marina Palmer from Matakana Island]. We went upstairs, and everything was so white and hygienic, like a hospital ward. Sister Jerome, or Jerry as we used to call her, was my first teacher. She took social studies and told me years later that she dreaded teaching us! We would challenge her about the 'Great Migration' regularly, especially my friend Rapai Te Hau (Sister's point being that we knew more about it than she did!).

Other teachers included Sister Raphael, Sister Crescentia, who was principal, and Sister Athanasius (Garry), with whom Georgina often got in trouble. Garry taught dressmaking:

> I hated sewing French seams and couldn't see the purpose of dressmaking. Sister Chanel, who was deaf, taught music; she taught us by vibration. She would know if you hit the wrong note when playing the piano. She also took the choir and had the girls singing the way she wanted them to. The girls couldn't read music, and everything was done by ear. She would become frustrated by what she called the "Māori whirl"; that is, we would add our own notes, especially when we harmonised. Singing in English was a nightmare. We would not sound our consonants. For example, how great thou art would become how grey thou are. (Nothing has changed – they still do this today!) I only took up piano so I didn't have to go to mass, as non-Catholics were able to go to practise then, until the East Coast girls were caught taking oranges from the convent garden during karakia. From that day to this, everyone goes to mass.

Top: Haka Pōwhiri for Georgina Kingi, 1987. Kuia H Henderson, E Henderson and H Reti.
Above left: Georgina Kingi being welcomed as the Principal of St Joseph's Māori Girls' College, 1987. Ngāti Awa with Georgina Kingi leading the whakaeke with her father, Romana Kingi, her son, Te Kani, and mother, Kani, following.
Above right: At Georgina's pōwhiri. Kaumātua John Koko. Tui Campbell-Swannenbeck with Korowai from Ngāpuhi. Hato Petera and St Joseph's presenting Korowai from Ngapuhi-Auckland Whānau Whānui.

One sister who had a lasting impact on Georgina was Mother Augustine, whose photo still hangs in her office:

> I look at her often. She was typically Irish, and being Irish, had an affinity with Māori. She would say that we shared similar practices such as the wake, our tangi and our takahi whare. She was a grammarian and strict but a very good teacher. She found my insistence on using the preposition "on" instead of "in", when referring to hopping "on" a car, frustrating. I would never contradict her but always thought, "Well you've got to hop 'on' to hop 'in' don't you?" We Māori are brighter than you Irish!

It was during her time that Georgina received her first taste of teaching. 'The sisters would say a teacher is born – not made.' She relieved for a short time in biology.

Following her time at St Joseph's, Georgina attended the University of Auckland and enrolled in a Bachelor of Arts. Lecturers and tutors included Pat Hohepa, George Ngata, Bruce Biggs, Merimeri Penfold, Hugh Kawharu and Ranginui Walker. Friends and contemporaries included Pete Sharples (a Te Aute old boy), Marama Kingi (née Paewai), Roimata Kirikiri (née Sinclair), Lauren Hunia and Aroha Sharples. Then there was a large contingent of ex-Tipene past pupils. Most Māori students had attended a Māori boarding school, and she enjoyed her times with the University of Auckland Māori Club.

In 1968, Georgina gave birth to Te Kani, her only child. Shortly afterwards, Anne Gillies persuaded Georgina to return to her alma mater. 'Auntie Anne rang me up because the sisters had phoned her, and she asked me to come back to St Joseph's. I returned because Sister Katarina [Mariu] was taking sabbatical leave. It was only supposed to be three months, but it turned into forty years.' Georgina began as an assistant teacher of te reo Māori and also relieved science and biology classes. At the time, there were very few teachers of te reo:

> Teaching te reo is not just about the language, it is also about tikanga. We [te reo Māori teachers] would meet regularly at the home of Erana Coulter from Ngāti Porou who taught at Napier Girls' High School, and Whare Tomoana, the Maori Education Advisor with the Department of Education from Te Whānau-ā-Apanui. We were whānau orientated and it didn't matter if you taught at primary, secondary or tertiary – we were all Māori teachers. That was the beginning of the Hawke's Bay Māori Language Teachers Association.

Professional development for teachers of te reo Māori back then took the form of national hui. Georgina credits these hui as moulding her into the teacher she is today. Georgina feels privileged to have been nutured by people of mana, quick wit and endearing humour.

Apart from the teaching of te reo Māori, many attribute the special sound of St Joseph's to Georgina, who is also responsible for tutoring the concert party: 'My whānau were definitely not musical and neither am I, but I know what I want, I know the sound we want, as it was the sound I had when I was a student here with the sisters. The sisters were the musicians. They could read music and they taught us how to sing.' When explaining the high notes the students are able to reach, Georgina explains: 'I didn't teach them [the students] to do that. They learn by experimenting. Try this note, try that note, and they eventually get the note. Māori are gifted musically. Sometimes I get Sister Sarah to come into the chapel to tell them how to breathe correctly, how to project their voices.' On the reason St Joseph's does not enter competitive kapa haka, Georgina responds:

Competition at a young age destroys the exuberance, the spontaneity, the enjoyment and the fun of the performance. The girls are from different iwi, and who am I to say that you have to do it this way or that? Taranaki have their tikanga, as does Ngāi Tūhoe and Ngāti Porou, whoever iwi the pupils belong to. To me, waiata, waiata ā-ringa and poi is about mahi-ngahau, enjoyment, not about competing.

Before students are accepted into St Joseph's, they are interviewed:

It is not so much what we want to know, it is about our expectations if they decide to study here. For some of the more recent arrivals, parents have this idea of St Joseph's being a finishing school. We are not. Our emphasis is on holistic well-being as well as academic success. Get the basics right and the rest will follow. We like to think that manaakitanga and whanaungatanga underpin all we do at the college.

Three hui have been instigated as permanent events on the St Joseph's calendar since Georgina has been the principal: the pōwhiri at the start of the year, the cultural festival and parent–teacher interviews in the middle of the year, and the wānanga during Labour Weekend.

The pōwhiri is for all manuhiri and based on my experience years ago of coming to St Joseph's with no seniors at the school to provide that mahana. Now the seniors return first, and the new entrants follow a few days later. St Joseph's cultural festival is an annual occasion. It first began in 1970 as an action song and poi competition among the ten groups or houses of the college. Nowadays, there are six groups at St Joseph's with about thirty girls in each group led by a prefect. Then there are the rōpū of pōtiki year 7 and 8 and year 13. It's no longer competitive, and the evening's entertainment is a festival of waiata, mahi-ā-ringa, poi and haka, of mahi-ngahau. The festival is a taste of the St Joseph's College spirit. The joy of working together in harmony, the discipline demanded, the co-operation, the laughter, the hard work, the reverence for the traditions of their tipuna and the enthusiasm of rangatahi. Getting the prefects to go back to their hapū and iwi is important in keeping their waiata alive and honouring our Māori composers.

Georgina enjoys the Labour Weekend wānanga, as do the whānau. 'They are pleased to contribute to their daughters' learning, to see the expectations placed on them, and to work together with staff.'

One observation made by a few former pupils was that Georgina is careful to separate her personal life from her professional life. 'A line has to be drawn. When immediate whānau enrol here, they are no longer your whānau but become part of a wider whānau that you are charged with caring for – each and every one of them.' There have been few bad experiences. 'My most traumatic year was undoubtedly 2015 when one of our girls committed suicide on the college grounds. It was a tragedy that took its toll personally on me, her friends, other students, staff and Hato Hohepa Whānau Whānui, yet it brought everyone so much closer. Kei te pōuri tonu, kei te tangi tonu.'

Very early on in her time as principal, the college expelled a student for bringing drugs into the hostel. The incident triggered a media frenzy, sensationalising it as a St Joseph's problem, even though it was a well-known issue in schools across the country. Early the following day, she received a call from Michael Laws, Member of Parliament for Hawke's Bay, who offered his help in dealing with the media. That was the beginning of the school's long and happy friendship with Michael Laws, who 'put his money where his mouth was' by sponsoring scholarships to the school. The 'drug' incident did have Georgina and the kāhui kaumātua of the college questioning the way Māori journalists handle 'Māori' issues. A hui was called by the Whānau Whānui, with the journalist being reminded by Waru Cooper and Te Ao Peehi of their expectation that the matter would be handled 'sensitively' and in a 'Māori' way.

Three great personal trials for Georgina were the deaths of her father in 2003, her mother in 2013, and her partner Jim Donnelly in 2015. Asked about her coping mechanisms, she responds, 'My faith, my work and my whānau.' Georgina now faces retirement after being at the helm for thirty years. She remarks: 'I was supposed to have retired earlier, but with the jubilee, I decided to stay until it was over.' Jim also looms large when Georgina discusses her damehood:

I refused the damehood first time round early in 2015. Jim had been overseas at the time, and later that year he asked if I had received anything in the mail about an award. I said, "Yes" and he then asked me, "What did you do?" I told him that I had binned it, and he said, "You selfish thing!" This time round, that conversation was in my head, and I accepted, acquiescing that Jim was probably right.

Before Georgina was awarded the damehood, she received other accolades such as the Suffrage Centennial Medal in 1993, a Queen's Service Medal in 2004 and the Benedict XVI Pont Maximvs in 2006 (the Papal Medal). When asked why she has remained at St Joseph's, her answer is simple. 'Because of my belief in the value of single-sex Māori education in the holistic environment of a Māori boarding school, I have stayed here. You can take the child out of the boarding school, but you cannot take the boarding school whanaungatanga out of the child.'

Cultural festival.

A Job For Life

Aroha Peakman-Walker
NÉE PEAKMAN
NGĀTI KAHUNGUNU KI WAIROA
1977–1981

Aroha Peakman-Walker was raised in Wairoa as the second eldest of eight children. Her grandmother took her to the marae in Frasertown for mass and for the rosary, so being Catholic was part of her upbringing:

> I believe I was sent to St Jo's to get away from an abusive father. I had no say in the whole decision. My grandmother and the principal at the time at St Joseph's in Wairoa decided between themselves that I would be sent to St Joseph's Māori Girls' College. Back in those days we were poor, we had no money, but the Maori Education Foundation funded my boarding.

Aroha loved the school, but she didn't get through University Entrance:

> I decided I wasn't going back to school, and off I went to apply for the dole. Georgina [Kingi] had sent a telegram to my mum that said, "What is Aroha up to? If doing nothing, send her back to school and worry about money later." So, I went back to St Jo's, and that was one of the best years of my life. I made sure that when I left college that year, I had my University Entrance, so I worked hard.

Her former principal continued to have a significant impact on her life:

> Georgina took me to my first job interview in 1981. I didn't want her to, but she insisted. I applied for a job with the State Services Commission, and back in those days, you had to tick one of three boxes: Housing, Inland Revenue or Social Welfare. I had no idea what Social Welfare was about, but I liked the social bit, so I ticked it, and two weeks later I got my first job. That has been my only job, and I had my 35-year anniversary in 2016. I owe so much of that to Georgina. I owe so much to that school.

For Aroha, her daughter was always going to attend St Joseph's. 'My daughter Teremoana was upset at the thought of going, but she persisted, and it has made all the difference to her. She'll send her daughters there too.'

Aroha Peakman-Walker.

Ngatoru Wall.

Kaitiaki

Ngatoru Wall
NGĀTI TŪWHARETOA
1989–1993

Pania Newton
WAIKATO, NGĀPUHI, TE WAI-O-HUA
2003–2004

Ngatoru Wall and Pania Newton are passionate about the whenua of their iwi and the rights of their people and are pleased to be labelled kaitiaki.

Ngatoru has been involved in numerous land occupations concerning her iwi of Ngāti Tūwharetoa, and Pania has fronted the protest at Ihumātao, land that sits near Auckland Airport and ground that Fletcher Construction wants to build on.

Ngatoru says that the role of Kaitiaki is not easy. 'I've been trespassed and chucked in jail. I'm just protecting the whenua.' As Pania explains:

> At the moment, I am working to protect our whenua, our whakapapa, our wāhi tapu and exercising my birthright. Fletcher's is looking to build out here and looking to desecrate the whenua. It's not only significant to the whānau, hapū and iwi of this whenua, it is also important to Auckland and Aotearoa history. This is where the first humans arrived in Aotearoa. This taonga has national significance with archaeologists saying that this is our Stonehenge.

The first protest Ngatoru was involved in actually took place at St Joseph's over Georgina Kingi not being allowed to participate in the running of the school's hostel. 'We said to the sisters, "We are not doing any chores." We organised the whole school because one of the sisters kicked up a stink about Miss Kingi being involved with the hostel. We protested for her, and we expressed our whakaaro to say why she should be involved.' She was given the moniker at St Joseph's of 'two back doors':

> I came through the back door. The first back door was that I didn't go through an interview process. My father, Nick, was on the board of Ngāti Tūwharetoa, and through Bishop Mariu, we asked Miss Kingi to let me in. The second back door was that my whānau lied on my enrolment form and said I was Catholic. I'm a patched up as Hāhi Rātana! The day after I arrived, I heard the girls singing in the chapel, and I knew I was in the right place.

Pania recalls her upbringing:

> We moved around a lot, and my two sisters and I were Māpihi Pounamu kids [students who were awarded a scholarship and were under the jurisdiction of Children, Young Persons and their Families service]. At-risk kids, that was the background I had come from, and I had been involved with CYFS and violence in the home. In my year, there were four other girls who were on the same scheme, and I migrated towards them because we had similar backgrounds. I was a naughty, cool kid, who wore red all the time and started getting involved in the gangs.

Pania was a pupil for only just over a year. 'Unfortunately, I did not finish at St Joseph's, and it is one of my biggest regrets to this day.' Despite Pania's compunctions, she credits the school with 'reigniting my longing to return to Te Ao Māori' and 'putting me on a scholarly path'.

Pania has maintained her love of language, graduating from the University of Auckland Law School with degrees in law and health science in 2015:

> During my last year of Law School, I was able to use my skills to help the campaign for Ihumātao. I helped lodge an urgent claim with the Waitangi Tribunal, and I am currently working on an urgent application for some injunctive relief at the Māori Land Court with other whānau who are staying here. I am using those skills to analyse and understand policy so we can interpret that and translate that to our whānau in easier terms.

Pania Newton.

Whetu Tirikatene-Sullivan at the opening of the gymnasium.

Building at the college has continued. In 1994, a new art and craft block and a classroom were opened,⁷⁵⁸ and on 15 February 1997, the long-awaited gymnasium and multi-complex hall was officially opened.⁷⁵⁹ In conjunction with the gym opening, extensions to the library and staffroom were completed. In 2005, the science and technology block was opened by Father Patrick Kinsella, the school's biggest building project since the completion of the gym almost a decade earlier.⁷⁶⁰

Academically, the school continued to go from strength to strength. In 1988, Shirley Simmonds achieved the best English and maths totals for Māori girls for School Certificate.⁷⁶¹ The following year, over 90 per cent of girls qualified for Sixth Form, and the college was able to add physics, chemistry and Japanese to the subjects on offer.⁷⁶² The art department, in 1989 and under the leadership of Ann Rafealov, appeared on *Te Karere*, with the sixth form presenting tapestries to the Women's Affairs Division in Wellington.⁷⁶³ In 1991, Georgina Kingi reported in her end-of-year speech that: 'It has been proved statistically over and over again that in Māori boarding schools we are succeeding academically where others fail ...'⁷⁶⁴

Rev. Sam and Noeline Paenga, Kura Wehipeihana (née Whā) and Heine Henderson (née Paenga) at the gymnasium opening.

Just over a decade later and following a visit from the Education Review Office (ERO), the college reported that it would plan to improve the technology curriculum, the only small criticism levelled at the school in what was otherwise an exemplar year of academic achievement.⁷⁶⁵ For the first time, the ERO monitored hostels and gave St Joseph's a rating of 100 per cent. Georgina Kingi wrote that the 'knocking machine' continues to denigrate the academic performance of Māori boarding schools.⁷⁶⁶ 'We all know what is required to improve this viability, i.e. an injection of funds ... so that our students would have living accommodation on an equitable basis with hostels in state schools.'⁷⁶⁷

284   I Ō MAHI KATOA, MAHIA

Kaumātua Tom Parker at pōwhiri day 2016.

Aroha Harris.

Rawinia Higgins.

Academics

Aroha Harris	Rawinia Higgins
TE RARAWA, NGAPUHI	NGĀI TŪHOE
1977–1980	1986–1989

Dr Aroha Harris is a senior lecturer in history at the University of Auckland and a member of the Waitangi Tribunal. Her most recent publication, *Tangata Whenua: An Illustrated History*, was a collaboration with Professor Atholl Anderson and the late Dame Judith Binney and is the most comprehensive single volume of Māori history to date, having won five national competitions, including the Non-Fiction category in the illustrious 2016 Ockham New Zealand Book Awards.

As a youngster, Aroha had been identified as a bright kid, but at times, she found the experience a lonely one:

It was a bit odd to be an academic Māori kid going to primary and intermediate. The classes were streamed, and I'd often end up being the only Māori in the top class. I was quite ill-fitting as a kid; some of the Pākehā kids were mean, and the Māori kids wondered why I was in a class all by myself.

Aroha's mother from Mitimiti, Margaret Leef, had attended St Joseph's during the 1950s.

There are certain aspects of school life at St Joseph's that have stuck with Aroha. 'Taha Māori was everywhere, and it was respected. From when you got up in the morning and do karakia with the meals. There was a lot of speaking Māori, singing, and kapa haka.' Aroha also noticed the uncompromising stance the school took on discipline. 'An observation I made was that St Jo's weeded out the bad girls when they first got to the school. Some of them were only a few months before they were out the door for issues involving theft, violence and aggression towards teachers. They held a line and stuck to it.'

Being punished at times seemed more militaristic to Aroha. 'I remember running around the hall, and a prefect would hit the floor with a rakau, and you had to jump at the time. Those kinds of punishments, I hadn't seen before.' The socialising at St Joseph's as a teenager also produces a particular person:

> I think that there's something in the way that we learnt to socialise at St Jo's that takes you into your adulthood in a different way. You're not caught up in the trappings of consumerism, and the girls I went to school with weren't necessarily rich, and it didn't matter. You competed on the sports field but not to see who had the latest jeans or shoes. You wouldn't be demanding the latest iPhone from your parents. You hated the rules at the time about what you could or couldn't wear, but you didn't have to eye each other up over the latest gears.

One aspect of the curriculum of St Joseph's that has remained with her were the type of subjects offered:

> I didn't understand why we would do typing, and I felt that they were setting us up for a job we would not be interested in. That was how it was in those days. Girls did cooking, sewing and typing, and the boys did woodwork and metalwork. In my mind, it was setting us up for motherhood or secretarial work.

The smaller class sizes and better relationships with the teachers, as opposed to some of the bigger state school classes, were positive features of her schooling at St Joseph's:

> In hindsight, it helped me academically. I think the teachers paid good attention to the students, which may have had something to do with the smaller class size as well (a bigger class was in the low twenties).

> The teachers were interested in what subjects you were taking for School Certificate. There is something about the size of it that means you get to know your teacher well and you get them for multiple years. You find out a little bit about the personal life of the teacher as well. Our economics teacher, Margo Woods, sometimes needed a baby-sitter and lived locally. There was a teacher in social studies. She was going to leave teaching and wanted to do wine trails in the Hawke's Bay, so in the sixth form at the

end of the year, she took us on the trail she was going to set up. I think it was a good education, and I didn't feel stifled. At St Jo's, there was something about it that kept me excited about learning. It's more than what they are teaching. It is also about how they taught.

As a historian today, Aroha looks back on how much she enjoyed her classes with Robert Curham, who taught history and English:

I really loved him; he made the subject interesting and challenging. He had a sarcasm that appealed to me, and he was provocative. I didn't know what a university was, and he asked me what I was going to do when I left school, and he suggested going to university. I was the first one from my mother and father's families to go.

The attraction to history has clearly continued for Aroha as a career.

Professor Rawinia Higgins, a fellow old girl and Waitangi Tribunal colleague of Aroha, has also enjoyed a successful career in academia, having recently been appointed Deputy Vice-Chancellor (Māori) at Victoria University of Wellington after having been the head of Te Kawa a Māui (Māori studies) at the same institution. Her career has been focused on the revitalisation of te reo Māori. Rawinia can still clearly remember attending the school's pōwhiri:

Principal Georgina Kingi with past pupils attending Otago University 2017:
Mere-Kingi Harvey-Brewster (2012-2016) – teaching early childhood;
Julie-Anne Campbell-Endicott-Davies (2009-2013) – midwifery;
Rereahu Jefferies (2009-2011) – dentistry;
Manurere Kiriona-Devonshire (2012-2013) – nursing;
Lyric Bird (2010-2015) – law;
Te Rena Vercoe-Aoina (2008-2012) – theology and science;
Orini Herewini-MacDougall (2009-2013) – health sciences;
Valerie Houkamau (2011-2015) – law;
Tali Wilson-Munday (2012-2015) – health sciences.
In front, Elsa Hug-Nicoll (2011-2015) – psychology.

After Mum and Dad brought me some lollies and an ice cream, I can remember being in the hongi line, and Miss Kingi must have heard me speaking Māori and asked me, "Nō hea koe?" She must have decided to make an example of the seniors because she told them that there was this third former who could run rings around them when speaking te reo Māori, which is her way of making you do better. I remember being dragged into the senior common room to translate *Te Karere* for them to test whether my language was as good as she said it was.

Rawinia was taught how to speak Māori at Ruatoki, where she lived with her nan:

I asked my parents if I could live in Ruatoki and learn Māori. St Jo's was not too dissimilar to where I had come from. At Nan's, there were thirteen of us in a two-bedroom house. During my time, the sisters were still the matrons of the hostel, and one sister I remember was Sister Monica. Because we couldn't go out in the weekends until netball started, she organised us to do activities with community organisations, and I did flower arranging.

Rawinia's final year at St Joseph's was the sixth form. 'I wanted to do seventh form, but at the time, you had to go to Sacred Heart, and my father didn't see the point. Uncle Pou Temara was at Victoria University, and said seventh form would be a waste of time, so aged sixteen, I enrolled at Victoria and got my degree.' Rawinia credits the school with equipping her with the skillset to succeed in tertiary study. 'The school spent a lot of effort getting us through School Certificate. If you had a School Certificate exam, you got a cooked breakfast, and they wanted you to do really well because if you did, then the school received a good quota for grades for the sixth form. It was strategic on the part of the school.'

Wānanga weekend.

CHAPTER ELEVEN

Swimming against the Tide

Since 1988, St Joseph's has been particularly affected by government policies and initiatives. The principal's report for 1988 observed the beginning of the implementation of Tomorrow's Schools, with Georgina believing the policy would be a positive change and would endorse the special character of the college.[768] She wrote that the curriculum had broadened the options available in terms of Māori culture and with subjects such as speech, clarinet and piano lessons.[769]

A little over a decade later, Georgina wrote of the government policy called Closing the Gaps (an attempt to address the inequality between Māori and the remaining population), saying that 'money alone or great plans will not close the gap' and that the 'wairua must be right'.[770] Highlighting the Integration Agreement of 1982 as being needed at the time, Georgina argued that the Closing the Gaps strategy should also apply to redeveloping the school hostel.[771]

In 2002, the new National Certificates of Educational Achievement (NCEA) assessment framework was introduced, replacing School Certificate, Sixth Form Certificate and University Entrance. The following year, Georgina wrote: 'We are not so intent on gathering exorbitant numbers of credits, when we miss out on learning the basics. I worry that our young people will have a collection of loosely gathered credits over an unplanned scheme of study – piecemeal success leading to piecemeal careers.'[772]

In 2006, the government released the draft New Zealand Curriculum. The new curriculum drew criticism from the principal due to the absence of any reference to the Treaty of Waitangi or associated principles. Citing the 1993 curriculum framework that did provide references to the Treaty, Georgina went further to say that she could hardly find any Māori words in the fifty-page document and that for the first time in a decade the Treaty component was excluded from Level 3 and bursary learning.[773] She was clear that it was her belief that the Treaty should be clearly stated and be compulsory learning for all schools.

Ka Hikitia (the Māori education strategy) was introduced in 2008. Georgina was responsive to the document. 'In my experience, Māori students do not want to be treated "differently", they just want to be treated as equals, as individuals, not to be patronised and "dumbed-down", to be understood – for "who" they are, not just what they are.'[774]

Georgina was seconded to the Ministry of Education for a year in 2010, where she worked on the professional development programme, He Kākano. Participating in He Kākano gave her time to reflect on what success and achievement is for Māori students. 'At St Joseph's success as Māori is more than just academic qualifications. A successful student here encompasses so much more. Tauira Māori here now know who they are and where they have come from, they are engaged with and empowered by use of te reo me ōna Tikanga and Māoritanga permeates all aspects of life.'[775] Georgina created a list of what she considered a successful student at St Joseph's to be:

- A respectful, mature young woman who has real pride in her culture, which she embraces, and passes on her knowledge to both peers and newcomers to the school.
- Humble and grateful to those who have helped her get to where she is.
- Have a sense of responsibility to her people.
- Able to demonstrate the ability to become a leader and meet challenges head on.
- Confident in Te Ao Tauiwi.
- One who finishes secondary school (and may not pursue tertiary education).
- Holding the tools she needs to begin building a successful life.[776]

Georgina describes a successful graduate in this way:

> Our vision of success for all girls at St Joseph's is the vision of confident, well-rounded, balanced and well-grounded women of integrity. We have a holistic approach to education and at the core of any success we may have is our uncompromising belief in our Māori and Gospel values – our tikanga Māori and our tikanga Hāhi. Proven and central to managing this success for Māori is "Personalising Learning", an approach that puts the student and their achievement at the heart of education – that places emphasis on a working partnership between professionals, parents and students and where the system must fit the student rather than the student fit the system.[777]

According to Georgina:

> ... the greatest barrier to real success for Māori is not the lack of resources or lack of caring but a lack of serious commitment from caregivers that should include making sure their children attend school right from early childhood education to the end of secondary. We have found that there is a correlation between poor performance and poor attendance.[778]

A decade after the introduction of NCEA, Georgina saw that the system promoted a 'scramble for credits rather than a pursuit of quality and meaningful qualifications'.[779] She also noted the increase in student absenteeism. She gave this advice at the end-of-year assembly:

> What we are seeing more and more however, are the number of parents who for various reasons allow themselves to be dictated to and blackmailed by their tamāhine. Here is a guide to improving the learning of your daughter:
>
> - Do not allow her to intimidate you into believing she is sick again. Remember the best medicine for her is a good education ...
> - Do not allow her to sleep in because she has spent all night watching DVDs and texting ...
> - Do not cover up for her by leaving weak excuses on the answer phone. Remember – we are not stupid, we know what is genuine and what is not, and you don't do yourself any favours by having us question your integrity.
> - Don't play the blame game or deal the "safety-card" every time your daughter deliberately breaks a rule ... Be the parent, not the pal.[780]

Also of frustration to Georgina was that Māori achievement, despite all the research and innovation, continued to lag behind. In 2012, another issue caught her attention:

> As I attend various hui (around the motu) and listen to whānau, friends, past-pupils, colleagues, pakeke and kaumātua, I have become only too aware of an emergent elitism

and a hierarchy in Māoridom, defined by an expertise in the language. However, making judgments about a person or persons or indeed an institution's "Māoriness", based solely on language proficiency is presumptuous and arrogant and does nothing for a language already in crisis ...[781]

During Georgina's time as principal, she has overseen the expansion of the school in several significant areas: the addition of a seventh form or year 13, the introduction of day students and the ability for girls to attend the college in years 7 and 8. John Bishara remembers the decision to allow day students to attend the college. 'That was a big thing to keep roll numbers up ... so we instituted day pupils. We refused, however, to become co-ed.' To Georgina, the introduction of day students brought another dynamic to the college:

> As a boarding school, one knew where your students were, and one never had issues with truancy. On the other hand, local whānau brought much appreciated support not only with transport and supervision, but by providing added pastoral care for the majority who live great distances from Greenmeadows. The college has many local nannies, koro, aunties and uncles that they can call upon.'

In 2013, a year 7 and year 8 cohort joined St Joseph's College, with the 'pōtiki' choosing to be five-day or seven-day boarders. The decision to take students at this level was based on the poor literacy and numeracy results of many girls entering at year 9. John Bishara recalls: 'Georgina had been observing that year 9 students were being presented with far more challenges than they had in the past, and Māori girls' entry levels in numeracy and literacy lagged way behind Tauiwi. She said, "Bring them in earlier, and it will be easier on them later."'

Spring in full bloom – years 7 and 8.

Tuterangi and Angela Nepe-Apatu.

Therese Nepe-Apatu.

Nepe-Apatu Whānau

Tuterangi Nepe-Apatu
NGĀTI KAHUNGUNU

Angela Nepe-Apatu
MUAŪPOKO

Therese Nepe-Apatu
1989–1993

Tuterangi Nepe-Apatu became associated with the school in 1978 through the Whānau Whānui. 'We became involved in the gala through Cyril and Waina Gotty and Mike Paku. They were involved with our Church.' Tuterangi, unlike his wife Angela, who was born Catholic, converted to Catholicism.

Tuterangi has nothing but praise for Georgina Kingi. 'You can tell a St Jo's girl anywhere in New Zealand. Georgina has high standards. They have a way of holding themselves and an air of confidence about them, and they are proud of who they are. Every shopkeeper in Taradale will tell you they can tell the difference between other Māori girls and a pupil from St Joseph's. It's about being a proud Māori lady who knows where she is going in life.' Tuterangi views himself as part of the korowai, a cloak that is wrapped around Georgina:

I became involved in the school when she came onto the school marae. I was asked to lead the pōwhiri with our club, Te Whetu-o-te-Rāwhiti. I led the pōwhiri, and Te Arawa came over us, so I came over the top of them again, and we kept the mauri. On that day, my father said because of that you have to stay with this woman. And that's why I've stayed here ever since. Our kaumātua wrapped themselves around her. Our kuia wrapped themselves around her. The boards have done the same. Her job is to manage the school and, if any conflict arose, we would intervene and handle the heat.

Tuterangi states that other Whānau Whānui and Board members also form part of the korowai for Georgina:

A HISTORY OF ST JOSEPH'S MĀORI GIRLS' COLLEGE

'People like the late Malcolm Mitchell, Martin Beveridge, Peter Peni, John Koko, Waru Cooper, Rere Unahi and Te Ao Peehi.' One very sad incident that Tuterangi had to deal with was the suicide of a student:

> Georgina called in every staff member and the Board to talk about what had happened. Thank God, we had the support of Flaxmere College who have had to sadly deal with suicide before.
>
> The principal there, Louise Anaru, took the Board through everything. The whānau brought the girl back to the school before she was taken back to her marae. The kaumātua led the karakia and blessed the college.

Angela's position in the school came about through Sister Mary Martin in 1987:

> There were only Pākehā in the hostel, and I was appointed as the manager of the kitchen. I walked in thinking I was going to be a manager, and the first place the Pākehā put me was at the kitchen sink for a week, and yet I was walking in as a boss; it took me a while to turn them around.

One year, Georgina Kingi placed the pupils on a diet:

> One of the main concerns, and the parents don't like me saying it, is their health. We have a lot of big girls coming in at year 9. I had some of them on a diet, just selected girls, and tried to educate them and their whānau about good eating habits. It's more about education. One girl in the front row of kapa haka was told she needed to do something about her size. The mother said, "God loves people of all shapes and sizes", and I said, "But I am not God".

As Angela remembers:

> We talked to the girls and gave them exercise, and I used to walk with them. We told Miss we could do it, but the problems weren't at school, they were in the home during the holidays. We have girls with a range of dietary needs such as being vegans or having nut, citrus or acid allergies. There is a girl here who can't eat pumpkin and another who can't eat white meat.

As for girls raiding the food cupboards, Angela 'knows all their tricks':

> They try and pinch food. They will walk past and grab food like butter or jam. I will tell them to get out, or I'll ask them to lift their plate and take their jerseys off. They get a good feed here: they get breakfast, morning tea, lunch, dinner and supper, and they have kai time after school at 4 p.m., when they eat their own kai.

Angela became known to the girls as 'Aunty Ange'.

Therese Nepe-Apatu didn't have much choice about whether she would attend St Joseph's. 'My mum's sisters were old girls, my cousins went here, my mum worked here and my dad was on the Board. I only lived down the road, and I cried the day I came here. My cousins asked when I arrived, "Why are you crying? At least your mum works here!"' Her father gave her some advice. 'He said if you ever come against the Board, he would stand me in front of the Marian Steps and give me a dressing down!' Therese is now a staff member at the local Tamatea High School.

Aunty Ange's Biscuit Recipe

Past and current pupils all rave about Angela Nepe-Apatu's biscuits. They are in such demand that it is not uncommon for past students of St Joseph's to ask Aunty Ange to cook a batch and send them by the boxful. Due to popular demand, and with some cajoling, here is her secret recipe for 280 biscuits.

Ingredients

Main ingredient	LOVE
Butter (semi-soft, not melted)	6 lb
Condensed milk	2 cans
Sugar	1 lb 1 oz
Self-raising flour	6 lb

Instructions

- Mix butter, sugar and condensed milk and beat until the sugar dissolves – it should look like fine caster sugar.
- Add the flour and mix until combined into a nice texture – not wet or dry.
- Cook at 130°C for 28 minutes.
- For peanut brownies, just add cocoa and peanuts.
- For chocolate chip cookies, just add chocolate chips.

The concert party often toured. Two memorable tours were in 1993 and 1994. In August 1993, they toured the South Island. As one pupil wrote: 'The adults were hanging out for smoking stops, so the bus was endlessly pulling up somewhere so they could drag away to their smokers' hearts' content.' When performing on the Interislander ferry: 'We thought it would be an easy mission. We were wrong. Trying to keep upright and do the poi at the same time isn't as easy as you think.'[782] At one point, they stopped at Queenstown Mall, where they opened up their guitar case to raise enough money for Danish Delights. As Te Rina Warren recalls: 'We performed in Queenstown Mall, and it's a couple of stories high. We performed, and we had a guitar case open, and money would literally be falling from the sky.'

After having been to Franz Joseph Glacier and Hokitika, the bus was involved in a crash with a car through the Inangahua Junction. Meriama Taufale recalls: 'The driver of the car had suffered a heart attack at the wheel. Mum was sitting second or third in the bus and spent three months in hospital.' Meriama's mother, Moana, remembers what happened. 'Martin and I had the privilege of going on that tour. An elderly gentleman came towards us as he had a heart attack and hit us. Mrs Unahi was very seriously injured, so herself, myself and one girl out of a whole bus of forty-eight, ended up in hospital.'

The following year, students toured Te Tai Tokerau, with the purpose of taking back the school's kuia, Rere Unahi, to her home at Te Kao. The first stop was at Waihi and then to the hot pools, before arriving in Rotorua where the pupils sang on the radio in front of an audience of old girls.[783] When in Auckland, the students toured TVNZ, visited a modelling agency and had a makeover, looked at the aquatic life at Kelly Tarlton's and then rode the attractions at Rainbow's End. When the tour arrived at Te Kao, Rere Unahi shared stories of her life, and they then visited Te Hāpua and Rāwene and went to see the famous Tāne Māhuta.[784]

Students have also gone on trips overseas. In November 1986, accompanied by Napier Jaycees, a group of eleven girls went on the school's first overseas trip to Japan. When in Japan, the pupils experienced the Japanese way of life, with going to the toilet being an experience they will never forget. Pupils observed that their language is similar to Māori but that they could not rely on 'Māori time' because the Japanese are always punctual.[785]

They visited Tokyo, Nagoya, Takayama, Tomakomai (Napier's Sister City) and Osaka. At Osaka, the girls caught a bullet train and performed a concert to promote New Zealand. Riria McDonald was one of the pupils lucky enough to travel to Japan:

> It was a real eye-opener and every girl had to be confident to sing or do poi by ourselves. Going to my host family, I went in a huge stretch limo. I wanted to sit up with the driver but you had to sit in the back and the father owned the whole street! They [the family] cleared the whole top of the house so I could sleep and they slept downstairs.

The purpose of the trip was to perform at the Jaycee International World Congress at Nagoya. The great success of the visit was marked by a triple award to their sponsors, the Napier Jaycees, for Best Planned and Executed Project, Best Cultural Project and Best Cultural Project in International Relations and in Economic Affairs.[786]

Right: Performing in Japan, 1986.
Standing: S Oliver, A Gotty, L Manaena, V Batistich, M Paaki, C Roberts, G Gray.
Kneeling: J Patea, R MacDonald, R Nuku, E Mason.

Centre: Horowai Wetini and Maria Smith in Singapore.

Bottom: Performing in China, 2009. Kimiora Atkins, Rangimarie Rautjoki, Te Amohaere Jefferies.

In 2001, the school made an educational visit to Singapore with the kapa haka group.[787] Year 13 student, Hinenui Tipoki-Lawton, explains that: 'The trip was an experience of a lifetime'.[788] Ani-Piki Tuari wrote an account of the school's trip to Sydney in 2005.[789] Upon arrival, students performed a pōwhiri at the Sydney University. After performing at Westmead Children's Hospital, the girls went for a cruise on Sydney Harbour. Another performance was with Aboriginal people, when the students participated at the pōwhiri for the NSW Māori Rugby League competition.[790]

In November 2009, the school embarked on their most ambitious overseas tour when twelve pupils travelled to China.[791] The first stop was Hong Kong, where the pupils visited Man Mo Temple, Aberdeen Fishing Village, Repulse Bay and Stanley Markets, before performing to one hundred ex-pats at New Zealand House.[792] Having been to Macau, the casino capital of Asia, the students arrived at Guilin, the Sister City to Hastings. There, they rode tuk-tuks, saw water buffaloes, visited the Reed Flute Caves and attended the Sanjie Show, the world's largest performance on water, with a cast of over six hundred farmers.[793]

The reason for the trip was to perform at the opening ceremony of the 2009 Guilin International Scenery, Culture and Tourism Festival.[794] The pupils were to perform the only live act for the opening. After five months of rehearsals and having been to the stadium for a practice run, the girls were treated like 'movie stars' before their performance. They sat opposite the Lord Mayor's table and enjoyed a banquet with gold cutlery and plates, and glasses with gold edging, as well as the world's largest indoor waterfall as a backdrop.

They had a police escort to the stadium, and then: 'They [the audience] were captivated with the singing, the poi and with Rangi's [Te Rangimarie Rautjoki] performance. We came off stage and there was paparazzi mayhem. We were mobbed, cameras flashing from all angles as everyone wanted photos with us. Inside our room, there were TV interviews and press photoshoots – the Chinese media couldn't seem to get enough Māori culture.'[795] The craving for Māori culture didn't end with their performance. The following night, there was a street parade. The pupils did an impromptu performance. They taught the crowd, which was six-deep for three kilometres, some of their songs. They described the experience as being the 'most exhilarating performance'.[796]

Another trip was a journey to Tōtara Point in February, 1988, to celebrate 150 years of the Catholic Church in New Zealand. Following the powhiri, there was a traditional planting of a grapevine from Greenmeadows and then a small concert.[797]

In March that same year, at Te Papa-o-Te Aroha Marae in Tokoroa, the school sent a delegation to the consecration of Max Mariu as the first Māori Catholic bishop.

In 1990, St Joseph's co-hosted the O'Shea Shield with Sacred Heart Napier and St John's College. Two years later, the college celebrated its 125th Jubilee. A commemoration mass was held in memory of the past pupils who had passed away. 'Women and girls stood to give the name of an aunty, a mother, a nanny, a sister or even a dear friend.'[798] Afterwards, a mini-concert was performed by the past pupils.

In November 2018, twenty-eight students accompanied by teachers and supporters departed for a twenty-one-day tour of Europe. Having taken in the sights and smells of Florence, the following day the pupils arrived in Rome to view the Colosseum before being hosted by the Sisters of the Lady of the Missions that evening, including former teacher, and now leader of the Order, Sister Josephine Kane. Early the next day, the entourage made their way to the Vatican and to St Paul's Basilica where the pupils broke into waiata, much to the pleasure of the waiting crowd who wished to get a peek of Pope Francis. 'We knew the Holy Father had entered when people began calling Papa! Papa!'[799] After one of his ten attendants gave St Joseph's Māori Girls College a 'shout out', the audience acknowledged the pupils by cheering and applauding. 'We may not have met the Holy Father but people world-wide knew we were there, especially the Welsh, the Irish and the Italians – we now have a fan-base,'[800] wrote year 10 student, Waikawa Sciascia.

After paying their respects to the fallen soldiers of the 28th Māori Battalion at Monte Cassino, the tour group arrived at Madrid to take in the sights of the Royal Palace and the Cathedral. The next day of leisure in Barcelona included an excursion to shop at the Maremagnum Mall but, as observed by year 11 pupil Te Ariki Turanga, 'I absolutely fell in love with it, but not the prices!'[801] From a bus ride around the Pyrenees mountain range, the students arrived at Lourdes, and then onwards to Lyon before arriving in Paris. The group saw all the sights in the capital of France: they climbed the Eiffel Tower, undertook a boat tour of the river Seine and rode the rides at Disneyland Paris. On their final day in Paris, they attended karakia at Notre Dame Cathedral, where year 12 pupil Te Orora Munroe-Waihape described the air in the cathedral as having '...a musty smell just like my Papa's old villa in Whakakī'[802] before their presence was formally acknowledged by the priests.

After arriving at night in London, a horrified Miss Kingi ordered the guides to find alternative accommodation, as the lodgings were a former prison. Despite being told there was nothing available in London on a Sunday night, their minders found room at the Royal National Hotel. The next day, the group went to Buckingham Palace and gained a bird's-eye view of England's capital via the London Eye. That night, the group was hosted by Ngāti Rānana at New Zealand House, where some of the girls had been desperate for some tastes of home and were pleasantly surprised when they saw boil-up on the menu. The following day, the group was given a tour of Oxford Street before having lunch with the New Zealand High Commissioner to the United Kingdom, Sir Jerry Mataparae.

Making their way back to New Zealand, the tour group made a two-day stopover in Dubai, where they had four-wheel-drive rides in the Arabian Desert, rode camels and, again, enjoyed spending time in luxurious shopping malls.

Students in Rome with the Vatican in the background.

Nadell Karatea.

Krystal Te Rina Warren.

Being a Pupil in the 1990s

Nadell 'Koka Nods' Karatea
NGĀTI KONOHI, NGĀTI RANGATAHI
NGĀTI MATAKORE,
NGĀTI PIKI-AHUWAEWAE
1989–1992

Kayleen Neho
TE RARAWA, NGĀTI TŪWHARETOA,
NGĀ RAURU
1989–1992

Krystal Te Rina Warren
RANGITANE, NGĀTI MATAKORE,
NGĀTI WHITIKAUPEKA
1990–1993

Janice Wall
WAITAHANUI, NGĀTI TŪTEMOHUTA
1993–1996

Kania Worsley
TE AITANGA A MĀHAKI, TE ĀTIAWA
1996–2000

Nadell Karatea was raised Catholic. 'Our grandmother and grandfather picked us up for church every Sunday without fail. We [her sister and herself] didn't like going because it was so repetitive, it was boring, it was old, and the singing was terrible.' Nadell reluctantly went to St Joseph's, as did her sister Cristina from 1991 to 1995, and that was where her learning of te reo Māori began (Nadell is now a qualified te reo Māori school teacher):

It was learning to write te reo at St Jo's. Miss Kingi would stand at the front of the class and you wrote subject, verb, extension. I absolutely love te reo Māori with a passion, and it has definitely developed my confidence, my independence, to have a voice for our kaupapa, and I thank Miss Kingi for that because she is always on my shoulder and my mum is on the side, so I take them wherever I go.

Nadell is also a regular performer at Te Matatini and recalls with fondness participating in the school's concert party. 'The cool thing about the concert party was that all the senior girls left their songs at the kura, and we would tour with those songs. The school would have over a million songs from those girls now.'

Kayleen Neho has a genealogical connection to St Joseph's. 'It was our grandmother, Mata Tahe Takuira, who went in 1914, and she married Hone Neho. From 1941 to 1942, our Auntie Tatiana attended the college.' As a pupil, following in the footsteps of the women in her family before her, she remembers the time when someone stole Sister Mary Martin's jandals.

'We all had to get up out of bed, all fifty-two of us in the third form, and we were marched out to the courts because she wanted to find her jandals.' One highlight was wearing her sister's blue blazer. 'A couple of years ago, I found out our blazer is still going around the school and in our family with our nieces who are attending St Joseph's.'

Krystal Te Rina Warren was much like Nadell Karatea in that there were plenty of old girls who had come from her home town of Taihape:

> The Christmas before I left, I was gifted a guitar that I took to St Joseph's, even though I didn't know how to play and was told that I would learn when I got there. With the local school struggling academically, my parents gave me the option of attending any secondary school. When I got there, Auntie Mereama Kereana was my Whaea Atawhai and Meriama Beveridge was messaged by my cousins to look after me, because they had attended the school with her. St Joseph's was the first place I learnt te reo. I grew up knowing words and hearing the old people speaking it. My grandmother was brought up by her grandmother and she couldn't speak te reo Māori. It was never spoken in the home and even though she pleaded with her to teach her, her grandmother refused because it wasn't a valued resource, it had no monetary benefit. So, to the credit of my grandmother, she followed the old people around and learnt the language.

Luckily for Te Rina, she received a scholarship for her last year of schooling. 'My sister was going to come and I was going to have to go home. I had a high academic success rate, and Georgina found me a scholarship.' Now, Te Rina Warren works with Nadell Karatea at Te Pūtahi a Toi, School of Māori Studies, Massey University.

One student who started in the same year as Te Rina was Janice Wall. Janice is thankful for the opportunities the school afforded her. 'I was the first student Board of Trustees representative. I did it because you got paid, and it was $25 per month. I'm on a board now and I don't have any kids, but the time spent at St Joseph's was my training ground.' Janice remembers Miss Kingi turning up to her parent's fish and chip shop, just out of Taupō. 'She came and got me for the seventh form because we couldn't afford it.' Janice says about her older cousin, Ngatoru: 'She was useless in the shop, so she was sent to St Joseph's.'

As for the contribution girls have made to Te Ao Māori, Janice observes: 'I've noticed a lot of them are on their Iwi Trusts: Ngāti Maniapoto, Ngāti Tūwharetoa, Ngāti Porou and Ngāti Awa. They are giving back to their people.'

Kania Worsley hadn't heard of St Joseph's before she arrived:

> I thought I was going to Lytton High School in Gisborne, but my parents wanted me to go to Te Aute College because, at the time, they were accepting girls. Brian Morris, the Tumuaki at Te Aute and former teacher from St Joseph's, suggested I attend St Jo's. I was

Kayleen Neho.

Kania Worsley.

sent here as I was the eldest and my parents didn't want me to worry about looking after my teina but to focus on my studies.

Dermott Kelly is a teacher Kania considered special:

He approached me to enter an essay competition that was sponsored by the Irish Consul General. At the time, I thought it was hōhā, and I learnt that the second prize was a Waterford Crystal set, so I thought, "Sweet! If I can come second and win that crystal, I could hock it off and buy my first car." I ended up coming first and going to Ireland for summer school for six weeks, and that was my first overseas experience!

Kania wasn't only gifted at writing; in 2001, she gained the top mark in Māori bursary with 96 per cent.[803] Kania taught at St Joseph's and was a member of staff for over ten years. At times Kania has been called on to perform special duties. 'Miss had a suspicion that girls were jumping out of a window. I was one of two old girls working at St Jo's at the time. We were a bit chubby and she wanted us to get through the window to prove it could be done, but we couldn't fit!' Kania now teaches at Tamatea High School, just down the road.

Teachers

Theresa Mariu, 'Sister Katarina'
NGĀTI TŪWHARETOA
1953–1968, 1987–1991

Maria van der Linden
1964–1990

Maureen Caffery
1981–2011

Te Rere o Kapuni Unahi
TE AUPŌURI
1973–2004

Ripeka Wiki
NGĀTI POROU
1996–PRESENT

Val Caffery-Tangimetua
2010–PRESENT

Theresa Mariu, otherwise known as Sister Katarina, was the school's first former pupil to become a sister.[804] In 1953, she re-joined her alma mater.[805] She returned to teach Māori, waiata and sewing, 'as well as growling and giving us a crack'.[806] She spent time in Christchurch during the late 1970s and early 1980s doing pastoral care work, before she was approached by a past student, Marion Boyles, to open a kōhanga reo. She was then transferred to the Petone Māori Missions Pastoral Care. She then went to Australia to study and returned to the school in 1987.[807] Sister Katarina passed away in 2015.

Kaa Daniels attended St Joseph's with Theresa Mariu:

> In my last year, we would see her go in the chapel and would ask, "What are you praying for Fish?" She said, "I think I'm getting the call." I said, "What call? I don't know what you are talking about." Before we left the college, she said, "I'm going to Christchurch and am going into the convent." I went to see Theresa in Christchurch. I asked her, "Do you wear all that stuff? Do they cut your hair so you are bald?" She said, "Stop it Kaa. We have to wear all our clothes for our sins." I said, "You're going to be heavy with my sins!" and she laughed. We were good mates.

Former pupil and Whaea Atawhai Miriama Kereama lived with Sister Katarina for a year at the convent. 'I had a lot of love for her. She was old school, staunch, and believed in the church like nobody. She was into keeping the old girls in the loop, communicating and letting them know what was happening.' Elsa Hug-Nicol made her first communion with Sister Katarina. 'She was always strict, but in a gentle way. Mum and I always used to go over to her house because she couldn't work a computer and couldn't log on to get her emails.'

One teacher most former pupils fondly remember is Nanny Rere. Brown Wiki, her nephew from Te Kao in the Far North, recalls being brought up with her on the opposite side of the creek. 'Her tipuna, Matiu Tupune, was one of the elder rangātira within the iwi.' Brown's wife and te reo Māori teacher and kuia at St Joseph's, Ripeka, remembers Nanny Rere as being loved by everyone:

> She was a huge influence and she taught the girls te reo Māori and raranga, Māori crafts, for nearly thirty years at St Joseph's. She was also a counsellor and a confidante. The younger Rere was a nurse and ended up contracting tuberculosis, staying at Pukeora in Waipukurau. That is where she met her husband, Miki Unahi, and they lived out at Haumoana. At the time she was employed at St Joseph's, Georgina wanted someone

1. Theresa Mariu (Sister Katarina).
2. Maria van der Linden.
3. Val Caffery-Tangimetua.
4. Te Rere o Kapuni Unahi.

with both taha wairua and taha reo, and she was that person.

Georgina explains: 'She was Rātana and no push-over. If it was wrong, she would not be afraid to tell you.'

Whaea Atawhai June Collins remembers Nanny Rere and her husband 'Darkie':

> He worked at the works and he liked to socialise at the "chemist", the Clive Hotel. Nanny Rere was always at the school and she was more than a teacher, she was a nanny. Whenever the girls went on tour, she would have all these pantyhose, hair ties and her bag of lollies. She could go onto a marae, as kaikaranga, and made the girls feel safe.

For Sister Maureen 'Doc' Richardson, Nanny Rere occupies a special place in her heart:

> I loved her for many reasons. I loved singing in Māori because that was easier than speaking. She would say, "Don't worry about it. You can't even pronounce my name properly yet." She was so positive and so down to earth.
>
> There was a serious accident at the school one day when hot oil was spilled on the kitchen floor and a member of the kitchen staff slipped over. She [Nanny Rere] grabbed everything she could from the deep freeze, wrapped her in a rug, and put her in the car. Because she couldn't drive, I drove and was stopped by a police officer. It was Nanny Rere's quick thinking that saved her.

Julie Tangaere has a more personal connection to the late kuia from Te Kao. 'She was one of our father's best friends. He was really sick for the last six months of his life. When we went into hospital, she would be there for 99 per cent of the time. That exemplified the relationship she had developed with the local parents.'

Rere Unahi's daughter, Debbie, remembers when Sister Patricia Huckle approached her mother to see if she would be interested in a part-time job at St Joseph's:

> Dad said she could go so long as they could pay her way to get there because she couldn't drive. She remained part-time for twenty-seven years! [Rere actually thought she was being asked to work in a voluntary capacity]. Mum was a registered nurse. Anything to do with health breakouts, like kutu, the girls would be called into the assembly hall and I'd see Mum there in her nurse's uniform, with them lined up and checking their heads.

Debbie didn't go to St Joseph's but knows the importance St Joseph's played in her mother's life. 'She loved the place. She would stay here all day, all night with the girls, and she would do anything for the girls. She was always very proud of any of her students.' Debbie also heard some stories at her mother's tangihanga:

> A lot of things came out that we as a family didn't even know, like the impact that she had. There was one girl who spoke and she was telling us that she and a friend got up on the roof with a fire escape ladder, and they didn't know Miss Kingi was on the premises, and she shut the entrance, during a freezing night. They got caught and called into a hostel management meeting, and they were going to be expelled because it was a fire hazard. They were crying, and Mum saved them because she told the Board, after they had decided to expel them, that they should not be expelled because the girls will become statistics and become uneducated. So those girls were not expelled.

In 1990, teacher Maria van der Linden retired after twenty-four years. In that year, she also wrote

Maureen Caffery.

Ngā Kōrero Mō Te Kura Māori o Hato Hohepa: St Joseph's Māori Girls' College 1867–1990.[808] Maria van der Linden was born in Poland. Her father was murdered by the Soviet secret police in 1940.[809] Maria became a Polish exile with her mother and younger brother Alek. Eventually, the family found their way to New Zealand as refugees in 1947, after having travelled through Kazakhstan, Uzbekistan, Turkmenistan, Iran and India.[810]

After graduating from Wellington Teachers' Training College, Maria completed her Bachelor of Arts degree from Victoria University of Wellington in 1958. In 1961, Maria and her young family shifted to a house diagonally opposite St Joseph's, where they were 'entertained by the sight of their marching teams trained by Mr Lynch'.[811] When Maria first began teaching, she was one of just four lay teachers.[812]

Maria was the school's guest speaker at the end-of-year assembly in 1990, the year she retired. 'This was a very emotional time for me, and I was glad of the support of my husband Wim and our six children, who were present on this memorable occasion. The beautiful pounamu, greenstone necklace and earrings presented to me by the board of trustees of the school will always be a treasured possession, a taonga for life.'[813] As the school farewell observed: 'Because of her own life experiences, she had a deep understanding of the problems and hardships experienced by the Māori people.'[814] Maria herself admitted: 'Working so closely with Māori students at St Joseph's and having suffered deprivation of human rights during my childhood, my empathy with tangata whenua increased over the years.'[815]

Wife and husband, Ripeka and Paraone (Brown) Wiki are focused on providing Māori pupils with values and a strong sense of identity. Former Hastings Boys' High School teacher and kaumātua of St Joseph's, Paraone explains:

> In the college here, they are taught day in, day out. The grounding, the shaping of a character through those values, that is much more important than their ABC.
>
> Knowledge can be picked up, but if you don't have those main values, you won't become anything. The welding of those two worlds, the physical and spiritual, they both go hand in hand and that is your spine for life.

Ripeka, current te reo Māori teacher and 'kuia on the spot' at St Joseph's, elaborates:

> If the taha wairua is strong, the learning falls into place more easily. If not, you will encounter many challenges unless you right it. We want the students to retain the tikanga. If the pupils only focus on their ABC, there will come a time when they will look back and not know who they are and lose their identity, and that's why it is so important to keep that basic foundation. This kura has that taha Māori and taha hāhi.

Both Ripeka and Paraone recall the impact of the closure of the Whakatu and Tomoana freezing works. Ripeka remembers: 'In 1987, it came over the television that Whakatu was going to close, and it came out of the blue. It seemed that people still wanted to send their girls to St Joseph's, but financially it was very difficult. People worked hard, not in one job, but two or three jobs.'

For Paraone, a native speaker from Te Hiku o te Ika where his family was 'blocked off from the world by the Mangamuka Range', the closure of the freezing works resulted in a change of career. A teacher at Colenso High School and the kaumātua for the Māori Teachers' Association in Hawke's Bay, Te Ao Peehi Kara, called him:

> He said, "Come on, boy, you're wasting your time here … You fill in that form and tomorrow I want it straight back." The following day we ended the kill [at the works], and it closed. The next day a phone call came from Te Ao Peehi, and he asked, "Where is that piece of paper because tomorrow I am going to Wellington and I need that paper so you can be a teacher."

Ripeka became a teacher at St Joseph's after a position had become vacant and she received a phone call from Georgina. Teaching te reo Māori brings with it its own challenges. Ripeka comments: 'There are a huge range of different backgrounds, and we have to ensure that our programme will cater for the different levels in class.' On the topic of teaching pupils from kura kaupapa, Ripeka observes:

> When you write the language, there are rules. Here is an example of how usage has become acceptable, contrary to how you would write it. The students will come in and say, "Taku Mama." I would say when you are writing it, you need to use "Tōku" because that shows that the person is older than you and it is about respect and mana. [For some children who have attended kura kaupapa] their attitude towards those who don't have the reo can be a bit arrogant and that is where the teaching of tikanga comes into it. Some of them say, "Why don't you use te reo Māori all the time in the classroom?" My answer is that it would be most unfair on the majority of them who don't know.

Another issue has been both pupils and parents who have come from a kura kaupapa background wanting to undertake a certain NCEA level:

> Sometimes we will get students who have achieved Level 3 Māori, but there are still gaps in their knowledge and they may not be able to cope with university level. When I started at St Joseph's, we had School Certificate, and sometimes we had girls coming in at Form III who already had the qualification. Unless they had great grades, Georgina and I would make them redo it, and some parents were incensed. I would explain, "Your daughter may have Level 1, but she should not do Level 2 yet; it could be that she is weak in an area of her learning."

Maureen Caffery began working at St Joseph's in 1981. Underpinning Maureen's passion for teaching was a perfectionist streak. Her daughter Val explans: 'At school, she worked really hard at setting up and building up the science department … She was very proud of the work she did with the Duke of Edinburgh Awards and [she] was pleased to be able to take a group of girls to Rarotonga in the mid 1990s.' Maureen did not teach past Level 1 and concentrated on ensuring that students at years 10 and 11 were given the best understanding possible of the basics of science so that achieving at a higher level would not be so difficult. Val also recalls her mother being very proud of her pupils. 'She kept the newspaper cut-outs of each of her science girls as they earned awards and went off to do extra study and showed the love of learning that she [had] shared with them.' Outside of school life, Maureen enjoyed working at the Hawke's Bay Racing Club, making jams and chutney, gardening and knitting.

Born with a congenital heart defect, Maureen's health was never strong, and twice she had to have open heart surgery. Her second operation was performed on her sixty-fifth birthday, resulting in her working part-time, until 2011, when she decided that she would retire. Sadly, Maureen was diagnosed with secondary cancer in the liver before embarking upon what she regarded as 'Her next big adventure'.

A committed teacher to the end, Maureen insisted that her daughter attend parent–teacher interviews at St Joseph's rather than stay at home and care for her. The following morning, after having had breakfast and reading some emails, she passed away. The first person Val rang was Georgina Kingi, who came within twenty minutes. Needless to say, the school provided the Caffery whānau with much love and support and her funeral was held in the chapel.

Following in her mother's footsteps, Val Caffery-Tangimetua first worked part-time at St Joseph's in 1987, teaching maths, before working full-time in Hastings. Over twenty years later, a position for a maths teacher at St Jo's was advertised and immediately Maureen rang her daughter, saying, 'You have to apply for it.' In 2010, Val was appointed and began working with her mother. To differentiate between the two Cafferys, the pupils called Maureen 'Big Miss Caffery' and Val was called 'Little Miss Caffery'. One of Maureen's favourite activities was putting flowers in the chapel. Val explains: 'My job was to carry the bucket around the garden to collect the flowers she cut, put the tarpaulin down in the chapel while the arrangement was made, and then tidy up afterwards. It was time with her that I have come to treasure.'

When reflecting on their time at St Joseph's together, Val remarks:

> In our family, no one else understood the choreography of the classroom or the politics of the staffroom, except Mum and I. It was something we discussed at great length and, while I know what she had to say supported me through difficult times in my career, I hope I was also able to give her support when she needed it.

Brown and Ripeka Wiki.

Sesquicentenary of St Joseph's Māori Girls' College

On the first weekend of October 2017, St Joseph's Māori Girls' College celebrated the school's 150th jubilee. Over 1000 people attended, most of whom were former pupils, with some travelling from Bahrain and China and 150 flying in from Australia.[816] Speakers at the pōwhiri included Bill Prentice, Haami Hilton, Henare Ngaia, Manahi Paewai and the Minister of Māori Affairs, Te Ururoa Flavell, with many commenting on the contribution the college had made to Māori development and highlighting the achievements of some of the old girls.[817] Following the evening meal, attendees were invited to the opening of an exhibition at the school's library that showcased the school's rich history.

The next morning began with a karakia, followed by historian Malcolm Mulholland providing an overview of the school's history, and many attending found themselves relating to the past activities and experiences he spoke of. The afternoon saw past pupils enjoy the best wine Hawke's Bay had to offer as they were given a tour of the many vineyards located near the college. Nearly 700 people participated in the official dinner that night held at the local Pettigrew Arena. Master of Ceremonies Julian Wilcox challenged each generation of students to take the stage and perform waiata ā-ringa, much to the delight of those attending.[818]

Sunday Mass was well attended by the numerous Mission Sisters who had travelled as far as Rome, Paris and India, as well as senior students who performed with the short poi. During the service, a framed blessing and message was received from Pope Francis and placed at the altar.[819] At the conclusion of the weekend, past pupils agreed to donate one dollar a month each to help towards costs to extend the college's buildings.

Former teachers at the Sesquicentenary event.
Back row: Anne Sklenars, Claire Murphy, Mary Maitland, Christina Cathro, Barbara Henley, Carmel Cassin, Mary Rose Holderness, Lidwina van Beers.
Front row: Jeanette McRae, Muriel Kivell, Raewyn Hogan, Margaret Purdie, Josephine Kane, Maureen Richardson, Sarah Greenlees, Maureen Duncan, Kathleen Prendergast, Colleen Edgecombe.

Sesquicentenary celebrations.
Kaumātua Heita Hiha,
Mrs Haami Hilton, Piri Prentice,
Haami Hilton, Enoka 'Togi' Waitoa.
Behind: Beverley Kemp-Harmer.

John Cribb, Hikurangi Edwards, Rueben Edwards, Kararaina Cribb, Tawhiwhirangi Skipper.

Skipper Whānau

John Cribb
NGĀTI RANGI, NGĀTI TŪWHARETOA,
NGĀTI KAUWHATA

Kararaina Cribb
NGĀTI POROU, NGĀTI KAUWHATA, NGĀPUHI,
NGĀRUAHINE

Tawhiwhirangi Skipper
NGĀTI POROU, NGĀTI KAUWHATA, NGĀPUHI,
NGĀRUAHINE, TE WHĀNAU Ā APANUI
1996–2000

Hikurangi Edwards
NÉE SKIPPER
1998–2002

Kararaina Cribb sent her two daughters, Tawhiwhirangi and Hikurangi, to St Joseph's because she wasn't happy with any of the Māori-medium education options available in Wellington. 'We were committed to kōhanga reo and kura kaupapa, but we weren't satisfied with what was on offer.' Kararaina's husband, John Cribb, was on the school's Trust Board between 1996 and 2002, when the girls attended the college. John would often drop the two sisters back to the school. 'I used to think they got homesick because they wanted me to take them back, so they wouldn't cry and get upset. It wasn't that, it was because I would take them grocery shopping and buy them heaps of kai. They used to rely on me to get them food.'

The eldest of the two daughters, Tawhiwhirangi, recalls: 'You spent all your spare time studying, and we did really well academically.' In terms of the religious aspect to the college, Tawhiwhirangi states: 'I once counted in third form how often we prayed, and it was thirteen times a day.' Tawhiwhirangi and her friend Briar Dargaville entered the Rockquest and Pacifica Beats Competition in Wellington under the name 'Maia' and came second.[820] Briar wrote the music and Tawhiwhirangi wrote the lyrics. The duo composed two songs: 'Tu Mai', a call for Māori youth to be strong, and 'Kaua E Kai Paipa', an anti-smoking song. 'We want to show the Māori side of things – I mean that's how we know how to do the stuff we do, through getting in touch with our Māoritanga.'[821]

Younger sister Hikurangi remembers the high expectations placed on them by their mother. 'Mum would ask why I was not in the top three in my subjects. I got first in class every year until I got to seventh form when I was pipped by Audrey Robin. Audrey had lost her mum, Auntie Sandy. We were all very close to that whānau, and we used to go to the Kohupatiki every weekend. In our final year Audrey and I both got Dux.'

Megan and Stephanie Gardner, moko, Ria Millen and Terry Gardner.

Gardner Whānau

Ria Millen
NGĀTI TOA, NGĀTI RAUKAWA,
NGĀTI MANIAPOTO,
TE AITANGA-A-HAUITI

Terry Gardner
NGĀTI KAHUNGUNU, TE ARAWA,
NGĀTI RAUKAWA, NGĀI TE RANGI,
NGĀTI HĀMOA (SAMOAN)

Megan Gardner
2001–2005

Stephanie Gardner
2002–2006

Ria Millen and Terry Gardner had both their daughters, Megan and Stephanie, attend St Joseph's. Ria says: 'We sent our daughters there because it is about excellence. I would always have a look at the statistics at the beginning of the year and compare them to other schools, and they are always right up there, so I would say to the girls this is the expectation and you have to keep it going into the future.' Another attraction is the focus on behaviour and presentation. 'Their presentation is always sharp. I always get comments on how they present themselves, both physically and in the manner they behave.'

The Gardner whānau are part of the wider Wellington Whānau Whānui:

> We found it difficult with transportation. It was expensive having the girls coming back home all the time, so what we did was we organised a local van, which is part of our waka ama club, and the girls paid $10 each. They were transported to and from school and then word got out and it got bigger. Then we got a bus.

Terry Gardner's cousin was Robert Koko, who did the Māori carvings that now adorn the Marian Steps. Some of his female cousins attended St Joseph's, giving his daughters a whānau connection to the school. Megan Gardner arrived at St Joseph's in 2001 and knew that her uncle had created the carvings on the Marian Steps. 'We used to go to the carvings all the time because we knew that my uncle did them, and I used to tell my friends because we thought we were so cool.' Megan enjoyed doing sports at St Joseph's and ended up being the sports prefect in her final year. 'I played representative netball for Napier under 13s and 19s. It gives you another opportunity to leave the school; one year for the Mission Cup we ended up in Christchurch.'

Megan is certain about what she wants to become, a policewoman, and she is already halfway there. 'I knew what I wanted to do at the age of sixteen and am already working at the Police Communications Centre in Wellington, taking the 111 calls. I draw inspiration from Uncle John Tangaere.' Megan got her first taste of enforcing the law when at St Joseph's:

> In the seventh form, we would buy groceries from Pak'n'Save on Friday evenings. One night we came back and the Whaea Atawhai asked me to put the van away because I could drive. With some friends, we saw some figures at the clothesline and they were taking the clothes and putting them over their shoulders.
>
> We thought they were pupils, so I drove the van up to the clothesline and put the lights on so we could help them get the clothes in. They were boys, so I drove through the clothesline and chased them. They were boys stealing girl's clothing! I felt like a cop then!

Younger sister Steph was one year behind Megan, and like her older sister, she became the sports prefect and the school guitarist:

> Our mail used to get checked, and Mum would sellotape $20 to the inside of the envelope because the Whaea Atawhai would open it, shake it, and if nothing fell out, then it would be given to you. Ten was the code word when Miss Kingi was coming because it was a quick word to say, and the whole school knew the number.

Kapa Haka at Education Excellence Awards 2015:
A Walker, M Harvey-Brewster, K Uruamo-Taiaki, L Bird, V Houkamau,
N Jonas, T Roberts-Thompson, R Albert, H Pou Poasa.

In 2006, twenty-nine out of thirty-two year 12 students achieved Level 2 NCEA, resulting in a pass rate of 91 per cent.[822] The following year, Georgina Kingi reported that a former student of St Joseph's, Christine Nepe, had become the very first practising Māori woman forensic scientist, and 'I was therefore appalled to hear some ministry officials in Wellington call into question our accomplishments because our school leavers favoured motherhood over professions ...'[823] In 2008, classical studies, media studies and mathematics with calculus were provided at Level 3.[824] Also in 2008, the 'Kanohi ki te kanohi' initiative began, a face-to-face, one-on-one conversational practice that developed the relationships between teacher and student, focusing on lifting self-esteem and assisting the student to set goals as she progresses into the senior school.[825]

At the 2009 end-of-year assembly, Georgina Kingi brought to people's attention that she had received a petition from the year 11 girls and dreaded that it would be a request for a ball – to which the answer would be 'No!' To her surprise, however, the petition was an appeal about increasing the subject load so that students could have a more comprehensive science pathway for 2010. The petition was received with favour, and it was announced that the timetable would be able to accommodate these courses.[826]

In 2013, the school enjoyed a 100 per cent pass rate for NCEA levels 1 to 3 and for University Entrance.[827] Ngapera Aperahama also gained an outstanding scholarship in the NZQA 2013 New Zealand Scholarship Awards for te reo Māori, an achievement that is normally reserved for years 12 or 13, not a year 11 student.[828] The following year, St Joseph's continued to produce outstanding academic results but was growing frustrated at the media's inability to focus on their achievements.[829]

Prefects 2016.
Left to right: Casey Webb, Danielle Wanoa-Kalepa, Hiraia Haami-Wells, Mārama Herewini-MacDougall, Hinewairere Sollitt-Mackey, Hineatatu Dorset, Paretao Tipoki-Hansen, Shanelle Smallman, Mereana Houkamou, Daria Bell, Virginia Tapara, Jessy-May Alo.

Millenial

Mere-Kingi Harvey-Brewster
NGĀTI KAHUNGUNU
2012–2016

Mere-Kingi Harvey-Brewster was born in Melbourne and was raised in Christchurch by her nan. Her nan's brother was keen to have the young woman exposed to her Māori culture, so she was placed at St Joseph's. 'It was daunting because everyone expected you to be Māori; I have a Māori name, and I was attending a Māori school.' Despite any initial reservations, Mere-Kingi confides that learning about te reo and tikanga has shaped her perspective about life. Mere-Kingi's first plan, however, was not met with approval by Georgina. Having been awarded a $15,000 Te Puawaitanga Scholarship in year 11, Georgina wanted to hear from the recipients what they intended to do as a career. 'I told her I wanted to be a fashion designer, and she said, "I'm not going to give you fifteen grand a year to be a fashion designer!" To her credit, however, she did let me take art to pursue being a fashion designer.'

Her plans are to become a teacher, and she is completing her Bachelor of Education at the University of Otago. 'I think that comes from here [St Joseph's]. Being a prefect was a deciding factor. Teaching those girls, connecting with them and seeing them learn when I taught them was something great to watch.' Mere-Kingi is referring to the time when she was appointed a group prefect:

> In year 9 our prefects were our role models. They looked after everyone really well, and we all wanted to be prefects because we wanted to be looked up to like that. I had thirty girls in my group when I was a prefect. Term two is the big term for prefects because that is when we have group comps. You have to go home, and within two weeks, you have to create a bracket of six songs, learn them and then teach the thirty girls, who could be on thirty different levels, over the space of ten weeks.

For Mere-Kingi, some of the challenges included finding suitable tunes with not too many slow or fast songs and finding her personal temperament when it came to both rewarding and disciplining the girls.

Mere-Kingi was also the public face of St Joseph's when she sang 'Marie Te Pō' ('Silent Night') with the backing of the kapa haka group for a television advertisement that promoted the school. 'With kapa I travelled all over the North Island; I loved it.' Performing kapa haka increased Mere-Kingi's confidence, as did competing in Ngā Manu Kōrero during year 12, where she won the regional competition for Senior English.

When thinking ahead, Mere-Kingi feels a tinge of sadness. 'Even though I have only just left, I cried and I already miss the school. I'm sad because I'm not coming back. It has been my home for the past five years. I know everyone so well, and Miss Kingi has done so much for me.'

Mere-Kingi Harvey-Brewster.

CHAPTER TWELVE

He Tuāhine Pūmau
Sisters for Life
'The Sisterhood'

The 1949 St Joseph's diary records: 'The fact that a Māori girl has been at St Joseph's has always united her with the other girls, by a bond that transcends religion and tribe.'[830] On leaving St Joseph's, most women express a sisterhood with their former peers that remains for life.

Jill Cotter compares the relationships formed at St Joseph's with being in a family. 'You all become family. We go to each other's weddings and it's like nothing has changed.' Another observation made by Jill is about the partners and husbands they choose to spend their lives with:

> We seem to look at similar values with our partners and they are all very similar, obedient and really good guys. They treat their partners very well and respect the relationship we all have. And they all get on really well – they are called the St Jo's brothers. When we go to weddings, the girls from St Jo's go to one table and the husbands go to one table.

Theresa McAlister agrees with Jill. 'There is a lot of loyalty attached to your year group. We went to each other's weddings and our children's birthdays. We are a family.'

Nadell Karatea and Hinewehi Mohi speak of the lifelong friendships that continue long after they have left their alma mater. Nadell says:

> One thing about St Jo's are my boarding school sisters, and we have been friends since 1989 and we are still the same to this day. We might have changed in size and weight but I tell you when we meet up, at least two to three times a year, it is like we are still at school with no one else around and I love that.

Hinewehi comments:

> The resounding memory I have of school was the friendships, the lifelong friendships you gained at school and being Māori women; we knew we were special and separate and different, but we were never allowed to get too full of ourselves. I've bumped into plenty of girls I went to school with along the way, and there is an immediate kind of connection because you have that common bond from that time, and you spent so much time together that you knew each other so well. They were just glorious years at St Jo's.

Kaapua Smith believes the relationship is formed when living with each other:

> It [attending boarding school] takes a while getting used to, but once you become friends, you are mates for life. My friends from high school are still my very best friends today. It takes a journey to get to that point. You have your run-ins, you figure people out, you have your dramas, and by the end of it you have learnt to live with one another.'

The deep connection St Joseph's holds with former pupils is another common theme expressed by most. Mere Roha-Stewart, who last attended in 1949, states: 'I looked at that place as my second home and most of the girls did.'

Heeni Bartlett supports Mere's view:

> St Joseph's is my second home. I had to yank myself away from here in 2015 because I knew if I didn't leave, I wouldn't be able to. That's how you feel because of all the love and success of this place, and you want to be a part of that. For me, it was having a purpose and being a part of that purpose and working as hard as Miss Kingi, and she is my inspiration, every day.

Stella Marr speaks of St Joseph's in glowing terms: 'They were probably the best years of my life. The whakawhanaungatanga. I can't tell you any lowlights; there weren't any. We loved each other, and the moment we see each other, it's like we were there yesterday.' Tira Ruru, who has graduated from Te Wānanga o Raukawa with a degree in Māori law and philosophy, sums up the effect St Joseph's has had on her life and hundreds of others who have walked through the college's gates at Greenmeadows:

> Our motto is "I o mahi katoa, mahia", so I would say I went on to make sure I did a really good job in whatever I do. I still don't know what I want to do yet as a career, but I know any jobs I will go into, I would just go hard and above and beyond what I was expected to do, and my bosses would always be grateful for that. I feel I got that from St Jo's.

St Joseph's Māori Girls College is well positioned to continue providing quality and holistic education to young Māori women. As history has shown, graduates of St Joseph's will go on and become leaders of their whānau, their communities, their people and their professions. The pioneering path that has been laid by those before them is set to continue long into the future.

Long may St Joseph's Māori Girls' College remain a leader in educating Māori women.

Endnotes

Introduction
1. Te Hau. 'I O Mahi Katoa Mahia'.
2. Ibid., pp. 47–69.

Chapter One
3. 1961 St Joseph's Māori Girls' College Magazine, Mulcahy, 'Centennial Sidelights', pp. 10–13; St Joseph's Māori Girls' College Series 9, College Magazines, Boxes 8 (1951–1967).
4. Ollivier & Grounds. *Missionary Beyond Boundaries*, p. 159.
5. Ibid.
6. Ibid.
7. Ibid.
8. Sisters of Our Lady of the Missions 125th Jubilee 1865–1990, p. 12; St Joseph's Māori Girls' College Series 4, Box 4: History of Our Lady of the Missions, SJMGC Archives.
9. Ibid.
10. Ford. *History of the Sacred Heart Province New Zealand*, p. 19; St Joseph's Māori Girls' College Series 4, Box 4: History of Sacred Heart Province, NZ, SJMGC Archives.
11. Ibid.
12. http://www.rndm.org/provinces/
13. Simmons. *A Brief History of the Catholic Church in New Zealand*, p. 26.
14. Ibid., pp. 50–51.
15. 1960 St Joseph's Māori Girls' College Magazine, Rev. Dr Mulcahy, 'St Joseph's Shares Napier's Catholic Centenary', pp. 12–15; St Joseph's Māori Girls' College Series 9, College Magazines, Boxes 8 (1951–1967), SJMGC Archives.
16. Ibid.
17. 1967 St Joseph's Māori Girls' College Magazine, 'Jottings of a Century', Taken from the Chronicle, p. 21; St Joseph's Māori Girls' College Series 9, College Magazines, Boxes 8 (1951–1967), SJMGC Archives.
18. Lecture – Rev. Dr M Mulcahy SM to Historical Section of Arts Society in Art Gallery, Napier, 3 September 1962, Subject: Father Euloge Reignier 'The Apostle of Hawkes Bay' in Acc 208/23A, MAW.
19. Reignier, 23 November 1886, Māori Schools – General Correspondence and Inspection Reports – St Joseph, Napier, BAAA A440 1001 Box 1025 a 44/6, NZNA.
20. ACGO 8333 IA 1 201 [35] 1859/1375 From: J Williamson, Superintendent, Auckland. To: Colonial Secretary, Auckland Date: 14 July 1859 Subject: Respecting expenses of constable at Turanga, NANZ.
21. AGCO 8333 IA 1 203 [9] 1859/1710 From: Governor, Auckland. To: [Colonial Secretary] Date (Received): 15 September 1859 Subject: Proclamation naturalising Thomas Topp, Nicholas Paul B Tunzelmann, Walter Pilliet and Euloge Reignier, NANZ.
22. *Hawke's Bay Herald*, 28 August 1888, Ibid.
23. *Napier Evening News*, 1 November 1888, Ibid.
24. Lecture – Rev. Dr M Mulcahy SM, 3 September 1962.
25. 1951 St Joseph's Māori Girls' College Magazine, 'Euphrasie Barbier', p. 17; St Joseph's Māori Girls' College Series 9, College Magazines, Boxes 8 (1951–1967), SJMGC Archives.
26. Notes on Euphrasie Barbier, Sister Norah Tobin, St Joseph's Māori Girls' College Series 4, Box 4: History of Our Lady of the Missions, SJMGC Archives.
27. http://www.rndm.org/history/
28. http://www.rndm.org/spirituality/
29. Euphrasie Barbier, 'Regulation of the Providence of Our Lady of the Missions, 1863–1865', Writings of Mother Mary of the Heart of Jesus, 1851–1870, vol. 1, in Smith. *Call to Mission*, p. 182.
30. Ibid., p. 627.
31. Coulomb. *Life of the Very Reverend Mother Marie Du Coeur De Jesus*, p. 446.
32. Notes on Euphrasie Barbier, Sister Norah Tobin, St Joseph's Māori Girls' College Series 4, Box 4: History of Our Lady of the Missions, SJMGC Archives.
33. Ibid.
34. Ibid.

Chapter Two
35. Binney. *The Legacy of Guilt*, p. 41.
36. Ibid., p. 42.
37. Ibid., p. 43.
38. Simon. 'The Place of Schooling in Maori-Pakeha Relations', p. 67.
39. McNab, Historical Records of New Zealand, Vol.1, p. 735 in Alexander. *The Story of Te Aute College*, p. 24.
40. Te Wananga, March, 1930, Ibid., p. 25.
41. Calman, R. 'Māori education – mātauranga – Māori church boarding schools', Te Ara - the Encyclopedia of New Zealand, http://www.TeAra.govt.nz/en/maori-education-matauranga/page-4 (accessed 28 April 2017).
42. Simon. 'The Place of Schooling in Maori-Pakeha Relations', p. 95.
43. An Ordinance for Promoting the Education of Youth in the Colony of N.Z., 7 October 1847.
44. Alexander. *The Story of Te Aute College*, p. 26.
45. Ibid., p. 27.
46. Mackey. *The Making of a State Education System*, p. 38.
47. Butchers. Young New Zealand, p. 120, Ibid.
48. An Act to grant the annual sum of Seven Thousand Pounds for a term of Seven Years from the 30th June, 1858, in aid of Schools for the education of the Aboriginal Native Race [21 August, 1858].
49. AJHR, 1862, E-4, p. 35, Ibid.
50. Barrington. *Separate but Equal?*, p. 19.

51. Ibid., p. 21.
52. Butchers. *Education in New Zealand*, p. 120.
53. 125th Jubilee of Sisters of Our Lady of the Missions, 1865–1990, SJMGC Archives, p.36; St Joseph's Māori Girls' College Series 4, Box 4: History of Our Lady of the Missions, SJMGC Archives.
54. 1960 St Joseph's Māori Girls' College Magazine, Rev. Dr Mulcahy, 'St Joseph's Shares Napier's Catholic Centenary', p. 12; St Joseph's Māori Girls' College Series 9, College Magazines, Boxes 8 (1951-1967), SJMGC Archives.
55. Ford. *Sacred Heart Province*, p. 54; St Joseph's Māori Girls' College Series 4, Box 4: History of Sacred Heart Province, NZ, SJMGC Archives.
56. Op. cit.
57. Ibid.
58. Ollivier. *Missionary Beyond Boundaries*, p. 184.
59. Ibid., p. 185.
60. 125th Jubilee of the Sisters of Our Lady of the Missions, 1865–1990, p. 28; St Joseph's Māori Girls' College Series 4, Box 4: History of Our Lady of the Missions, SJMGC Archives.
61. Op. cit., p. 187.
62. Coulomb. *Life of the Very Reverend Mother Marie Du Coeur De Jesus*, p. 122.
63. Ibid.
64. Ford. *Sacred Heart Province*, p. 55; St Joseph's Māori Girls' College Series 4, Box 4: History of Sacred Heart Province, NZ, SJMGC Archives.
65. 1967 St Joseph's Māori Girls' College Magazine, 'Jottings of a Century taken from the Chronicle', p. 21; St Joseph's Māori Girls' College Series 9, College Magazines, Boxes 8 (1951-1967), SJMGC Archives.
66. van der Linden. *Nga Korero Mo Te Kura Māori o Hato Hohepa*, p. 16.
67. 'And God Gave the Increase', Napier 1865–1965, Centenary of the Congregation of Our Lady of the Missions, St Joseph's Māori Providence p.28; St Joseph's Māori Girls' College Series 4, Box 4: History of Our Lady of the Missions, SJMGC Archives.
68. Reverend E Reignier to Superintendent of Hawke's Bay Donald McLean, 31 July 1867 in Letter 6 in Folder 349, MAW.
69. Object #1018910 from MS-Papers-0032-0525 2 pages written 3 August 1866 by Rev. E Reignier in Napier City From: Inward letters - E Reignier, Reference Number MS-Papers-0032-0525.
70. Keys. *Philip Viard: Bishop of Wellington*, pp. 85–86.
71. Simon. 'The Place of Schooling in Maori-Pakeha Relations', p. 78.
72. Object #1006813 from MS-Papers-0032-0525 4 pages written 20 August 1866 by Rev. E Reignier in Napier City to Sir Donald McLean. From: Inward letters - E Reignier, Reference Number MS-Papers-0032-0525.
73. Ibid.
74. Ibid.
75. Ibid.
76. Reverend E Reignier to Superintendent of Hawke's Bay Donald McLean, 2 September 1867 in Letter 7 in Folder 349, MAW.
77. Reverend E Reignier to Superintendent of Hawke's Bay Donald McLean, 13 September 1867 in Letter 8 in Folder 349, MAW.
78. Ibid.
79. Origins of Hawkes Bay Mission, Acc 208/23A MAW.
80. *Hawke's Bay Herald*, 21 January 1868, p. 2.
81. *Hawke's Bay Herald*, 22 October 1867, p. 2.
82. 1960 St Joseph's Māori Girls' College Magazine, Rev. Dr Mulcahy, 'St Joseph's Shares Napier's Catholic Centenary', p.13; St Joseph's Māori Girls' College Series 9, College Magazines, Boxes 8 (1951-1967).
83. St Joseph's Providence Registration Book 1867, St Joseph's Māori Girls' College Series 1, Box 1: Ledger containing early admissions, accounts, correspondence/Admission Registers No. 1-10/Attendance Register 1941, 1910, SJMGC Archives.
84. Object #1000294 from MS-Papers-0032-0525 3 pages written 14 August 1868 by Rev. E Reignier to Sir Donald McLean.
85. Reverend E Reignier to Superintendent of Hawke's Bay Donald McLean, 29 July 1868 in Letter 9 in Folder 349, MAW.
86. Op.Cit.
87. Object #1020135 from MS-Papers-0032-0525 2 pages written 9 September 1868 by Rev. E Reignier to Sir Donald McLean From: Inward letters - E Reignier, Reference Number MS-Papers-0032-0525.
88. STATEMENT OF OPERATIONS UNDER 'THE NATIVE SCHOOLS ACT, 1867'. Appendix to the Journals of the House of Representatives, 1868 Session I, A-06a.
89. Dans la lettre du p. Reignier à Mgr Viard du 29 octobre 1868 il écrit: Notre Providence est ouverte. Je commence à rassembler les enfants, MAW.
90. Donald McLean, 28/02/1872, Māori Schools – General Correspondence and Inspection Reports – St Joseph, Napier, BAAA A440 1001 Box 1025 a 44/6, National Archives of New Zealand, Auckland.
91. 1967 St Joseph's Māori Girls' College Magazine, 'Jottings of a Century', p. 29, St Joseph's Māori Girls' College Series 9, College Magazines, Box 8 (1951-1967), SJMGC Archives.
92. Trust estates for religious, charitable and educational purposes. Appendix to the Journals of the House of Representatives, 1898 Session I, H-21a.
93. Reignier to Aubert, 13/11/1870 APM Z 208, in Munro. *Letters on the Go*, p. 53.
94. Papers relating to native schools. Appendix to the Journals of the House of Representatives, 1872 Session I, F-05.
95. Ibid.
96. Native schools. Appendix to the Journals of the House of Representatives, 1873 Session I, G-04a.
97. Op. cit.
98. Ibid.
99. Ibid.
100. Ibid.
101. Ibid.
102. Native schools. (FURTHER REPORTS OF INSPECTING OFFICERS.) Appendix to the Journals of the House of Representatives, 1875 Session I, G-02a.

103. Ibid.
104. Ibid.
105. Keogh. *Fruit of the Vine*, p. 26.
106. Ibid.
107. Ibid., p. 28.
108. Ibid., p. 32.
109. John Hislop, Department of Education, to Father E Reignier, 31 January 1882 in SJMGC Archives.
110. Father E Reignier to John Hislop, Department of Education, 08 February 1882 in SJMGC Archives.
111. Ollivier. *Missionary Beyond Boundaries*, p. 338.
112. Letter of Fr Yardin to Fr Forest, Lyon, 26 March 1867, APM W HDS (CF1) 17, in Ibid.
113. Ford. *Sacred Heart Province*', p.79; St Joseph's Māori Girls' College Series 4, Box 4: History of Sacred Heart Province, Ford, M, SJMGC Archives.
114. Smith. *Call to Mission*, p. 182.
115. Bishop Moran to Father Reignier, 15 September 1873, SCH 1, MAW.
116. Bishop Moran to Father Reignier, 24 October 1873, Ibid.
117. Father Reignier to Bishop Moran, 24 October 1873, Ibid.
118. Bishop Moran to Father Reignier, 27 October 1873, Ibid.
119. Agreements between Rev. Fr Reignier, the Superior General of the Religious of Our Lady of the Missions and Bishop Moran, concerning the "Providence" for Māori children and young Māori girls, 26 September 1873, APMW SCH 1.26 in Ollivier. *Missionary Beyond Boundaries*, p. 338.
120. Letter of Euphrasie Barbier to Hon. Donald McLean, 28 October 1873, Ibid, p. 183.
121. Father Reignier to Bishop Moran, 28 October 1873, SCH 1, MAW.
122. Bishop Moran to Father Reignier, 29 October 1873, SCH 1, MAW.
123. Donald McLean to Mother Superior, 31 October 1873, SCH 1, MAW.
124. Ollivier. *Missionary Beyond Boundaries*, p. 338.
125. Ibid.
126. Ibid.
127. Father Reignier to Bishop Moran, 05 November 1873, Ibid.
128. Ibid.
129. List of documents outlining the history of 80 acres of land at Greenmeadows, St Joseph's Māori Girls' College Series 3, Box 3: History of College, SJMGC Archives.
130. Father Dr Victor Geaney to Archbishop Panico, 15 March 1943, Ibid.
131. Apostolic Delegate in Sydney to Father Geaney, 26 August 1934, Ibid.
132. Op. cit.
133. Ibid.
134. Ibid.
135. Ibid.
136. Ibid.
137. Memorandum of Agreement 9 February 1944, Ibid.
138. 'Mission Farm at Meeanee Sold to Crown', *Daily Telegraph*, 24 September 1969.
139. 'Near-century link broken by sale of Mission Farm', *Daily Telegraph*, 25 September 1969.
140. Butchers. *Education in New Zealand*, p. 9.
141. Ibid., pp. 12–13.
142. Ibid., p. 120.
143. Appendix to the Journals of the House of Representatives, 1880 Session I, H-01f.
144. Ibid; Education Department, Wellington, 4 June 1880.
145. *Hawke's Bay Herald*, 18 March 1880, p. 1.
146. John Hislop, Department of Education to Father E Reignier, 10 April 1880 in St Joseph's Māori Girls' College Series 1, Box 1: Ledger containing early admissions, accounts, correspondence/Admission Registers No. 1-10/Attendance Register 1941, 1910, SJMGC Archives.
147. Redwood to Habens, 16 July 1892, Māori Schools – General Correspondence and Inspection Reports – St Joseph, Napier, BAAA A440 1001 Box 1025 a 44/6, NANZ.
148. John Hislop, Education Department, Wellington, 10 February 1880 to Reverend E Reignier, St Mary's, Napier.
149. Father E Reignier to John Hislop, Department of Education, 19 February 1880, Ibid.
150. Ibid.
151. Hislop to Reignier, 8 February 1882, Māori Schools – General Correspondence and Inspection Reports – St Joseph, Napier, BAAA A440 1001 Box 1025 a 44/6, National Archives of New Zealand, Auckland.
152. Father E Reignier to John Hislop, Department of Education, 07 January 1881 in St Joseph's Māori Girls' College Series 1, Box 1: Ledger containing early admissions, accounts, correspondence/Admission Registers No. 1-10/Attendance Register 1941, 1910, SJMGC Archives.
153. John Hislop, Department of Education, to Father E Reignier, 13 April 1881, Ibid.
154. Father E Reignier to John Hislop, Department of Education, 19 April 1881, Ibid.
155. 23 September 1880, Māori Schools – General Correspondence and Inspection Reports – St Joseph, Napier, BAAA A440 1001 Box 1025 a 44/6, NANZ.
156. Habens to Thomas Dick, 27 December 1882, Ibid.
157. John Hislop, Department of Education, to Father E Reignier, 1 July 1884 in St Joseph's Māori Girls' College Series 1, Box 1: Ledger containing early admissions, accounts, correspondence/Admission Registers No. 1-10/Attendance Register 1941, 1910, SJMGC Archives.
158. 7 October 1939, To Rev. Mother from Education Department, BAAA A440 1001 Box 1026: Māori Schools – General Correspondence and Inspection Reports – St Joseph. Napier 1916-1949.
159. 5 April 1899, Māori Schools– General Correspondence and Inspection Reports – St Joseph, Napier, BAAA A440 1001 Box 1025 a 44/6, NANZ.
160. John Hislop, Department of Education to Father E Reignier, 26 July 1880 in St Joseph's Māori Girls' College Series 1, Box 1: Ledger containing early admissions, accounts, correspondence/Admission Registers No. 1-10/Attendance Register 1941, 1910, SJMGC Archives. SJMGC Archives.

161. John Hislop, Department of Education, to Father E Reignier, 27 September 1880 in St Joseph's Māori Girls' College Series 1, Box 1: Ledger containing early admissions, accounts, correspondence/Admission Registers No. 1-10/Attendance Register 1941, 1910, SJMGC Archives.
162. Ibid.
163. Māori Schools – General Correspondence and Inspection Reports – St Joseph, Napier, BAAA A440 1001 Box 1025 a 44/6, National Archives of New Zealand, Auckland; Māori Schools – General Correspondence and Inspection Reports – St Joseph, Napier, BAAA A440 1001 Box 1026 a 44/6, NANZ.
164. School Report, 1 October 1880, Māori Schools – General Correspondence and Inspection Reports – St Joseph, Napier, BAAA A440 1001 Box 1025 a 44/6, NANZ.
165. John Hislop, Department of Education to Father E Reignier, 8 April 1881 in St Joseph's Māori Girls' College Series 1, Box 1: Ledger containing early admissions, accounts, correspondence/Admission Registers No. 1-10/Attendance Register 1941, 1910, SJMGC Archives.
166. Father E Reignier to John Hislop, Department of Education, 16 April 1881, Ibid.
167. John Hislop, Department of Education, to Father E Reignier, 26 April 1881, Ibid.
168. John Hislop, Department of Education, to Father E Reignier, 31 January 1882, Ibid.
169. Ibid.
170. EDUCATION: NATIVE SCHOOLS. [In Continuation of E.-2, 1883.] Appendix to the Journals of the House of Representatives, 1884 Session I, E-02.
171. Pope, 18 December 1885, Māori Schools – General Correspondence and Inspection Reports – St Joseph's, Napier, BAAA A440 1001 Box 1025 a 44/6, NANZ.
172. Inspection of School, 10 February 1888, Ibid.
173. E O Gibbes to Father Grogan, 14 February 1899 in St Joseph's Māori Girls' College Series 1, Box 1: Ledger containing early admissions, accounts, correspondence/Admission Registers No. 1-10/Attendance Register 1941, 1910, SJMGC Archives.
174. George Hogben to Father Grogan, 10 April 1899, Ibid.
175. James Pope to Mother Superior, 6 August 1899, Ibid.
176. Inspection Report, 7 December 1882, Māori Schools – General Correspondence and Inspection Reports – St Joseph, Napier, BAAA A440 1001 Box 1025 a 44/6, NANZ.
177. 'Native schools'. *Hawke's Bay Herald*, 6 September 1882, p. 2.
178. *Daily Telegraph*, 8 September 1884; *Daily Telegraph*, 8 September 1884.
179. Ibid.
180. Ibid.
181. 'Education of natives'. *Hawke's Bay Herald*, 21 August 1886, p. 2.
182. Ibid.
183. *Hawke's Bay Herald*, 29 December 1898, p. 2.
184. Ibid.
185. E Gibbes, Secretary, Department of Education to Father E Reignier, 6 February 1886 in St Joseph's Māori Girls' College Series 1, Box 1: Ledger containing early admissions, accounts, correspondence/Admission Registers No. 1-10/Attendance Register 1941, 1910, SJMGC Archives.
186. 31 March 1886 Reignier to Hislop, Māori Schools – General Correspondence and Inspection Reports – St Joseph, Napier, BAAA A440 1001 Box 1025 a 44/6, NANZ.
187. St Joseph's Providence to Reignier, ND, Ibid.
188. W J Habens to Mother Superior, 5 April 1886 in St Joseph's Māori Girls' College Series 1, Box 1: Ledger containing early admissions, accounts, correspondence/Admission Registers No. 1-10/Attendance Register 1941, 1910, SJMGC Archives.
189. EDUCATION: NATIVE SCHOOLS. [In continuation of E.-2, 1887.] Appendix to the Journals of the House of Representatives, 1888 Session I, E-02.
190. Pope to Habens, 26 March 1886, Māori Schools – General Correspondence and Inspection Reports – St Joseph's, Napier, BAAA A440 1001 Box 1025 a 44/6, NANZ.
191. Habens to Mother Superior, 20 February 1888, Ibid.
192. George Preece to Under-Secretary of the Department of Education, 5 April 1885, Ibid.
193. Ibid.
194. W J Hobens to Mother Superior, 5 April 1886 in St Joseph's Māori Girls' College Series 1, Box 1: Ledger containing early admissions, accounts, correspondence/Admission Registers No. 1-10/Attendance Register 1941, 1910, SJMGC Archives.
195. Ballara, A. 'Mangakahia, Meri Te Tai', Te Ara – the Encyclopedia of New Zealand, http://www.TeAra.govt.nz/en/biographies/2m30/mangakahia-meri-te-tai (accessed 30 April 2017).
196. Ibid.
197. Macdonald, Penfold, & Williams. *The Book of New Zealand Women*, p. 413.
198. Coney. *Standing in the Sunshine*, p. 22.

Chapter Three

199. Inspection of School, 7 February 1890, Ibid.
200. John Hislop, Department of Education, to Father E Reignier, 29 October 1880 in St Joseph's Māori Girls' College Series 1, Box 1: Ledger containing early admissions, accounts, correspondence/Admission Registers No. 1-10/Attendance Register 1941, 1910, SJMGC Archives.
201. John Hislop, Department of Education, to Father E Reignier, 7 May 1881, Ibid.
202. W Gibbes, Department of Education, to C C Soulas, 07 March 1882, Ibid.
203. Ibid.
204. W J Hobens to Rev. Lepeche, 3 October 1889, Ibid.
205. W Gibbes, Department of Education, to C C Soulas, 7 March 1882, Ibid.
206. Ibid.
207. John Hislop, Department of Education, to Father E Reignier, 11 March 1882, Ibid.

208. EDUCATION: NATIVE SCHOOLS. [In Continuation of E-2, 1883.] Appendix to the Journals of the House of Representatives, 1884 Session I, E-02.
209. Ibid.
210. Education Department to St Joseph's Providence, 29 August 1883 in St Joseph's Māori Girls' College Series 1, Box 1: Ledger containing early admissions, accounts, correspondence/Admission Registers No. 1-10/Attendance Register 1941, 1910, SJMGC Archives.
211. EDUCATION: NATIVE SCHOOLS. (In continuation of E-2, 1884.) Appendix to the Journals of the House of Representatives, 1885 Session I, E-02.
212. EDUCATION: NATIVE SCHOOLS. (In Continuation of E-2, 1886.) Appendix to the Journals of the House of Representatives, 1887 Session I, E-02.
213. Ibid.
214. Ibid.
215. EDUCATION: NATIVE SCHOOLS. [In Continuation of E-2, 1891.] Appendix to the Journals of the House of Representatives, 1892 Session I, E-02.
216. 'St. Joseph's, Napier (Roman Catholic), Native Girls' School'. *Daily Telegraph*, 23 July 1896, p. 4.
217. Ibid.
218. Hislop to Pope, 30 July 1885, Māori Schools – General Correspondence and Inspection Reports – St Joseph, Napier, BAAA A440 1001 Box 1025 a 44/6, NANZ.
219. Pope, 4 June 1891, 22 February 1894, Ibid.
220. Māori Schools – General Correspondence and Inspection Reports – St Joseph, Napier, BAAA A440 1001 Box 1025 a 44/6, National Archives of New Zealand, Auckland; Māori Schools – General Correspondence and Inspection Reports – St Joseph, Napier, BAAA A440 1001 Box 1026 a 44/6, National Archives of New Zealand, Auckland.
221. Ollivier & Grounds. *Missionary Beyond Boundaries*, p. 628.
222. Euphrasie to Reignier, 1 October 1873, ARNDM, FII. Letter Press, Volume IV, p. 284, Ibid, p. 334.
223. Inspectors' Report, 12 December 1889, BAAA A440 1001 Box 1025 a 44/6, NANZ.
224. W J Habens to Rev. L, 15 January 1892 in St Joseph's Māori Girls' College Series 1, Box 1: Ledger containing early admissions, accounts, correspondence/Admission Registers No. 1-10/Attendance Register 1941, 1910, SJMGC Archives.
225. Pope, 4 June 1891, Ibid.
226. Pope, 22 February 1894, Māori Schools – General Correspondence and Inspection Reports – St Joseph, Napier, BAAA A440 1001 Box 1025 a 44/6, NANZ.
227. W J Habens to Reverend Sir, 26 January 1896 in Op. cit.
228. E O Gibbes to Madam, 12 January 1899, Ibid.
229. http://teataarangi.org.nz/?q=welcome
230. Winitana. *My Language: My Inspiration*, p. 69.
231. Ibid.
232. Ibid., p. 76.
233. http://news.tangatawhenua.com/2011/07/dame-katerina-mataira-champion-of-te-reo-maori-passes/
234. Op. cit.
235. Ibid., p. 71.
236. Ibid., p. 68.
237. Ibid., p. 75.
238. W Gibbes, Department of Education, to C C Soulas, 7 March 1882 in St Joseph's Māori Girls' College Series 1, Box 1: Ledger containing early admissions, accounts, correspondence/Admission Registers No. 1-10/Attendance Register 1941, 1910, SJMGC Archives.
239. 'St. Joseph's, Napier (Roman Catholic), Native Girls' School'. *Daily Telegraph*, 23 July 1896, p. 4.
240. Habens, 19 December 1885, Māori Schools – General Correspondence and Inspection Reports – St Joseph's, Napier, BAAA A440 1001 Box 1025 a 44/6, NANZ.
241. School Inspection, 16 October 1884, Ibid.
242. School Inspection, 7 February 1890, Ibid.
243. 'Convent Schools'. *Hawke's Bay Herald*, 19 December 1879, p. 3.
244. School Inspection, 16 October 1884, Māori Schools – General Correspondence and Inspection Reports – St Joseph, Napier, BAAA A440 1001 Box 1025 a 44/6, NANZ.
245. Pool, I, & Kukutai, T. 'Taupori Māori – Māori population change - Decades of despair, 1840–1900', Te Ara - the Encyclopedia of New Zealand, http://www.TeAra.govt.nz/en/taupori-maori-maori-population-change/page-2 (accessed 7 May 2017).
246. NATIVE SCHOOLS. (FURTHER REPORTS OF INSPECTING OFFICERS). Appendix to the Journals of the House of Representatives, 1875 Session I, G-02a.
247. Father E Reignier to John Hislop, Department of Education, 3 August 1880 in St Joseph's Māori Girls' College Series 1, Box 1: Ledger containing early admissions, accounts, correspondence/Admission Registers No. 1-10/Attendance Register 1941, 1910, SJMGC Archives.
248. Father E Reignier to John Hislop, Department of Education, 28 August 1880, Ibid.
249. W J Habens to The Teacher, St Joseph's School, 30 April 1894, Ibid.
250. Ibid.
251. Ibid.
252. W J Habens, 23 January 1895, Māori Schools – General Correspondence and Inspection Reports – St Joseph, Napier, BAAA A440 1001 Box 1025 a 44/6, NANZ.
253. Telegram, 16 December 1897, Ibid.
254. 4 January 1898, Māori Schools – General Correspondence and Inspection Reports – St Joseph, Napier, BAAA A440 1001 Box 1026 a 44/6, National Archives of New Zealand, Auckland.
255. School Inspection, 21 February 1899, Op. cit.
256. Ibid.; Marie St Winifred to the Director of Education, 19 November 1918, Ibid.
257. 1967 St Joseph's Māori Girls' College Magazine, 'Jottings of a Century', p.21, St Joseph's Māori Girls' College Series 9, College Magazines, Box 8 (1951-1967) SJMGC Archives.
258. Ibid.
259. Ibid.
260. Ibid.

261. Ibid.
262. Secretary of the Napier Hospital Board to the Inspector of the Native Schools, 31 May 1898 in St Joseph's Māori Girls College Series 1, Box 1: Ledger containing early admissions, accounts, correspondence/Admission Registers No. 1-10/Attendance Register 1941, 1910, SJMGC Archives.
263. W J Habens to Mother Superior, 22 June 1898, Ibid.
264. Ibid.
265. 1967 St Joseph's Māori Girls' College Magazine, 'Jottings of a Century', p. 38; St Joseph's Māori Girls College Series 9, College Magazines, Boxes 8 (1951–1967), SJMGC Archives.
266. Lange. *May the People Live*, p. 166.
267. Ibid.
268. James Pope to Mother Superior, 13 July 1899 in St Joseph's Māori Girls' College Series 1, Box 1: Ledger containing early admissions, accounts, correspondence/Admission Registers No. 1-10/Attendance Register 1941, 1910, SJMGC Archives.
269. Ibid.
270. George Hogben to Reverend Mother, 25 August 1899, Ibid.
271. James Pope to Reverend Mother, 6 October 1899, Ibid.
272. St Joseph's to Habens, 30 June 1892, Māori Schools – General Correspondence and Inspection Reports – St Joseph, Napier, BAAA A440 1001 Box 1025 a 44/6, NANZ.
273. Sargison, P A. 'Hei, Akenehi'. Te Ara - the Encyclopedia of New Zealand, http://www.TeAra.govt.nz/en/biographies/3h13/hei-akenehi (accessed 30 April 2017).
274. 1967 St Joseph's Māori Girls' College Magazine, 'Jottings of a Century', p. 21, St Joseph's Māori Girls College Series 9, College Magazines, Boxes 8 (1951–1967), SJMGC Archives.
275. Op. cit.
276. Coney. *Standing in the Sunshine*, p .92.
277. Lange. *May the People Live*, p. 176.
278. Sargison. 'Hei, Akenehi'.
279. Ibid.

Chapter Four

280. SJMGC School Inspection, Porteous, 14 December 1920, BAAA A440 1001 Box 1026: Māori Schools – General Correspondence and Inspection Reports – St Joseph. Napier 1916-1949, NANZ.
281. Inspection Report, 27 February 1900, Ibid.
282. Report on School, Hobgen, 12 December 1900, Ibid.
283. SJMGC School Report, William Bird, 20 December 1909, Ibid.
284. SJMGC School Inspection, Porteous, 9 December 1910, Ibid.
285. SJMGC School Inspection, William Bird, 18 December 1912, Ibid.
286. SJMGC School Inspection, William Bird, 6 December 1913, Ibid.
287. SJMGC Inspection Report, William Bird, 16 December 1916, Ibid.
288. Memorandum from James Pope to E O Gibbes, 11 February 1902, Ibid.
289. Pope, 4 April 1902, Ibid.
290. E O Gibbes (Assistant Secretary, Education) to Prioress, 1902, Ibid.
291. Letter from Hone Heke to Minister of Education, 6 October 1902, Ibid.
292. Ibid.
293. Ibid.
294. Walker to Heke, 16 October 1902, Ibid.
295. D T Hamilton to Pope, 4 April 1902, Ibid.
296. Pope to Hamilton, April 1902, Ibid.
297. Hogben to Prioress, 29 December 1904, Ibid.
298. 1904 School Inspection, Ibid.
299. William Bird, 1906 School Inspection, Ibid.
300. E Issac, 1907 School Inspection, 6 July 1907, Ibid.
301. W Bird, 1907 Inspection Report, 17 December 1907, Ibid.
302. Ibid.
303. Ibid.
304. Secretary of Education to the Prioress, 5 September 1908, Ibid.
305. Ibid.
306. Memo from Department of Education to St Joseph's Māori Girls' College, 8 March 1910, E1 42 44/6 St Joseph's Māori Girls College, NANZ.
307. Ibid.
308. Prioress to Hogben, 20 May 1910, Ibid.
309. Hogben to Prioress, 10 June 1910, Ibid.
310. SJMGC School Inspection, William Bird, 16 December 1911, Ibid.
311. King. *Whina*, p. 59.
312. Sister Bernadine to Heremia Te Wake, 1 May 1908, Received: 9 June 1908. From: Heremia te Wake, Kohukohu, Hokianga. Subject: Forwarding letter from nuns of St Josephs College, Napier, re maintenance of his daughter, Hohiwhinia te Wake, ACIH 16036 MA 1 948/1908/276.
313. Heremia Te Wake to Native Minister James Carroll, 12 May 1908, Ibid.
314. Under Secretary of Native Affairs to Sister Bernadine, St Joseph's Māori Girls College, 09 June 1908, Ibid.
315. Under-Secretary of Native Department to Sister Bernadine, 29 March 1909, Ibid.
316. Under-Secretary of Native Affairs to Heremia Te Wake, 22 June 1909, Ibid.
317. King. *Whina*, p. 59.
318. Ibid., pp. 61–62.
319. Ibid., p. 69.
320. Ibid., p. 61.
321. Ibid., p. 75.
322. King, M. 'Cooper, Whina', Te Ara – the Encyclopedia of New Zealand, http://www.TeAra.govt.nz/en/biographies/5c32/cooper-whina (accessed 29 April 2017).
323. Ibid.
324. Ibid.
325. Ibid.
326. ACIH 16068 MA51 7/ 35 St Joseph's College for Māori Girls, NANZ.
327. Ibid.

328. MPFB to SJMGC, 29 September 1925, Ibid.
329. Balneavis to SJMGC, 19 December 1930, Ibid.
330. John Porteous to Director of Education, 11 March 1933, Ibid.
331. Ibid.
332. AJHR, 1881, E-7:1, p. 95. in Simon. 'The Place of Schooling in Maori-Pakeha Relations'.
333. Op. cit.
334. Ibid.
335. Ibid. It should also be noted that ten scholarships were available at Sacred Heart College, Auckland, but none had been taken.
336. Ibid.
337. Ibid.
338. Balneavis to Porteous, 24 October 1931, Ibid.
339. Butterworth. *Māori Affairs*, p. 70.
340. SJMGC School Inspection, GM Henderson, 19 December 1922, Ibid.
341. Ibid.
342. Ibid.
343. SJMGC School Inspection, G M Henderson, 2 December 1924, Ibid.
344. SJMGC School Inspection, Porteous, 3 December 1926, Op. cit.
345. SJMGC School Inspection, Porteous, 16 December 1927, Ibid.
346. SJMGC School Inspection, D G Ball, 6 June 1929, Ibid.
347. Ibid.
348. Memorandum to Director of Education from D G Ball, 7 December 1929, Ibid.
349. Ibid.
350. Ibid.
351. SJMGC School Inspection, D G Ball and T A Fletcher, 18 November 1931, E1 42 44/6 St Joseph's Māori Girls' College, NANZ.
352. SJMGC School Inspection, T A Fletcher, 15 December 1932, Ibid.
353. SJMGC School Inspection, D G Ball, 26 November 1934, Ibid.
354. D G Ball to Director of Education, 8 December 1930, Ibid.
355. Ibid.
356. Ibid.
357. McSaveney, E. 'Historic earthquakes – The 1931 Hawke's Bay earthquake', Te Ara – the Encyclopedia of New Zealand, http://www.TeAra.govt.nz/en/historic-earthquakes/page-6 (accessed 7 May 2017).
358. Ibid.
359. Sisters of the Lady of the Missions 125th Jubilee, 1865–1990, p. 19, St Joseph's Māori Girls' College Series 4, Box 4: History of Our Lady of the Missions, SJMGC Archives.
360. Ibid., p. 21.
361. NZ *Tablet*, 11 March 1931, in Ford. *Sacred Heart Province*, p. 79; St Joseph's Māori Girls' College Series 4, Box 4: History of Sacred Heart Province, NZ, SJMGC Archives.
362. Op. cit.
363. Sister M Vergine, Ibid., p. 26.
364. Ibid., p. 21.
365. Op. cit.
366. Prime Minister to Acting Native Minister, 16 March 1943, Ibid.
367. Prioress Venatius to Ngata, 11 October 1929, Ibid.
368. Ibid.
369. Balneavis to the Prioress, 22 July 1929, Ibid.
370. 5 June 1930, in Memorandum to the Prime Minister from MPFB, 31 August 1939, Ibid.
371. Principal to Ngata, 29 October 1934, Ibid.
372. Riordan to Masters, 20 March 1935, Ibid.
373. Masters to Riordan, 31 May 1935, Ibid.
374. Masters to Riordan, 31 May 1935, in Prime Minister to Acting Native Minister, 16 March 1943, Ibid.
375. Ibid.
376. Ngata, 26 September 1935, in Prime Minister to Acting Native Minister, 16 March 1943, Ibid.
377. Riordan to Savage, 16 June 1939 in Prime Minister to Acting Native Minister, 16 March 1943, Ibid.
378. Ibid.
379. Ibid.
380. Livingstone to Riordan, 8 March 1937, Ibid.
381. Livingstone to Principal, 9 October 1937, Ibid.
382. Minister of Education to Acting Minister of Native Affairs, 19 November 1941, Ibid.
383. Ibid.
384. Ibid.
385. Ibid.
386. Ibid.
387. Ibid.
388. 18 November 1941, in Prime Minister to Acting Native Minister, 16 March 1943, Ibid.
389. Ibid.
390. Ibid.
391. Ibid.
392. Under-Secretary of the Native Department to the Minister of Native Affairs, 5 December 1941, Ibid.
393. Memorandum for the Prime Minister, 26 May 1943, Ibid.
394. SJMGC School Inspection, D G Ball and T A Fletcher, 18 November 1931, E1 42 44/6 St Joseph's Māori Girls' College, NANZ.
395. Ibid.
396. 1932 SJMGC School Diary, St Joseph's Māori Girls' College Series 2, Box 2: Chronicles – Diaries, 1904, 1910, 1912, 1944, 1939–1950, 1940–1946, 1951–1952, 1953–1955, 1957–1959, SJMGC Archives.
397. Ibid.
398. Ibid.
399. Ibid.
400. Ibid.
401. Ibid.
402. Ibid.

Chapter Five

403. Director of Education to Mother Prioress, 12 February 1934, Ibid.
404. Ibid.

405. Ibid.
406. Sisters of the Lady of the Missions 125th Jubilee 1865–1990, p. 58; Ford. *History of Sacred Heart Province*, p. 29, St Joseph's Māori Girls' College Series 4, Box 4: History of Our Lady of the Missions, History of Sacred Heart Province, NZ.
407. Ibid.
408. 10 December 1935, 1935 SJMGC School Diary, St Joseph's Māori Girls' College Series 2, Box 2: Chronicles – Diaries, 1904, 1910, 1912, 1944, 1939–1950, 1940–1946, 1951–1952, 1953–1955, 1957–1959, SJMGC Archives.
409. Ibid.
410. Ibid.
411. 1935 SJMGC School Diary, Ibid.
412. 12 March 1935, Ibid.
413. 'Great Progress on School Grounds', ND, unnamed newspaper clipping, Ibid.
414. 'Māori Girl's College', ND, unnamed newspaper clipping, Ibid.
415. *Daily Telegraph*, ND, Ibid.
416. 'A New Māori College: Advance in Māori Education, ND, unnamed newspaper clipping, Ibid.
417. ND, unnamed newspaper clipping, Ibid.
418. Ibid.
419. 1937 School Inspection of SJMGC, Ibid.
420. Ngata to Fraser as Minister of Education, 20 February 1937, Ibid.
421. 16 March 1952, 1952 SJMGC School Diary, St Joseph's Māori Girls' College Series 2, Box 2: Chronicles – Diaries, 1904, 1910, 1912, 1944, 1939–1950, 1940–1946, 1951–1952, 1953–1955, 1957–1959, SJMGC Archives.
422. 17 March 1952, Ibid.
423. Lillian Taylor, 'St Joseph's Day', 1963 St Joseph's Māori Girls' College Magazine, p.16, St Joseph's Māori Girls' College Series 9, College Magazines, Box 8 (1951–1967), SJMGC Archives.
424. Ibid.
425. 8 September 1940, 1940 SJMGC School Diary, St Joseph's Māori Girls' College Series 2, Box 2: Chronicles – Diaries, 1904, 1910, 1912, 1944, 1939–1950, 1940–1946, 1951–1952, 1953–1955, 1957–1959, SJMGC Archives.
426. 31 July 1942, 1942 SJMGC School Diary, Ibid.
427. 6 October 1948, 1948 SJMGC School Diary, Ibid.
428. 5 May 1951, 6 May 1961, 1951 and 1961 SJMGC School Diaries, Ibid.
429. Ibid.
430. 12 April 1939, 1939 SJMGC School Diary, Ibid.
431. 13 June 1954, 1954 SJMGC School Diary, Ibid.
432. 8 October 1951, 1951 SJMGC School Diary, Ibid.
433. Ibid.
434. Ibid.
435. 9 May 1944, 1944 SJMGC School Diary, Ibid.
436. ND, 1935 SJMGC School Diary, Ibid.
437. 12 October 1941, 1941 SJMGC School Diary, Ibid.
438. 21 October 1957, 1956 SJMGC School Diary, Ibid.
439. Ibid.
440. Ibid.
441. Ibid.
442. 11 September 1951, 09 May 1951, 26 July 1942, 29 May 1942, 17 September 1946, 1951, 1942 and 1946 SJMGC School Diaries, St Joseph's Māori Girls' College Series 2, Box 2: Chronicles – Diaries, 1904, 1910, 1912, 1944, 1939–1950, 1940–1946, 1951–1952, 1953–1955, 1957–1959, SJMGC Archives.
443. 13 March 1949, 1949 SJMGC School Diary, Ibid.
444. 04 November 1949, 1949 SJMGC School Diary, Ibid.
445. 'Mr Corbett Visits the School', 1951 St Joseph's Māori Girls' College Magazine, pp. 22–23, St Joseph's Māori Girls' College Series 9, College Magazines, Box 8 (1951–1967), SJMGC Archives.
446. 'The Winds of Change in Maoridom', 1963 St Joseph's Māori Girls' College Magazine, p. 30, Ibid.
447. Ibid.
448. Ibid.
449. Ibid.
450. 27 April 1956, 1956 SJMGC School Diary, St Joseph's Māori Girls' College Series 2, Box 2: Chronicles – Diaries, 1904, 1910, 1912, 1944, 1939–1950, 1940–1946, 1951–1952, 1953–1955, 1957–1959, SJMGC Archives.
451. Ford. *Sacred Heart Province*, p. 17, St Joseph's Māori Girls' College Series 4, Box 4: History of Sacred Heart Province, NZ, SJMGC Archives.
452. 'Apostolic Delegate to St Joseph's', 1956 St Joseph's Māori Girls' College Magazine, pp. 6–7, St Joseph's Māori Girls' College Series 9, College Magazines, Box 8 (1951–1967), SJMGC Archives.
453. 'The Visit to Our College', 1956 St Joseph's Māori Girls' College Magazine, p. 9, Ibid.
454. Ibid.
455. 1957 St Joseph's Māori Girls' College School Magazine, pp. 9–10, Ibid.
456. 'The New Chapel', 1958 St Joseph's Māori Girls' College School Magazine, pp. 7–9, Ibid.
457. Ford. *Sacred Heart Province*, p. 20, St Joseph's Māori Girls' College Series 4, Box 4: History of Sacred Heart Province, NZ, SJMGC Archives.
458. 13 July 1958, 1958 SJMGC School Diary, St Joseph's Māori Girls' College Series 2, Box 2: Chronicles – Diaries, 1904, 1910, 1912, 1944, 1939–1950, 1940–1946, 1951–1952, 1953–1955, 1957–1959, SJMGC Archives.
459. Ibid.
460. 'The New Chapel', 1958 St Joseph's Māori Girls' College Magazine, pp. 7–9, St Joseph's Māori Girls' College Series 9, College Magazines, Box 8 (1951–1967), SJMGC Archives.
461. 1959 St Joseph's Māori Girls' College Magazine, p. 20, Ibid.
462. Ibid.
463. Ibid., pp. 142–144.
464. Ibid.
465. Higgins, Q. 'We Are The Lay Apostle', *The Marist Messenger*, 01 December 1941, St Joseph's Māori Girls' College Series 2, Box 2: Chronicles – Diaries, 1904, 1910, 1912, 1944, 1939–1950, 1940–1946, 1951–1952, 1953–1955, 1957–1959, SJMGC Archives.
466. 26 October 1946, 1946 SJMGC School Diary, Ibid.

467. 19 September 1945, 1945 SJMGC School Diary, Ibid.
468. 08 September 1946, 1946 SJMGC School Diary, Ibid.
469. 10 August 1940, 1940 SJMGC School Diary, Ibid.
470. 01 June 1942, 1942 SJMGC School Diary, Ibid.
471. 15 March 1942, 19 March 1942, 1942 SJMGC School Diary, Ibid.
472. 21 September 1946, 1946 SJMGC School Diary, Ibid.
473. 'Women's Auxiliary Air Force founded', https://nzhistory.govt.nz/foundation-of-the-womens-auxiliary-air-force (Accessed 9 March 2017).
474. Ibid.
475. 19 June 1942, 1942 SJMGC School Diary, St Joseph's Māori Girls' College Series 2, Box 2: Chronicles – Diaries, 1904, 1910, 1912, 1944, 1939–1950, 1940–1946, 1951–1952, 1953–1955, 1957–1959, SJMGC Archives.
476. Unnamed newspaper Clipping, 1932 SJMGC School Diary, Ibid.
477. Ford. *Sacred Heart Province*, p. 2, St Joseph's Māori Girls' College Series 4, Box 4: History of Sacred Heart Province, NZ, SJMGC Archives.
478. 24 August 1946, 1946 SJMGC School Diary, Op. cit.
479. 19 February 1957, 1957 SJMGC School Diary, Ibid.
480. 25 September 1957, 1957 SJMGC School Diary, Ibid.
481. 'Softball', 1954 St Joseph's Māori Girls' College Magazine, p.22, St Joseph's Māori Girls' College Series 9, College Magazines, Box 8 (1951–1967), SJMGC Archives.
482. 26 July 1949, 19 August 1952, 28 July 1954, 28 April 1956, 19 June 1956, 1949, 1952, 1954 and 1956 SJMGC School Diaries, St Joseph's Māori Girls' College Series 2, Box 2: Chronicles – Diaries, 1904, 1910, 1912, 1944, 1939–1950, 1940–1946, 1951–1952, 1953–1955, 1957–1959, SJMGC Archives.
483. 19 June 1956, 1956 SJMGC School Diary, Ibid.
484. 09 June 1951, 1951 SJMGC School Diary, Ibid.
485. 17 June 1955, 1955 SJMGC School Diary, Ibid.
486. 18 June 1955, 1955 SJMGC School Diary, Ibid.
487. 19 June 1955, 1955 SJMGC School Diary, Ibid.
488. 1955 St Joseph's Māori Girls' College Magazine, pp. 10–11, St Joseph's Māori Girls' College Series 9, College Magazines, Box 8 (1951–1967), SJMGC Archives.
489. 02 May 1933, 1933 SJMGC School Diary, Op.Cit.
490. 02 April 1956, 1956 SJMGC School Diary, Ibid.
491. 10 March 1954, 1954 SJMGC School Diary, Ibid.
492. 06 July 1933, 20 February 1939, 1933 and 1939 SJMGC School Diaries, Ibid.
493. 29 March 1950, 1950 SJMGC School Diary, Ibid.
494. 10 February 1951, 1951 SJMGC School Diary, Ibid.
495. 24 May 1952, 1952 SJMGC School Diary, Ibid.
496. 1955 SJMGC School Diary, Ibid.
497. 26 July 1952, 1952 SJMGC School Diary, Ibid.
498. 1947 SJMGC School Diary, Ibid.
499. 25 July 1945, 1945 SJMGC School Diary, Ibid.
500. Notes, pp. 8–9, St Joseph's Māori Girls' College Series 4, Box 4: History of Our Lady of the Missions, SJMGC Archives.
501. 17 June 1953, 1953 SJMGC School Diary, Op. cit.
502. 14–17 August 1950, 1950 SJMGC School Diary, Ibid.
503. 14 February 1953, 1953 SJMGC School Diary, Ibid.

Chapter Six

504. 'As Others See Us', 1951 St Joseph's Māori Girls' College Magazine, p. 16, St Joseph's Māori Girls' College Series 9, College Magazines, Box 8 (1951–1967), SJMGC Archives.
505. 1949 SJMGC School Diary, Op.Cit.
506. 10 February 1953, 1953 SJMGC School Diary, Ibid.
507. 02 December 1947, 1947 SJMGC School Diary, Ibid.
508. 13 May 1947, 1947 SJMGC School Diary, Ibid.
509. 29 July 1947, 1947 SJMGC School Diary, Ibid.
510. 07 February 1951, 1951 SJMGC School Diary, Ibid.
511. 01 February 1955, 1955 SJMGC School Diary, Ibid.
512. 24 October 1952, 1952 SJMGC School Diary, Ibid.
513. 11 February 1951, 1951 SJMGC School Diary, Ibid.
514. Ford. *Sacred Heart Province*, p. 12, St Joseph's Māori Girls' College Series 4, Box 4: History of Our Lady of the Missions, History of Sacred Heart Province, NZ, SJMGC Archives.
515. 18 February 1951, 1951 SJMGC School Diary, Op. cit.
516. Ibid.
517. Ford. *Sacred Heart Province*, p. 2, St Joseph's Māori Girls' College Series 4, Box 4: History of Our Lady of the Missions, History of Sacred Heart Province, NZ, SJMGC Archives.
518. Ibid., pp.6–7.
519. 10 September 1944, 1944 SJMGC School Diary, St Joseph's Māori Girls' College Series 2, Box 2: Chronicles – Diaries, 1904, 1910, 1912, 1944, 1939–1950, 1940–1946, 1951–1952, 1953–1955, 1957–1959, SJMGC Archives.
520. Op. cit., p. 3, SJMGC Archives.
521. 30 April 1948, 1948 SJMGC School Diary, Op. cit.
522. Op. cit., p. 9.
523. 23 February 1952, 1952 SJMGC School Diary, Op. cit.
524. 1954 Entry, Op.Cit. Sisters of the Lady of the Missions 125th Jubilee 1865–1990, p. 58, St Joseph's Māori Girls' College Series 4, Box 4: History of Our Lady of the Missions, SJMGC Archives.
525. 31 March 1953, 2 February 1954, 6 March 1954, 1953 and 1954 SJMGC School Diaries, St Joseph's Māori Girls' College Series 2, Box 2: Chronicles – Diaries, 1904, 1910, 1912, 1944, 1939–1950, 1940–1946, 1951–1952, 1953–1955, 1957–1959, SJMGC Archives.
526. 'Modern Wing', 1954 St Joseph's Māori Girls' College Magazine, pp. 10–12, St Joseph's Māori Girls' College Series 9, College Magazines, Boxes 8 (1951–1967), SJMGC Archives.
527. 1954 St Joseph's Māori Girls' College Magazine, Ibid.
528. Ibid.
529. 11 April 1954, 1954 SJMGC School Diary, St Joseph's Māori Girls' College Series 2, Box 2: Chronicles – Diaries, 1904, 1910, 1912, 1944, 1939–1950, 1940–1946, 1951–1952, 1953–1955, 1957–1959, SJMGC Archives.
530. 1967 St Joseph's Māori Girls' College Magazine, St Joseph's Māori Girls' College Series 9, College Magazines, Boxes 8 (1951–1967), SJMGC Archives.

531. Education Department to SJMGC, 19 October 1944, BAAA A440 1001 Box 1026: Māori Schools – General Correspondence and Inspection Reports – St Joseph. Napier 1916–1949, NANZ.
532. Ford. *Sacred Heart Province*, St Joseph's Māori Girls' College Series 4, Box 4: History of Our Lady of the Missions, History of Sacred Heart Province, NZ, SJMGC Archives.
533. Inspectors' Report on St Joseph's Māori Girls College, Greenmeadows, 1946, BAAA A440 1001 Box 1026: Māori Schools – General Correspondence and Inspection Reports – St Joseph. Napier 1916–1949, NANZ.
534. Ibid.
535. 16 August 1943, 1943 SJMGC School Diary, St Joseph's Māori Girls' College Series 2, Box 2: Chronicles – Diaries, 1904, 1910, 1912, 1944, 1939–1950, 1940–1946, 1951–1952, 1953–1955, 1957–1959, SJMGC Archives. 18 September 1954, 1954 SJMGC School Diary, Ibid.
536. History of the Sisters of Our Lady of the Missions, Notes, p. 2, St Joseph's Māori Girls' College Series 4, Box 4: History of Our Lady of the Missions, SJMGC Archives.
537. Education Department, Inspectors' Report on St Joseph's Māori Girls' College, Greenmeadows, visited 3 and 4 March, 1949, Ibid.
538. Ibid.
539. Ibid.
540. Ibid.
541. Ibid.
542. Ibid.
543. Ibid.
544. 29 August 1949, 1949 SJMGC School Diary, Ibid.
545. Ibid.
546. 24 August 1950, 1950 SJMGC School Diary, Ibid.
547. 'Whaikorero Competition', 1951 St Joseph's Māori Girls' College Magazine, p. 48, St Joseph's Māori Girls' College Series 9, College Magazines, Box 8 (1951–1967), SJMGC Archives.
548. 'English Oratory Competition', 1953 St Joseph's Māori Girls' College Magazine, p. 6., Ibid.
549. Ibid.
550. Lillian Taylor, 'Our Problem', 1963 St Joseph's Māori Girls' College Magazine, pp. 13–14, Ibid.
551. Unnamed newspaper clipping, ND, St Joseph's Māori Girls' College Series 12, Box 11: Ephemera, Newspaper Cuttings, SJMGC Archives.
552. Ibid.
553. 'A Survey of the Catholic Church in Hawkes Bay', 1940 Centennial Exhibition Entry, SJMGC Archives.
554. Unnamed newspaper clipping, ND, St Joseph's Māori Girls' College Series 12, Box 11: Ephemera, Newspaper Cuttings, SJMGC Archives.
555. 24 March 1952, 1952 SJMGC School Diary, St Joseph's Māori Girls' College Series 2, Box 2: Chronicles – Diaries, 1904, 1910, 1912, 1944, 1939–1950, 1940–1946, 1951–1952, 1953–1955, 1957–1959, SJMGC Archives.
556. 16 April 1959, 1959 SJMGC School Diary, Ibid.
557. 11 June 1956, 1956 SJMGC School Diary, Ibid.
558. 04 October 1954, 1954 SJMGC School Diary, Ibid.
559. 22 May 1953, 1953 SJMGC School Diary, Ibid.
560. 16 November 1933, 1933 SJMGC School Diary, Ibid.
561. 16 February 1947, 1947 SJMGC School Diary, Ibid.
562. Ibid.
563. 01 July 1958, 1958 SJMGC School Diary, Ibid.
564. 27 August 1952, 1952 SJMGC School Diary, Ibid.
565. 02 March 1955, 1955 SJMGC School Diary, Ibid.
566. 11 April 1957, 1957 SJMGC School Diary, Ibid.
567. 'Junior Red Cross', 1957 St Joseph's Māori Girls' College Magazine, p. 13, St Joseph's Māori Girls' College Series 9, College Magazines, Box 8 (1951–1967), SJMGC Archives.
568. 29 March 1955, 1955 SJMGC School Diary, Op. cit.
569. 30 March 1955, Ibid.
570. 05 June 1955, Ibid.
571. van der Linden, *Nga Korero Mo Te Kura o Hato Hohepa*, p. 145.
572. 18 September 1953, 1953 SJMGC School Diary, Op. cit.
573. Dominion Special Service, 10 March 1946, Ibid.
574. 23 September 1947, 1947 SJMGC School Diary, Ibid.
575. 18 October 1951, 1951 SJMGC School Diary, Ibid.
576. 12 September 1954, 1954 SJMGC School Diary, Ibid.
577. 1955 St Joseph's Māori Girls' College Magazine, pp. 13–14, St Joseph's Māori Girls' College Series 9, College Magazines, Box 8 (1951–1967), SJMGC Archives.
578. Ibid.
579. 'Mr Lynch Tribute', 1964 St Joseph's Māori Girls' College Magazine, p. 34, Ibid.
580. 23 February 1953, 1953 SJMGC School Diary, St Joseph's Māori Girls' College Series 2, Box 2: Chronicles – Diaries, 1904, 1910, 1912, 1944, 1939–1950, 1940–1946, 1951–1952, 1953–1955, 1957–1959, SJMGC Archives.
581. 18 August 1959, 1959 SJMGC School Diary, Ibid.
582. 29 July 1945, 1945 SJMGC School Diary, Ibid.
583. 27 October 1947, 1947 SJMGC School Diary, Ibid.
584. 03 August 1952, 1952 SJMGC School Diary, Ibid.
585. 'Our Visit to Hato Paora', 1953 St Joseph's Māori Girls' College Magazine, p. 16, St Joseph's Māori Girls' College Series 9, College Magazines, Box 8 (1951–1967), SJMGC Archives.
586. 20 June 1951, 1951 SJMGC School Diary, Op. cit.
587. 18 October 1952, 1952 SJMGC School Diary, Ibid.
588. 12 August 1952, 1952 SJMGC School Diary, Ibid.
589. 02 June 1956, 1956 SJMGC School Diary, Ibid.
590. 'Mother M Athanasius', 1956 St Joseph's Māori Girls' College Magazine, p. 10, St Joseph's Māori Girls' College Series 9, College Magazines, Box 8 (1951–1967), SJMGC Archives.
591. Ibid.
592. 1954 SJMGC School Diary, St Joseph's Māori Girls' College Series 2, Box 2: Chronicles – Diaries, 1904, 1910, 1912, 1944, 1939–1950, 1940–1946, 1951–1952, 1953–1955, 1957–1959, SJMGC Archives.
593. 1967 St Joseph's Māori Girls College Magazine, p. 11, Op. cit.

594. Ibid.
595. Greenlees, S. 'St Joseph's Māori Girls' College 1867–2007', p. 13, St Joseph's Māori Girls' College Series 3, Box 3: History of College, SJMGC Archives.
596. 22 November 1950, 1950 SJMGC School Diary, St Joseph's Māori Girls' College Series 2, Box 2: Chronicles – Diaries, 1904, 1910, 1912, 1944, 1939–1950, 1940–1946, 1951–1952, 1953–1955, 1957–1959, SJMGC Archives.
597. 16 June 1950, Ibid.
598. Newspaper article, St Joseph's Māori Girls' College Series 12, Box 11: Ephemera, Newspaper Cuttings, SJMGC Archives.
599. 'Lions Visit', 1959 St Joseph's Māori Girls' College Magazine, pp. 25–26, St Joseph's Māori Girls' College Series 9, College Magazines, Box 8 (1951–1967), SJMGC Archives.
600. 03 August 1951, 1951 SJMGC School Diary, Op. cit.
601. 04 August 1956, 1956 SJMGC School Diary, Ibid.
602. 18 August 1956, Ibid.
603. 12 May 1954, 1954 SJMGC School Diary, Ibid.
604. 13 May 1954, Ibid.
605. 'Vienna Boys Choir', 1964 St Joseph's Māori Girls' College Magazine, p. 21, St Joseph's Māori Girls' College Series 9, College Magazines, Box 8 (1951–1967), SJMGC Archives.
606. 29 May 1953, 1953 SJMGC School Diary, Op.Cit.
607. 02 June 1953, Ibid.
608. 1963 St Joseph's Māori Girls' College Magazine, pp. 8–10, St Joseph's Māori Girls' College Series 9, College Magazines, Box 8 (1951–1967), SJMGC Archives.
609. Ibid.
610. Ibid.
611. 1960 St Joseph's Māori Girls' College Magazine, p. 43, Ibid.
612. Ibid.
613. 'Foundress of the Congregation of the Sisters of Our Lady of the Missions', edited by Tobin, M. 'The New Zealand Story, Centenary of the Congregation of Our Lady of the Missions', p. 33, St Joseph's Māori Girls' College Series 4, Box 4: History of Our Lady of the Missions, SJMGC Archives.
614. Ibid.
615. 30 November 1932, 1932 SJMGC School Diary, Ibid.
616. 7 October 1945, 1945 SJMGC School Diary, Ibid.
617. 24 October 1955, 1955 SJMGC School Diary, St Joseph's Māori Girls' College Series 2, Box 2: Chronicles – Diaries, 1904, 1910, 1912, 1944, 1939–1950, 1940–1946, 1951–1952, 1953–1955, 1957–1959, SJMGC Archives.
618. 15 April 1939, 1939 SJMGC School Diary, Ibid.
619. 25 September 1944, 1944 SJMGC School Diary, Ibid.
620. 12 June 1946, 1946 SJMGC School Diary, Ibid.
621. Ibid.
622. 4 October 1941, 1941 SJMGC School Diary, Ibid.
623. 1947 SJMGC School Diary, Ibid.
624. 1967 St Joseph's Māori Girls' College Magazine, p. 24, St Joseph's Māori Girls' College Series 9, College Magazines, Box 8 (1951–1967), SJMGC Archives.
625. Ibid.
626. 'Australian Reporter's Visit', 1961 St Joseph's Māori Girls' College Magazine, p. 41, Ibid.
627. 16 May 1956, 1956 SJMGC School Diary, St Joseph's Māori Girls' College Series 2, Box 2: Chronicles – Diaries, 1904, 1910, 1912, 1944, 1939–1950, 1940–1946, 1951–1952, 1953–1955, 1957–1959, SJMGC Archives.
628. 1 March 1937, 1937 SJMGC School Diary, Ibid.
629. 17 April 1939, 1939 SJMGC School Diary, Ibid.
630. 7 September 1957, 1957 SJMGC School Diary, Ibid.
631. 10 September 1953, 1953 SJMGC School Diary, Ibid.
632. 15 August 1945, 1945 SJMGC School Diary, Ibid.
633. 06 August 1952, 1952 SJMGC School Diary, Ibid.
634. 1935 SJMGC School Diary, Ibid.
635. 13 February 1952, 1952 SJMGC School Diary, Ibid.
636. 16 October 1942, 1942 SJMGC School Diary, Ibid.
637. 30 October 1942, 1942 SJMGC School Diary, Ibid.
638. 22 August 1939, 1939 SJMGC School Diary, Ibid.

Chapter Seven

639. 'A Visit to St Joseph's Māori Girls' College', *Te Ao Hou*, November 1964, p. 28.
640. Ibid.
641. Ibid.
642. Ibid.
643. Ibid.
644. Accommodation and Equipment – School Visits: St Joseph's Māori Girls' College 1965–1984, ABRX W4612 6880 Box 15, NANZ.
645. Ibid.
646. Notes on Girls Interviewed by Miss N P Witana on 09 June 1965, Ibid.
647. Ibid.
648. ABRX W4612 8472 Box 17 School Profiles – St Joseph's Māori Girls' College 1990, NANZ.
649. 16 February 1944, 1944 SJMGC School Diary, St Joseph's Māori Girls' College Series 2, Box 2: Chronicles – Diaries, 1904, 1910, 1912, 1944, 1939–1950, 1940–1946, 1951–1952, 1953–1955, 1957–1959, SJMGC Archives.
650. 4 February 1956, 1956 SJMGC School Diary, Ibid.
651. 26 February 1956, Ibid.
652. 1933 SJMGC School Diary, Ibid.
653. 20 July 1955, 1955 SJMGC School Diary, Ibid.
654. 24 February 1955, 1955 SJMGC School Diary, Ibid.
655. 'St Joseph's Queen Carnival', 1959 St Joseph's Māori Girls' College Magazine, p. 3, St Joseph's Māori Girls' College Series 9, College Magazines, Box 8 (1951–1967), SJMGC Archives.
656. 'Swimming Baths', 1961 St Joseph's Māori Girls' College Magazine, p. 67, Ibid.
657. 'Jottings of a Century', 1967 St Joseph's Māori Girls' College Magazine, p. 22, Ibid.
658. Ibid.
659. Ibid, p. 24.
660. 8 September 1939, 1939 SJMGC School Diary, St Joseph's Māori Girls' College Series 2, Box 2: Chronicles – Diaries, 1904, 1910, 1912, 1944, 1939–1950, 1940–1946, 1951–1952, 1953–1955, 1957–1959, SJMGC Archives.

661. 1946 SJMGC School Diary, Ibid.
662. 16 September 1943, 1943 SJMGC School Diary, Ibid.
663. 25 September 1954, 1954 SJMGC School Diary, Ibid.
664. Ford. *Sacred Heart Province*, p. 4, St Joseph's Māori Girls' College Series 4, Box 4: History of Sacred Heart Province, NZ, SJMGC Archives.
665. 27 May 1946, 1946 SJMGC School Diary, Op. cit.
666. 15 August 1949, 1949 SJMGC School Diary, Ibid.
667. Ibid.
668. Ibid.
669. 'Old Girls Notes', 1954 St Joseph's Māori Girls' College Magazine, p. 17, St Joseph's Māori Girls' College Series 9, College Magazines, Box 8 (1951–1967), SJMGC Archives.
670. 'Past Pupils of the College', 1956 St Joseph's Māori Girls' College Magazine, p. 33, Ibid.
671. 1964 St Joseph's Māori Girls' College Magazine, p. 63, Ibid.
672. 'The Reunion', 1964 St Joseph's Māori Girls' College Magazine, p. 15, Ibid.
673. 14 July 1960, 1960 SJMGC School Diary, St Joseph's Māori Girls' College Series 2, Box 2: Chronicles – Diaries, 1904, 1910, 1912, 1944, 1939–1950, 1940–1946, 1951–1952, 1953–1955, 1957–1959, SJMGC Archives.
674. 9 August 1950, 1950 SJMGC School Diary, Ibid.
675. 'Jottings of a Century', 1967 St Joseph's Māori Girls' College Magazine, p. 23, St Joseph's Māori Girls' College Series 9, College Magazines, Box 8 (1951–1967), SJMGC Archives.
676. Ibid.
677. Ibid.
678. van der Linden. *Nga Korero Mo Te Kura Māori o Hato Hohepa*, p. 56.
679. 'St Joseph's Centennial', *Te Ao Hou*, 1 March 1968, p. 42.
680. *Te Ao Hou*, 1 December 1967, p. 24.
681. Ibid.
682. 1967 St Joseph's Māori Girls' College Magazine, p. 38, St Joseph's Māori Girls' College Series 9, College Magazines, Box 8 (1951–1967), SJMGC Archives.
683. 'Miss Aotearoa', 1964 St Joseph's Māori Girls' College Magazine, p. 32, Ibid.
684. 'The Welcome', *Te Ao Hou*, 1 June 1966, p. 26.
685. 'Consecration of New Bishop of Aotearoa', *Te Ao Hou*, 1 December 1968, p. 34.
686. 'Māori Song Competition', *Te Ao Hou*, 1 March 1967, p. 26.
687. David Burgess, 'Tops for Māori Enterprise', newspaper article, 2001, St Joseph's Māori Girls' College Series 12, Box 11: Ephemera, Newspaper Cuttings, SJMGC Archives.

Chapter Eight

688. van der Linden. *Nga Korero Mo Te Kura Māori o Hato Hohepa*, p. 66.
689. Ibid., p. 67.
690. Ibid., p. 66.
691. St Joseph's Māori Girls' College Greenmeadows 15 August 1971, MACINTYRE1W1187 4, NANZ.
692. Ibid.
693. 'Principal's Report', 1973 St Joseph's Māori Girls' College Magazine, p.3, St Joseph's Māori Girls' College Series 9, College Magazines, Boxes 8A (1973–1993).
694. Ibid.
695. Ibid.
696. Ibid.
697. Ibid.
698. 'Principal's Report', 1974 St Joseph's Māori Girls' College Magazine, p. 3, Ibid.
699. Ibid., p. 33.
700. Ibid., p. 35.
701. Ibid., p. 38.
702. Ibid., p. 42.
703. 1977 St Joseph's Māori Girls' College Magazine, Ibid.
704. 1978 St Joseph's Māori Girls' College Magazine, Ibid.
705. Ibid.
706. Ibid.
707. Ibid.
708. Ibid., p. 36.
709. *Daily Telegraph*, 7 July 1979, St Joseph's Māori Girls' College Series 12, Box 11: Ephemera, Newspaper Cuttings, SJMGC Archives.
710. 'Gold Disc Award', 1976 St Joseph's Māori Girls' College Magazine, pp. 33–34, Op. cit.
711. http://www.moananz.com/music.html
712. Ibid.
713. Ibid.
714. http://maiseyrika.com/
715. Ibid.
716. 17 August 1985, Paul McAlister Papers.
717. March 1988, Ibid.

Chapter Nine

718. Smith, S., 'Māori and Mission Sisters in New Zealand Since 1865: Changing Approaches'. *International Bulletin of Missionary Research*, Vol. 31, No. 2, April 2007, p. 77.
719. Ibid., p. 89.
720. 1980 St Joseph's Māori Girls' College Magazine, p. 2, St Joseph's Māori Girls' College Series 9, College Magazines, Boxes 8A (1973–1993).
721. 1986 St Joseph's Māori Girls' College Magazine, p. 2, Ibid.
722. 1985 St Joseph's Māori Girls' College Magazine, p. 2, Ibid.
723. Ibid.
724. 1981 St Joseph's Māori Girls' College Magazine, p. 5, Ibid.
725. 1981, *Hawke's Bay Herald*, St Joseph's Māori Girls' College Series 12, Box 11: Ephemera, Newspaper Cuttings, SJMGC Archives.
726. Ibid.
727. Ibid.
728. Ibid.
729. Ibid.
730. Ibid.
731. Ibid.

732. 1954 Entry, Sisters of the Lady of the Missions 125th Jubilee 1865–1990, p. 58, St Joseph's Māori Girls' College Series 4, Box 4: History of Our Lady of the Missions, SJMGC Archives.
733. Ibid.
734. 3 July 1982, Paul McAlister Papers.
735. AGM 9 July 1983, Ibid.
736. April 1990, Ibid.
737. 22 March 1986, Ibid.
738. 4 July 1987, Ibid.
739. 1988, Ibid.
740. March 1989, Ibid.
741. 1990, Ibid.
742. November 1987, Ibid.
743. 30 March 1985, Ibid.
744. 1989, Ibid.
745. 1990, Ibid.
746. November 1987, Ibid.
747. 30 March 1985, Ibid.
748. Ibid.
749. 'Principal's Message', 2009 St Joseph's Māori Girls' College Magazine, St Joseph's Māori Girls' College Series 9, College Magazines, Box 8B (1994–2016), SJMGC Archives.

Chapter Ten

750. 1987 St Joseph's Māori Girls' College Magazine, p. 12, St Joseph's Māori Girls' College Series 9, College Magazines, Box 8A (1973–1993).
751. Ibid., p. 13.
752. April 1987, Paul McAlister Papers.
753. 1987 St Joseph's Māori Girls' College Magazine, p. 14, St Joseph's Māori Girls' College Series 9, College Magazines, Box 8A (1973–1993).
754. Ibid., p. 15.
755. 4 October 1988, P A Atkinson to Sister Mary Martin, ABEP W4262 7750 Box 3653 8/1 1 Integration and State Aid – Private Schools – General-St Joseph's Māori Girls, Greenmeadows 1982–1988.
756. Ibid.
757. 1963 St Joseph's Māori Girls' College Magazine, Oratory and Debating Contest, p. 32, St Joseph's Māori Girls' College Series 9, College Magazines, Box 8 (1951–1967), SJMGC Archives.
758. 1994 St Joseph's Māori Girls' College Magazine, St Joseph's Māori Girls' College Series 9, College Magazines, Box 8B (1994–2016).
759. 'Board of Trustees Report', 1997 St Joseph's Māori Girls' College Magazine, Ibid.
760. 2005 St Joseph's Māori Girls' College Magazine, Ibid.
761. 1988 St Joseph's Māori Girls' College Magazine, pp. 6–7, St Joseph's Māori Girls' College Series 9, College Magazines, Box 8A (1973–1993), SJMGC Archives.
762. 1990 St Joseph's Māori Girls' College Magazine p.7; 1991 St Joseph's Māori Girls' College Magazine, p. 23, Ibid.
763. Ibid.
764. 1991 St Joseph's Māori Girls' College Magazine, p. 23, Ibid.
765. 'Principal's Report', 2002 St Joseph's Māori Girls' College Magazine, pp. 1–2, St Joseph's Māori Girls' College Series 9, College Magazines, Box 8B (1994–2016), SJMGC Archives.
766. Ibid.
767. Ibid.

Chapter Eleven

768. 'Principal's Report', 1988 St Joseph's Māori Girls' College Magazine, pp. 6–7, St Joseph's Māori Girls' College Series 9, College Magazines, Box 8A (1973–1993), SJMGC Archives.
769. Ibid.
770. 'Principal's Report', 2000 St Joseph's Māori Girls' College Magazine, St Joseph's Māori Girls' College Series 9, College Magazines, Box 8B (1994–2016), SJMGC Archives.
771. Ibid.
772. 'Principal's Report', St Joseph's Māori Girls' College Magazine 2003, p. 1, Ibid.
773. Ibid.
774. Ibid.
775. 'Principal's Report', St Joseph's Māori Girls' College Magazine 2010, pp. 2–3, Ibid.
776. Ibid.
777. 'Principal's Report', 2013 St Joseph's Māori Girls' College Magazine, Ibid.
778. Ibid.
779. Ibid.
780. Ibid.
781. 'Principal's Report', 2012 St Joseph's Māori Girls' College, p. 6, Ibid.
782. 'South Island Tour', 1993 St Joseph's Māori Girls' College Magazine, St Joseph's Māori Girls' College Series 9, College Magazines, Box 8B (1973–1993), SJMGC Archives.
783. 1994 St Joseph's Māori Girls' College Magazine , St Joseph's Māori Girls' College Series 9, College Magazines, Box 8B (1994–2016).
784. Ibid.
785. 1986 St Joseph's Māori Girls' College Magazine, pp. 38–39, St Joseph's Māori Girls' College Series 9, College Magazines, Box 8A (1973–1993).
786. 1954 Entry, Sisters of the Lady of the Missions 125th Jubilee 1865–1990, p. 58, St Joseph's Māori Girls' College Series 4, Box 4: History of Our Lady of the Missions, SJMGC Archives.
787. 2001 St Joseph's Māori Girls' College Magazine, pp. 1-2, 4, St Joseph's Māori Girls' College Series 9, College Magazines, Box 8B (1994–2016).
788. Ibid., p. 35.
789. 2005 St Joseph's Māori Girls' College Magazine, Ibid.
790. Ibid.
791. 2009 St Joseph's Māori Girls' College Magazine, Ibid.
792. Ibid.
793. Ibid.
794. Ibid.

795. Ibid.
796. Ibid.
797. 'Totara Point', 1988 St Joseph's Māori Girls' College Magazine, p. 30, St Joseph's Māori Girls' College Series 9, College Magazines, Box 8A (1973–1993).
798. Hato Hohepa 125th Jubilee Celebrations 1992, St Joseph's Māori Girls' College Series 7, Box 7: Jubilees, Celebrations and Hui, SJMGC Archives.
799. Sciascia, W. 'Te Ekenga ki Ūropi', St Joseph's Māori Girls' College, p.3.
800. Ibid.
801. Turanga, Te Ariki, in Ibid, p. 6.
802. Munro-Waihape, Te Oraora, in Ibid, p .8.
803. March 2001, unnamed newspaper article, St Joseph's Māori Girls' College Series 12, Box 11: Ephemera, Newspaper Cuttings, SJMGC Archives.
804. 14 August 1952, 1952 SJMGC School Diary, Ibid.
805. 1953 SJMGC School Diary, Ibid.
806. 'Jubilee Profiles: Sister Katarina', 1992 St Joseph's Māori Girls' College Magazine, p. 102, St Joseph's Māori Girls' College Series 9, College Magazines, Box 8B (1994–2016), SJMGC Archives.
807. Ibid.
808. van der Linden. *Nga Korero Mo Te Kura Māori o Hato Hohepa.*
809. van der Linden. *An Unforgettable Journey*, p. 231.
810. Ibid.
811. Ibid., p. 185.
812. Ibid., pp. 188–189.
813. Ibid., p. 222.
814. 'Farewell to Maria van der Linden', 1990 St Joseph's Māori Girls' College, p. 6, St Joseph's Māori Girls' College Series 9, College Magazines, Box 8A (1973-1993), SJMGC Archives.
815. Op. cit., p. 203.
816. Harfield, R. 'Old Girls Meet for Tales of School', *Hawke's Bay Today*, ND.
817. Harfield, R. 'College Celebrates 150 Years', *Hawke's Bay Today*, ND.
818. Hickey, P. 'Māori College Celebrates 150 Years in Style', *NZ Catholic*, 5–18 November 2017, p. 4.
819. Ibid.
820. 'Māori Focus Strong For Duo', newspaper article, St Joseph's Māori Girls' College Series 12, Box 11: Ephemera, Newspaper Cuttings, SJMGC Archives.
821. Ibid.
822. 2006 St Joseph's Māori Girls' College Magazine, Ibid.
823. 'Principal's Report', 2007 St Joseph's Māori Girls' College Magazine, Ibid.
824. 'Chairperson's Report', Ibid.
825. Ibid.
826. Ibid.
827. 'Principal's Report', 2014 St Joseph's Māori Girls' College Magazine, pp. 4–5, Ibid.
828. Roger Moroney, *Hawke's Bay Today*, 2014, SJMGC Archives.
829. 'Board of Trustees', 2014 St Joseph's Māori Girls' College Magazine, pp. 2–3, St Joseph's Māori Girls' College Series 9, College Magazines, Box 8B (1994–2016), SJMGC Archives.

Chapter Twelve
830. 15 August 1949 SJMGC School Diary, St Joseph's Māori Girls' College Series 2, Box 2: Chronicles – Diaries, 1904, 1910, 1912, 1944, 1939–1950, 1940–1946, 1951–1952, 1953–1955, 1957–1959, SJMGC Archives.

Select Bibliography

Archives

Alexander Turnbull Library (ATL)
Inward letters – E Reignier, Reference Number MS-Papers-0032-0525 Series 1 Inward letters (English), Reference Number Series 1 Inward letters (English) McLean Papers, Reference Number MS-Group-1551.

Society of Mary – Marist Archives, Wellington (MAW)
Acc 208/23A Dans la lettre du p. Reignier à Mgr Viard du 29 octobre 1868 il écrit: Notre Providence est ouverte. Je commence à rassembler les enfants.

Reverend E Reignier to Superintendent of Hawke's Bay Donald McLean, Folder 349.

Bishop Moran to Father Reignier, 15/09/1873, SCH 1, MAW.

National Archives of New Zealand (NANZ)
AUCKLAND
BAAA A440 1001 Box 1025 a 44/6 Māori Schools – General Correspondence and Inspection Reports – St Joseph's, Napier.

BAAA A440 1001 Box 1026 a 44/6 Māori Schools – General Correspondence and Inspection Reports – St Joseph's, Napier.

WELLINGTON
ABEP W4262 7750 Box 3653 8/1 1 Integration and State Aid – Private Schools – General- St Joseph's Māori Girls College, Greenmeadows 1982–1988.

ABLG W3781 Box 56 5455 St Joseph's Māori Girls' College History.

ABRX W4612 6880 Box 15 Accommodation and Equipment – School Visits – St Joseph's Māori Girls' College 1965–1984.

ABRX W4612 8472 Box 17 School Profiles – St Joseph's Māori Girls' College 1990.

ACGO 8333 IA 1 201 [35] 1859/1375 From: J Williamson, Superintendent, Auckland. To: Colonial Secretary, Auckland Date: 14 July 1859 Subject: Respecting expenses of constable at Turanga.

AGCO 8333 IA 1 203 [9] 1859/1710 From: Governor, Auckland. To: [Colonial Secretary] Date (Received): 15 September 1859 Subject: Proclamation naturalising Thomas Topp, Nicholas Paul B Tunzelmann, Walter Pilliet and Euloge Reignier.

ACIG 17240 E1 42/44/6 St Joseph's Māori Girls' College.

ACIH 16036 MA 1 948/1908/276 Received: 9 June 1908. From: Heremia te Wake, Kohukohu, Hokianga. Subject: Forwarding letter from nuns of St Josephs College, Napier, re maintenance of his daughter, Hohiwhinia te Wake.

ACIH 16068 MA51 7/ 35 St Joseph's College for Māori Girls.

AEFU 19640 W1187 MACINTYRE1W1187 4/ St Joseph's Māori Girls' College, Greenmeadows – 15 August 1971.

BAAA A440 1001 Box 1026: Māori Schools – General Correspondence and Inspection Reports – St Joseph's. Napier 1916–1949.

St Joseph's Māori Girls' College Archives (SJMGC)
St Joseph's Māori Girls' College Series 1, Box 1: Ledger containing early admissions, accounts, correspondence/Admission Registers No.1–10/ Attendance Register 1941, 1910.

St Joseph's Māori Girls' College Series 2, Box 2: Chronicles – Diaries, 1904, 1910, 1912, 1944, 1939–1950, 1940–1946, 1951–1952, 1953–1955, 1957–1959.

St Joseph's Māori Girls' College Series 3, Box 3: History of College.

St Joseph's Māori Girls' College Series 4, Box 4: History of Our Lady of the Missions, History of Sisters Our Lady of the Missions, History of Sacred Heart Province, NZ, Sister M M Ford.

St Joseph's Māori Girls' College Series 7, Box 7: Jubilees, Celebrations and Hui.

St Joseph's Māori Girls' College Series 9, College Magazines, Boxes 8 (1951–1967), 8A (1973–1993), and 8B (1994–2016).

St Joseph's Māori Girls' College Series 12, Box 11: Ephemera, Newspaper Cuttings.

Private Papers
Paul McAlister, Parents, Teachers and Friends Association of St Joseph's Māori Girls' College Minutes 1982–1990.

Newspapers and Periodicals
Daily Telegraph
Hawke's Bay Herald
Hawke's Bay Today
International Bulletin of Missionary Research
Te Ao Hou
The Marist Messenger
The New Zealand Tablet
Zealandia

Unpublished Theses
Girdwood-Morgan, K B. 'Jean-Baptise Pompallier, Instructions pour les travaux de la mission, 1841, Catholic Diocese of Auckland Archives, translated from the French with an introduction'. Research exercise presented in partial fulfilment for Diploma of Social Sciences in History. Massey University, 1985.

Simon, J A. 'The Place of Schooling in Maori–Pakeha Relations'. Thesis for PhD in Anthropology. University of Auckland, 1990.

Te Hau, R J. 'I O Mahi Katoa Mahia: An Analysis of Sustained Success'. Thesis presented in partial fulfilment for Master of Education. University of Auckland, 2006.

Thompson, J. 'The Roman Catholic Mission in New Zealand 1838–1870'. Thesis for Master of Arts in History. Victoria University of Wellington, 1966.

Appendices to the Journals of the House of Representatives
Appendix to the Journals of the House of Representatives, 1880 Session I, H-01f.

EDUCATION: NATIVE SCHOOLS. [In continuation of E.-2, 1883.] Appendix to the Journals of the House of Representatives, 1884 Session I, E-02.

EDUCATION: NATIVE SCHOOLS. [In continuation of E.-2, 1884.] Appendix to the Journals of the House of Representatives, 1885 Session I, E-02.

EDUCATION: NATIVE SCHOOLS. [In continuation of E.-2, 1886.] Appendix to the Journals of the House of Representatives, 1887 Session I, E-02.

EDUCATION: NATIVE SCHOOLS. [In continuation of E.-2, 1887.] Appendix to the Journals of the House of Representatives, 1888 Session I, E-02.

EDUCATION: NATIVE SCHOOLS. [In continuation of E.-2, 1891.] Appendix to the Journals of the House of Representatives, 1892 Session I, E-02.

NATIVE SCHOOLS. Appendix to the Journals of the House of Representatives, 1873 Session I, G-04a.

NATIVE SCHOOLS. (Further reports of inspecting officers.) Appendix to the Journals of the House of Representatives, 1875 Session I, G-02a.

PAPERS RELATING TO NATIVE SCHOOLS. Appendix to the Journals of the House of Representatives, 1872 Session I, F-05.

STATEMENT OF OPERATIONS UNDER 'THE NATIVE SCHOOLS ACT, 1867'. Appendix to the Journals of the House of Representatives, 1868 Session I, A-06a.

TRUST ESTATES FOR RELIGIOUS, CHARITABLE, AND EDUCATIONAL PURPOSES (SECOND REPORT OF THE COMMISSION OF INQUIRY INTO THE CONDITION AND NATURE OF). Appendix to the Journals of the House of Representatives, 1898 Session I, H-21a.

Publications
Alexander, R R. *The Story of Te Aute College*. Wellington: A H & A W Reed, 1951.

Anderson, A, Binney, J, & Harris, A. *Tangata Whenua: An Illustrated History*. Wellington: Bridget Williams Books, 2015.

Ballantyne, T. *Entanglements of Empire: Missionaries, Māori and the Question of Body*. Auckland: Auckland University Press, 2015.

Ballantyne, T. *Webs of Empire: Locating New Zealand's Colonial Past*. Wellington: Bridget Williams Books, 2012.

Barrington, J. *Separate but Equal? Māori Schools and the Crown 1867–1969*. Wellington: Victoria University Press, 2009.

Beeching, J. *An Open Path: Christian Missionaries 1515–1914*. Auckland: Hutchinson & Co., 1979.

Belich, J. *Making Peoples: A History of the New Zealanders: From Polynesian Settlement to the End of the Nineteenth Century*. Auckland: Allen Lane/The Penguin Press, 1996.

Binney, J. *The Legacy of Guilt: A Life of Thomas Kendall*. Auckland: Oxford University Press, 1968.

Bokenkotter, T. *A Concise History of the Catholic Church*. Auckland: Image Books, 2004.

Butchers, A G. *Education in New Zealand*. Wellington: Coulls, Somerville, Wilkie Ltd, 1930.

Butchers, A G. *Young New Zealand*. Dunedin: Coulls, Sommerville, Wilkie Ltd, 1929.

Butterworth, G V. *Māori Affairs*. Wellington: GP Books, 1990.

Clisby, E. *Marist Brothers and Māori 1838–1988*. Auckland: Marist Publications, 2002.

Coney, S. *Standing in the Sunshine: A History of New Zealand Women Since They Won the Vote*. Auckland: Penguin Books, 1993.

Coulomb, l'Abbe. *Life of the Very Reverend Mother Marie Du Coeur De Jesus*. Mechlin, Belgium: H. Dessain, 1914.

Davidson, A K, & Lineham, P J (Eds). *Transplanted Christianity* (2nd Ed.). Palmerston North: Department of History, Massey University, 1995.

Faggioli, M. *Vatican II: The Battle for Meaning*. Mahwah, NJ: Paulist Press, 2012.

Ford, M. *Sacred Heart Province*. Sisters of Our Lady of the Missions, 1980.

Gallagher, P. *The Marist Brothers in New Zealand, Fiji & Samoa 1876–1976*. Auckland: Marist Trust Board and Pegasus Press, 1976.

Gilling, B (Ed.). *Godly Schools? Some Approaches to Christian Education in New Zealand*. Hamilton: Waikato Studies in Religion Volume 4, University of Waikato, 1993.

Goulter, M C. *Sons of France: A Forgotten Influence on New Zealand History*. Christchurch: Whitcombe and Tombs Ltd, 1957.

Historic Royal Palaces. *The Really Useful Guide to Kings and Queens of England*. Surrey: Historic Royal Palaces, 2015.

Jenkins, K, & Matthews, K. *Hukarere and the Politics of Māori Girls' Schooling 1875–1995*. Palmerston North: Dunmore Press, 1995.

Keogh, D. *Fruit of the Vine: The Story of St Mary's Parish 1850–2003*. Napier: CHB Print, 2004.

Keys, L. *The Life and Times of Bishop Pompallier*. Christchurch: The Pegasus Press, 1957.

Keys, L. *Philip Viard: Bishop of Wellington*. The Pegasus Press, 1968.

King, M. *God's Farthest Outpost: A History of Catholics in New Zealand*. Auckland: Penguin Books, 1997.

King, M. *Whina: The Biography of Whina Cooper*. Auckland: Penguin Books, 1991.

Lange, R. *May the People Live: A History of Māori Health Development 1900–1920*. Auckland: Auckland University Press, 1999.

Laurenson, G I. 'Te Haahi Weteriana: Three Half Centuries of the Methodist Māori Missions 1822–1972', in *Proceedings of the Wesley Historical Society of New Zealand*. Vol. 27, Nos 1 & 2, 1972.

Macdonald, C, Penfold, M, & Williams, B (Eds). *The Book of New Zealand Women: Ko Kui Ma Te Kaupapa*. Wellington: Bridget Williams Books, 1991.

Mackey, J. *The Making of a State Education System: The Passing of the New Zealand Education Act 1877*. Geoffrey Chapman, 1967.

Marshall, P. *Reformation England 1480–1642*. London: Hodder Arnold, 2003.

Mooney, K D. *Faith-Family and Friends: 150 Years of St Patrick's Catholic Parish Napier, New Zealand 1859–2009*. Napier: St Patrick's Parish, 2009.

Mooney, M. 'And God Gave The Increase, Napier 1865–1965: Centenary of the Congregation of Our Lady of the Missions'. *Daily Telegraph*, 1964.

Morrell, W. *The Anglican Church in New Zealand: A History*. Dunedin: Anglican Church of the Province of New Zealand, 1973.

Munro, J (Ed.). *Letters on the Go: The Correspondence of Suzanne Aubert*. Wellington: Bridget Williams Books, 2009.

Nichol, C, & Veitch, J (Eds). *Religion in New Zealand*. Wellington: Tertiary Christian Services Programme and The Religious Studies Department, Victoria University, 1983.

Ollivier, M, & Grounds, B. *Missionary Beyond Boundaries: Euphrasie Barbier 1829–1893*. Rome: Istituto Salesiano Pio XI, 2007.

O'Malley, V. *The Meeting Place: Māori and Pākehā Encounters, 1642–1840*. Auckland: Auckland University Press, 2012.

Orange, C. *The Treaty of Waitangi*. Wellington: Bridget Williams Books, 1987.

O'Sullivan, D. *Faith, Politics and Reconciliation: Catholicism and the Politics of Indigeneity*. Wellington: Huia Publishers, 2005.

Purchas, H T. *The English Church in New Zealand*. Christchurch: Simpson & Williams Ltd, 1914.

Reed, A H. *The Story of Hawke's Bay*. Wellington: A H & A W Reed, 1958.

Reese, T. *Inside the Vatican: The Politics and Organisation of the Catholic Church*. Cambridge, MA: Harvard University Press, 1996.

Simmons, E R. *A Brief History of the Catholic Church in New Zealand*. Catholic Publications Centre, 1978.

Simmons, E R. *Pompallier: Prince of Bishops*. CPC Publishing, 1984.

Sisters of the Lady of the Missions, *Sisters of the Lady of the Missions 125th Jubilee 1865–1990*. Jubilee Committee, 1991.

Smith, S. *Call to Mission: The Story of the Mission Sisters of Aotearoa New Zealand and Samoa*. Auckland: David Ling Publishing, 2010.

Smith, S. *Zeal for Mission: The Story of the Sisters of Our Lady of the Missions 1861–2011*. Auckland: David Ling Publishing, 2012.

Stock, E (Ed.). *The History of the Church Missionary Society: Its Environment, Its Men, and Its Work, Vol.1*. London: Church Missionary Society, 1899.

Van der Linden, M. *An Unforgettable Journey*. Palmerston North: Dunmore Press, 1992.

Van der Linden, M. *Ngā Kōrero Mō Te Kura Māori o Hato Hohepa: St Joseph's Māori Girls' College 1867–1990*. Palmerston North: Dunmore Press, 1990.

Waitangi Tribunal. *Te Whanganui-a-Orotu Report*. Wellington: Brookers Ltd, 1995.

Wakeman, H. *An Introduction to the History of the Church of England*. London: Rivingtons, 1955.

Williment, T M I. *John Hobbs 1800–1883: Wesleyan Missionary to the Ngapuhi Tribe of Northern New Zealand*. Wellington: Government Printer, 1985.

Winitana, C. *My Language: My Inspiration*. Wellington: Huia Publishers and Te Taura Whiri i te Reo Māori, 2011.

Wright, M. *Hawke's Bay: The History of a Province*. Palmerston North: Dunmore Press, 1994.

Wright, O. *The Voyage of the Astrolabe 1840*. Wellington: A H & A W Reed, 1955.

Image Credits

Unless specified below, all images are supplied courtesy of St Joseph's Māori Girls' College.

Key:
Alexander Turnbull Library (ATL)
Society of Mary – Marist Archives, Wellington (MAW)

Opposite half-title page Ans Westra

p. viii Kataraina Millen

pp. 4–5 Seas Cookson

p. 9 Mere Roha-Stewart

p. 12 MAW

p. 13 Molly Rose Mulholland

p. 14 *Pope Pius XI*: MAW

p. 14 *Jean-Baptiste Francois Pompallier*: Auckland Catholic Diocesan Archive

p. 14 *Father Louis Catherin Servant*: MAW

p. 14 *Bishop Philippe Viard*: MAW

p. 16 MAW

p. 17 Henry Bates, Non-ATL-P-0099, ATL

p. 21 *Sister Maureen Richardson*: Molly Rose Mulholland

p. 23 Robert Park, A-114-012, ATL

p. 24 Molly Rose Mulholland

p. 27 Shontelle Bishara

p. 28 Molly Rose Mulholland

p. 29 *Maraea and Moengarau Taiaroa*: Molly Rose Mulholland

p. 29 *John Bishara, Nastasia Kopa and Shontelle Bishara*: Shontelle Bishara

p. 31 Olive Prince

p. 33 *Both*: Molly Rose Mulholland

p. 39 Monika Barker

p. 39 Stella Marr

p. 40 MAW

p. 43 *Thomas Kendall*: G-618, ATL

p. 43 *Books*: B-K-1049-COVER, ATL

p. 44 *James Richmond*: 1/2-031822-F, ATL

p. 44 *George Grey*: 1/2-005087-G, ATL

p. 46 MAW

p. 47 1/2-103970-F, ATL

p. 50 *Bottom*: MAW

p. 51 *Top*: MAW

p. 53 1/4-017170-G, ATL

p. 58 *Te Aute*: 1/1-013163-G, ATL

p. 58 *Hukarere*: PAColl-1761-05, ATL

p. 58 *St Stephen's*: Tipene Old Boys

p. 59 *Waerenga-a-Hika*: AWNS-19370414-44-2, JD Richardson, Sir George Grey Special Collections, Auckland Libraries

p. 59 *Te Waipounamu Māori Girls' College*: Lord Family Photos courtesy Belinda Lansley

p. 60 *Queen Victoria School*: 4-2663, Sir George Grey Special Collections, Auckland Libraries

p. 60 *Hikurangi College*: 1/2-092651, ATL

p. 60 *Ōtaki Māori College*: NZG-119091013-23-1, Muir and MacKinlay, Sir George Grey Special Collections, Auckland Libraries

p. 60 *Turakina*: PAColl-5736, ATL

p. 61 *Hato Petera*: Sir George Grey Special Collections, Auckland Libraries

p. 61 *Wesley College*: Wesley College

p. 61 *Hato Paora College*: Stuff Limited

p. 65 PAColl-0408-3, ATL

p. 68 *Meri Te Tai Mangakahia*: Jill Williams

p. 68 Reihana Ruka/Williams whānau

p. 78 *Right*: Charisma Rangipunga

p. 82 Te Mihinga Komene

p. 85 GNS Science

p. 86 CCL-PhotoCD11-IMG0062, Christchurch City Libraries

p. 88 *Kiriana Bird*: *Mana* magazine

p. 88 *Maia Melbourne-Wilcox*: *Tū Mai* magazine

p. 89 Audrey Robin

p. 94 1/2-030877-F, ATL

p. 95 35mm-00188-a-F, ATL

p. 98 *Both*: Māori Women's Welfare League

p. 101 *125th Anniversary*: Henderson whānau

p. 102 Evie O'Brien

p. 107 Tineka Hall

p. 109 *Napier left:* PAColl-6585-73, ATL

p. 109 *Napier right:* 1/2-048343-G, ATL

p. 110 1/2-002945-F, ATL

p. 112 *Apirana Ngata:* 1/2-028390-F, ATL

p. 113 1/4-020106-F, ATL

p. 117 *Artwork:* Tūhoe – Te Uru Taumatua

p. 131 Mere Stewart

p. 139 1992,1170, National Army Museum, NZ

p. 140 *Left:* Linda Mastny

p. 140 *Right:* Jill Cotter

p. 143 *Senior A Team 2015:* Seas Cookson

p. 144 *Left:* Ramona Belmont

p. 144 *Right: Tammi Wilson-Uluinayau:* Gitto Photography

p. 147 *Senior A Basketball Team 2015:* Seas Cookson

p. 147 *Hockey 1976:* Amiria Tibble

p. 147 *Tira Holland:* Seas Cookson

p. 149 *Estelle Sword:* Kataraina Millen

p. 151 Collection of Hawke's Bay Museums Trust, Ruawharo Tā-ū-rangi, 11093

p. 152 *Left:* Margaret Walsh

p. 152 *Right:* Molly Rose Mulholland

p. 156 Molly Rose Mulholland

p. 159 *Left:* Api Hemi

p. 159 *Mere Roha-Stewart:* Molly Rose Mulholland

p. 161 *Monty and Kaa Daniels:* Stacey Daniels

p. 163 Henderson whānau

p. 165 Molly Rose Mulholland

p. 175 *Patrick Hickey:* Molly Rose Mulholland

p. 175 *Lillian Taylor:* Kathy Bates

p. 179 Molly Rose Mulholland

p. 189 Alamein Shoulten

p. 190 Kathy Bates

p. 193 Collection of Hawke's Bay Museums Trust, Ruawharo Tā-ū-rangi, 10502

p. 203 *1:* Collection of Hawke's Bay Museums Trust, Ruawharo Tā-ū-rangi, 12469

p. 206 *Katrina Bates:* Noreen Pakinga

p. 206 *Unaiki Lawton:* Sharon Melrose

p. 206 *Kim and Horowai Wetini:* Kim Wetini

p. 210 Molly Rose Mulholland

p. 213 Molly Rose Mulholland

p. 214 Te Arani Barrett

p. 221 *Duncan McIntyre:* WA-70820-25-F, ATL

p. 228 Amiria Arapere

p. 229 *Moana Maniapoto-Jackson: Mana* magazine

p. 229 *Centre:* Hinewehi Mohi

p. 229 *Right:* Maisey Rika

p. 233 Wiki Baker

p. 236 Maisey Rika

p. 238 Nikayla Jonas

p. 248 Kimiora Kaire-Melbourne

p. 249 *Left:* Iulia Leilua

p. 249 *Right:* Ani-Piki Tuari

p. 250 Mereana Hond

p. 252 Stephanie Tibble

p. 253 Hond whānau

p. 258 Paul McAlister

p. 263 Molly Rose Mulholland

p. 264 Julie Tangaere

p. 265 *Left:* Beth Dixon

p. 265 *Right:* Riria McDonald

p. 266 *Top:* Te Aranga Rolleston

p. 266 *Centre:* Taria Tahana

p. 266 *Bottom:* Charlie Mackey

p. 275 Georgina Kingi

p. 277 Georgina Kingi

p. 281 Aroha Peakman-Walker

p. 282 Ngatoru Wall

p. 283 Molly Rose Mulholland

p. 286 *Left:* Aroha Harris

p. 286 *Right:* Rawinia Higgins

p. 288 Georgina Kingi

p. 299 Georgina Kingi

p. 302 *Left:* Nadell Karatea

p. 302 *Right:* Krystal Te Rina Warren

p. 304 *Left:* Kayleen Neho

p. 305 *Right:* Kania Worsley

p. 306 *Val Caffery-Tangimetua:* Seas Cookson

p. 306 *Te Rere o Kapuni Unahi:* Georgina Kingi

p. 310 Molly Rose Mulholland

p. 312: Molly Rose Mulholland

p. 313 Molly Rose Mulholland

p. 316: Molly Rose Mulholland

p. 318: Seas Cookson

p. 321: Molly Rose Mulholland